To:

Know

The

Truth

About

ISLAM

Copyright © 2018 Usama Dakdok, Venice, Florida
Published in 2018 by Usama Dakdok Publishing, LLC
P.O Box 1144, Marble Hill, MO 63764

All rights reserved. No part of this book may be reproduced, stored in a retrieval system, or transmitted in any form or by any means – printed, electronic, mechanical, photocopy, recording or otherwise – without written permission of the copyright holder.

For copyright information:
Usama Dakdok Publishing, LLC
P.O Box 1144
Marble Hill, MO 63764

All Scripture quotations, unless otherwise indicated, are taken from the New King James Version®. Copyright © 1982 by Thomas Nelson, Inc. Used by permission. All rights reserved.

ISBN: 978-0-9824137-1-5

Dewey decimal system number: 297, Islam
Published in the United States of America

Exposing the Truth about Jihad

Volume One: Holy War in the Bible

Usama Dakdok

Vol. 1 of 2

CONTENTS

Dedication	v
Foreword	vii
Introduction	1

Vol 1, Book 1: Old Testament

Chapter 1: The Origin of Jihad
   1. First Organized War: Genesis 14-15 ----------------------------- 17
   2. Jihad of Fire: Genesis 18-19 -- 21
   3. Killing in the Bible: Exodus 4, 12-14 ----------------------------- 23
   4. Holy War or Jihad? --- 30

Chapter 2: Rules of Jihad
   5. Rules of Jihad in the Old Testament: Deuteronomy 20 ------ 31
   6. Rules of Jihad According to Christian Theologians ------------ 34
   7. First Holy War – Amalek vs Israelites: Exodus 17-23 ---------- 40
   8. Golden Calf: Israelites vs Levites: Exodus 32 -------------------- 42
   9. Unholy Jihad: Numbers 13-14 -------------------------------------- 49
   10. Three Holy Wars: Numbers 21 ------------------------------------ 55

Chapter 3: Why Jihad?
   11. Result of the Hebrews Breaking the Commands -------------- 61
   of God: Exodus 33-34
   12. Continuation of Results of the Hebrews Breaking the ------- 66
   Commands of God: Numbers 25
   13. The Final Jihad Performed by Moses: Numbers 31 ---------- 69

Chapter 4: The Saga Continues
   14. Joshua and Holy War: Joshua 1-4 -------------------------------- 79
   15. How God Gave Jericho to the Israelites: Joshua 5-6 --------- 84
   16. The Sin of Achan and the City of Ai: Joshua 7-8 -------------- 91
   17. Gibeonites and the Kings across the Jordan River: ----------- 97
   Joshua 9-10
   18. A Continuation Through the Conclusion of Joshua's --------- 104
   Holy Wars: Joshua 11-23

Chapter 5: The Art of War

19. Othniel, the First Judge: Judges 1-3 ---------------------------- 112
20. Judges Ehud, Deborah, and Gideon: Judges 3-6 -------------- 116
21. The Story of Abimelech --- 131
22. The Cycle Continues --- 133
23. The Story of Jephthah -- 134
24. The Story of Samson -- 136
25. The Account of Jews Killing Other Jews ---------------------- 146

Chapter 6: The Jihad of King Saul

26. Holy War in the Book of Samuel ------------------------------- 155
27. Samuel and King Saul: 1 Samuel 8-10 ------------------------- 162
28. King Saul and the Ammonites: 1 Samuel 11 ------------------ 164
29. Saul's Attacks on the Philistines and the Amalekites: ------- 167
1 Samuel 13-15
30. King Saul Rejected and King David Anointed: ----------------- 173
1 Samuel 15-16
31. A Kingdom with Two Kings: Saul and David: ------------------- 177
1 Samuel 16:15-17

Chapter 7: The Jihad of King David

32. David's First Holy War and the Killing of Goliath: ------------- 180
1 Samuel 17
33. Relationship Between King Saul and David: ------------------ 182
1 Samuel 18-23
34. David's Second Holy War with the Philistines: ---------------- 184
1 Samuel 23
35. David Shows Mercy and Spares Saul's Life: ------------------- 185
1 Samuel 24-26
36. David Lives Among the Enemy While Performing ----------- 188
Many Holy Wars: 1 Samuel 27
37. Last War of King Saul with the Philistines: ---------------------- 190
1 Samuel 28-29
38. Amalekites Invasion of Ziklag and the Victory of David: ---- 192
1 Samuel 30
39. Death of Saul: 1 Samuel 31 -------------------------------------- 193
40. David Becomes King and Fights Many Battles ---------------- 195
with the Philistines: 2 Samuel 1-8

Chapter 8: Jihad in Transition
41. David's Desire to Build the House for the Lord: -------------- 200
2 Samuel 7, 9-10
42. Solomon Builds the Temple: 2 Samuel 7 ---------------------- 206
(Short Term Prophecy Fulfillment-Jesus the True Fulfillment)

Vol 1, Book 2: New Testament

Chapter 9: Prelude to the Final Conflict
43. Sacrifices in the Old Testament Leads --------------------------- 217
to the New Testament
44. Adam and Eve and the First Sacrifice -------------------------- 220
45. Cain and Abel and the Acceptable Sacrifice ------------------- 224
46. Noah and Sacrifices after the Flood --------------------------- 228
47. The Sacrifices of the Covenant Between ---------------------- 231
God and Abraham: Genesis 15
48. Abraham Offers Isaac as a Sacrifice: --------------------------- 232
Genesis 22:1-9 vs Qur'an 37:99-113
49. Jacob Offered Sacrifices: Genesis 31 --------------------------- 239
50. The Biblical Account of Job Offering Sacrifices --------------- 239
and Job's Story in the Qur'an

Chapter 10: Battle Plans Unfolding
51. Sacrifices of Moses and the Plagues in Exodus --------------- 243
and in the Qur'an
52. The Passover Meal --- 246
53. Sacrifices Required to Be Clean Animals or Birds ------------ 248
54. Mohammed's Bright Yellow Cow Is Not ---------------------- 249
the Bible's Heifer
55. The Red Heifer Offering: -------------------------------------- 254
Numbers 19:1-9 and Deuteronomy 21:1-9
56. The Herd, Flock, and Bird Sacrifices: Leviticus 1 ------------- 257
57. Rejected Sacrifices: Isaiah 1 and 43 --------------------------- 259
58. Rejected Sacrifices: Jeremiah 7 and 17:26-27 ---------------- 265
59. Elijah the Prophet of God vs the Prophets of Baal: ----------- 271
1 Kings 16:29-18

Chapter 11: Battle Plans Revealed

60. Old Testament Prophecies and New Testament Fulfillment of Christ's Coming -------------- 282

61. Prophecies and Fulfillment Concerning the Childhood of Jesus: Luke 2 ------------------------ 293

62. Prophecies and Fulfillment Concerning Jesus' Ministry: Isaiah 40 ---- 295

63. Miracles of Jesus' Healing, Creating, and Raising People from the Dead: Isaiah, Psalms, and 1 Peter -- 300

64. Prophecies on the Nation of Israel Rejecting Jesus and Gentiles Believing in Jesus: Isaiah and 1 Peter ----- 305

65. Prophecies of the Last Week of Jesus on Earth: Zechariah 9, Psalm 41, Matthew 21, Luke 19 -------------- 307

66. Prophecies of the Death of Jesus Fulfilled --------------------- 310

Chapter 12: The Point of the Sword

67. Jesus' Death on the Cross: Psalms, Zechariah, Matthew, John ---------------- 321

68. The Holy War of the New Testament: Isaiah, Psalms, Matthew, Hebrews ------- 322

69. The Resurrection of Jesus Christ: Luke ------------------------ 325

Chapter 13: Clearing the Fog of War

70. Muslims Claim Christianity Was Spread by the Sword in Matthew 10:34 ------------------------ 332

71. The True Teaching of Jesus in Matthew 10:34 ---------------- 337

72. More Verses that Muslims Say Teach Jihad or War in the New Testament: Luke 12:49-51 and Luke 22:36 and 38 ---------- 347

73. The True Teachings of Jesus Instructing His Disciples to Buy a Sword: John 18:36 and Matthew 26:52 ------- 350

74. The Slaughter of Those Who Refused to Believe in Jesus: Luke 19:27 -- 353

Chapter 14: Summary -- 360

DEDICATION

Over the many years of this ministry, hundreds of friends and fellow-believers have graciously given of themselves and their time so that our message and our materials could go forth.

But, as I look back, I see that the Lord mightily provided one wonderful woman to assist in this work from the beginning, and that is my beloved wife, Vicki. I love you more than words can say, and I dedicate this book in your honor due to your patience, faithfulness, and loving support.

May the Lord richly bless you for your often unseen yet always necessary work in this ministry.

Usama K. Dakdok

FOREWORD

Death.
Violence.
Bloodshed.

Humanity's history is a long and winding trail, often marred with fighting and tainted with blood. This dark trail began with rebellion and murder in our first family and has continued, unbroken and unrepentant, until our modern world. From the time that Cain lifted up his hand and slaughtered his own brother, mankind has never departed from hatred, greed, and war. There have been battles for lust, for land, for money, for power, and for revenge. But what about religious wars? What about killing in the (supposed) name of God or a particular religious persuasion?

It is perhaps quite telling that the first murder in history was related to religion. This ruthless attack was carried out due to the intolerance of a religious view that sought to justify itself instead of simple trust in the provision of the Lord. It was the first of many unholy wars that would be fought to wipe out those who worshiped the Creator according to His mercy and grace. Cain killed his "infidel" brother to seek to establish his own religion of power. It was the beginning of countless unholy "jihads."

But, let me ask an important question: is war ever "holy"? Is it possible for there to be justified bloodshed according to God's judgment? It is undeniable that the Bible records many instances of the Lord bringing death and judgment through various "holy" wars. What is the difference (if any) between these battles and the violent history of Islam over the past fourteen centuries?

In this two-volume series, Usama Dakdok provides both an important overview and an insightful examination of the details surrounding death and killing in both the Bible (Volume One) and the Qur'an (Volume Two). The reader will see the pattern of justified killing in the Bible (judgment due to sin) versus the arbitrary and unjustified murders carried out in Islam as commanded by Allah.

RLM

PART ONE:
JIHAD IN THE OLD TESTAMENT

Introduction

Until the tragic events of September 11th, 2001, many in the West had not even heard of the term jihad. Yet today, we hear or read about jihad on (what seems to be) a daily basis. Various definitions for this word are passed around in the media and in casual conversation. Most people would probably say that this Arabic word means something like "holy war." In this first of a two-book series, we will examine the topic of jihad as found in the Bible. In our second volume, we will explore the term jihad as found in the Qur'an. There are many passages in the Bible where God performed jihad. The Jewish nation, God's chosen earthly people, also performed jihad in the Bible.

Make no mistake—there is *killing* in the Bible. There is *war* in the Bible. There were hundreds of thousands who were killed by the sword, disease, and by various other ways. We can read about this throughout the Old Testament and even in the New Testament. In addition to prophecy and spiritual instruction, the Bible also contains detailed historical information, and as such, it speaks about death in a historical sense as well.

During my radio broadcasts concerning the topics of jihad and war within Islam, I spoke about hundreds of verses from the Qur'an and shared many of the sayings of Mohammed in the hadith that clearly demonstrate that Islam is not a "religion of peace." It is not a religion of love. In fact, the opposite is true. In terms of murder and violence, Islam is possibly the most barbaric cult that has ever existed on planet Earth. Cities, nations, and even entire regions of the world have been bathed in blood during the last fifteen centuries of Muslim aggression and domination.

Many Muslims have written to me asking why I ignore or disregard the killing and violence in the Bible. They have written to me about war, killing, and the shedding of blood in the Bible and claim that both books, the Bible and the Qur'an, teach hate, war, and killing. However, is this true?

I have written this book to respond to the Muslims' claim, to contrast what is written in the Bible to what is written in the Qur'an, and to see if the killing in the Bible is similar to the killing we read about throughout the Qur'an. Does the Bible teach hate, violence, and killing like what we find in the Qur'an? It is time to investigate and expose the truth about jihad in the Bible (and jihad in the Qur'an in our second volume).

We must understand the reason for the chaos and misery that is in the world. The Bible answers this very clearly...it is the result of *sin*. Man's rebellion against God has led to our sad history of violence, greed, and hate. To properly understand killing or jihad in the Bible, we must understand that the biblical use of jihad is the shedding of blood. Jihad is any kind of killing.

Let me ask you...did God create man just to kill man? Did God bring jihad to humanity just for the purpose of shedding blood, for waging war and to kill, or was this the outcome of the sins and rebellion of man?

According to the Scripture, when God created Adam and Eve and placed them on the earth, it was not in His plan that their descendants would kill each other or that some of their descendants would wage war or perform jihad against others. God's plan was for Adam and Eve and their offspring to live on the earth forever and to have an unending relationship with God. It was His desire that mankind (in the context of a "free will") would serve, worship, and commune with Him eternally. However, that is not how Adam and Eve chose to live. God created us in perfection, but He also gave us free will. We can choose to accept, reject, love, or hate.

You see, the God of the Bible is not a god who forces people to believe in Him or to love Him. He is not a god who gives you an option to believe in Him or else to kill you by the sword. Yet, in Islam, we clearly see this teaching in the Qur'an by Allah.

The God of the Bible is the God of freedom. He gives us the freedom to worship or not to worship Him, to believe or not to believe Him, or to serve or not to serve Him. He will not force anyone to worship, believe, or serve Him. We have a free will.

With this is mind, let us study the topic of jihad in the teachings of both the Old and New Testaments in the Bible.

In this discussion, we must begin with *sin*...because sin is the cause of ALL death. Therefore, sin (or rebellion against our Creator) is the foundation of jihad/killing in the Bible. Sin is the reason why jihad must exist in the Bible. As 1 John 3:4 states: **Whoever commits sin also commits lawlessness, and sin is lawlessness.** This is a very simple verse. From it we can understand what sin is. Sin is to commit transgression, to violate God's law. Muslims believe in small sins and in large sins. The Bible makes no such distinction. Sin is sin, and all sin is serious in the eyes of a holy God.

However, when we study what a "small sin" is or what a "large sin" is in Islam, Allah in the Qur'an (and Muslim scholars) teaches that even a really wicked sin, a most unacceptable and ungodly sin, is not really a large sin. It is just a small sin. For example, lying in Islam is not a big sin. There is no command in the Qur'an "Thou shalt not lie." Instead, Mohammed in the hadith stated, "It is lawful to lie in three cases: a man to his wife that she would be pleased, at the time of war, for war is deception, or to make peace between people." Which means in Islam that you can lie to your wives, to your enemies, and to your friends. In other words, it is okay to lie to everyone all the time.

What is sin in the Bible? It is disobedience to God's word and His command. The law was given, and anyone who disobeys the law has committed sin. In James 2:10-11, the Bible states: **[10]For whoever shall keep the whole law, and yet stumble in one point, he is guilty of all. [11]For He who said, "Do not commit adultery," also said, "Do not murder." Now if you do not commit adultery, but you do murder, you have become a transgressor of the law.**

I personally know that some Muslims believe there are white lies, gray lies, black lies, small lies, and large lies. However, in reality, in the eyes of God, lying equals killing. Let me share an example of this with you.

Imagine someone going to court. They stand before the judge, and then lie by stating, "So-and-so killed so-and-so." This is a simple lie. He did not kill anyone. He just lied and accused this person of killing someone. Then the judge sentences the accused person to be put to death. So you see, as a result of a lie, someone lost his life.

The opposite is also true. If someone goes before the judge and lies by saying, "No, this person could not be the killer because he was with me at the time of the crime," then the guilty person will be freed instead of being put to death by this simple lie. Sin is sin. If you did not commit adultery, but you killed, you are still guilty because you broke the law. If you did not commit adultery or kill but you lied, you are still guilty because you broke the law. The same law of God that condemns murder also condemns adultery and lying. A holy God is offended by every wicked act and thought of mankind. Some actions may seem better or worse to us, but we are not a perfectly righteous God.

Sin in the Bible is very serious. The Bible does not teach that sin has sizes, large or small, or a light or a dark color. Sin is sin. Sin is disobedience to God's command.

Sin is transgressing the law. It doesn't matter which law we break. As we read the Bible, we find that not only doing evil is sin (commission), but the Bible also teaches that those who know to do good but then choose not to do good (omission) are also committing sin. So, it is not just breaking the Ten Commandments, but if we know of an opportunity to do good and we choose not to do good (such as helping someone in need), then we are also sinning against God. We have disobeyed God's word and His law. It is not just about what we DO, it is also about what we DO NOT do.

If we look at James 4:17, the Bible states: **Therefore, to him who knows to do good and does not do it, to him it is sin.** That is exactly what the Bible teaches about sin. Sin is not only committing evil deeds but also neglecting to do the good deeds. God's word is very clear. Those who know to do good and then don't do it are committing sin against Him.

Now, how did sin come into the world? The Bible makes this very clear as well. It was when Adam and Eve disobeyed the plain command of God. The command was very simple. It had nothing to do with the Ten Commandments. Those laws came many thousands of years later during the time of Moses. God's command was for them to not eat from the Tree of the Knowledge of Good and Evil. This single prohibition was obviously a test. God said that they could do almost anything they wanted, except for this one act; and they chose, of their own free will, to disobey God's one command.

Some people try to justify their sin by claiming that it was only a small sin, not a large sin. Do you know how large Adam's sin was that has now affected the entire human race all the way down to you and me? He simply ate a piece of fruit! He did not harm anyone. He did not kill anyone. He did not commit adultery. He did not lie. He simply ate some fruit and thereby chose to disobey God's command.

It was not the last tree in the garden. It was not the last piece of fruit in the garden. The garden was full of trees, and the description of the trees was not any different from the Tree of Knowledge of Good and Evil. We read about this in Genesis 2:9: **And out of the ground the Lord God made every tree grow that is pleasant to the sight and good for food...**

However, Adam disobeyed God when he ate from the tree that God had commanded him not to eat, not because there wasn't any other good fruit in the garden but because Adam yielded to the subtle deceptions of Satan. Satan deceived Adam and Eve by making them believe that this one forbidden tree would make them wise and ultimately make them like God Himself. He offered them the tempting prospect of becoming their own gods. Many religions in the world today still deceive millions of people by offering them the tempting promise of one day becoming a god (such as Mormonism).

However, the command of God was very simple. They could eat from all the trees of the garden except this one tree. However, Adam and Eve disobeyed God. They ate from this tree which God had commanded them not to eat. The tree wasn't really special; rather, it was what the tree represented: obedience to God or rebellion against God. It was a test.

So, how did sin and rebellion and evil come into the world? How did sin move from the first man who committed sin (Adam) to the rest of mankind? We read about this in Romans 5:12: **Therefore, just as through one man sin entered the world, and death through sin, and thus death spread to all men, because all sinned.**

So, what do we learn from this verse? It was because of Adam, the one man who ate from the tree, the one man who disobeyed God, the one man who sinned, that sin entered into God's perfect world. Look carefully once again at this verse which explains to us how death entered into the world through sin. Death is the result of sin. Death is the consequence of sin and rebellion. Yes, Adam sinned, and the result was death. Why is that? The Scripture explains this as well.

Let us read the word of God in Genesis 2:15-17: **¹⁵Then the Lord God took the man and put him in the garden of Eden to tend and keep it. ¹⁶And the Lord God commanded the man, saying, "Of every tree of the garden you may freely eat; ¹⁷but of the tree of the knowledge of good and evil you shall not eat, for in the day that you eat of it you shall surely die."**

This was justice. The law was given. The punishment for breaking the law is death; and that is, in essence, jihad in the Bible. It was a just (fair) and righteous jihad. It was the punishment for evil. It was the punishment for sin. Death in the Bible is ultimately the result of sin and rebellion.

There were plenty of tasty, healthy, and beautiful trees from which Adam could eat. All Adam had to do was to obey God's one command and enjoy life in the garden…free from hardship, difficulty, and sweat. He was to live and enjoy life forever. He only had to obey God's command. If he chose to eat from this tree, he would die. This was a just law, and it was a just punishment.

As we read in Romans 5:12, Adam ate from the tree. Therefore, death came as a result of his sin because that was the right and just punishment for his sin, and so death came to all mankind. Why? It is because all mankind have sinned against God. Adam became a sinner. This "sin nature" has been passed down to all of his descendants. Some call this Original Sin, but let's be clear…God does not hold anyone responsible for the sins that others have committed, including Adam. Adam was the original sinner of the human race, but we also have used our free will and have chosen to sin against God. Because Adam sinned, you and I have a nature that is rebellious against God; and **because of our sin (not Adam's sin), we must be put to death.**

God revealed to Adam that to eat from the tree was to bring death. If it had not been Adam, but you and me in the garden, there is no doubt that we would have eaten from the tree as well. As we live today outside of the garden, we still sin against God, and we still deserve the punishment for our sin which is death. All have sinned. That is the truth. No one has lived a life free from sin. The only one, in all of human history, who did not sin is our Lord and Savior Jesus Christ.

Romans 3:23 makes it abundantly clear that not even one perfect human has ever walked on earth, except for Jesus Christ. This verse states: **For all have sinned and fall short of the glory of God.** All have sinned. That is A-L-L. That is you and I. That is your father and my father. That is your mother and my mother. That is your sons and daughters and my sons and daughters. Everyone has sinned. There is not one perfect person outside of Christ, our Savior. We all have sinned. So what is the punishment for us?

Let's look at another verse found in Romans 6:23: **For the wages of sin is death, but the gift of God is eternal life in Christ Jesus our Lord**. Romans 3:23 reveals to us that all have sinned. Romans 6:23 reveals to us that the wages (payment) for sin is death. It is very simple. There is a consistency of teaching in the Bible. Sin came into this world, the wages/payment for sin is death, all have sinned, and so all must be put to death.

When we talk about death in the Christian faith, we talk about three types of death. First, there is *spiritual* death. This is to be separated spiritually from the presence of God. That is when people follow their own desires, wishes, and the will of a fallen nature and continue to rebel against God.

We read about this fallen condition in Job 15:16: **How much less man, who is abominable and filthy, who drinks iniquity like water!** Have you ever had difficulty in drinking a glass of water? We enjoy drinking water. All humans drink water. Animals and birds and nearly all creatures drink water. This is how wicked man has become. We are living in sin, and we enjoy sin just as we enjoy drinking water. This sin that we live in separates us from a holy God, for in His presence there is no unholiness or any unrighteousness. He is perfect…we are not.

Isaiah 59:2 states: **But your iniquities have separated you from your God; and your sins have hidden His face from you, so that He will not hear.** This is a fact. This is the truth. Because of our sin, we have been separated from God, and now we are dead spiritually, separated from the presence of God.

God used to walk and commune with Adam and Eve in the garden as friend with friend. God used to have fellowship with them. However, after Adam and Eve ate from the Tree of the Knowledge of Good and Evil, the Bible states that they started hiding from God. They became afraid of God. This is evidence of that first type of death...*spiritual* death. They had become stained with sin (law-breakers) and that separated them from a holy God.

The second type of death that the Bible mentions is *physical* death. This is the punishment which everyone must go through. We all must die because we all have sinned, and we descend from Adam who passed on his rebellious nature. We came into this world with a sinful nature. We read of the punishment given to Adam for his disobedience to God's command in Genesis 3:19: **In the sweat of your face you shall eat bread till you return to the ground, for out of it you were taken; for dust you are, and to dust you shall return.**

When God created Adam, he was created to live forever as long as he did not fall into sin by disobeying God's command. However, since Adam did disobey God's command, the punishment (which was a just punishment since God warned Adam prior to his disobedience of eating from the tree) must be fulfilled. The punishment is from dust to dust. This is the second type of death as the Bible teaches, *physical* death. Because you and I sin, we are dead *spiritually* and are separated from God. Then, secondly, we must die *physically* and our bodies must return to dust.

Now we come to the third and final type of death which the Bible calls *eternal* death. In Mark 9:43-44, Jesus tells us: **"If your hand causes you to sin, cut it off. It is better for you to enter into life maimed, rather than having two hands, to go to hell, into the fire that shall never be quenched [44]where 'Their worm does not die and the fire is not quenched.'"**

Jesus continued his teaching by speaking figuratively of cutting off a foot and plucking out an eye, for in these verses Jesus is explaining that the punishment of our sin (whether it is the work of the hand or the walk of the foot or even the lust of the eye) will cause us to spend eternity in Hell and perish forever. This is what the Bible calls *eternal* death. It is the justice concerning the final punishment of the rebellious sinner.

The rule has been set. The day we sin, we begin to die, and this happened to Adam, our example and prototype. The very day (moment) that he sinned, he was separated from God (*spiritual* death). His body began to decay and he later suffered *physical* death. All who reject God's salvation will ultimately experience *eternal* death. This is the foundation of our research into the biblical teaching of jihad. We must have this fact in mind as we continue investigating jihad in the Bible.

[5]Then the Lord saw that the wickedness of man was great in the earth, and that every intent of the thoughts of his heart was only evil continually. [6]And the Lord was sorry that He had made man on the earth, and He was grieved in His heart. [7]So the Lord said, "I will destroy man whom I have created from the face of the earth, both man and beast, creeping thing and birds of the air, for I am sorry that I have made them." [8]But Noah found grace in the eyes of the Lord.

This is the description from Genesis 6:5-8 of the first recorded jihad that was performed by God in the Bible, i.e. the killing of the wicked people on the earth. Christians and Jews are familiar with the famous account of Noah. The story of the Genesis account has been copied and corrupted in the pages of the Qur'an. Sadly, Muslims do not know the actual truth and the details of this account of God's righteous judgment.

We see in this passage that the earth had become corrupted because the descendants of Adam and Eve were committing sin, and the wickedness of mankind was great on the earth. Not just their physical actions, but even the thoughts of man also became constantly evil as we read in Genesis 6:5. After man sinned in the garden, God created a conscience within us, an inner witness to right and wrong behavior, and all of mankind rebelled against their conscience (God's law in their hearts) and chose to do evil.

God was grieved in His heart for the wickedness and rebellion of man. This is what Genesis states in 6:6, but then in verse 7, God brought the judgment on man whom He had created by His own hand. God decided to execute His judgment by destroying every creature, man, bird, and animal that lived on earth. The Flood was **a fulfillment of God's righteous judgment: sin brings death.**

As I stated earlier, there are three different types of death. Spiritual death is separation from God. It occurs when a person enjoys living in sin just as he enjoys drinking a glass of water. The second death is physical death, from dust to dust where man must return. The third death is eternal death -- punishment in Hell forever.

As we see, God's law was known in the hearts of people. Yet people were doing every evil act on the face of the earth. That is why, I believe, that this is the first jihad ever mentioned in the Bible. This jihad was accomplished by God Himself, and He used water in this jihad to destroy life on the earth.

However, we read in verse 8: **But Noah found grace in the eyes of the Lord.** Who is this Noah that the Bible is talking about? The Bible states in Genesis 6:9-10: **This is the genealogy of Noah. Noah was a just man, perfect in his generations. Noah walked with God. ¹⁰And Noah begot three sons: Shem, Ham, and Japheth.**

When we read the Bible, we see how God described Noah to be a perfect man. This was not because Noah did not fall into sin or did not break God's command. Noah was a sinner. However, God spoke so highly of him because he walked with God. This means that he did what God commanded men to do at the time.

If we go back to the account of Adam and Eve, after they ate from the tree, they were then kicked out of the Garden of Eden. However, the Bible does not stop there. The Bible states that God showed His grace and gave His mercy to Adam and Eve by providing a temporary solution for their sin in a symbolic way. When Adam and Eve ate from the tree, they suddenly had awareness that they were naked because they now knew evil from good. They felt naked and hid themselves among the trees of the garden.

In Genesis 3:21 the Bible states: **Also for Adam and his wife the Lord God made tunics of skin, and clothed them.** This was the first sacrifice offered on behalf of sinful people. Through the blood of this sacrifice (the killing of the animal to make the tunics), Adam and Eve were able to receive symbolic covering for their sin. I am not saying forgiveness for their sin but a simple covering. This is the theme, as we read throughout the entire Bible, from the days of Adam until the time the Lamb of God, Jesus Christ, our Lord and our Savior, was offered as a true sacrifice for our sins two thousand years ago.

How do we know that Noah was living in obedience to God? It was because he listened to the voice of God and did exactly what God commanded him to do. We read a very important verse in Genesis 8:20: **Then Noah built an**

altar to the Lord, and took of every clean animal and of every clean bird, and offered burnt offerings on the altar. This is why I believe, according to the teaching of the Bible, that Noah was a just man, "perfect" (complete) in his generation. Why? It was because he walked with God. Not because he had not sinned. The Bible is very clear in Romans 3:23 that everyone has sinned, including Noah. Noah sinned just as everyone who has walked upon the earth, with the single exception of our Lord and our Savior Jesus Christ.

How do we know that Noah was perfect in his generation? It was because he covered his sin with a sacrifice (as God had instructed). How do we know this? As we read in Genesis 8:20, Noah sacrificed animals and birds. Any kind of animals or birds? No, Noah sacrificed only clean, pure animals and birds. As for the rest of the people of Noah's day, they were not living right before God. They were a wicked generation. They disregarded God and any of His laws.

So who taught Noah to offer sacrifices? It was the same way that the two sons of Adam, Cain and Abel, learned. It was from their father, Adam, who learned it from God Himself. God revealed to Adam that the only way to cover sin is with the death of an innocent victim (an animal). God was teaching mankind, in symbolic form, that one day the ultimate innocent victim would die for the sins of the whole world…the Lamb of God, the Lord Jesus Christ.

Now, let's go back to the first jihad that was ever recorded in Scripture. God is the one who destroyed all life on earth, and now we know why from the Scriptures. It was because the earth was corrupted in sin. The earth was full of violence and rebellion. That is why God decided to bring all life on earth (all humans, animals, and birds) to an end. We read this in Genesis 6:11-13. However, in verse 14, God gave a command to Noah to build an ark: **"Make yourself an ark of gopherwood; make rooms in the ark, and cover it inside and outside with pitch."** God then gave Noah the exact description of how to build the ark: how many floors it was to have, its dimensions, and where to place the door and window. It is interesting that none of these important details and descriptions are found in the Qur'an.

Notice here that Noah's ark represents Christ. As Noah and his family were saved from death in the ark, we also are delivered from death through our Lord, Jesus Christ.

Why did God ask Noah to build this ark? The reason is that God spoke to Noah and told him that He was going to send a flood. This flood would cover the entire earth and destroy every creature on the face of the earth. That is what we read in Genesis 6:17: **"And behold, I Myself am bringing floodwaters on the earth, to destroy from under heaven all flesh in which is the breath of life; everything that is on the earth shall die."**

The Bible states that every air-breathing creature, including the people, died. Everything that had breath of life on the face of the earth was destroyed in the flood, with the exception of those on the ark. From the Scripture we read that only Noah, his wife, his three sons, Shem, Ham, and Japheth, and their three wives were saved from the flood. Only eight people were saved. We read this in Genesis 7:13. Only these eight people were saved from the flood plus the animals, birds, and creeping things of the earth that were on the ark. We read this in Genesis 7:2-3 where God instructed Noah: **"You shall take with you seven each of every clean animal, a male and his female; two each of animals that are unclean, a male and his female; ³also seven each of birds of the air, male and female, to keep the species alive on the face of all the earth."** These are the remnants of all the animals, all the birds, and all the creeping things of the earth. They also had to take food for themselves, the animals, and the birds as written in Genesis 6:21.

Now we must ask some questions. Did God warn the people on the earth? Did Noah preach to the people on the earth? Did Noah do this for a couple of weeks or a couple of months or maybe even a couple of years?

The answer to these questions is very clear in the Bible. We know that God gave people plenty of time to do what was right and repent of their wickedness. He gave them one hundred twenty years, not a hundred twenty weeks or a hundred twenty months, but one hundred twenty *years*. We read in Genesis 6:3: **And the Lord said, "My Spirit shall not strive with man forever, for he is indeed flesh; yet his days shall be one hundred and twenty years."** That's exactly the amount of time God warned them and allowed man to live on the earth before the flood took place. God is willing for people to repent and be saved. The Scripture teaches that God is patient and withholds judgment for as long as possible.

In Genesis 7:11-12, we read that water gushed up from the fountains of the earth and that it began to rain from above. It rained for forty days and nights (and the whole time water rushed up from caverns deep in the crust). Then, in verse 20 we see that the water covered every high mountain of the earth. All humans, birds, and creeping things on the earth died, and God removed from the face of the earth all air-breathing living things, except for those on the ark. All that was left alive after the flood was Noah, his wife, his three sons, his sons' wives, and all the creatures on the ark.

In Genesis 8:1-12, we read that God remembered Noah and those who were with him on the ark. The rain stopped, the water receded slowly, and after one hundred fifty days, the ark rested on Mount Ararat. Forty days later, Noah opened the window and sent out a raven. The raven flew back and forth, so then Noah sent out a dove. The dove returned. Then Noah sent the dove out again a week later, and the dove returned with an olive leaf in its beak. Noah sent the dove out a third time, but this time the dove did not return. Then Noah knew that the waters had abated from the face of the earth, for the dove had found a dry home.

We read, beginning in Genesis 8:16, that God spoke to Noah and told him, along with his family and all the animals, birds, and creeping things, to come out of the ark. The creatures left the ark and began to multiply. Noah's sons also began to have children and grandchildren and great-grandchildren and so on. The earth's population exploded.

Another important fact, which we read earlier, is stated in Genesis 8:20: **Then Noah built an altar to the Lord, and took of every clean animal and of every clean bird, and offered burnt offerings on the altar.** Then continuing with verse 21: **And the Lord smelled a soothing aroma. Then the Lord said in His heart, "I will never again curse the ground for man's sake, although the imagination of man's heart is evil from his youth; nor will I again destroy every living thing as I have done."**

So what do we learn from this account? There was a jihad (killing), and this jihad was performed by the hand of God directly. In Noah's day, all people on the earth had a warning and had time to repent from their sin, but because they refused to repent and chose to live in their wickedness, God brought judgment. This is what I call a just jihad, a just punishment, a righteous judgment. God is the Creator of all human life; and therefore, He has the right to decide when and how each physical life will end. He can end it through nature, as through the flood, or He can choose to use people as instruments of His justice, as we will read about later, but it is important to remember that God has the right to choose the time and manner of the end of physical life for each person.

Getting back to the flood, Noah and his family had done what was right. They offered the sacrifices as instructed, lived right before God, listened to His voice, and obeyed the command of God.

However, all the other people who did not obey God, did not listen to the command of God, and did not even seek refuge in Noah's ark, simply rejected God. Because they rejected God and rebelled against Him, the flood came over a hundred years later, and all of these creatures, all humans, birds, animals, and creeping things, were destroyed. They were killed by the waters of the flood. That was a just jihad. As it is written in the Scripture, if we disobey and sin, we must die.

Someone may complain and say that this is not just. "What about all the little children or the women, especially the pregnant women who died in this flood?" No, my dear friends, God is God. He is sovereign. He can do as He sees fit and right. Can the clay say to the potter, "What are you making out of me?" (Romans 9:20) God can choose to do whatever He wishes.

However, the good news is that God is a just and fair God. He will not punish anyone with the eternal punishment (the death of Hell), unless they are guilty of sin without repenting, and then they will be punished for their sin. The overall teachings in the Bible indicated that all the young children who were killed in the flood will be in Heaven because they did not actually commit any sin. We read about this in Ezekiel 18:20: **The soul who sins shall die. The son shall not bear the guilt of the father, nor the father bear the guilt of the son.**

Sometimes we look at things happening all around us and across the world, such as little children dying in bad accidents or by diseases. We say that this is not just or right. Remember, physical death must take place. All people will experience physical death. The question is this: "Are you dead spiritually?" This is a serious and solemn question, because, if you die the physical death while you are dead spiritually, then guess what? The eternal punishment, the eternal death, will be yours. Jihad, as mentioned in the Bible, is a 100 percent just and fair jihad. **That's why I call it Holy Jihad.** When we sin, we must die, spiritually, physically, and eternally. This is not the same as the unholy jihad of Mohammed in Islam, which we will talk about in Volume 2.

The Origin of Jihad

First Organized War: Genesis 14-15

The first organized war recorded in the Bible is found in Genesis 14. Someone may ask, "Why does the Bible record this war? Does the Bible want to teach us to engage in war, to perform jihad, or to kill other people?" No, it was written in the Bible because it is actual history, the events that happened in the life of Abraham and his nephew, Lot.

The Bible teaches us many things, things to do and things NOT to do. When we hear about bad behaviors and sin (as even in the lives of some of the prophets, kings, messengers, and spiritual leaders), that does not mean that their sin is an example for us to follow. Instead, their sin and shortcomings are to teach us so that we will not do the same. God is honest about the lives of His servants. He doesn't hide their failures, but they are recorded for our benefit and learning to show us that God is a forgiving God and a God of second chances.

It is amazing how quickly Muslims will attack the Bible and accuse it of being an ungodly book. Why? It is because the Bible mentions the sins and faults of this person or that person. They don't understand that it is written for us to learn from these sins and not to copy or practice them.

The more we see the sins and shortcomings of the people in the Bible, the more I know for sure that the Bible is the true word of God. Contrary to what some Muslims claim, the Bible has never been changed or corrupted. If there had been any corruption/changes in the Bible, I guarantee you, it would have been the removal of the sins of their prophets, kings, and other important leaders in the Bible. Abraham lied, David committed adultery and murder, and the apostle Peter denied the Lord three times. God does not hide the failures of His servants.

In the first organized war in Genesis 14, there were four kings who were united together to engage in war against five other kings. According to Genesis 14:1-2: ¹**And it came to pass in the days of Amraphel king of**

Shinar, Arioch king of Ellasar, Chedorlaomer king of Elam, and Tidal king of nations, ²that they made war with Bera king of Sodom, Birsha king of Gomorrah, Shinab king of Admah, Shemeber king of Zeboiim, and the king of Bela (that is, Zoar).** Abraham's nephew, Lot, was living in Sodom at this time.

During this time, there was much abuse and evil in the land because for years these four kings had been taking advantage of the people by invading their lands and enslaving them. According to Genesis 14:3-12, the abused people rebelled against these four oppressive kings. The king of Sodom and his four allies went to war against the other four kings. During this war, the four kings won the battle, and the king of Sodom and the king of Gomorrah escaped and ran for their lives. Some of the men escaped to the mountain. However, the people in the city of Sodom were captured and carried off as a spoil of war. Lot, the nephew of Abraham (called Abram at this time in his life), was also taken along with all of his possessions.

However, one of the men who had escaped came and told Abraham about what had happened. Abraham took over three hundred and eighteen of his strong, young men who were trained to fight and followed these four kings to the land of Dan. Once there, Abraham attacked them at night, smote them, took all of the spoils, and returned all the people and their spoils taken in the first battle back to the city and the king of Sodom.

The king of Sodom met Abraham, and he offered to give Abraham all of the spoils as a reward. All that the king of Sodom wanted from Abraham was the people, but Abraham refused to take any of the spoils. Abraham only took the food that his men had eaten and their portion, but Abraham himself did not take anything from the king of Sodom.

So what do we learn from this war? Was Abraham performing jihad for the sake of Allah just to kill their men and take their women and their children as a spoil of war so that he may also get their camels, their gold, their silver, and their land? No, this was a just war. Abraham got involved in this war to deliver his nephew and also to restore the land and the people and to give the spoils back to the owners who had been unjustly taken by these four wicked kings.

Was Abraham doing this for the purpose of receiving spoils? No. He was offered all the spoils by the king of Sodom, but he refused to take any of the spoils. Was this war about taking land? No. Abraham left the land and returned back to his own home. Was this war about forcing people to believe in the God of Abraham, in the religion of Abraham? No, because Abraham did not do so, it was a just war to bring an end to the wickedness of these four evil kings and to bring back that which had been taken from the land. Justice was served in that war. Because of sin and greed, sometimes war is necessary to end wickedness and to bring liberty to those oppressed. God does not delight in violence and war, but sometimes a greater good comes from this lesser evil. War and killing can be justified.

Now, let us move on to Genesis 15. There is a very important event in this chapter, and I will elaborate using this same chapter later when we examine the taking of the Promised Land and the sacrifices in the Old Testament. According to Genesis 15:1, after Abraham restored back to the land of Sodom the people and the spoils which had been taken by the four wicked kings (including his nephew along with his possessions), God appeared to Abraham in a vision in which God told him that his reward would be great.

Then Abraham asked God: "What reward? I am a man without children. When I die, all that I have and all my blessings will be given to the steward of my house, Eliezer of Damascus." So, we can see here that Abraham was, in effect, complaining to God about not having anyone to inherit all the riches he had. God told Abraham that Eliezer would not inherit his possessions but that a child of his own flesh and blood would get the inheritance. Then God told Abraham to look at the stars and asked him to count them. God told him that the number of his descendants would be like the number of stars, impossible to count. Abraham simply believed God, and God counted it to him as righteousness, according to Genesis 15:6.

In this vision in Genesis 15:7, God reminded Abraham that He was the Lord God who had relocated Abraham from the land of the Chaldeans to give him this new land to inherit. What land was God speaking of? This is the Promised Land that now, thousands of years later, all the eyes of the world are focused on, the land of Israel. It is the only property given by God in a written deed. It is interesting that this deed is found not only in the Bible but also in the Qur'an as Allah, the god of Mohammed, gave it to Moses and his people in Qur'an 5:20-26.

It is incredible that many Muslims do not know their own book, the Qur'an. They call Israel "the land that is occupied by the Jews." No, my dear readers, if you have read the Qur'an, you will see that the Promised Land was given by Allah to Moses and his people. The Bible for the Christians and the Jews (and the Qur'an for the Muslims) both clearly declare that the Promised Land was given by God, the God of Abraham (or Allah the god of Mohammed) to the children of Israel. People today might be confused about whose land it is, but God, the Creator, has clearly revealed the people to whom He has given it.

In Genesis 15:8-10, Abraham asked God about how he would get assurance that he would inherit the land. It was then, that God and Abraham made a covenant of blood as Abraham sacrificed a three-year-old ram, a three-year-old goat, a three-year-old heifer, a young pigeon, and a turtledove. Then continuing in the vision, Abraham sacrificed these animals, divided them down the middle, and laid these pieces opposite from each other. When the vultures came down to feed on the carcasses, Abraham would drive the vultures away.

The rest of the vision, as we read in Genesis 15:12-15, was a scary moment for Abraham as he saw the sun go down. He fell into a deep sleep and a terrible darkness fell upon him. God spoke to Abraham and revealed to him what would take place in the lives of his children and his grandchildren far off into the future. They would be strangers in a land that would not belong to them (Egypt), and they would be enslaved in this land for four hundred years. However, God would judge this land that would enslave his descendants. His descendants would then leave this land with great riches. Then God revealed to Abraham that he would die at an old age and be buried, but in the fourth generation, after four hundred years, his descendants would return back to the Promised Land that He had given to Abraham.

Why did God have the descendants of Abraham wait four hundred years before they would be able to return to the Promised Land that God had given to Abraham? The answer is found in Genesis 15:16 where God told Abraham: **"But in the fourth generation they shall return here, for the iniquity of the Amorites is not yet complete."** God is speaking to Abraham and revealed to him that his descendants would come back to this land from Egypt. They will inherit this land but not yet. It will happen four

Chapter 1: The Origin of Jihad

hundred years later. God had the descendants of Abraham wait for four hundred years until the sins (iniquities) of the people in this land were completed. As a punishment for their sins, God would remove them from the land and give the land to the descendants of Abraham. God allowed the Canaanites/Amorites four centuries to repent of their incredible wickedness, but they only increased their evil. God's law is that sin brings death, and four hundred years later judgment finally fell, for God is patient.

In Genesis 15:17-21, God made a covenant with Abraham and gave to him and his descendants all of the land from the Nile River of Egypt to the Euphrates River. All this land would be given to the descendants of Abraham.

So who were the people living in the land at this time? This is very important. According to verses 19-21 they were: [19]**the Kenites, the Kenezzites, the Kadmonites,** [20]**the Hittites, the Perizzites, the Rephaim,** [21]**the Amorites, the Canaanites, the Girgashites, and the Jebusites.** Notice that we did not read the word *Palestinian* in this list of names.

None of the original people of the land were Palestinians. Today, there is a false claim of the Arab Palestinians that they were the original "owners" of the land. The Bible refutes this claim. It lists the original tenants of the land, and then those peoples were replaced by the children of Israel. We see the promise of God was delayed for only one reason, the sin of these people who lived in the land was not fulfilled until the time of Moses, and that was the perfect time for the punishment of their sin. Not only would they lose their land, but they would lose their lives by the sword of Moses and God's chosen people, the Jews. As Creator, God can use whatever means to execute His judgment as He sees fit...whether supernatural or natural. In this case of the wicked Canaanites/Amorites, God used the sword of the children of Israel as His means of judgment.

Jihad of Fire: Genesis 18-19

Now, I would like to share with you another jihad that is recorded in the Bible. This jihad is the jihad of fire which God Himself performed by the power of His own hand (supernatural). We read about this jihad beginning in Genesis 18:22, where there is a conversation taking place between God and Abraham. Abraham tried to intercede on behalf of the people of the cities of Sodom and Gomorrah (because his nephew Lot lived there), but God revealed to him that their evil was ripe for judgment. The Bible declares that these cities were so wicked as God stated in Genesis 18:20-21: [20]"**Because the outcry against Sodom and Gomorrah is great, and because their sin is very grave,** [21]**I will go down now..."**

As mentioned earlier, the wages of sin is death, and there are three different kinds of death. First is spiritual death, which was the condition of every man and woman in these cities. Next, is physical death, which is exactly what happened when God burned these cities with fire and brimstone. Then finally, there is eternal death which is separation from God forever for all those who have committed sin without repenting and receiving the salvation that God offers.

Early in the morning, God sent two angels who quickly removed Lot, his wife, and their two daughters, causing them to leave so that they would not be destroyed with the wicked people of the city. Once again, we see people who are going to be destroyed because of their sin. Everything was destroyed by fire and brimstone. In Genesis 19:24, the Bible states: **Then the Lord rained brimstone and fire on Sodom and Gomorrah, from the Lord out of the heavens.** This was the judgment of God for the sins of the people who lived in this land.

As for the children and babies who died in the fire of Sodom and Gomorrah, the Bible makes it clear that they will not die the *third* death, the death of eternal Hell. Obviously, everyone in the city perished on that day because of their disobedience to God. This is the true nature of jihad in the Bible. It is a justified killing as a justified punishment for their willful sin and repeated rebellion. Remember, physical death does not mean "cease to exist." No person ever ceases to exist since God says that we have an eternal soul. Every person who has ever lived is still alive, right now, at this very moment. Unfortunately, many of them are separated from God and will be cast into Hell. Every baby and every child who has ever died at a young age is still alive, right now, and they are in the presence of the God Who created them and loves them.

Chapter 1: The Origin of Jihad

Killing in the Bible: Exodus 4, 12-14

God's promise was that Abraham's descendants would come back to the Promised Land after living in a foreign land as slaves for four hundred years. In the fourth generation, they would return to take the Promised Land. God's promise must be fulfilled.

Then, after four hundred years, because of their sin and God's punishment, they had to die, physically. Then all those who had lived ungodly lives and had done every evil in the eyes of the Lord would be punished with eternal death and spend all of eternity in the fire of Hell.

Now, let me take you to Egypt, the country of my birth. We read in the Bible that there was a famine in the land (a lack of crops and food). Joseph, a descendant of Abraham, had been sold as a slave into Egypt, where he later interpreted the dreams of Pharaoh concerning the seven years of plenty followed by seven years of famine.

Joseph's family came from the Promised Land to Egypt. They were there not just for the seven year of plenty and the seven years of famine, but they and their descendants remained there for four hundred years. The Jewish population grew tremendously. The Egyptians worried that if the Hebrews continued to grow in numbers they might join with an enemy nation and rebel. The Egyptians were concerned that they could lose their land and their lives if the Hebrews rose up from within and helped Egypt's enemies.

To reduce the population of the Hebrews, Pharaoh decided to kill all the boys born to Hebrew women (since the males could grow up to be fighters against them). Pharaoh also made the Hebrews slaves. The Egyptians humiliated the Hebrews for the remainder of the four hundred years. However, the harsher Pharaoh treated the Hebrews, the more the Hebrews grew and multiplied.

We read the account of Moses in Exodus 2. A Levite man and his wife had a baby boy, and they hid him for three months (since the Egyptians were killing male babies). Then the mother placed her son in a basket and put him into the river where the daughter of Pharaoh found the boy, retrieved him, and named him Moses. The baby's sister, Miriam, who had watched to see what would become of her brother, asked Pharaoh's daughter if she needed a nurse for the boy. Pharaoh's daughter told the girl to find a

Hebrew nurse. So Miriam took Moses back to their own mother for him to be breastfed by her.

Moses grew up in the house of Pharaoh. As a young man Moses witnessed two men fighting. One was an Egyptian, and the other was a Hebrew. Moses looked to the right and to the left and saw that no one was watching, so he killed the Egyptian and buried him. Another day he saw two Hebrews fighting. As he went to speak to them to counsel them not to fight, he discovered that his secret of killing the Egyptian was known. Even Pharaoh found out about it according to Exodus 2:15 where it says that Pharaoh decided to kill Moses. However, Moses escaped from Egypt and went to live in the land of Midian. He found work and a wife and stayed there forty years.

Then God spoke to Moses through the famous burning bush, commanding him to go back to Egypt to lead the Hebrew slaves to the Promised Land. God told Moses that He had heard the groaning of His people and remembered His covenant with Abraham, Isaac, and Jacob. What covenant? It was the covenant to give the Promised Land to the descendants of Abraham.

We read in Exodus 4:21-23: [21]**And the LORD said to Moses, "When you go back to Egypt, see that you do all those wonders before Pharaoh which I have put in your hand. But I will harden his heart, so that he will not let the people go.** [22] **Then you shall say to Pharaoh, 'Thus says the LORD: "Israel *is* My son, My firstborn.** [23] **So I say to you, let My son go that he may serve Me. But if you refuse to let him go, indeed I will kill your son, your firstborn."'"**

The warning of God here is very clear. God asked Moses to go to Pharaoh and tell him that (after four hundred years of slavery) he must let God's firstborn, God's chosen people, Israel, go free and leave the land of Egypt. However, God knew that Pharaoh would harden his heart and not let them go. That is why God gave the warning, and here is the law – let the Hebrew people go. Pharaoh must let God's firstborn, the children of Israel, go free.

God told Pharaoh that if he chose to disobey, that is, if he refused God's command, that God would kill Pharaoh's firstborn son as a judgment for this sin. The word of God was clear, and the punishment of disobedience to the command of God was also clear.

We know from the Scripture that God brought ten different plagues upon Egypt. Every time God performed one of these plagues, Pharaoh called Moses and asked him to pray to God to remove the punishment and the plagues from him and the Egyptian people. Pharaoh promised that then he would free the children of Israel.

However, after Moses interceded and God removed the plagues from the Egyptian land and the Egyptian people, Pharaoh once again changed his mind, hardened his heart, and did not let the Hebrews go. This was repeated nine times as Pharaoh refused to let God's people go. That is when Pharaoh's opportunity for repentance was over.

God called upon Pharaoh and his people to do what is right. That is exactly how God has always been from the beginning of life here on earth until today. God is gracious in that He still gives us a second chance, a third chance, a fourth chance, and many more chances to do what is right. Remember, He waited in Noah's days for one hundred and twenty years. He waited from the days of Abraham until the days of Moses (over four hundred years) for the original people of the Promised Land to do what is right. God waited on Pharaoh during these nine plagues to do what is right and let the people go.

Let us look at Exodus 13:15-16: [15]**"'And it came to pass, when Pharaoh was stubborn about letting us** (*us* here is obviously Moses and his people) **go, that the LORD killed all the firstborn in the land of Egypt, both the firstborn of man and the firstborn of beast. Therefore I sacrifice to the LORD all males that open the womb** (Moses is talking about the firstborn of the animals)**, but all the firstborn of my sons I redeem.'** [16] **It shall be as a sign on your hand and as frontlets between your eyes, for by strength of hand the LORD brought us out of Egypt."**

God had warned Pharaoh earlier in Exodus 4 that if he would not let the Hebrew people go, God would punish Pharaoh by taking the life of his firstborn. That is exactly what took place as is written in Exodus 13.

Let me remind you of the promise that God had given to Abraham four hundred years earlier in Genesis 15:14. The nation that would enslave

Abraham's descendants would be judged by God, and Abraham's descendants would come out of that nation with great substance and great abundance. That is exactly what happened. After the firstborn of all the Egyptian people and animals died, Pharaoh called Moses and told him that the Hebrews could now go free. Do not forget the sacrifice of the unblemished lamb and the blood which was applied to the door posts and lintels on the night of the first Passover which is a picture for the sacrifice of the Lamb of God (Jesus Christ).

We read this account in Exodus 12:31-35: **³¹Then he called for Moses and Aaron by night, and said, "Rise, go out from among my people, both you and the children of Israel. And go, serve the Lord as you have said. ³²Also take your flocks and you herds, as you have said, and be gone; and bless me also. ³³And the Egyptians urged the people, that they might send them out of the land in haste. For they said, "We shall all be dead." ³⁴So the people took their dough before it was leavened, having their kneading bowls bound up in their clothes on their shoulders. ³⁵Now the children of Israel had done according to the word of Moses, and they had asked from the Egyptians articles of silver, articles of gold, and clothing.**

We read in the Scriptures that the Egyptians were begging and urging the Hebrews to leave their land because they were afraid that they would all die. The children of Israel did exactly as Moses instructed them. The Egyptians were even willing to give the descendants of Abraham precious jewelry and costly items, so that these former slaves left the land of their bondage as wealthy pilgrims headed for the Promised Land.

This took place at the end of four hundred thirty years after Joseph's family came to Egypt. Now, someone will say that we have an error in the Bible. God told Abraham that his descendants would be slaves for four hundred years, but we read in Exodus 12:41 that they stayed in Egypt for four hundred and thirty years. However, there is no such contradiction in the Bible. The four hundred and thirty years is the length of time the Hebrews lived in the land of Egypt, but they only served the Egyptians as slaves for four hundred years for they lived the first thirty years as the family of Prince Joseph (he was a powerful and respected leader). None of the Hebrews served as slaves as long as Joseph was alive.

As a matter of fact, they lived in the best part of the land of Egypt. During the life of Joseph, all the Egyptians served as slaves for Pharaoh after they sold their animals and land for food. However Joseph's family was free. Then we read in the Bible, that after Joseph's death, a new Pharaoh came into power who did not know Joseph or his people. This was the time when slavery began for the Hebrew people in Egypt.

Now, did Pharaoh really let the Hebrews leave the land of Egypt? The answer is actually "no" because he followed them with his armies. The Hebrew people left and camped near the Red Sea. Pharaoh followed them because he thought the Hebrew slaves would leave just for a few days to worship their God and then come back. However, he discovered, as we read in Exodus 14:5, that the Hebrew slaves had escaped and fled from Egypt and had no intention of returning.

That is why Pharaoh rose up, took his soldiers, and followed after the Hebrews to bring them back to Egypt. As we read in Exodus 14:7-9: **[7]Also, he took six hundred choice chariots, and all the chariots of Egypt with captains over every one of them. [8]And the LORD hardened the heart of Pharaoh king of Egypt, and he pursued the children of Israel; and the children of Israel went out with boldness. [9]So the Egyptians pursued them, all the horses and chariots of Pharaoh, his horsemen and his army, and overtook them camping by the sea beside Pi Hahiroth, before Baal Zephon.**

God allowed the hardened heart of Pharaoh to desire to bring the Hebrews back to Egypt to continue to serve him, and Pharaoh thought that he had the strength and power to do so. When Pharaoh drew near to the Hebrews, they saw the Egyptian army behind him. They became afraid crying out to the Lord.

They complained to Moses, asking if there were no graves in Egypt in which they could be buried. Had Moses brought them to the wilderness to be killed by the hand of the Egyptians? Don't forget that they had asked Moses to leave them alone in Egypt, so that they would serve the Egyptians and live.

Moses answered as we read in Exodus 14:13-14: **[13]And Moses said to the people, "Do not be afraid. Stand still, and see the salvation of the LORD,** which He will accomplish for you today. For the Egyptians whom you see today, you shall see again no more forever. ¹⁴ The LORD will fight for you, and you shall hold your peace."** The battle was the Lord's. It was not about Moses. It was not about the Egyptians. None of the Hebrews were prepared to do any fighting, and they didn't need to.

The Egyptians and their mighty army and with the leadership of Pharaoh were about to crush the Hebrew slaves. If this was just a normal battle, it was certain that the Egyptians would win and crush every last one of the Hebrews who dared to fight them and then take the rest back to slavery in Egypt. Surely the untrained Hebrews would be no match for the mighty armies of Egypt.

However, this is not the lesson we learn from this study. It was the Lord's battle. God was the one who would fight. From day one, it was God who would fight for the Hebrew people as they journeyed back to take the Promised Land.

We read in verses 19-27 that God commanded Moses to stretch out his hand over the sea and to strike the water with his rod. The Lord sent a strong wind from the east that caused the water to divide, and the Hebrew people walked to the other side on dry land. Pharaoh, his chariots, his soldiers, and his horseman followed the Hebrews onto the dry land in the middle of the parted sea.

A pillar of fire stood between the Hebrews and the Egyptian army, separating them during this long crossing. After the Hebrews left the dry land of the sea and arrived on the other side, the water returned. Pharaoh and all his army drowned. They were all killed on that day because the Lord fought the battle against the Egyptians. That happened when Moses stretched out his hand once again over the waters of the sea, the water returned to its place and the Egyptians drowned, delivering Israel from the hand of the Egyptians. According to Exodus 14:30: **"So the Lord saved Israel that day out of the hand of the Egyptians…,"** and the Hebrews saw the dead bodies of the Egyptians on the shore of the sea. That was when God's chosen people feared God, and they believed in the Lord and in His servant, Moses.

Here in Exodus 14 we see that the Lord fought for the children of Israel. Just as He used the flood waters with Noah, God used the water of the sea to destroy Pharaoh and his mighty Egyptian army. It was a jihad, a holy war which God performed. It happened in one day. The children of Israel did not touch one Egyptian for it was the Lord Himself who fought against their enemies.

This was the beginning of the journey of Moses and his people to return to the Promised Land so that the promise of God would be fulfilled. He gave His word to Abraham, Isaac, and Jacob that their descendants would come back to receive the Promised Land.

This was the first battle in which the Jewish nation, God's chosen people, was involved. As we have seen, these men who had left Egypt with their wives and children, the old and the young, carrying everything they owned, were not prepared for such a battle. They were slaves not soldiers.

It was God's war. If it had not been God's war, they would have lost the battle. However, they won the battle without one strike of a Hebrew sword. They won the battle without any spear or any weapons of war. They simply won the battle when God chose to pick up the water of the sea to crush Pharaoh and his host. All of these Egyptians drowned; all of them were dead. Not one of the Hebrews died in this battle, and not one of the Egyptians left this battle alive.

This was the first organized attack against the Jewish nation. They escaped by simply walking across the dry sea floor. God destroyed the entire army of Pharaoh. It was a true and just jihad that we see in the Bible. It was **God's war, not Moses' war.**

God fought the battle for the Hebrews, and they won the battle and were able to obtain their freedom. It was a battle for the Jewish nation to be set free from slavery in Egypt. It was a battle to begin the journey to the Promised Land. The Hebrews had to win this battle, because if they did not win, they would continue to be slaves in the land of Egypt, **and God's** promise given to Abraham, Isaac, and Jacob would never have been fulfilled.

In Volume 2 of this series we will see the difference between the battle of the Lord and the wars of Mohammed. There we will see the difference between the holy jihad in the Bible and the unholy jihad in the Qur'an. Notice here, the Egyptians had enslaved the Hebrew nation (consisting of over two million men, women, and children) for over four hundred years. It was an act of justice for these people to leave Egypt and go on with their lives, especially when we know that these were not just any ordinary people. These were God's chosen earthly people, the people who would bring us the Scriptures, and one day, the Savior. These were the people who lived a godly life even though they lived in a pagan land. The Egyptians worshiped their Pharaohs and a host of false gods, but this chosen nation worshiped Yahweh (Jehovah), the God of the Bible.

All Moses said to Pharaoh was: "Let my people go." If Pharaoh had let the Hebrews go freely and leave peacefully, not one of his army would have drowned. Since Pharaoh was stubborn and had hardened his heart, God allowed all of this to happen to the Egyptians. Don't forget that it was Pharaoh who had chased after the Hebrews and it was God who took Pharaoh out, as well as all of his soldiers. The victory was given to the Jewish nation so that they may leave and inherit the Promised Land as God had promised to Abraham.

Holy War or Jihad

What is meant by jihad (holy war) in the Bible? It is a war to bring holiness and to punish sin. It is a war to get rid of evil. It is the Lord's battle. It is God's war. We have learned that it was because of the wickedness of man, that God chose to wipe out every living creature in the Flood of Noah. God made the land more "holy" simply by getting rid of evil men.

Scripture shows us a similar situation in the case of the people living in Sodom and Gomorrah. Their sin and their wickedness were beyond the measure of correction. As we see in the Bible, there were not even ten godly men in this entire area. That is the reason God chose to destroy Sodom and Gomorrah by killing everyone in the land by fire and brimstone. That is what is meant by jihad (holy war) in the Bible.

Rules of Jihad

Rules of Jihad in the Old Testament: Deuteronomy 20

I would like to share two important passages regarding the rules of war as set forth by God. The first is taken from a passage in Deuteronomy 20. In verse 1 we read: **"When you go out to battle against your enemies, and see horses and chariots *and* people more numerous than you, do not be afraid of them; for the LORD your God *is* with you, who brought you up from the land of Egypt."**

Here is the first rule of a battle against an enemy: it is not about your numbers or their numbers. As we study these wars in the Bible, so many times the number of the enemy was much larger than the number of Jews who went to fight. Nonetheless, the Jews won the battle because it was God who fought the battle for them and through them. As we read in Deuteronomy 20:2: **"So it shall be, when you are on the verge of battle, that the priest shall approach and speak to the people."**

Here is a very important rule: the Jewish priest will speak to the people who are about to go into battle, encouraging them by letting them know that the Lord will go with them and fight the battle for them, and they will have victory. We see this clearly in Deuteronomy 20:3-4: ³**And he shall say to them, "Hear, O Israel: Today you are on the verge of battle with your enemies. Do not let your heart faint, do not be afraid, and do not tremble or be terrified because of them;** ⁴**for the LORD your God is He who goes with you, to fight for you against your enemies, to save you."**

It is God's war. It is God's battle. He will win it because it is a holy war against sin. It is His work. That is why the Jews had to understand that there was no reason to be faint-hearted, no reason to fear, no reason to tremble, and no reason to be terrified because God is the one who will lead them in holy war. They will win it no matter how strong or how large the enemy is.

Now, according to the second set of rules, before a war began, their officers went before the people to tell them who was and who was not exempt from fighting in the war. In Deuteronomy 20:5-7 we see the rules for those who are exempt from fighting in war. These are the men who have just built a new house, the men who have planted a vineyard but have not eaten from it, and the men who are engaged to a woman but are not married yet. These three groups must be exempt from the battle because they must dedicate their homes, they must harvest their vineyards, and they must complete their marriage. They must accomplish these three objectives in life before they go off to war and maybe die in battle before they can fulfill their duty to their homes, their farms, and their fiancées.

We see also in Deuteronomy 20:8-9 when it comes to those about to engage in jihad and perform holy war, there must not be any weak men in the army, such as those who are afraid to die in war. If such men were in the battle, they could cause other men to be afraid and perhaps retreat from the war. These men must return to their homes because their attitudes are not good for the well-being of the army.

Now, let us look at the people the Jews were going to engage in war. There were two different groups: those who lived in the Promised Land and those who lived in faraway lands. To those who lived in a faraway land, God gave them a way out so that the Jews would not have to fight them and eliminate them. If they surrendered to the Hebrews, they could live. We read about this in Deuteronomy 20:10-12: [10]**"When you go near a city to fight against it, then proclaim an offer of peace to it.** [11] **And it shall be that if they accept your offer of peace, and open to you, then all the people who are found in it shall be placed under tribute to you, and serve you.** [12] **Now if the city will not make peace with you, but makes war against you, then you shall besiege it."**

So what will the Hebrews do to all the men of the city who go to war against them? We read about this in Deuteronomy 20:13-14: [13]**"And when the LORD your God delivers it into your hands, you shall strike every male in it with the edge of the sword.** [14] **But the women, the little ones, the livestock, and all that is in the city, all its spoil, you shall plunder for yourself; and you shall eat the enemies' plunder which the LORD your God gives you."** These rules were set only for the people who lived far from the Promised Land as we read about in Deuteronomy 20:15: **"Thus you shall do to all the cities which are very far from you, which are not of the cities of these nations."**

What about the cities that existed in the Promised Land? God said to Moses and the Hebrew people that they must kill every one of them. Why? We see the reason in Deuteronomy 20:16-17: [16]**"But of the cities of these peoples which the LORD your God gives you as an inheritance, you shall let nothing that breathes remain alive,** [17]**but you shall utterly destroy them: the Hittite and the Amorite and the Canaanite and the Perizzite and the Hivite and the Jebusite, just as the LORD your God has commanded you,** Why did God want to strike down all of these people? The answer is in verse 18 which states: **lest they teach you to do according to all their abominations which they have done for their gods, and you sin against the LORD your God."**

These were the wicked people. These were the sinful people whom we read about in Genesis 15 where God told Abraham that his descendants would return to inherit the Promised Land (not in Abraham's time but after their four hundred year sojourn in Egypt). Why? The sin of the original inhabitants of the land had not yet been fulfilled. Now Moses was coming out of Egypt to take this Promised Land, and these evil people had to perish. These ungodly people had to be eliminated, and every one of them must be put to death because of their sin and for their wickedness. If the Hebrews did not remove them, then God's chosen people would have sinned according to the wickedness of the Canaanites and the Jews would have to be put to death.

We will see that this is exactly what happened as we continue to study jihad in the Bible. We will see that when God's chosen people sinned against God and disobeyed God's command, they themselves were put to death because God is no respecter of persons (impartial). It doesn't matter who it was who sinned. If the Amorites and Hittites and all the other "ites" sinned against God, they must be put to death because the wages of sin is death. We are talking about *physical* death here. They had already died spiritually, separated from God, and they must be put to death physically. Because God is not a respecter of persons, even when His own chosen people sinned against Him, they must also be put to death, just as we see throughout the teachings in the Old Testament.

What about the rules for the cities with which the Hebrews were about to engage in war? What about the trees, the houses, and all the things inside? Should the Jews do whatever they wished with them or burn the city and

everything in it? The Bible gives the answer in Deuteronomy 20:19-20:
¹⁹**"When you besiege a city for a long time, while making war against it to take it, you shall not destroy its trees by wielding an ax against them; if you can eat of them, do not cut them down to use in the siege, for the tree of the field *is* man's *food*.** ²⁰ **Only the trees which you know *are* not trees for food you may destroy and cut down, to build siegeworks against the city that makes war with you, until it is subdued."** So these are the rules concerning the trees in a holy war. The Jews were not to cut down fruit trees, but they could cut down other trees to use the wood to fight in the battle against their enemy.

Rules of Jihad According to Christian Theologians

Now, let's examine a set of rules according to a biblical scholar. I would like to share a quick summary from *The New American Commentary*. D.K. Stuart (Volume 2, 2006) of the book of Exodus. On pages 392-397 the author stated that holy war could be summarized by twelve propositions:

Proposition #1: no standing army was allowed. The battles were fought by amateur volunteers who had to depend upon God for their success and could not boast in their own accomplishments.

Proposition #2: no pay for soldiers was allowed. These fighters were going to war as God's agents of justice, not as people seeking their own advantage.

Proposition #3: no personal spoil or plunder could be taken. The general rule of a worldly war (not a holy war) was that a soldier could keep anything that he could take from an enemy; but in a holy war, a Hebrew soldier could not personally take any of the spoils of war.

Proposition #4: a holy war could only be fought for the conquest or defense of the Promised Land. Israel had no right to any other land or to go to war for any other purpose. A good example of this is when David tried to expand his empire and God punished him as we read in 2 Samuel 24:1-17.

Proposition #5: only at the Lord's direction could a holy war be launched. No king or even a high priest could make a decision to initiate a holy war. Only God alone could.

Proposition #6: only through a prophet could that divine call come. Prophets were spokespersons for God. Only through a prophet could the decision about going to war (or not going to war) come.

Proposition #7: the Lord did the real fighting in a holy war because the war was always His. Holy war is ultimately a war to defeat Satan and his angels. Holy war is a spiritual war to deal with evil and sin.

Proposition #8: a holy war was a religious undertaking involving fasting, abstinence from sex, and/or other forms of self-denial. It was an act of obedience to God and not of national pride or military strategies.

Proposition #9: the goal of a holy war was the total annihilation of an evil culture. Let me remind you again that this was the main issue concerning the taking of the Promised Land. It was because the original people of the land had sinned without repentance. God punished these people by annihilating them because of their sins. We can read this in Genesis 15:12-16. Obviously, this is when the original people of the land had become so corrupted that God could do nothing else except to exterminate them. We saw this in the Flood, we saw this in Sodom and Gomorrah, and we will see this in the wars led by Moses and his people. (As a side note, historians who study these Canaanite civilizations have often said that their practices were so evil and utterly barbaric that the extermination brought about by the armies of Israel did the world a great favor. These wicked nations were like a societal cancer, dangerous and malignant. God, in His righteous wisdom, performed surgery and removed them from the world.)

Proposition #10: anyone who becomes a violator of the rule of holy war will be an enemy. That means if any of the Jews would not obey all the rules, they would become an enemy and be punishable by death. During our study, we will show many examples where the Jewish people sinned against God and did not obey these rules and how He punished them for sinning against Him.

Proposition #11: exceptions and limitations were possible, especially in the case of combat with those who were not original inhabitants of the Promised Land, and therefore were not automatically exterminated. We will see a wonderful example of this when we look at the first war led by Joshua between the Hebrews and the Amalekites.

Proposition #12: a decisive, rapid victory characterized a holy war. It was expected that if God was behind a war then that war would be concluded in a day, the day of Yahweh or the Day of the Lord.

We will compare these rules in Volume 2 with the rules that Mohammed gave to the Muslims when they went into battle and invaded other countries. You will see that they are quite the opposite.

We have read that there were rules and regulations as to the manner in which the Jewish people treated the far (distant) and near (close) original inhabitants of the Promised Land and also those who began living in the Promised Land at a later date. The original people were to be annihilated due to their sins against God. The people who lived close to the Jewish settlements had to be eliminated. Those inhabitants who lived farther away could have the option to have peace if they would accept the terms of surrender. If they chose to fight, the Jews were given permission by God to kill all the men.

Why were the Jews commanded to kill all of these original inhabitants? Once again, it was because of the promise of God to Abraham and because of the sin and wickedness of the original people. If they were allowed to live among the Jewish people, the Jewish people would intermarry with them, worship their gods, and fall into the same sin that the original people had. These wicked nations were like a malignant, spiritual cancer. The evil and wickedness of the original people would eventually cause the Jews to sin, and therefore they would also have to be killed.

Now, someone may say, "Doesn't the Bible say, 'Thou shall not commit murder'?" Yes, indeed, it does. The Bible clearly states in Exodus 20:13: **"You shall not murder."** It also states in Exodus 23:7: **"Keep yourself far from a false matter; do not kill the innocent and righteous. For I will not justify the wicked."** This is God's word; this is God's command.

Here are some questions. What if someone commits murder, killing an innocent soul? Should we just let them go free or maybe put them in a nice hotel for forty years with full health care, good food, a nice bed to sleep in, TV programs to watch, and allow them to have fun? No. The same Bible which teaches us (as individuals) not to murder also teaches very clearly that if someone commits a murder, you must kill that person (capital punishment by the government). We read this in Exodus 21:14: **"But if a man acts with premeditation against his neighbor, to kill him by treachery, you shall take him from My altar, that he may die."**

This is the true justice of the Bible. Sin must be punished. If someone commits a murder, that person must be put to death. The wages of sin is death. It does not matter who the person is who has committed the atrocity. If he is a Hebrew or if he is from another people (like the original people living in the Promised Land), he/she must be put to death because this is the punishment for their sin. It is God's physical judgment on earth.

Notice that the Bible does not limit capital punishment to just murder, but there are also many other sins that should be punished by physical death. Notice that these laws were given to all mankind, not just the Hebrews. That is what makes it a just law, i.e. a moral, righteous law.

Anyone who sins must be put to death. If God was willing to enforce this law on His own chosen people, Israel, the people that He is about to take to the Promised Land, then He is going to enforce it on other people who likewise commit any of these sins without repentance. They must also be put to death.

Where can we find a list of some of these sins that must be punished by death? We can look in Exodus 22:18-24. Let's read these verses to understand that God punishes sin no matter who the person is who commits these sins. Remember that the original people in the land were living and practicing these sins long before Moses and that he was instructed to wipe them out so that the Israelites could inherent the land promised to Abraham. In verse 18: **"You shall not permit a sorceress to live."** Anyone who practices sorcery (Satanic witchcraft) must be put to death. Many of the original people living in the Promised Land were practicing all sorts of demonic sorcery and seeking satanic power, and that is why they must be put to death by the hand of Moses and his people.

Then in verse 19, the Bible states: **"Whoever lies with an animal shall surely be put to death."** God forbids abnormal and deviant sexual behavior, such as bestiality. By the way, in the teaching of Islam, there is no such punishment for men who have sexual relations with an animal.

In verse 20, the Bible states: **"He who sacrifices to any god, except to the Lord only, he shall be utterly destroyed."** It is hard to imagine, but these wicked nations were not only offering animals to other (false) gods, but they were also offering *their own children* to these gods! That is why God told Moses that he must annihilate these people completely from the Promised Land. If any Israelite did the same thing, then he must also be put to death as well because this was God's rule.

Verse 21 states: **"You shall neither mistreat a stranger nor oppress him, for you were strangers in the land of Egypt."** God commanded that any strangers (foreigners) who came to the Jewish land in peace were to be treated justly, treated well, and treated with generosity by the Israelites. God reminded the Israelites that they themselves had been strangers in a strange land in Egypt, had been oppressed, and therefore were forbidden from treating strangers as they had been mistreated.

Then in verses 22-24: **"You shall not afflict any widow or fatherless child. ^{23}If you afflict them in any way, and they cry at all to Me, I will surely hear their cry; ^{24}and My wrath will become hot, and I will kill you with the sword; your wives shall be widows, and your children fatherless."** This was the command of God for the Hebrews as well as anyone else. God is sovereign, and these are His rules. God cares about those who are suffering and in need. We are forbidden from oppressing the less fortunate or from taking advantage of those destitute and suffering, such as widows and orphans.

As we look at these righteous laws and compare them against the Canaanites who lived in the Promised Land for hundreds of years, these people were living in wickedness and practicing all of these sins. That is why, as I have already stated, holy war (jihad) in the Bible is a justified war. It is a justified killing because the wicked are being held accountable for their sins. In it justice is served. Holy war gets rid of evil (like removing a spiritual cancer) by eliminating the people who commit these sins. It is God's rules, and He knows what is best for the world.

It is important to note that these are not the same rules as we find in the cult of Islam. In Islam, Mohammed engaged in war (by the command of Allah/Satan) to help his cult grow and to take over Jews, Christians, and

Chapter 2: Rules of Jihad

Christianity. Therefore, it was not to fulfill the will of God but the will of Satan, to eliminate those who believe in Jesus Christ as Lord and Savior.

To summarize holy war in the Old Testament, we have to understand that it was necessary for two important reasons. First, it was for the Hebrews to be able to defend themselves against anyone who was trying to harm them. Second, it was to get rid of the wicked people in the land who were living in unrepentant wickedness. Therefore, the Hebrews were commanded to annihilate these people completely in order that they would not influence the Hebrews and cause them to sin against God in the same manner.

Now, let's continue our study to see what happened to Moses and the Hebrews after they crossed the Red Sea on their way to the Promised Land. There is a very important verse we need to look at in Exodus 13:17: **Then it came to pass, when Pharaoh had let the people go, that God did not lead them *by* way of the land of the Philistines, although that *was* near; for God said, "Lest perhaps the people change their minds when they see war, and return to Egypt."**

The distance from the land of Goshen in Egypt, which is where the Hebrews had lived in slavery, to the Promised Land is roughly a twelve day's journey by foot. However, God did not lead the Hebrews out of Egypt by the shorter path. Instead, God actually took them in a wide arc.

Many skeptics have mocked the account of the Exodus from Egypt and claimed that it never really happened. Some have even claimed that the Hebrews only crossed a shallow body of water in the Red Sea. This is **ludicrous. As an Egyptian, I don't know how dumb my ancestors would have been** in order to all drown in shallow water. Remember, my Egyptian people are the ones who had the intelligence and wisdom to build the mighty pyramids and invent the incredible process of mummification. So, skeptics out there, how stupid do you think my Egyptian people were?

I believe the main problem for the archeologists who have denied the crossing of the Red Sea is due to the fact that they have searched in the wrong place. Many of them have speculated that the Hebrews crossed the Red Sea near or in the Gulf of Suez. However, it is far more likely that they crossed at the Gulf of Aqaba. So, obviously, if you are searching for any evidence of the crossing of the Red Sea, but are looking in the wrong location, you will never find it.

Recently, many other archeologists have discovered evidences of the crossing of the Red Sea simply because they were searching in the right place. (If you are interested, many of these evidences are available online for those who wish to investigate it.)

The point I would like to make from this passage is that God did not take the Hebrews on a short route from Egypt to the Promised Land. Instead, He took them on a longer route because God knew that if they were to get into a war they would run back to Egypt, they would not fight, they would not obey His command, and then they would miss God's blessing of living in the Promised Land. God knows the decisions we *would* make in any given situation, and in His omniscience, He knew that His own people would rebel if they faced war at this point in their experience.

First Holy War – Amalek vs Israelites: Exodus 17-23

Having said all that, let us begin our study of the first war mentioned in the book of Exodus. The Bible states in Exodus 17:8-13: **⁸Now Amalek came and fought with Israel in Rephidim. ⁹And Moses said to Joshua, "Choose us some men and go out, fight with Amalek. Tomorrow I will stand on the top of the hill with the rod of God in my hand." ¹⁰So Joshua did as Moses said to him, and fought with Amalek. And Moses, Aaron, and Hur went up to the top of the hill. ¹¹And so it was, when Moses held up his hand, that Israel prevailed; and when he let down his hand, Amalek prevailed. ¹²But Moses' hands became heavy; so they took a stone and put it under him, and he sat on it. And Aaron and Hur supported his hands, one on one side, and the other on the other side; and his hands were steady until the going down of the sun. ¹³So Joshua defeated Amalek and his people with the edge of the sword.**

Now, before I begin interpreting these verses, I would like to draw your attention to an important point. When we read the Qur'an, we read its interpretations by Muslim scholars. I will do the same here because we have biblical scholars who help us to understand the Bible just as Muslim scholars help us to understand the Qur'an. I am always amazed at Muslims who read the Bible and interpret it for themselves without seeking the wisdom of legitimate scholars. They need to read the interpretation of the Bible by its own scholars. Thus we will be looking at the understandings and views of various Christian scholars as we go through this study.

Let us first look at the description of Amalek according to Christian scholar Douglas K. Stuart and his interpretation of the above verses in the book of Exodus. In *The New American Commentary* (volume 2, 2006) on page 393, he describes the Amalekites as the ones who started the fight with Moses and the Hebrews. We read about them in Genesis 36:12 which states that they were the descendants of Amalek, the grandson of Esau, and they organized themselves into an early national nomadic group. As a matter of fact, they were the first among the nations according to words of Balaam in Numbers 24:20.

Another fact about the people of Amalek is that they lived partly by attacking other population groups and plundering their wealth. We read about this in Judges 3:13. The Amalekites had domesticated the camel and used its swiftness effectively in surprise attacks. They not only attacked the Israelites in this battle at Rephidim but a year later they attacked them again in Hormah when the Israelites had been driven out of southern Canaan and were on the run after their foolish attempt to enter the Promised Land in spite of God's command through Moses that they could not win the battle and they should not go into battle. We read about this in Numbers 14:43-45.

From the reading of the Bible, we discover that the Amalekites were the ones who started the fight. They were a well-trained people of war; they knew that the Israelites had no defenses. That is why they decided to attack the Israelites. That was their business; that was their way of life.

As we read from the text, every time Moses lifted up his hand with the rod of God, the Israelites would prevail; but every time Moses lowered the rod of God, the Israelites began to lose. Obviously, we can learn that it was God who was giving the victory to the Israelites against these well-trained, well-equipped Amalekites. It was not about the power of Israel, but it was actually the power of God which is represented here in the rod of Moses.

Another crucial fact is that the Israelites had only one day to prepare for the battle after Moses asked Joshua to pick out some of the men to fight the Amalekites, even though the Amalekites were well-trained and well-prepared. This was their lifestyle, the way they made their living. Even so, God helped the weak Israelites to have victory over these professional warriors. The Amalekites were well-equipped with all kinds of weapons, but the Hebrews (who had just come out of Egypt) likely did not have a significant supply of weapons. They were not equipped for war because their Egyptian masters surely would not let them carry weapons. So, obviously, they were fighting with whatever crude weapons they were able to fashion to be able to defend themselves.

As I shared earlier in the 12 Propositions of a Holy War, I would like to emphasize Proposition #11 which stated that "exceptions and limitations were possible, especially in the case of combat with those who were not original inhabitants of the Promised Land, and therefore were not automatically exterminated."

Accordingly, the Amalekites (who were not original inhabitants of the Promised Land) were added to this list of who must be annihilated by the hands of the Israelites. I personally believe this was because the Amalekites had attacked the Israelites, and that is why the Israelites had the right to defend themselves and wipe them out. That is exactly what happened as we read in Exodus 17:13: **So Joshua defeated Amalek and his people with the edge of the sword.** This was the first holy war, a war of defense, against the Amalekites. Through this victory, God was protecting His chosen people so that His promises to Abraham would be fulfilled. The Jews were God's messengers for bringing His Word and ultimately His Son, our Savior, the Lord Jesus Christ, to the rest of the world.

<u>Golden Calf - Israelites vs Levites: Exodus 32</u>

Another account in the Bible where God utilized jihad is found in Exodus 32. God implemented jihad because of the sin of the Israelites (His chosen people). In this tragic event, God used the Levites to execute three thousand other Israelites who had sinned wickedly. According to Exodus 32:1: **Now when the people saw that Moses delayed coming down from the mountain, the people gathered together to Aaron, and said to him, "Come, make us gods that shall go before us; for as for this Moses, the man who brought us up out of the land of Egypt, we do not know what has become of him."**

Chapter 2: Rules of Jihad

When the Hebrews left Egypt, they were given plenty of gold and silver from my people, the Egyptians. When Moses remained away from them for an extended period, the Hebrews asked Moses' brother, Aaron, to forge for them a god to worship. The ladies took the gold from their ears and their hands, their necks, from their sons and their daughters giving this gold to Aaron. We see this in Exodus 32:2-3. In verse 4, Aaron took this gold and made a golden calf for them and said to them: **"This is your god, O Israel, that brought you out of the land of Egypt!"** It is difficult to imagine the extreme grief that this brought to the heart of God, the God who had lovingly rescued them from enslavement in Egypt.

Not only did Aaron make them a golden calf, but he actually built an altar for it as well. Then Aaron announced to the people that the following day was going to be a day of celebrating and feasting to the Lord. In verse 6, we read that the Hebrews rose up early the next morning, offered sacrifices of peace, ate and drank, and then played.

All of this took place while Moses was still on the top of the mountain speaking with God. Since nothing is hidden from God, God told Moses in verse 7: **"Go, get down! For your people whom you brought out of the land of Egypt have corrupted themselves."**

Verse 8 is a crucial verse because someone might say that maybe the "ignorant" Hebrews did not know that this was a sin and that it was wrong to worship other gods. No. God had already told them not to do such things. Verse 8 clearly states that the Hebrews had quickly turned from what God had commanded them not to do and made for themselves a golden calf which they worshiped and sacrificed to by saying: **"This is your god, O Israel, that brought you out of the land of Egypt!"** The reaction of God in verses 9 and 10 is very clear. A righteous and holy God became offended at their wickedness. He declared to Moses, because the people were stubborn and sinful, to let Him alone take out His anger against them and destroy them. Then He would raise up from Moses a great nation, just as He had raised up a nation from Abraham. Since Moses was a direct descendant of Abraham, this would not break God's original promise.

However, Moses reacted differently to this than one might expect. He became humble as he interceded before God on behalf of the Hebrews, those who had sinned against God, broke His covenant, and had done the opposite of what God had commanded them to do. We see this written in Exodus 32:11-12: ¹¹**Then Moses pleaded with the Lord his God, and said: "Lord, why does Your wrath burn hot against Your people whom You have brought out of the land of Egypt with great power and with a mighty hand? ¹²Why should the Egyptians speak, and say, 'He brought them out to harm them, to kill them in the mountains, and to consume them from the face of the earth'? Turn from Your fierce wrath, and relent from this harm to Your people."**

Someone may seek to reject these words of the Bible by asking, "Is this how easy it is for the God of Israel to change His mind? Is this a God who deserves to be respected and worshiped by the Israelites? What kind of God is this who changed His mind and repented just because His prophet asked Him to do so?"

Did God change His mind and repent? No. God in His sovereignty will not let this happen. As the Scripture declares, God is not a man who can change His mind or a man who would lie about what He is about to do. Here we see the reaction between the God of Israel in His might and strength and the God of Israel in His grace and compassion. As a just and righteous God, the entire nation of Israel (minus one) must be wiped out because they had sinned. Once we look at the God of Israel as a loving and kind God, He has the right to show His mercy to His people. Moses interceded on behalf of his people exactly as Christ interceded on behalf of the Church concerning their sin as He went to the cross, died, was buried, and arose from the grave. For in reality, all of us Christians deserve to spend eternity in Hell because all of us have sinned. This is the *third* death, the *eternal* death, separation from God because of our sin. What Christ did on our behalf on the cross gives us the opportunity to live eternally in Heaven. Jesus was separated from His heavenly Father due to our sin, and He died for us on the cross. He suffered separation and death so that we would not have to suffer them. God can now offer a free pardon to any who will receive it because of what Christ has done for us.

Getting back to this sin of Israel in worshiping the golden calf, in verse 13, Moses reminded God of His promises which He had given to the early fathers, Abraham, Isaac, and Jacob. He reminded God of the Old Covenant, not because God had forgotten, but because Moses believed the promises of God as he interceded. Moses reminded God, "You promised Abraham,

Chapter 2: Rules of Jihad

Isaac, and Israel that You swore by Yourself that You will make their children and their descendants as numerous as the stars in the heaven. You will give to their children this Promised Land that they may inherit it. How can You destroy all of them in Your anger? Show Your mercy and grace even though Your people have sinned against You."

That is why we see in verse 14 that God chose *NOT* to destroy the Hebrews. In simple words, God had two options. Option one is that He may use His justice and will destroy every one of the Hebrews who had sinned against Him by worshiping this golden calf. Option two is that He may use His grace, His mercy, and His love which means He will spare their lives for a little bit longer even though He knows that they are a stubborn and "stiff-necked" people.

As we continue with the account, Moses went down from the mountain with the two tablets of the Law that God had made by His own hand (the famous Ten Commandments). As Moses came down from the mountain, he first met Joshua who was unaware of what the people had done. Joshua heard a voice which he thought was a noise of war. Obviously, Joshua did not know what had taken place, but God had already told Moses what had happened. That is why in verse 18 Moses said that this was not a voice of war but a noise of singing.

In verse 19, when Moses drew near the camp and saw the golden calf and the people dancing, he himself became angry. This is why he cast the two tablets down, and they broke upon the ground. Not only did God become angry because of the sinful acts of the Hebrews, but his loyal servant Moses also grew incensed at their folly. Through the dropping of the stone tablets, we see the level of frustration in Moses. One thing about the Egyptian culture in which I grew up is that when people get upset, they break whatever they have in their hands.

The Hebrews had sinned against the God of Israel by breaking the first two commandments. They made a god of the golden calf. Then they worshiped it by offering sacrifices to it instead of worshiping the true God, the God of Israel.

In verse 20 we read that Moses then took their golden calf and melted it with fire, ground it into powder, and scattered the powder of gold in the water. Then Moses gave the water to the Hebrews and told them to drink it. There goes my Egyptian ancestors' gold into the bellies of the Hebrews. Maybe that is why we never got our gold back!

So imagine with me that what Moses did was a picture, a mocking of their foolishness. "You made this golden calf," he was saying, "and I am going to smoke it for you, I am going to burn it for you, I am going to grind your god into powder, and you are going to drink this foolish act which you have done." They all drank their golden calf. Then the people, if you can imagine with me, were saying to Moses, "Well, it was your brother Aaron who made this golden calf for us." This is so true of human nature, we always try to place the blame and guilt on others, rather than ourselves. It happened in the Garden of Eden with Adam and Eve, and it has continued down through the ages until today.

Then a very tense conversation took place between Moses and Aaron. In verses 21-24, Moses asked Aaron (so to speak), "What is wrong with you, man? What did these people do to you to make you sin in this terrible way?"

Well, Aaron, the man who was about to become the high priest of the children of Israel, told his brother, "Don't get angry with me. You know these people. They are evil."

So here was Aaron pointing a finger of blame at the people, and yet he was supposed to be the spiritual leader for them! Just like many spiritual leaders of today, he yielded to the ungodly desires of his flock and tried to be a people-pleaser. He told Moses, "Well, they told me to make gods for us. You went to the top of the mountain, you delayed, and we didn't know what had become of you. So, I told them to give me their gold. They gave me the gold, I threw it into the fire, and here this golden calf came out of the fire." What a foolish excuse (and lie) that Aaron tried to give to Moses. As I have already stated, Aaron was supposed to be the spiritual leader, the one who was to lead the people to do what was right, but he actually led them into further sin by making the golden calf. Woe to spiritual leaders who lead their flocks away from the truth of God in order to be popular or to gain some earthly reward!

Then, according to verse 26, Moses drew a line to divide the camp between those who were faithful to the Lord God and those who were worshiping the golden calf. The children of Levi joined Moses in their loyalty to God, and this is where we see God's jihad performed.

God's chosen people sinned against Him by making and worshiping a golden calf. Remember, the wages of sin is spiritual death, physical death, and eternal death. In this true account we see the three deaths taking place. The people sinned spiritually when they worshiped a false god (golden calf). Then those Hebrews suffered the physical death by the sword of the Levites. Obviously, those who purposefully sinned against God and did not repent, even after physical death, will suffer an eternal death in the fires of Hell. The wages of sin is death.

Where do we read about this in the Bible? In verses 27-28: [27]**"Thus says the Lord God of Israel: 'Let every man put his sword on his side, and go in and out from entrance to entrance throughout the camp, and let every man kill his brother, every man his companion, and every man his neighbor.'"** [28] **So the sons of Levi did according to the word of Moses. And about three thousand men of the people fell that day**.

Not only do we see God's justice, but we also see His grace because if it had been only God's justice, none of these men would have been spared from death. However, because of God's grace and the intercession of Moses, only three thousand men died on that day. There were over two million Hebrews who left Egypt. So, even though there were three thousand men killed, hundreds of thousands of lives were spared.

In verses 29-30, we see God's blessing on the Hebrews whom He had just spared. Then Moses spoke to the people. He explained to them that they had sinned against God. So he interceded on their behalf for God to forgive their sin in verses 31-32. Moses confessed the sins of his people to God and sought forgiveness for them. Once again, God accepted his intercession.

However, God told Moses, in verses 33-35, that all those who had sinned against Him will be blotted out of His book. He was speaking of the eternal punishment in Hell. God also told Moses that the Angel of the Lord will walk before His people. In addition, God said that He will not let their sin go completely unpunished. That is exactly what we read in Exodus 32:33-

35: ³³**And the Lord said to Moses, "Whoever has sinned against Me, I will blot him out of My book.** ³⁴**Now therefore, go, lead the people to *the place* of which I have spoken to you. Behold, My Angel shall go before you. Nevertheless, in the day when I visit for punishment, I will visit punishment upon them for their sin."** ³⁵**So the Lord plagued the people because of what they did with the calf which Aaron made.**

So, what do we learn from this account concerning killing (jihad) in the Bible? We see here that God performed a justified jihad by using the sons of Levi as His sword of justice to kill three thousand Hebrew men who had sinned against Him. That is the justice of God.

As I have shared with you before, God is no respecter of persons. When the Hebrews sinned and worshiped the golden calf, He became angry and commanded Moses to use the sons of Levi to kill three thousand of them. When the original people of the land, the Hittites, the Canaanites, and all the other "ites," sinned against God by worshiping other gods by offering their own children as sacrifices to these gods, God's justice would surely be served. We see that He is the same God, with no partiality.

I know that it is easy for Muslims to open the Bible and show verses in which the Hebrews used the sword, killed women and children, and destroyed lands according to the command of God. Then our Muslim friends will say, "Look with me; read with me. Here in the Bible is the exact same teaching which Allah gave to Mohammed in the Qur'an. It is exactly like what we have in the Qur'an." No, it is not. The Bible contains exactly the opposite of what is written in the Qur'an. In the Bible, God allowed this to happen as a punishment for the sins of the people of the earth.

However, in the Qur'an, Allah (who is Satan by his own admission), ordered Mohammed and his believers to go and kill. Whom are they to kill? It is the Christians, those who are living godly lives because they simply believe that Jesus Christ is God Almighty who came in the flesh, died on the cross, was buried, and arose from the grave.

So jihad in the Bible is a justified jihad. People sin, Hebrews or Gentiles, and the punishment of their sin is death. That is exactly the justice of God.

However, according to the **teaching of the Qur'an**, it is the opposite in Islam. The god of Mohammed (Satan) is called to literally annihilate the

Christians and the Jews, God's chosen people and God's true believers, because they are living right and are in obedience to the holy words of God in the Bible. One could say that the Qur'an teaches that "the wages of righteousness is death."

I am glad that the Lord God included Chapter 32 in the book of Exodus. For if we did not have this passage, some might think that God is not treating all people the same, but here is a true historical account of what happened in the life of Moses before the Hebrews began to fight against and kill the original people of the land as a justified punishment for their sin. God punished His own people when they sinned against Him by worshiping the golden calf. This scene will be repeated throughout this study about jihad in the Old Testament. God is impartial.

Unholy Jihad: Numbers 13-14

¹**And the Lord spoke to Moses saying,** ²**"Send men to spy out the land of Canaan which I am giving to the children of Israel; from each tribe of their fathers you shall send a man, every one a leader among them."** ³**So Moses sent them from the Wilderness of Paran according to the command of the Lord, all of them men who were heads of the children of Israel.** Numbers 13:1-3

God spoke to Moses and instructed him to send out spies from every tribe to check out Canaan, the Promised Land, the land which God had promised to Abraham, Isaac, and Jacob. Moses did as God instructed and picked out twelve men, one from each tribe, to send them to the Promised Land. However, before sending them out, he gave them a list of things to look for and to investigate.

Remember, the original people living in the Promised Land were wicked people, and their time to be judged had arrived. God did not choose to punish them by a flood as in the days of Noah or by fire as in the days of Sodom and Gomorrah. Instead, God chose to use His people, the Hebrews, to judge them by the edge of the sword. That is why we see Moses sending the spies to investigate the land to see what strategy should be used to engage in war against these people.

The instructions which Moses gave to the spies are found in Numbers 13:18-20. Moses told the spies to see what the land is like, see what kind of people live there, and see if they are strong or weak or are large or small in numbers. He told them to look at the land itself to see if it is good or a bad land. He asked them to see if the people were living in flimsy tents or in stone strongholds. He also instructed them to investigate the land to see if it is fat or lean and what kind of trees and fruit are grown there. He encouraged them to bring back some of the fruit since it was roughly between July and September, the time of the harvest.

So they went, as written in verses 21-29, and investigated the land. There they saw the children of Anak. When the spies arrived at the Valley of Eshcol, they took one cluster of grapes so large that it took two of the spies to carry it on poles. They also brought back some figs and pomegranates.

After forty days, the twelve spies returned from their appointed mission. They reported the *good* news to Moses and the Hebrew people about the land. It was "flowing with milk and honey" and showed the people the fruit which they had taken from the land. Then they gave the *bad* news about the land. They reported that the people were strong, the cities were walled, and they had seen the children of Anak there. They stated in verse 29: **"The Amalekites dwell in the land of the South; the Hittites, the Jebusites, and the Amorites dwell in the mountains; and the Canaanites dwell by the sea and along the banks of the Jordan."**

Here we see the spies were divided into two groups, a group of two men and a group of ten. Caleb and Joshua encouraged the people and Moses to go and take the land. Caleb told the people in verse 30: **"Let us go up at once and take possession, for we are well able to overcome it."** However, the other ten spies told the people in verse 31: **"We are not able to go up against the people, for they are stronger than we."** They spread fear among the Hebrews when they told the people that the men of the land were giants compared to the small and weak Hebrews.

Chapter 14:1 gives the reaction of the people when they heard the report about the Promised Land: **So all the congregation lifted up their voices and cried, and the people wept that night.** Why were the Hebrew people crying? Why were they weeping? It was simply because they had heard the negative report, the evil report about the Promised Land, and they believed it. They had waited a long time to come to the Promised Land, and here they heard this bad report.

Maybe the Hebrews thought that the inhabitants living in the land might be weak people dwelling in tents and then they could take over the people and the land by their own might and strength. They did not count on or look to the Lord God who had led them out of Egypt, taken care of them, and performed great miracles. They thought they could do it through their own power and their own strength. So this bad report bothered them because they had already forgotten the mighty hand of God.

Then the Hebrews began to grumble against Moses and Aaron and complained in verses 2 and 3 saying: **"...If only we had died in the land of Egypt! Or if only we had died in this wilderness! ³Why has the Lord brought us to this land to fall by the sword, that our wives and children should become victims? Would it not be better for us to return to Egypt?"** Then in verse 4: **So they said to one another, "Let us select a leader and return to Egypt."**

As I was studying this passage, I discovered that not only were these grumbling Hebrews rejecting Moses and Aaron's leadership (and Joshua and Caleb's good report about the Promised Land), but they were rejecting God Himself. They wanted their own leader to take them back to Egypt and back to slavery!

Remember, God did not take the Hebrews on the shortest path from Egypt to the Promised Land. He took them on a longer route because He knew that they would grumble and that when they would be threatened with war, they would want to return to Egypt. They said it would be better to live as slaves in Egypt than to be the owners of all the blessings of the Promised Land, the land full of milk and honey. That is why God did not take them on the shortest route to the Promised Land. If He had, they would have already returned to slavery in Egypt. The familiar past, even when that past was slavery, was preferable to an unknown future!

What was the reaction of Moses and Aaron when they saw what was happening? We read in verse 5: **Then Moses and Aaron fell on their faces before all the assembly of the congregation of the children of Israel.** Here we see the humility and brokenness of the hearts of Moses and Aaron at the direction the entire nation wanted to take. The Hebrews were once again living in disobedience to the command of the Lord. God wanted them to take the Promised Land. He wanted to bless them. However, they rejected blessing and chose not to take the Promised Land.

They forgot the mighty hand of God. They forgot that God had drowned Pharaoh and his entire host in the sea. They forgot all the miracles God had performed before their eyes. Now they were weeping and wanting to leave the Promised Land and return to Egypt and slavery!

What was the reaction of Joshua? What was the reaction of Caleb? These were the two spies who saw the Promised Land, believed in God, and were willing to live in obedience to God's command to take the Promised Land. Their reaction was very clear in verse 6: **But Joshua the son of Nun and Caleb the son of Jephunneh, who were among those who had spied out the land, tore their clothes.**

In my Egyptian culture (and in most of the Middle East), tearing one's clothes often means a great deal of sorrow and frustration because of some great sin which has been committed. Both Joshua and Caleb believed that the Hebrews had sinned wickedly against God by not obeying His command to go into Canaan and take the Promised Land, and not only that, but the Hebrews also wanted to leave the Promised Land, appoint a *new* leader, and return to Egypt to live as slaves.

Once again, Joshua and Caleb spoke to the people and explained to them how beautiful and excellent this land was. They told the people that, if the Lord is pleased with them and they are in obedience to Him, He will freely give them this land.

In verse 9, Joshua and Caleb told them not to rebel against the Lord. They told the Hebrews not to fear the people of the land. At the end of verse 9, Joshua and Caleb told the people that the Lord is with them and not to fear the people of the land because the Lord is with the Hebrews. It was not about the strength of the Hebrews. It was not about the weakness of the enemy. It was about the strength of the Lord Yahweh who commanded them to go up and take the Promised Land.

Instead of listening to Joshua and Caleb, the people picked up rocks to stone the two who were willing to obey God's command, the two who trusted the Lord God of Israel. In verse 10, a visible form of the Lord's glory appeared in the tabernacle before all the children of Israel. Then God spoke to Moses in verses 11-12: **11"How long will these people reject Me? And how long will they not believe Me, with all the signs which I have performed among them? 12I will strike them with the pestilence and disinherit them, and I will make of you a nation greater and mightier than they."**

That is exactly what the Hebrews did. They rejected Moses. They rejected Aaron. They rejected the opinion of Joshua and Caleb. They even rejected God Himself. They were about to appoint a leader of their own choosing, to leave the promises of God, and to go back to Egypt to be slaves once again.

What was Moses' reaction? His reaction was the same as before. This kind man, with a humble heart before God and before the people, interceded once again on behalf of the disobedient Hebrew people. He reminded God that the Egyptians would hear about what He had done to the Hebrew people (if he annihilated them). To summarize, Moses spoke to God saying, "You are the one who covered them with a cloud by day and traveled before them with a pillar of fire by night. If You kill the entire people, the Hebrews, what will the inhabitants of the land say when they hear about this? They will say that the Hebrews' Lord was not able to take His people to the Promised Land which He had sworn to give to them and killed them in the wilderness."

Once again, we see Moses beg God not to destroy the Hebrews because of their disobedience and their sin. He reminded God of His power, His might, His long suffering, and His great mercy. Moses begged God to forgive their sin. Moses said to God in verse 19: **"Pardon the iniquity of this people, I pray, according to the greatness of Your mercy, just as You have forgiven this people, from Egypt even until now."**

The answer of God was, once again, truly amazing. Sometimes people look unfairly at the God of the Old Testament as a harsh and mean God, and sometimes people look at the God of the New Testament as a loving and merciful God. However, we see throughout the Old Testament that God was merciful and showed His grace so many times to His people (and even to the wicked people of the land) if they repented of their sin.

Remember, God had made a promise to Abraham more than four hundred years earlier that He would give this land to His people. Throughout all of these years, the inhabitants living in the land were living in sin, but God had not destroyed them. It would have been very easy for God to send fire from heaven or send one of His angels to wipe out the wicked people of the land, but God chose to show His mercy and patience for all of these years. He had not judged the people of the land, but now He wants to use His chosen people (the Israelites) to bring judgment to the wicked people of the land and also bless His people by taking the Promised Land. By doing this, not only would God punish sin, but He would teach His own people a lesson (and us as well) about the seriousness of sin and of the judgment of a righteous God.

The Lord said to Moses in verses 20-24: [20]**"...I have pardoned, according to your word;** [21]**but truly, as I live, all the earth shall be filled with the glory of the Lord—** [22]**because all these men who have seen My glory and the signs which I did in Egypt and in the wilderness, and have put Me to the test now these ten times, and have not heeded My voice,** [23]**they certainly shall not see the land of which I swore to their fathers, nor shall any of those who rejected Me see it.** [24]**But My servant Caleb, because he has a different spirit in him and has followed Me fully, I will bring into the land where he went, and his descendants shall inherit it."**

Obviously, the judgment of God here is justified. These people did not believe God when He told them that they could take the Promised Land with His help. Except for Caleb and Joshua, these unbelieving Hebrews will not see the Promised Land. God told Moses to tell them that all the people twenty years old and older (the age of men eligible to fight) will fall dead in the wilderness, according to verses 29-30. None of them will enter the Promised Land, except for Caleb and Joshua and the children.

All those adults who had rejected God and didn't believe Him, all of them would die in the desert and never enter the Promised Land. The judgment of God caused them to wander in the desert aimlessly for forty years. That was one year for every day that the spies had spent in the Promised Land. That is what is written in verse 34. As for the other ten men who spied out the land of Canaan and gave a bad report, verses 36-37 tell us that they all died with a plague.

Then we see a jihad which the Hebrew people decided to do, but it was NOT according to God's word. That is why I will not call this jihad a "holy jihad" but an "unholy jihad." Why is that? It is because, as we see in verses

39-40, after Moses spoke and told the children of Israel what the Lord had told him, they mourned greatly; but early in the morning they decided to go up to the mountain to begin this foolish plan.

Moses asked them in verse 41 why they had transgressed against the commandment of the Lord. Moses continued in verses 41-43 to tell the Hebrews that this "jihad" they were about to perform would not succeed because God was not in it. They would not win the battle, so they were not to go up and fight. They were warned that they would be defeated by their enemies because they had rejected the Lord. The Lord would not be with them.

However, as we read in verses 44-45, they decided to go to the mountain to battle anyway, but Moses and the Ark of the Covenant did not go with them but remained at the camp. Then the Amalekites and the Canaanites came down, attacked, and drove the Hebrews back as far as Hormah.

The Hebrews lost the war for the simple reason that they disobeyed and did not believe God. Because they engaged in this war, not according to the Lord's will, and they disobeyed His command, God punished them by not allowing them to enter the Promised Land. Because they went in their own strength, they could not win the battle. This was not a holy jihad simply because God was not in it. It was just an unholy war, and they lost.

Three Holy Wars: Numbers 21

Unlike the unholy war in Numbers 13 and 14, there are three "holy" wars found in Numbers 21 in which the Hebrews performed jihad according to the will of God and received victory in each of these battles. Also, we will see what happened when the Hebrews once again grumbled against God. They experienced the punishment of God, which was a justified punishment even towards His own chosen people, because the wages of sin is death.

First, let's look at Numbers 21:1-3. The king of Arad, a Canaanite king who lived in the South, heard that the Israelites were coming. They were coming along the road to Atharim. So the king of Arad started the fight against Israel and won, and he took many prisoners of war. This time the Israelites did the right thing, and this is why we can call this fight a holy war. How do we know that this was a holy war? If they called upon the Lord and He gave them permission to go and fight, then that was a holy war, a righteous war.

In verses 2-3, we see that the Israelites made a vow to the Lord God of Israel, and in their vow they said to the Lord that if He delivered the Canaanites into their hands, then the Hebrews would utterly destroy them and their cities. The Lord listened to their cry and delivered up the Canaanites, and the Hebrews utterly destroyed them and their cities.

The Israelites won this battle simply because they sought the Lord, and He gave them the victory. The Canaanites were ungodly people, and the punishment of their sin was by the hand of the Lord even though they attacked the Israelites first and took many of them as spoils of war. However, when the Hebrews sought the help of God and gave Him the glory for this battle, the Lord gave the Canaanites into their hands, and they had a great victory in this battle.

Notice what happened next in verses 4 and 5. The Hebrews continued to travel from Mount Hor by the way of the Red Sea and then had to go around the land of Edom. They became discouraged as they traveled. Once again, they began to complain and grumble against God and Moses by saying, "Why did you take us out of Egypt so that we may die here in this wilderness? There is no food. There is no bread. There is no water. We hate this ridiculous food we are eating. Manna in the morning. Manna in the afternoon. Manna in the evening. We are getting sick and tired of this manna. We need something else!"

I can imagine the Hebrew people grumbling against Moses, somehow wishing to be slaves once again in Egypt. They remembered the smell of onions and garlic that they used to cook for their Egyptian masters. They hated what God had given them as they remembered the tasty food of Egypt.

So what happened to God's chosen people when they sinned against God and against Moses? The punishment of their sin was death. I think it is safe to say that the Hebrews hadn't learned this crucial lesson yet. How many times, as we have studied the history of this stubborn and stiff-necked people, do we see that they have not learned their lesson? The Apostle Paul tells us in 1 Thess. 5:18 to "give thanks (not grumbling or complaining) in all circumstances; for this is the will of God."

Every time they sinned against God and complained and grumbled against Him and Moses, God punished their unbelief. Once again, here is the justice of God, no matter who the person is who is committing the sin. When it was the Canaanites, the inhabitants of the land, who sinned against God, He destroyed them by the hand of the Hebrews. When it was the Hebrews who sinned against God, He destroyed them as well. In this case, as we see in verses 6-9, God used snakes (serpents). The Lord sent fiery serpents upon the Hebrews, and anyone who was bitten by the serpents died. Because of their rebellion, many Hebrews died in the wilderness. When the people realized that they had sinned, they confessed their evil to Moses. They asked him to pray to the Lord and to ask Him to take away the serpents so that they would not be destroyed. Once again we see Moses, the man with the heart of humility, the man who quickly runs to intercede on behalf of the people, go to the Lord. The Lord gave him the answer. The answer was very simple. God instructed Moses to make a fiery serpent from bronze and lift it up on a staff. If any person who was bitten by a serpent looked up at the bronze serpent, he would be healed.

This takes us to the account in John 3:14-16 about Nicodemus, a Pharisee, who came to Jesus at night. **Jesus told him: **[14]**"And as Moses lifted up the serpent in the wilderness, even so must the Son of Man be lifted up, **[15]**that whoever believes in Him should not perish but have eternal life. **[16]**For God so loved the world that He gave His only begotten Son, that whoever believes in Him should not perish but have everlasting life."**

In the days of Moses, those who were bitten by the fiery serpent would die unless they looked up at the bronze serpent. If they looked at the bronze serpent, expecting to be healed, they were saved. Looking at the bronze serpent was a **statement of faith saying, "We trust in the answer and provision of the Lord for our problem. We believe that He will heal us."**

Faith was what saved them. There was no magic or medicine in the bronze serpent. It was because they *trusted* in the God of Moses. They trusted in the God of Moses by looking at the bronze serpent because that was the way to be set free from the poison. That was the way to be set free from death. Just look at the bronze serpent by faith and be healed. It was their job to believe and God's job to do the miraculous healing.

So it is the same way for us today. By trusting and believing in Jesus Christ, who was lifted up on that cross, we have eternal life because that is the love of God to the world. Whoever looks at Jesus on the cross, believing that He died on that cross for us, was buried, and arose from the grave, and trusts in Jesus Christ alone will have eternal life. That is the promise of God to every person. Look in faith and live.

The Hebrews continued to travel from one part of the land to another. This was a long journey, and the Hebrews traveled all of it as Moses led them. In verse 21, Israel sent messengers to Sihon, the king of the Amorites. The message was very simple. The Hebrews told the Amorites to let them go through their land. The Hebrews said that they would not turn to the right or to the left in the fields or in the vineyards of the Amorites. They would not drink the water from the Amorites' wells. All that the Israelites were doing was asking for permission to safely travel through their land.

However, instead of King Sihon allowing them to travel through his land, he decided to war against Israel. The king gathered his people at Jahaz to fight against the Jews. Here in Chapter 21, we see another war. The Hebrews did not start it. The enemy king started it. King Sihon, the king of the Amorites, did not allow the Israelites to travel through his land even though they made a commitment not to eat from his fields or drink from his wells. In verses 24-26: "**[24]Then Israel defeated him with the edge of the sword, and took possession of his land from the Arnon to the Jabbok, as far as the people of Ammon; for the border of the people of Ammon was fortified. [25]So Israel took all these cities, and Israel dwelt in all the cities of the Amorites, in Heshbon and in all its villages. [26]For Heshbon was the city of Sihon king of the Amorites, who had fought against the former king of Moab, and had taken all his land from his hand as far as the Arnon.**"

Victory was given to the Hebrews because God was with them and because they were doing what was right. The wicked people of the land did not allow the Hebrews to travel through their land to go to the Promised Land. Instead they started a war with the Hebrews without provocation.

However, the Hebrews not only defeated the Amorites but also took all their cities and villages. Then Moses sent out spies to the land of Jazer, and they took its villages and kicked out the Amorites who lived there as well.

Now we come to the last holy war which Moses and his people performed. This account is found in Numbers 21:33-35. The Hebrew people turned and went to the land of Bashan. King Og of Bashan and all his people went out to fight the Hebrews. Now the Lord spoke to Moses and told him in verse 34: **"Do not be afraid of him. I will give him into your hand, he and all of his people and his land; and you will do to him exactly as you did with King Sihon, the king of the Amorites, who lived in the land of Heshbon."** Here we see that it is the Lord's fight for He is the One who will give the victory to Moses and his people. That is exactly what happened in verse 35, for the Bible states: **"So they defeated him, his sons, and all his people, until there was no survivor left him; and they took possession of his land."**

The promise of God (the covenant He made with Abraham over four hundred years earlier) that this land would be given to the descendants of Abraham, Isaac, and Jacob, began to be fulfilled. As these kings, one after another, came to fight against Israel and the Lord of Israel, God gave the Hebrews courage. God gave the victory to His people over all the kings of the land. When the Hebrews obeyed God and did not grumble and murmur and complain against God and Moses, they had victory.

Three victories were given to the Hebrews in this chapter. However, in this same chapter, as we saw earlier, when the people sinned against God and complained and grumbled against Moses, they were killed…sometimes by the sword of the Hebrews, sometimes by the sword of the enemy, sometimes by a plague, and sometimes by fiery snakes.

These wars for the Lord were why the Hebrews won each one of them. These wars were against evil, against wicked men, the inhabitants of the land. God's patience and grace waited on both peoples. When the Hebrews sinned, God punished them, but He also gave them grace and did not destroy all of them. When the original people of the land sinned, God was patient with them for hundreds of years so that they may repent; but when they refused to repent, He destroyed them with the sword in these three battles with Moses and his people. Sometimes the enemy began the fight, and sometime God's people began the fight. In either case, it was justice because the wages of sin is death. As I stated earlier, spiritual death leads to physical death and eternal death.

Once again, I would like to remind you that the holy war of the Bible is holy because through it God punished sin (which as Creator, He has the right to do). God removed wicked, sinful people in any way He saw fit through natural death, natural disasters like fire, flood, earthquakes, by the angel of the Lord, by a plague, or by the sword. It was however God willed it. It was justified since the wages of sin is death.

However, this is not the case in the Qur'an. In the Qur'an, Allah, the god of Mohammed, commanded Mohammed and his Muslim believers to kill the righteous ones, meaning the Jews who are God's chosen people and the Christians who believe in Jesus Christ and trust in the love of God through the death and the resurrection of our Lord and Savior Jesus Christ. We will see this in more detail in Volume 2.

Why Jihad?

Result of the Hebrews Breaking the Commands of God: Exodus 33-34

Now let us look at what happened to the Jewish people after they sinned against God and broke His first two commandments. We learn from Exodus 33:1-3 that God told Moses that He would take the Hebrew people to the Promised Land. This was the land He had promised to Abraham, Isaac, Jacob, and their descendants. However, God told Moses that He Himself would not go with them directly but instead would send His angel to go before them to drive out the Canaanites, the Amorites, the Hittites, the Perizzites, the Hivites, and the Jebusites. God told Moses that He would let His people take this land filled with milk and honey.

In verse 4, we see the reaction of the Hebrews when they heard the disappointing news. They mourned. The people were sorrowful because they needed God to go before them. This holy war to take the Promised Land from all the original people of the land could not be accomplished without faith in God. God Himself needed to be the leader of this war. So why would God Himself not go with them? The Lord told Moses and the people in verse 5 that the reason was because they were a stubborn, stiff-necked people.

Now let us see Moses' reaction to God not going but instead sending His angel before them. In paraphrasing verses 12-14, Moses spoke to God saying that "You told me to lead these people out of Egypt. You said to me that I had found grace in Your eyes. So if I have found grace in Your eyes, show me the way that I may know You. Give me grace that I may know how to look after this nation." Then God replied to Moses saying that His presence would go before Moses and give him rest.

In verses 15-16, Moses told God: [15]**"If Your Presence does not go with us, do not bring us up from here.** [16]**For how then will it be known that Your people and I have found grace in Your sight, except You go with us? So we shall be separate, Your people and I, from all the people who are upon the face of the earth."**

The difference between God's chosen people and the rest of the people living on the earth at this time was that God went with His people. He was the One who led them. He was the One who fought their battles. He was the One who performed jihad on their behalf. That was how the Jews could have victory. That was how the promise of God, His covenant which He had given to Abraham, Isaac, and Jacob, could be fulfilled. They could inherit a good land filled with milk and honey.

The response of God was amazing in verse 17. God told Moses: **"I will also do this thing that you have spoken; for you have found grace in My sight, and I know you by name."**

God would go before the Hebrews and fight the battles for them, not the angel of the Lord, but God Himself. That is one of the great differences between jihad in the Bible and jihad in the Qur'an. In summary, the Bible's battles were won by God. They were fought by God for His glory to remove evil because the wages of sin is death.

Then we see the rest of the story in Exodus 34 as God told Moses to carve out two new tablets and go to the top of the mountain so he could have the Ten Commandments once again. This was literally a picture of God giving the Hebrews a second chance. The tablets, which had been broken earlier, would be rewritten, and the people would fulfill what was written in the law so that **the blessing of God could be applied to God's chosen people.**

God told Moses to go to the top of Mt. Sinai early in the morning and that no one was to go with him. No one was to even be near the mountain, not even their cattle or livestock.

Moses did exactly as God instructed him, and the Ten Commandments were given once again. Also, God gave Moses new commandments which were to be fulfilled, and these commandments are very important. **If the Hebrew people lived according to God's commands, they would live in peace.** However, if they broke these commandments, God would punish them simply because they would be like the original inhabitants of the land, the ones God was about to annihilate from the Promised Land.

In Exodus 34:11-17, God told Moses to obey His commands. He told Moses that He was going to drive out the people of the land, the Amorites, the Canaanites, the Hittites, the Perizzites, the Hivites, and the Jebusites.

Chapter 3: Why Jihad?

Why was God going to drive out these people? It was so that the Hebrews would not make a covenant with the inhabitants of the land. God did not want these people to be a snare to the Hebrews. The Hebrews were to destroy their altars and their idols of wooden images. Why? In verses 14-16 God told Moses: **¹⁴for you shall worship no other god, for the Lord, whose name is Jealous, is a jealous God, ¹⁵lest you make a covenant with the inhabitants of the land, and they play the harlot with their gods and make sacrifice to their gods, and one of them invites you and you eat of his sacrifice, ¹⁶and you take of his daughters for your sons, and his daughters play the harlot with their gods and make your sons play the harlot with their gods.** They were not to make any false gods which they would foolishly worship.

This was the command God gave to Moses during his second time on the mountain top. God asked him to write it down. So Moses brought it down to his people. God said that He would drive out the original people of the land before Moses, fight the battles for him, and give him the Promised Land. However, there was a catch. God told **Moses that he must keep God's** commandments. God was going to remove the original people because they worshiped false gods and because of their evil. This was why God commanded Moses to never make a covenant with the original, sinful people of the land. Not only was he not to make a covenant with them, but Moses must also destroy their altars and places of worship by breaking and demolishing the images that the original inhabitants had been worshiping. God was clear. The Hebrews were not to worship any other gods beside Himself.

You see, the whole idea of taking the Promised Land from the original people was very simple. It was because these people were worshiping false gods. So if the Hebrews were going to worship the same false gods as the original people were doing, then why should God give them this land? The only reason God was fighting this holy war for the Hebrews was to make the land holy by getting rid of the evil ones. God did not want the Hebrews to become evil like the people living there.

Why was God doing all of this? It was because God was setting the **Hebrews apart as God's special, chosen people. They were not like the rest** of the people of the earth. The people of the earth worshiped and sacrificed to false gods. If the Hebrews made a covenant with them, most likely the

Hebrews would marry their daughters to the inhabitants' sons and the inhabitants' daughters to their sons.

Because the inhabitants of the land were people who worshiped false gods, they would cause the Hebrews' sons and daughters to worship these false gods. The Hebrews would then make idols and false gods just like the inhabitants of the land were doing. Just as the Hebrews were about to destroy the inhabitants of the land by the edge of the sword, God would then have to punish His own people by the edge of the sword for making and worshiping false gods.

This is the theme throughout the Old Testament. We see this in the book of Judges and in the history of the Hebrew people because they disobeyed God, not just once, but continually by not destroying the people of the land completely as God commanded. The Hebrews allowed some of them to live, then married their sons and daughters, and then finally worshiped the gods of the inhabitants of the land.

That was why God punished the Hebrews each time they disobeyed His commands. As I have mentioned before, God is not a respecter of persons. When the inhabitants of the land sinned against God by worshiping false gods, God commanded His own chosen people to perform holy war and kill them by the edge of the sword. Then, when God's chosen people sinned against God, He used some of His own chosen people to destroy those who had sinned against Him. As we study the history of the wars in the Bible, we see that God has chosen many ways to punish His own people, both naturally and supernaturally.

Now, let us look at Numbers 25:1-4 to see if the Hebrews obeyed God's word. **Israel was at Acacia Grove** (Acacia comes from the Hebrew word *Shittim*). Here is where the Hebrews began to commit harlotry with the women of Moab. The Bible states: ²**They invited the people to the sacrifices of their gods, and the people ate and bowed down to their gods.** ³**So Israel was joined to Baal of Peor, and the anger of the Lord was aroused against Israel.** ⁴**Then the Lord said to Moses, "Take all the leaders of the people and hang the offenders before the Lord, out in the sun, that the fierce anger of the Lord may turn away from Israel."**

What do we read in these verses? Just exactly what God had warned the Israelites. This is what would happen if they left alive any inhabitants of the land. If they did not kill every last one of them, the hearts of the Jews will be attached to the inhabitants of the land. If the Hebrews make any covenant with the people of the land, the Hebrews would end up worshiping their gods. A modern version of that is the Inter-faith movement.

When the Hebrews were invited for dinner to eat sacrifices offered to other gods, they ate and bowed down to these gods of the land! They sinned against God. Once again, let me remind you that the wages of sin is death. That was why God commanded Moses to kill the leaders of the people, the offenders, those who had sinned against the God of Israel.

Quite often Muslims will go to the Bible and find some of the passages describing the Israelites killing the inhabitants in the Promised Land. Then the Muslims will say, "See. Look. It is the same. Mohammed and the Muslims killed people, and Moses and his people killed people."

The fact is, that none of these Muslims dare to be honest enough to read all the other passages in the Bible where God did the same thing to His own chosen people when they sinned against Him. You will never see a Muslim read a passage describing Moses killing the leaders of his own people who had sinned against God because if a Muslim is sincere and reads the entire Bible without choosing one passage over another, he will see clearly that the God of the Bible never changes. He is impartial.

God does not have two sets of rules, one for the wicked inhabitants of the land and another set of rules for His own chosen people. If God would kill His own people when they sinned against Him by worshiping false gods, **why wouldn't God punish the people who invented the worship of these false gods?** These evil and wicked ones led God's chosen people to sin against Him.

As a matter of fact, if God's own chosen people had obeyed His command by eliminating these people from the Promised Land and eliminating their worship of false gods, they would not have fallen into the sin of worshiping these false gods. Then they would not have been punished by the hand of God. They sinned in not fully obeying the Lord, and now that disobedience had returned to ensnare them, just as God had foretold.

The Hebrews, as we read in Numbers 25:1-4, did not obey God's command. They did not kill the Moabites, they did not remove the altars, and they did not destroy the false gods. Instead, they made a covenant with the Moabites, and in the end, they committed adultery with the Moabite women. They broke all of God's commandments, all God's rules, once again.

The punishment was death. Yes, indeed, that was what happened in verse 5. Moses told the judges of Israel: **"Every one of you kill his men who were joined to Baal of Peor."**

We read in Numbers 25:6-15 that upon hearing this, the Israelites wept at the door of the tabernacle. Then a heroic man, Phinehas the son of Eleazar, the son of Aaron the priest, took a javelin and thrust it into an Israelite man named Zimri and the Midianite woman with whom he was committing adultery inside a tent. The name of the woman was Cozbi, the daughter of Zur, a leader of Midian. Because of the action of Phinehas, the plague was stopped among the Israelites. The Lord punished all those who had committed adultery, and on that day twenty-four thousand died from the plague. The Lord then blessed Phinehas because of what he did. The Lord gave the priesthood to him and his descendants because he obeyed the Lord's command to bring an end to the wickedness that God's people were committing.

In Numbers 25:16-18, we read that the Lord gave Moses a new command. He commanded the Hebrews to harass and attack the Midianites because of their plot to seduce Israel to sin, just as in the matter of Cozbi and Peor.

Continuation of Results of the Hebrews Breaking the Commands of God: Numbers 25

Let me remind you that holy war, jihad, in the Bible is about killing. It is about justice. As I have already shared with you, as we read throughout the Bible, we see that the God of the Bible is no respecter of persons. We can read this in 2 Chronicles, Proverbs, Romans, Ephesians, Colossians, and James. So, no matter who the person is who has sinned, he must be punished for his sins because the Bible states that the wages of sin is death. When a person dies spiritually, that person must also die physically and perish eternally in the fires of Hell unless he repents of his sins. This is the true account of God in the Bible. God doesn't "pick" on people, God doesn't play "favorites."

Now I would like to share with you the final holy jihad that Moses performed before he died. I know it is very simple for Muslims to open many passages of the Bible which point out that the Hebrews killed people in the land: the men, women, children, the old, and the young. Muslims use these passages from the Bible to justify all the killing which took place in the life of Mohammed as we see in the pages of the Qur'an and Mohammed's teaching in the hadith. However, we need to understand that the people which God commanded Moses to kill were wicked people, but Mohammed was commanded by Allah to kill the Christians, the godly ones, the ones who believe in Jesus Christ as their Lord and Savior. That is the opposite story. Mohammed was killing idol worshipers to force them to submit to him in order to create a larger army. He used this army to kill the Jews and the Christians simply because they refused to submit to him. He killed the Christians especially because they believed in the person and work of Jesus Christ.

As I have shared with you earlier, Muslims will often not read the other passages in the Bible where God punished His chosen people the same way that He punished the original inhabitants of the land because of their sin. That is what we read in Numbers 25, where twenty-four thousand Hebrews perished because of their own sin. Throughout the Bible, we see that many tens of thousands of Hebrews were killed because of their disobedience. God used the Hebrews to kill Hebrews. God used serpents to kill Hebrews. God used the angel of the Lord to kill Hebrews. God used plagues to kill Hebrews.

Here is a fact that all Muslims need to know. Every time the Hebrews sinned in the Bible, God punished them by death. Therefore, if it was just for God to kill His own people when they sinned, it was also just for God to kill the original inhabitants of the land for their sins.

As we have seen in Numbers 25, when God's people sinned against God with the Moabite people, God punished them for their sins. To understand the true justice of God through jihad in the passage of Numbers 31, we must first know about the sins of the Moabites. How did they sin against God, and how did they cause the Hebrews to sin against God? When we read about their sins, then we see that the vengeance of Moses and the vengeance of God was a justified vengeance.

This entire account in found in Numbers in chapters 22-25. The account begins with the king of Moab, Balak, who was the son of Zippor. In chapter 22, King Balak saw how the Hebrews walked throughout the land and literally took one city after another and wiped out the people of the land. He was terrified because of the large number of Israelites. So Balak sent messengers to the Prophet Balaam and asked him to come and curse the Israelites so that the king could have victory over them and drive them away.

When the messengers of Moab met and gave Prophet Balaam the words of their king, the Prophet Balaam told these men that he could not do what King Balak wanted him to do. He could not curse God's people for these were the people God had blessed. However, King Balak did not give up and sent more messengers, men of higher positions than the earlier messengers, to ask the Prophet Balaam to come and curse God's chosen people. This time the Lord told Balaam to go to King Balak, but he could only say what the Lord wanted him to say.

When the Prophet Balaam was on his way to see the king, the Angel of the Lord blocked his way three times. The Angel told Balaam to continue on and to only say what the Lord commanded him to say. Balaam continued on his way and met with King Balak. Three times King Balak built seven altars. He offered seven oxen (bulls) and seven sheep (rams). Each time, instead of the Prophet Balaam cursing the Hebrews, he blessed them. In Numbers 23:8, Balaam said: **"How shall I curse whom God has not cursed? And how shall I denounce whom the Lord has not denounced?"**

That was why the Prophet Balaam did not curse the children of Israel. As King Balak took Balaam to different places asking him to curse the Israelites, Balaam could not curse them. I believe a very important verse is found in Numbers 23:21: **He has not observed iniquity in Jacob, nor has He seen wickedness in Israel. The Lord his God is with him, and the shout of a King is among them.** That was the reason why the Prophet Balaam could not curse Israel. It was because God, the God of Jacob (Israel), did not find iniquity in Jacob. If Jacob sinned, then Jacob would be cursed. If Jacob lived righteous before God, then Jacob would not be cursed.

Balak, the king of Moab, was not very happy at the end of the account because he had brought the Prophet Balaam to curse the Israelites. Instead, Balaam blessed them, not once but three times. Then the Prophet Balaam reminded King Balak that when he sent his messengers to him, Balaam told them that even if the king had given him a house full of gold and silver, Balaam would still only do what God told him to do.

God chose to bless Israel **if** Israel chose to live right before God, but **if** Israel chose to sin against God, then God's curse would come upon Israel. That is exactly what we covered earlier in Numbers 25 when the Hebrews sinned against God by committing adultery with the Moabite women and worshiping the Moabite gods. As a result, God punished them and caused twenty-four thousand Hebrews to perish, for the wages of sin is death. Now, it was time for God and Moses to take vengeance on Moab.

The Final Jihad Performed by Moses: Numbers 31

Therefore, we come to the final jihad (holy war) performed by Moses, the servant of the Lord. Moses left Egypt when he was forty years old, after he killed the Egyptian. He returned to Egypt when he was eighty years old to lead the Hebrew people out of Egypt to the Promised Land. Now Moses was about one hundred twenty years old. This was the final battle he must perform before he died and was gathered to his people.

The passage in the Bible we are going to read is one of the most controversial passages. Muslims use it to try to "prove" that the Bible is a violent book, just as in the case of the Qur'an. The fact is that this final battle performed by Moses' people, according to the direction of God, was a justified war because the Midianites had sinned against God, not only by living ungodly lives and worshiping false gods but also by causing the Hebrews to sin against God by involving the Israelites in immorality with the Moabite women, eating the sacrifices to their false gods, and worshiping these false gods. As a result of these sins, God killed twenty-four thousand by a plague.

Now the time had come for the Hebrews to take God's vengeance against the Midianites because of their sin, for the wages of sin is death, and they had led the Hebrews to sin against God. Numbers 31:1-2 states: ¹**And the Lord spoke to Moses, saying:** ²**"Take vengeance on the Midianites for the children of Israel. Afterward you shall be gathered to your people."**

Before we continue with verse 3, I would like to refer you to *The New American Commentary* by R.D. Cole (2000, page 494) where he states that G. E. Mendenhall had defined the contents of this instruction as punitive vindication.

"Mendenhall is right in suggesting that the word *avenge* or *revenge* with God as the subject reflects an improper theology based of a low view of God, rather God vindicates the righteous and punishes the sinner as an essential part of His ethical, moral, and just character. God is not out for retaliatory revenge but for vindication of the honor of His people and Himself and ultimately for restoration of the well-being of humanity."

In simple words, as we read in the Old Testament and will see in the New Testament, God does not take "revenge." God does not get even with people. God is a just judge, and He executes justice. Remember when Adam and Eve were told that the day they ate from the tree they would die? After they ate from the tree, it was justice for God to punish them by causing them to die, the spiritual death, the physical death, and the eternal death. That does not mean God was taking revenge on Adam and Eve. No, God was applying the law that had been given to Adam and Eve. They both understood it very well that they must die. They sinned by their will. Therefore, it was justified for God to punish both of them.

From Adam and Eve, until the last person who walks on the face of the earth, if God punishes each one of them by death, that is a just punishment. We cannot say here that God is taking revenge. God has the right to punish those who sin against Him, physically and eternally, by death. He is the Creator, and God has the right to take physical life.

Therefore, in chapter 31, the people of Midian, had already sinned against God for hundreds of years by living in sin and worshiping false gods. The time for their punishment had now come. God told Abraham, over four hundred years earlier, that the day would come when the sins of the inhabitants would be fulfilled and that God would destroy them and give their land to Abraham's descendants. Now it was time for Moses to bring justice, to perform one last holy war, and to kill the Midianites as a punishment for their sin and as a punishment on behalf of the children of Israel whom the Midianites had led to sin against the God of Israel.

In verses 3-4 we read: **³So Moses spoke to the people, saying, "Arm some of yourselves for war, and let them go against the Midianites to take vengeance for the Lord on Midian. ⁴A thousand from each tribe of all the tribes of Israel you shall send to the war."** The total number of Israelite men who would fight was twelve thousand since there were twelve tribes and a thousand men from each tribe. By doing this, the burden of the holy war would be shared equally among the community. Midian's sin had affected them all, so they all shared in the judgment of God against Midian.

R.D. Cole stated: "When the nation acts in obedience to their God, victory, blessing, and fulfillment of life was theirs." (*The New American Commentary*, R.D. Cole, 2000, page 496)

The command was given by God to Moses to perform a holy war against the Midianites. Moses was in obedience because he instructed the Hebrews to gather twelve thousand men to fight the battle and to obey the commands of God. Therefore, the wages of the sins of the Midianites would be fulfilled, and the wages were death.

In verses 6-8 we read that Moses sent the twelve thousand Hebrew men to war along with Phinehas, the son of the priest Eleazar, and the holy articles and trumpets. The Hebrews fought against the Midianites and killed all the males as the Lord had commanded Moses. They also killed the five kings of Midian along with Balaam, the son of Beor.

This was the holy war which the Jews would use as a model for future battles. Later, as we study other wars fought by the Jewish people to take the Promised Land and to bring the justice of God to the sinful nations of the land, we will see that the Hebrews followed the same method according to verses 6-8.

This was not a holy war because Phinehas, the high priest, was in the war with the holy articles and the **trumpets but because of God's presence with** them. A holy war was a war won by the hand of God, according to the command of God, in one day. That was called the Day of the Lord.

"Here we see Phinehas, once again, acting as the antidote to Balaam, just as he countered Balaam's plan to seduce the Israelites at Baal-peor." (*The New American Commentary*, R.D. Cole, 2000, page 495) One of the five kings who was killed in this final battle was Zur. Cole also stated that Zor (or Zur in NKJV) was the father of Cozbi, the Midianite woman who was killed by Phinehas, the son of Eleazar, the high priest, along with her Israelite partner, Zimri, son of Salu. (*The New American Commentary*, R.D. Cole, 2000, page 433) We read this in Number 25:14-18.

Now, let us take a look at the killing of the Prophet Balaam. As we read before in Number 24:25, King Balak asked Balaam to curse the Hebrew people, but Balaam refused and actually blessed them three times. A simple reading of this verse could cause the reader to make the assumption that after Balaam refused to curse the Israelites, he left and went back to his home.

However, in *The New American Commentary*, R.D. Cole stated in his interpretation that "The verb sequence *arose* and *went* is a common narrative idiom...Likewise, the statement, "He returned to his place, or he returned on his way," is a common way of completing a narrative cycle." (*The New American Commentary*, R.D. Cole, 2000, page 432)

Let me put it in simple words. Let's say I was inside your living room, and I said that I was leaving and going home now. However, as I walked out to your driveway, I met with some of your children and talked with them for another half hour or so. While I stood on your driveway, a friend came by and invited me to go have a cup of coffee, so we went to McDonalds to have a cup of coffee. While we were there, my wife came by and wanted to go to Walmart to do some shopping, so we went to Walmart. This could go on for hours and hours, from early morning to late evening, until I finally arrived home much later after leaving your house.

So, the common statements of "I am going home" or "I am on my way home" do not necessarily mean that I left and went straight home. That was what happened with the Prophet Balaam, as we read in Numbers 31:16. He was actually killed in the Midianite land. He did not leave and go immediately home, as we assume in Numbers 24:25.

However, before Balaam left to go home and after he refused to curse the Israelites, he provided some additional advice to the Midianite and Moabite leaders about how he could cause the Israelites to fall into sin against God. That way the Midianites and the Moabites could have victory over the Israelites because Prophet Balaam knew that if the Israelites sinned against God, then God would be the One to curse them, and they would be defeated in war. They would be destroyed by the hand of God.

Balaam advised the Moabite women to seduce the Hebrew men into sexual immorality and lead the Hebrew men to the feast of the sacrifices made to their false gods. Balaam knew that by doing so, the women might be able to lead the Hebrew men to then worship their false gods. If they were successful in doing this, then God's anger would be upon His people.

According to Numbers 25, that was what happened. The Hebrew men were invited to the sacrifice, they worshiped these false gods, they were involved in sexual immorality with the daughters of Moab, and then God's anger was on them. Then, because they had sinned against God, God punished them by killing twenty-four thousand of their men.

Now we understand why the Israelites killed the Prophet Balaam. They killed him because he was the one who instructed the Moabites to seduce the Israelite men into sexual immorality so that they would be defeated in battle.

In Numbers 31:15-20, we read that the twelve thousand Hebrew warriors that Moses sent out to perform this battle killed the five kings, killed all the males, killed the Prophet Balaam, and then came back to camp with all the spoils of war, including all the women and all the children.

Let us see the reaction of Moses to these men in verses 15-20. Moses asked the Hebrews why they had kept all the women alive. He reminded the Hebrews that these women, through the advice of Balaam, were the ones who caused the Hebrew men to sin, and God punished the Hebrews for their sin. So Moses told them to kill every male child and every woman who had known a man intimately. Moses went on to instruct the Hebrews that whoever among them had killed someone or touched a dead body were to remain outside the camp until the time of purification was completed. Not only were they to purify themselves but also their garments, leather items, goats' hair items, and everything made of wood.

When Muslims read Numbers 31:15-20, they come to many conclusions without having studied what we have covered previously about jihad in the Bible. They say, "See. What we read in Number 31 is exactly the same as what we read in Qur'an chapters 8, 9, and 47. It is the same message. There is nothing wrong with killing because that is Allah's way of life. Even Mohammed stated this many times in the Qur'an when Allah said, 'This is the way of the ancients.' Nothing has changed. God is Allah. What God caused Moses to do in the Old Testament in the book of Numbers is the same as what Mohammed practiced throughout the pages of the Qur'an."

I have also had Muslims tell me that, in the Qur'an, Mohammed never killed women or children (which is not true, as we will prove in Volume 2). Here we read that Moses commanded the people to kill the women, but Muslims forget a very important fact. These women were killed by Moses because they were the women who had seduced the Israelite men with sexual immorality and the false worship of their gods. Because of these women, twenty-four thousand Jews were killed; therefore, these women must die for their sins. That was the justice of the Old Testament.

I remember one time I was debating with a man on the internet. I was sharing with him that Mohammed's (the prophet of Islam) immoral life does not fit the criteria for a man to be called a prophet because he was married to his young wife Aisha. Many people are shocked to learn that fifty-one-year-old Mohammed married her when she was only six years old.

The Muslim man's response was that he had read the above passage. He said, "See, here is God telling Moses to kill all the women who had known men intimately but to keep the little children." He emphasized the words *little children*, which means God, the God of the Bible, gave permission for the Israelite men to be involved with little children sexually. Therefore, if it was good in the days of Moses, it must be good in the days of Mohammed. Since God allowed it in the Old Testament, there was nothing wrong with it in the case of Mohammed.

No, my dear readers. No, dear Muslims. The Bible does not tell us that the Israelites kept the little children to be involved with them sexually! The children were not kept for that purpose at all. The whole idea here of killing the women and all the males was that these wicked people would not reproduce any new generation who would live in sin as their parents did. The physical punishment from God's perspective was concerning their sin.

As for the women who had already had intimate relationships with men, the command of Moses to kill them was to ensure that none of these women, who might be pregnant, would produce a new generation. Then that generation would live in the sin of their parents and lead the Israelites in the future to sin against God. God commanded Moses, and Moses commanded his people to kill these women as a punishment of their sins and to end the cycle of the false worship of the false gods.

Another important reason why the Israelites killed all the young men and the women was to destroy the means of future rebellion in Midian as stated in *The New American Commentary*: "Only young girls were allowed to live so that they could be taken as wives" (obviously, when they come to the age of marriage), "or they may be taken as slaves, according to the principles of a holy war…By this they could be brought under the umbrella of the covenant community of faith." (*The New American Commentary*, R.D. Cole, 2000, page 498).

In simple words, when these young virgins grew up and came to the age of maturity, they could be taken as wives by the Israelites, or they could be taken as servants by the Israelites. If they were brought into the faith, they would have children who would also grow up in the faith.

A good example of this in Scripture was Ruth, the Moabite, who was from the same people of Moab. She joined the Jewish community of faith, and eventually, out of her lineage came King David and our Lord and Savior Jesus Christ according to the flesh.

The whole purpose of performing jihad in the Bible was to get rid of the immorality, to get rid of the worship of false gods, and to get rid of the influence of these people's wicked ways. The Israelites, the people of the covenant, were to live in righteousness before God.

This is exactly what God told Moses to tell the children of Israel in Leviticus 18. In verse 3, we read that God commanded the children of Israel not to act like the people of Egypt or the people of the land of Canaan

(Promised Land). In verses 4-5, they must keep the commands of God so that they may live. The immoral sins which the Egyptians and the original people of the Promised Land practiced are mentioned in verses 6-24. God emphasized to Moses that the original people would be destroyed because of these sins, and God commanded the children of Israel and the foreigners who would be living among them to not commit these wicked practices as stated in verse 26, for the earth was defiled because of these ungodly, immoral sins. If the children of Israel committed these same sins, they must be put to death. Therefore, God's chosen people must live in obedience to the commands of God, or they would become defiled as stated in verses 27-30.

As we continue to study the Hebrews and their history, we see that when the Hebrews did not obey God and sinned against Him, God punished them. The whole idea of holy war, in the Bible in the Old Testament, was to get rid of sin and evil because the wages of sin is death. When people die spiritually, they must die physically, and they also must die eternally in the fire of Hell, unless they repent of their sin and disobedience and turn to live in obedience before the Lord God Jehovah, no matter who the person is who is committing the sin, Hebrew or Gentile, for that is the justifiable holy war.

Another great difference between the holy war recorded in the Bible and the holy war taught in the Qur'an is the purification. We read in Numbers 31:19-20 that there were rules set for the Hebrews. The unclean Hebrew men who had been involved in the battle and had killed or touched a dead body had to go through a purification ritual for seven days before they could re-enter their camp. They and their captives had to be purified and washed in pure water. They also had to purify their clothes and other material made of goats' hair, leather, and wood with water. Anything that they were going to bring back into camp had to be purified and cleansed.

Purification is not something seen or read about in the pages of the Qur'an or in the teachings of Mohammed in the hadith. Cleansing and purification were very essential according to the laws of Moses.

In Numbers 31:21-24, Eleazar, the priest, told the men which materials should first be purified with fire, such as objects made of metal. Anything that could not be purified by fire had to be purified by water. Everything had to be purified before they could enter their camp.

That is what happened in Numbers 31:25-31. God told Moses, Eleazar the priest, and the leaders of the congregation to count the spoils that were taken, including people and animals. They were to divide the spoils into two groups, those who fought in the war and then the rest of the congregation. They were to levy a tribute from the spoils of the two groups. From the group who fought in the battle, one of every five hundred of the spoils of people, donkeys, sheep, and cattle was to be taken from their half and be given to Eleazar as an offering to the Lord. The congregation was to give one of every fifty of their half of the spoils and give that portion to the Levites in charge of the tabernacle.

In simple words, all the spoils were divided equally between the warriors who had fought in the battle and the congregation. A tax tribute was levied unto the Lord from the warriors and from the congregation. The tax tribute amount on the warriors was much smaller than the tax tribute from the congregation. The warriors only gave one for every five hundred, but the congregation gave one of every fifty. For example, if there were one thousand sheep taken as spoils of war, five hundred sheep would be given to the warriors who had fought the battle and five hundred to the congregation. The tax tribute for the soldiers would be one out of the five hundred sheep, but the congregation would give ten out of their five hundred sheep. This tax tribute was a very small amount compared to the tax tribute Muslims give. **According to the teaching of the Qur'an, Muslims must give 20 percent of the spoils.**

One of the amazing things about this final jihad performed through Moses and his people was that not one of the Hebrew warriors perished. All twelve thousand warriors returned alive. This proved that Yahweh, the God of Israel, was in complete charge of the war. He gave them the victory without the loss of a single soul. Such a victory gave the Jewish people the confidence and the assurance that they would receive the Promised Land because God is the One who would give them the victory. This was the last victory God gave to Moses during his lifetime. This was the end of the Prophet Moses' legacy.

However, before Moses died, the sons of Reuben and the sons of Gad, because they had such a large amount of cattle, asked Moses if they could stay in the land of Gilead, which was an excellent land for raising cattle. Moses agreed to give them this land to be their inheritance of the Promised Land under one condition. The sons of Reuben and the sons of Gad had to promise to cross the Jordan River to fight and help the rest of their brothers to receive their own portion of the inheritance of the Promised Land. They agreed. They gave their word to Moses that they would leave their wives and children and their cattle in the land of Gilead, and all the men who were trained and equipped to fight would cross the river to help their brothers gain their possession of the Promised Land. Then they would return to their families and their land.

It is very important to note that, while the Hebrews were living under the leadership of Moses, they had been eating the manna and the quail which God had provided for them. Up until this point, the Hebrew men had not harvested any land.

Another important fact is that all the men who had left Egypt, twenty years of age and older at that time, had died, including Aaron and Moses, with two exceptions. The only two men that were older than twenty years old when they left Egypt and were still alive when they crossed over the Jordan River into the Promised Land were Joshua and Caleb, the two spies who had believed the Lord and trusted that He would give the inhabitants of the land into their hand. These are the two men who would continue to lead the Hebrew people as they crossed the Jordan River to continue to perform holy jihad on the behalf of God after the death of His servant, Moses.

The Saga Continues

Joshua and Holy War: Joshua 1-4

Let's continue our study of jihad in the Old Testament to learn about holy war in the book of Joshua to see how the Hebrews received the rest of the Promised Land. First, let me share with you a quick summary of what took place after the death of Moses. In the first chapter in the book of Joshua, we learn that following Moses' death, God spoke to Joshua, telling him that His servant Moses had died. Then God commanded Joshua to lead the people to the Promised Land which He was giving to the children of Israel.

God promised Joshua that every place the children of Israel would walk would be given to them as God had told Moses and promised Abraham, Isaac, and Jacob. God told Joshua to have courage and to be strong and not to fear any man. God promised Joshua that wherever he went, he would prosper and be successful.

God also asked Joshua to keep the law. He was cautioned to meditate on the law day and night and live according to the law. Obedience was the only way Joshua could be successful in taking the Promised Land. It was not about the strength of the Hebrews. It was not about the weakness of the enemy. It was about being obedient to the command of God, to the Torah, and to the words of God as written in the law.

Joshua then began to lead the Hebrews to take the Promised Land. He told them that in three days they would cross the river to possess the Promised Land. Joshua talked to the children of Reuben, the children of Gad, and half of the tribe of Manasseh and reminded them of their promise which they gave to Moses that they would cross the river with the rest of the tribes to take the Promised Land. Then they would return to their lands on the eastern side of the Jordan River after the battles.

In the second chapter of the book of Joshua, Joshua sent two men to spy on the land of Jericho. When they arrived, they entered the house of a prostitute named Rahab. The king of the city had heard about the men, so he sent word to Rahab asking her to give up the two men. However, she hid the men on the top of her roof. She told the two spies that she knew the Lord had given the Jews the land because the people of the land were living in fear of them. She knew (as the rest of the people of the land knew) how God went before the Hebrews, how God divided the Red Sea, and how they crossed over on dry land. They also knew how the Lord had given the Hebrews victory over all the kings on the eastern side of the Jordan River. Good news travels fast…bad news even faster.

Rahab asked these two men to spare her life and the lives of her household when they came back to take over the city. The two men gave an oath that, if she would not expose them, they would give their lives for her and that she and her household would be spared when the Hebrews came to take the city of Jericho. She let the two spies down through her window because her house was built into the city wall. The spies asked her to leave a mark on her window, and she bound a scarlet line in the window.

The two spies then returned to Joshua. We read in Joshua 2:23-24: **[23]So the two men returned, descended from the mountain, and crossed over; and they came to Joshua the son of Nun, and told him all that had befallen them. [24]And they said to Joshua, "Truly the Lord has delivered all the land into our hands, for indeed all the inhabitants of the country are fainthearted because of us."**

This reminds us of the first twelve spies who had been sent by Moses to spy on the land of Canaan. Joshua and Caleb were the only spies who believed God's promise of possessing this land which was overflowing with milk and honey. Now Joshua himself sent the two spies to the city of Jericho. They came back with a wonderful report that the people were living in fear. Now it was no longer the Hebrews afraid of the inhabitants of the land because of their size. This time it was the inhabitants who were afraid of the Hebrews because the Lord had given them this land.

Let us move on in our study to the third chapter of Joshua. We read that early in the morning all the people, under the leadership of Joshua, traveled from Shittim to the Jordan River. They slept there that night. After three days, Joshua sent the officers throughout their camp and gave the command to all the people that when they saw the Ark of the Covenant of the Lord and the priests and the Levites carrying it, they must follow behind the Ark

Chapter 4: The Saga Continues

of the Covenant. Also, they were warned to be careful. They had to follow behind the Ark of the Covenant at a distance of two thousand cubits and to not come near it. Notice here that it is the Lord leading the Hebrews to the Promised Land. They are about to accomplish another holy war by their new leader, Joshua. The Lord (Who is represented by the Ark of the Covenant) will lead them to take this Promised Land.

It is very important to realize that this was also a holy war. Joshua commanded the Hebrews in Joshua 3:5 to be holy and to sanctify themselves before the Lord because, on the following day, the Lord would do great wonders among them. Yes, indeed, it was the Lord's battle, and wonders were about to take place in their lives.

If we look at this battle and compare it to everything that Mohammed accomplished and all the wars he led and all the wars and invasions led by Muslim believers throughout the history of Islam, there is nothing in comparison. This is a great example of a holy war that was led by the Lord, as we see how Jericho fell into the hands of the Hebrews.

Remember the great miracle God performed by Moses in which the entire nation of Israel left my home country of Egypt and was able to cross through the Red Sea? Not one of them was harmed, not one of them was killed, and not one of them was drowned. However, the entire Egyptian army, with its leaders and Pharaoh, drowned in the water as the Hebrews watched.

Here, in the same way, God performed another great miracle. In it we see that the God of Moses is now the God of Joshua. He is the One who performed the first miracle to cross the Red Sea, and He is about to perform another great miracle to cross the Jordan River at the time of harvest, which means that the river was full to the top of its banks. God spoke to Joshua in verse 7 and told him that He would make Joshua great in the eyes of the entire people of Israel. Just as God was with Moses, He would also be with Joshua.

In Joshua 3:8, we read that the Lord said to Joshua: **"You shall command the priests who bear the ark of the covenant, saying, 'When you have come to the edge of the water of the Jordan, you shall stand in the Jordan.'"** Then Joshua told the Israelites to come and hear the words of the Lord their God. In doing so, they would know that the living God was among them. They would know that God would drive out the Canaanites, the Hittites, the Hivites, the Perizzites, the Girgashites, the Amorites, and the Jebusites, all the original inhabitants of the Promised Land. These are the same people that God told Abraham, over four hundred years earlier, that these were wicked, sinful people must perish for their sin. Here is another opportunity for Joshua and his people to perform jihad to eliminate these evil people and take their land.

The Ark of the Covenant of the Lord was on the shoulders of the priests on the eastern side of the Jordan River. Joshua told the Israelites that all the original people must be destroyed and removed from the Promised Land because of their sins and because of the promise that God gave to Abraham, Isaac, and Jacob concerning this land. Joshua emphasized that the Ark of the Covenant would travel in front of the people as they crossed the Jordan River.

Joshua asked the twelve tribes to choose one man from each tribe. Each of these twelve men were to pick up one stone from the bottom of the Jordan River. They were not going to dive into the water to pick up twelve stones. No, they would just simply bend down, as you would walk on the floor of the river, and pick up twelve stones to be a memorial for their children and their grandchildren. Then, as the children grew older in the years to come, they would remember by these twelve stones the great day in which the living God of Israel performed a great miracle when He dried the Jordan River and their fathers and grandfathers crossed it to take the Promised Land.

Once again, I must remind you that this was not a shallow river. It was not the dry time of the year when the level of the water in the river was low enough so that people could just walk across the river. No, as we read in Joshua 3:15: **And as those who bore the ark came to the Jordan, and the feet of the priests who bore the ark dipped in the edge of the water (for the Jordan overflows all its banks during the whole time of harvest),**... The river was flowing at its highest level. So what happened? We see this great miracle performed by God as Joshua was about to cross the river with the Israelites to take the Promised Land.

The Bible states in 3:16: **that the waters which came down from upstream stood still, and rose in a heap very far away at Adam, the city that is beside Zaretan. So the waters that went down into the Sea of the Arabah, the Salt Sea, failed, and were cut off; and the people crossed over opposite Jericho.** Then the priests, who carried the Ark of the Covenant of the Lord, stood in the midst of the river on dry land. All the Israelites crossed the river on dry land until the very last one of the people stood on the opposite shore.

Then we read next in Joshua 4:5 that these twelve chosen men, one from each tribe, lifted up a stone on his shoulder and took it to the western shore of the Jordan River. The twelve stones were piled on top of each other as a memorial for their children and grandchildren for the years to come. Whenever they would look upon these stones, they would then ask, "What are these stones for? What is the story behind these stones?" The parents and grandparents would then tell their children and grandchildren that these stones were a memorial about the mighty hand of God and the miracle He did on that day.

This is something you will never see in any of the battles in which Mohammed led his Muslim followers as they invaded many cities. This did not happen in Mohammed's lifetime nor even after his death. Neither did this happen with the rest of the caliphs (the new leaders who came after him) or with all of their military invasions. Mohammed and the caliphs never performed any miracle like this as we will see in volume 2 of this book. Throughout the history of the Muslim invasions around the world, there is not one miracle to **accompany Muslims in Mohammed's days or after Mohammed's days or even today in which they were able, by the power of a god, to take over a city or to accomplish any of their invasions.**

That is another one of the great differences between jihad in the Old Testament and jihad in the Qur'an in which Mohammed and his followers perpetrated against godly Christians and the Hebrew people. They have been the ones who refused to submit to Mohammed as a prophet and refused to accept Islam as a true religion from God. No miracles whatsoever accompanied the Muslims in any of their invasions. There were no miracles by any Muslim similar to the ones we see in the account of Joshua in the Old Testament.

After the Hebrew people had crossed over the Jordan River, the priests, who carried the Ark of the Covenant, left the river and headed to the west bank of the river. It was then that the water returned as it was before their crossing of the Jordan as written in Joshua 4:18.

On that day, the Lord magnified His servant Joshua in the eyes of Israel, and the Israelites respected Joshua exactly as they had respected Moses before him. About forty thousand men, who were prepared for war, crossed the Jordan River and were ready to take over the city of Jericho.

Chapter 4 ended with God telling the Hebrews they must teach these facts and this history to their children. They were to tell their children that their ancestors crossed the Jordan River on dry land because the Lord their God had dried the river before them just as He did in the case of Moses and the entire Hebrew nation when they crossed the Red Sea forty years earlier. Why?

We read the answer in verse 24: **"That all the peoples of the earth may know the hand of the Lord, that it is mighty, that you may fear the Lord your God forever."** It was not about the strength or the might of the Hebrews. It was not about how large their numbers were. It was about the mighty hand of the Lord God, and He is strong forever.

How God Gave Jericho to the Israelites - Joshua 5-6

In Joshua 5:1, when the kings of the Amorites and the kings of the Canaanites heard about what had taken place and how the Jordan River had dried up before the children of Israel, their hearts melted so to speak. They had no spirit left in them for the fear of the Lord had fallen on them. Now they knew that the crossing of the Jordan River with Joshua was a miracle similar to the miracle of the crossing of the Red Sea with Moses. The mighty hand of God was with His people. He was and is the One who can perform great miracles. He will give their land to the children of Israel.

Next, the children of Israel celebrated the first Passover across the Jordan River. On the following day, as we read in verse 11, they ate of the corn of the land. That was when the manna stopped coming down to them from heaven. That was when the children of Israel ate the food of the land of Canaan for the first time. God's supernatural provision lasted until His natural provision began.

In Joshua 5:13-15, we read of a mysterious encounter in which Joshua met a Man who had a sword in his hand. Joshua asked the Man if He was for them or for their enemy. The Man told Joshua that He was the Commander of the host of the Lord. That is when Joshua fell down on his face and worshiped the Man. Joshua asked what the Lord wanted to tell his servant. In verse 15, we read that the Commander of the Lord's army said to Joshua: **"Take your sandal off your foot, for the place where you stand is holy."** Joshua did so. That was a great meeting between God and Joshua.

In *The New American Commentary*, we read there are three different opinions of who the Commander of the army of the Lord was. As stated: "He may be simply an angel with a special mission or maybe he was a momentary descent of God Himself into visibility or this angel was the Logos Himself. This angel was a manifestation of Christ before He came in the flesh." (*The New American Commentary*, R.D. Cole, 2000, Excursus page 160) This is exactly what I personally believe.

This was no ordinary "angel." For just as it was in the case of Moses, when he drew near the burning bush, God spoke to him from the fire and asked him to take off his shoes. This Angel also commanded Joshua to take off his shoes because the ground cannot be holy simply because an angel appeared, but by the appearance of God Himself. As we see throughout the Bible, angels never commanded people to take off their shoes. Also, Joshua bowed down and worshiped this Angel which means this was not an ordinary angel. This was the moment where God declared Joshua to be the new leader for the Hebrew people and to fight and win the battle. Moses began his ministry by taking off his shoes in the presence of a holy God, and now Joshua, at the beginning of his ministry, in like manner, meets with a holy God with unshod feet.

It was by the sword of God and by the power of God that Joshua would have victory over Jericho. Joshua knew now that the Commander of the army of the Lord had come to give him and his people victory over the people of Jericho. There was no fear, for the Commander of the Lord's army and Joshua were on the same side.

How did the people of Jericho take this news? They were living in fear. How do we know this? In Joshua 6:1, we read that they closed all the doors because of the children of Israel. No one was able to go out, and no one was able to go in. The Lord told Joshua in verse 2: **"See, I have given Jericho into your hand, its king, and the mighty men of valor."**

We all know Joshua to be the military leader, but what kind of military leader was he? He was the military leader for the Lord of hosts. Let us examine this. First, God instructed Joshua on the tactics of war to use, and it was…*strange*. When I read this unusual account years ago as a child, I could not help but laugh. What in the world were these Jewish people doing? The command of God to Joshua and to all the Jewish people was to do *what?* It was to go quietly in a circle around the city one time every day, and they must repeat this for six days! Just imagine with me, here are the priests carrying the Ark of the Lord and going around the city of Jericho and all the people are following behind them. The only noise heard was the sound of the seven trumpets being blown by the priests. They did this every day for six days.

However, on the seventh day, they did not do it just one time but seven times. On the seventh pass, Joshua gave the command that when the priests blew the trumpets that all the people were to shout. They were to shout with a great shout; and when they shouted, the walls of the city would fall down, and that is when the fight would begin. That was exactly what Joshua told the people in verse 16.

Verses 17-19 are very important. The Hebrews were to take Jericho. The Lord was giving Jericho to them because the inhabitants of the land were wicked and sinful people, and God had been patient with these people for hundreds and hundreds of years. Now the time had come when their sin was ripe for judgment. Now God would be giving their city and lands to the Jews.

God gave the Israelites a law and told them not to break this law, because if they did, the punishment would also be on them. We read in these three verses, Joshua 6:17-19: [17]**"Now the city shall be doomed by the Lord to destruction, it and all who are in it. Only Rahab the harlot shall live, she and all who are with her in the house, because she hid the messengers that we sent.** [18]**And you, by all means abstain from the accursed things, lest you become accursed when you take of the accursed things, and make the camp of Israel a curse, and trouble it.**

Chapter 4: The Saga Continues

¹⁹But all the silver and gold, and vessels of bronze and iron, are consecrated to the Lord; they shall come into the treasury of the Lord."

God commanded Joshua and the entire people of Israel that no one was to touch anything from the city. It was forbidden. If they took any spoils from the city, they would be cursed. It was the command of God, a law not to be broken. Only the metal, the silver, gold, bronze, and iron were to be taken to the house of the Lord. It was not for the people to keep.

So, as the Israelites went around the city on the seventh day, on the seventh pass, all the people shouted, and the city of Jericho was given to the Lord. The entire city was completely destroyed. Every man, woman, and child, the young and the old, every sheep, cow, and donkey, *everything* was killed by the edge of the sword except the prostitute Rahab and her entire household.

Now, wait a minute. Did the Jewish people who fought at the battle of Jericho not take anything out of the city for themselves? Did they kill all the women and the old and the young? Did they kill all the animals and not keep any of the camels or sheep or goats or cows? Did the Jewish people burn the entire city?

That is not how Mohammed and his people performed jihad. There were two reasons Mohammed went to battle to perform jihad. The first reason was to kill Christians and Jews so as to get rid of any truth which could stand against his cult. The second reason was to get the spoils of war. He enticed his men with the blonde women from the Romans and the Greeks. He enticed his people with all the children they could obtain to enjoy as slaves and concubines. Even if Muslims died while performing jihad, Mohammed taught that they would get seventy-two virgins in paradise. You see, jihad in Islam is a win-win case. If they win, they get the spoils; and if they die, they get the virgins.

So if the Israelites did not get anything out of Jericho, then why did they go to war in the first place? Why did they perform jihad against Jericho if they were commanded by God and their leader Joshua not to take any of the spoils?

When we answer this question, we find a significant difference between **jihad in the Bible and jihad in the Qur'an. Here is an example of the great** difference between the holy war of Joshua with the city of Jericho and all the battles and fighting Mohammed led for Islam.

As we stated earlier, holy war according to the Bible must be commanded by God and for the purpose of punishment of sins or of eliminating an evil act. Holy war must be about cleansing the land from the wickedness of the work of Satan. Holy war must be performed by miracles of God so that the battle would be won in one day. We know it as the Day of the Lord.

A holy (justified) war was performed through miracles as in the case of Joshua fighting against Jericho. The Hebrews crossed the Jordan River at its highest level, miraculously, on dry ground simply by walking behind the Ark of the Covenant. Holy war meant circling the fortified city once a day for six days and seven times on the seventh day, and then the walls of Jericho fell down. It was not about the might or strength of the Jews. It was about the mighty hand of God.

Holy war was about obedience to God's command. It was not about spoils. It was not about having women, children, camels, sheep, and goats. No, it was simply a life of obedience to God's command.

That is not the same in the case of Muslims. Muslims go and fight only to get the women. They only go and fight to get the children. They only go and fight to get the cows, camels, sheep, and donkeys. There is not one place in the history of Muslims' **fighting where they were forbidden from taking the spoils of a city.** This was the opposite of the command of God in Joshua 6.

You see, the Hebrews were not fighting to get the spoils because this war did not include any spoils at all. They were not fighting to get the gold and the silver. They were fighting to bring the justice of God concerning the people of Jericho.

The people of Jericho were ungodly people who had sinned against God. They had worshiped false gods, and the wages of their sin was death. For hundreds of years God had been patient with these people, but now, when the right time came for judgment, they must all be put to death by the edge of the sword.

Joshua sent two men, the same two spies he had sent earlier to Jericho, to go to the house of the harlot Rahab once again. They took her, her father, her

Chapter 4: The Saga Continues

mother, her brothers, and those relatives who were with her in her house and removed them to Israel's camp. They fulfilled their promise to her as they had sworn to her earlier.

The entire city, according to verse 24, was burned by fire. Everything in the city was burned except the gold, silver, bronze, and iron which was taken and put in the treasury of the house of the Lord.

We read in Joshua 6:26-27: [26]**Then Joshua charged them at the time, saying, "Cursed be the man before the Lord who rises up and builds this city Jericho; he shall lay its foundation with his firstborn, and with his youngest he shall set up its gates."** [27]**So the Lord was with Joshua, and his fame spread throughout all the country.**

It is striking that when Muslims read this same passage of the account of Joshua and Jericho in the Bible, they shout, "'Allah Akbar.' The truth is showing. Here is the great evidence that the Qur'an and the Bible are the same. Yes, Mohammed in the Qur'an killed infidels, and here we see Joshua killing infidels. It is Allah's word. It is the same in the Qur'an as it is in the Bible. There is no difference whatsoever. War and jihad in both books are the same."

It is amazing that even atheists use this passage and compare it to the Qur'an to say, "Look, the God of the Bible is the same as the god of Islam. It is hate and killing, the shedding of blood. Innocent women and children and the old and young were killed by the hand of the Jews and by the hand of the Muslims. Even in the Crusades, the Christians, those who claim to be a loving, peaceful people, have done the same thing."

We must answer the claim by Muslims stating that jihad in the Bible is the same as jihad in the Qur'an. In other words, is the claim of the Muslims true? Is the God of Joshua the same god of Mohammed just because both of them killed *innocent* women and children?

Let me repeat myself once again. I pray that, by the end of this book, our dear readers will understand and lay hold of the truth fully. Jihad in the Bible is true. Killing in the Bible is true, but it is a justified killing, a justified jihad. We are talking about a physical annihilation of the people of the land. Which people? Not the Christians or the Jews as Mohammed did simply because they did not submit to Mohammed, the self-proclaimed prophet, nor did they believe in the teaching of the Qur'an because they did not believe in the god of Mohammed, Allah. In the days of Joshua, it was the annihilation of the wicked people of the land. In the eyes of God, they were not innocent. They had disobeyed his commands and worshiped false gods.

The command was clearly given in the Bible. Don't eat of the tree. For the day you eat of the tree, Mr. Adam and Mrs. Eve, you will surely die. Death is a just punishment for the wages of sin. Remember, there are three levels of death in the Bible, spiritual death, physical death, and eternal death. If you think it was bad for all the people of Jericho to be killed by the edge of the sword, you need to reconsider it again. After these people were killed by the edge of the sword by Joshua and his men, they went to Hell to spend eternity in the fiery lake forever. That is the third death which is a justifiable punishment for all the wicked people of the land. Obviously, this was not for the little children, but for those who were mature and understood what sin was and yet continued in their rebellion.

That is not the jihad of Mohammed. Once again, Mohammed killed Christians, and Allah yet today commands Muslims to kill Christians because, in the Qur'an, Allah called Christians infidels. If you believe that Jesus Christ is the Son of God, God Almighty who came in the flesh, died on the cross, was buried, and arose from the grave, then you are an infidel according to the teaching of the Qur'an in 5:72 and 5:73.

If you are a Christian, according to Allah's word in the Qur'an, Mohammed and all Muslims are commanded to kill you by chopping off your head. That is known as decapitation punishment. These are not my words, but it is the word of Allah according to Qur'an 47:4 and many other verses as we will see in depth in volume 2 of this book series.

This is one of the significant differences between jihad in the Bible and jihad in the Qur'an. Jihad in the Old Testament was a justified jihad. It was the punishment of people for their wickedness and their sins, regardless of who they were. They could be a Jew or someone else. However, jihad in the Qur'an is to kill and get rid of the godly people, especially the Christians, who believe in Jesus Christ as Lord and Savior and reject Mohammed to be a true prophet.

Chapter 4: The Saga Continues

To prove my point that the God in the Old Testament is no respecter of persons, we will study the next battle of the Jews. We must begin with this question: were the Hebrew people faithful to the commands of God at Jericho?

The Sin of Achan and the City of Ai - Joshua 7-8

God instructed Joshua concerning His prohibition of the spoils, and Joshua passed the command of God along to all the children of Israel. They were not to touch any animal, any gold, any silver, or any spoil of any kind. Not one person was to take any of the spoils. Also, the entire city was to be destroyed and burned to the ground.

So, were the Jewish people faithful and obedient to God in this command? The answer, sadly, is no. According to Joshua 7:1: **But the children of Israel committed a trespass regarding the accursed things, for Achan the son of Carmi, the son of Zabdi, the son of Zerah, of the tribe of Judah, took of the accursed things; so the anger of the Lord burned against the children of Israel.**

So you see that here, once again, when the Hebrew people sinned, God became displeased; and when the Gentile people sinned, God became displeased. It does not matter who sins. With the righteous anger of God against wickedness there is a just punishment, and the just punishment is the loss of life. It is always death.

In verse 2, Joshua sent out some spies to another smaller city called Ai. As usual, that was how war always began. Spies were sent to check out a city to see how strong the city was, how many people lived there, and what the land was like. Then the leaders planned a strategy of war, such as how many men to send, how to attack the city, and how to win the battle. Now, in this case, Joshua sent some spies to Ai. When they returned, these spies told Joshua that it would be a "piece of cake" and not to send all the people to fight. Just send a few thousand men and do not burden the entire nation to fight such a small city as Ai.

So what happened? Here is what the Bible states in verses 4 and 5: ⁴**So about three thousand men went up there from the people, but they fled before the men of Ai. ⁵And the men of Ai struck down about thirty-six men, for they chased them from before the gate as far as Shebarim, and**

struck them down on the descent; therefore the hearts of the people melted and became like water.

Do you see what happened here? Once again, when there was sin in the land, there was the punishment of God. Holy jihad in the Bible was not about how much might the Jews had, how large their numbers were, or how weak or strong their enemy was. It was to fight to get rid of sin. It was to fight to get rid of evil.

Yes, the people of Ai were a sinful people, and God wanted the Jewish people to go to war with them to annihilate them. Yet, at the same time, God cannot overlook a sinful people when punishing another sinful people. He is impartial. When there was "sin in the camp," there was no blessing from God, and then there would be a defeat by their enemies. The shameful and humiliating defeat (which involved some of the Hebrew soldiers dying) was part of God's punishment for their rebellion at Jericho earlier.

So what happened next? Joshua tore his clothes and fell on his face to the ground before the Ark of the Lord until evening. The elders also tore their clothes and put dust on their heads. The tearing of clothes and putting dust on their heads was a sign of great sorrow. It was a sign of brokenness before God, and the heart of the people melted like water, so to speak. What a sorrowful state of the people just after the great victory they had accomplished against Jericho.

Joshua spoke to the Lord in verse 7: **And Joshua said, "Alas, Lord God, why have You brought this people over the Jordan at all – to deliver us into the hand of the Amorites, to destroy us? Oh, that we had been content, and dwelt on the other side of the Jordan!"**

This was a prayer of lamentation from the humble leader Joshua to the Lord concerning this simple battle in which thirty-six Jewish men were killed and the rest of the three thousand men turned their backs and ran as cowards before their enemy. The Lord spoke to Joshua, who had been prostrate on his face, and told him to stand up. God announced that Israel had sinned. They had transgressed the Lord's covenant. They had stolen from the forbidden things. Not only had they stolen from the forbidden spoils, but they also had denied what they had done and put what they had stolen among their things. That was why the Hebrews could not stand firm against

Chapter 4: The Saga Continues

their enemy. They turned their backs against their enemy because they themselves were accursed. The Lord told Joshua in verses 12 and 13 that He would not be with them anymore unless Joshua removed the accursed from among them. He told Joshua to get up and to sanctify the people for they must be judged for their sin. Because of the accursed thing in their camp, Israel could not stand before their enemies until it was removed. So then God had Joshua investigate the twelve tribes of Israel to find out who had brought sin upon the people of Israel.

As we look at the rest of chapter 7, we read that Joshua found out the reason why the Hebrews were accursed. It was because of what Achan had done. He confessed to Joshua and the elders of Israel. In verse 21, Achan told Joshua: **"When I saw among the spoils a beautiful Babylonian garment, two hundred shekels of silver, and a wedge of gold weighing fifty shekels, I coveted them and took them. And there they are, hidden in the earth in the midst of my tent, with the silver under it."**

That was the sin of Achan. He took what was forbidden just as Adam had eaten from what was forbidden, the tree in the garden from which God told him not to eat. Here Achan took from the spoils which God told the Hebrews not to take. In both cases, they sinned in disobeying a simple and direct command, and the punishment in both cases was death. That was why the Hebrews could not win the battle against the small city of Ai.

There is a great difference between jihad in the Bible and jihad in the Qur'an. Jihad in the Bible must be a holy war, meaning there is no sin in the camp. If one man sins against God, he will bring a curse on the entire people of Israel, and then they will lose the battle. The punishment in the Bible is always justified, no matter who the person is who sinned.

So how was the curse removed from the camp of Israel? What was the punishment for Achan? Did the Jews have another chance to win the battle with Ai?

When Achan confessed to Joshua and the elders of Israel about what he had stolen and had done to bring the curse upon the camp of Israel, he had to face just punishment. We read in Joshua 7:24-26a: [24]**Then Joshua, and all Israel with him, took Achan the son of Zerah, the silver, the garment, the wedge of gold, his sons, his daughters, his oxen, his donkeys, his** sheep, his tent, and all that he had, and they brought them to the Valley of Achor. ²⁵And Joshua said, "Why have you troubled us? The Lord will trouble you this day." So all Israel stoned him with stones; and they burned them with fire after they had stoned them with stones. ²⁶Then they raised over him a great heap of stones...**

This was the just punishment for this man and for his family because of his sin. When he stole that which was forbidden, he brought a curse upon himself, his family, his tribe, and ultimately the entire people of Israel.

I know it is very easy for Muslims to attack the passages in the Bible about the Jews killing other people inhabiting the land, but will they have a sincere heart to study the rest of the passages of the Bible? For here we see Joshua and his people killing one of their own. Achan was a Hebrew. Achan was a Jewish man. He was from the tribe of Judah.

Because Achan sinned, Achan must die. When the Amorites, the Hittites, the Jebusites, and the Canaanites sinned, they must be put to death. It did not matter who committed the sin. The person who sinned must die.

That was the just law of the Old Testament as we continue to see in one holy war after another. It was not because of the land. It was not because of the spoils. It was not for whatever reason, but it was a just punishment for the people's sin. When the Hebrew people sinned, God punished them with death. When other nations around them sinned, God punished them with death.

Now let us continue our study in chapter 8 where we see the victory of Joshua and his people over the people of Ai. Israel lost the first battle with Ai simply because there was sin in their camp. Then sanctification (cleaning and restoration) took place. That is why they could now have victory over Ai. As we read in Joshua 8:1: **Now the Lord said to Joshua: "Do not be afraid, nor be dismayed; take all the people of war with you, and arise, go up to Ai. See, I have given into your hand the king of Ai, his people, his city, and his land."**

This was a holy war, and God gave victory to Joshua and Israel. God is the One who gave the king, the city, the people, and the land to Joshua and his mighty men. Then we read the command of God in verse 2: **And you shall do to Ai and its king as you did to Jericho and its king...**

Chapter 4: The Saga Continues

That meant total annihilation of the people of Ai. Why was that? Is the God of the Old Testament a cruel God? No. These were the sinful nations that God had told Abraham over four hundred years earlier that, when the sin of these nations was fulfilled, they would perish. They would be punished for their sin by the hand of the Israelites, and the Israelites would then inherit the "cleansed" land.

In this battle, God told Joshua that the spoil of this city, the cattle and all the booty, were to be taken by the people of Israel. This city was forbidden in regards to the people of the city, but it was not forbidden as for the spoil. The Hebrew people could take all the spoil out of the city.

Here was the command of God, and they must obey it. If they sinned against God, as we will see in future battles, then that was when God punished the Hebrew people. This war was a holy war ordered by God and the victory given by God. As we see throughout Scripture, there were rules for each war. The Jewish people must obey each one of God's laws because when they sinned against God by disobeying any of His commands, they themselves would be punished.

As we look at the rest of chapter 8, we see that God told Joshua how to win this war by setting an ambush for the city. So Joshua, on the night before he attacked the city of Ai, sent thirty thousand men out into the night to lay in ambush between Bethel and Ai, behind the city of Ai. He told them not to go very far from the city and be ready to attack.

In verse 10, Joshua rose early in the morning. He and the elders led the people to the north side of Ai. There was a valley between them and the city. So Joshua sent five thousand men to set up another ambush on the west side of the city. So now there are three groups of Israelites. Thirty thousand men were on the north side of Ai, five thousand men were on the west side of the city, and Joshua with the rest of the people were in the midst of the valley.

Here is a summary of what took place in verses 17-20: there were no men left in Ai or Bethel as they left the city open when they pursued Joshua and his soldiers in the valley. The Lord told Joshua to stretch out the spear in his hand toward Ai because the Lord would give the city into Joshua's hand. So Joshua did as the Lord commanded. Then those who were waiting in ambush quickly rose up and ran to enter the city. They took the city and set it on fire. When the men of Ai saw the smoke coming out from their city, they tried to flee. However, they were surrounded by the Israelites. They could not find a place to escape, not to the east or to the west or to the north or to the south because the Israelites had completely surrounded them.

According to verse 21, when Joshua and the Israelites saw that the ambush had worked and the smoke was rising from the city of Ai, they turned and began to strike down their enemies. The Israelites did not let any of them remain alive or escape, with the exception of the king of Ai, and they brought him to Joshua.

In verse 24, we read that the Israelites killed all the inhabitants of Ai, those in the fields and those in the wilderness and those still left in the city. All the people of Ai were killed by the edge of the sword.

So we see that the Hebrews were faithful to the command of God. According to verse 25, the number of people in Ai that were killed that day was twelve thousand men and women. Joshua continued to stretch out the spear in his hand until the entire people of Ai were destroyed. As for the animals and the spoils of the city, the Hebrews took them for themselves as the Lord God had commanded Joshua. Joshua once again burned the entire city of Ai and made the city a heap.

As for the king of Ai, he was killed and hung on a tree until evening. When the sun set, Joshua commanded that the king's body be taken down and put in the entry of the city. Then they covered him with a great number of stones. That was a great victory for Joshua and the Israelites against another wicked people, the people of Ai. After this victory was won, Joshua built an altar and offered many peace offering sacrifices to the Lord, the God of Israel.

In verse 33, we see the people of Israel standing on top of two mountains. Half of the Israelites stood on Mount Gerizim, and the other half stood on Mount Ebal. Then Joshua read the blessing and the curse of the law of the Lord according to the Torah. We read in verse 35: **There was not a word of all that Moses had commanded which Joshua did not read before all the assembly of Israel, with the women, the little ones, and the strangers who were living among them.**

Did you see that one word? Strangers. Strangers? Now, where did these strangers come from who heard the word of the Lord? These strangers were the female children who Moses had kept alive, as we read in Numbers 31, from the battle which he had won against the Midianites and also Rahab and her people who were saved as Joshua fought the battle with Jericho.

All the strangers who had joined the Jewish community were listening to the word of the law as they are now entering into the new community of the Jewish faith. What a great picture, to receive the blessing by the servant of the Lord, Joshua, simply by reading the word of the law.

I can only imagine Joshua telling the Hebrews, once again, that if they obey the word of the Lord, they will be blessed; but if they disobey the word of the Lord, they will be cursed. This is the theme we will continue to study throughout the Old Testament.

Gibeonites and the Kings across the Jordan River: Joshua 9-10

As we continue our study in Joshua 9, we see that the kings of the Hittites, the Amorites, the Canaanites, the Perizzites, the Hivites, and the Jebusites (those living across the Jordan River in the mountains, in the valleys, and on the coast of the Mediterranean Sea near Lebanon) heard about what had taken place with Joshua because his fame had become so great. So they decided to unite together to engage in war with Israel.

There was also another group, the Gibeonites. As we read beginning in Joshua 9:3, when they heard what had taken place in Jericho and Ai, they decided to try and deceive the Israelites. They came to Joshua at Gilgal and pretended to be from a faraway land because they had old sacks and old wineskins, dressed in old, worn sandals and garments, and only had dry and moldy bread to eat. They met with Joshua and asked the Israelites to make a covenant with them. They told the Israelites, "Look at us. We come from a faraway land. Please make a covenant with us that you will not harm us."

The Israelites asked them, "How can we make a covenant with you? Perhaps you live near us." They answered Joshua, "We are your servants." Joshua asked, "Where are you from?" They replied (lying), "From a far faraway land. We are coming to you in the name of your Lord God for we have heard of what your Lord did to Egypt and to the kings of the Amorites on the other side of the Jordan River and the other kings who the Lord your

God gave you victory over. So our elders sent us to you and gave us supplies for our trip to come all this way to make a covenant with you. Look at our supplies. See how moldy and dry our bread is, and our supplies are almost gone because we have traveled a long journey to come to you."

The Hebrew men listened to these lies, fell for their deception, and believed their story. However, the Hebrews did not seek the counsel and direction of the Lord. In verse 15 we see that Joshua made a peace covenant with them to allow them to live, and the Hebrew leaders swore to them. Then three days later, after the covenant had been made between Israel and these people, it was discovered that they were neighbors and actually lived in the midst of the Israelites in the cities of Gibeon, Beeroth, Chephirah, and Kirjath Jearim.

We see in verse 18 that the Israelites could not attack the Gibeonites because they had sworn to the Lord that they would not attack them and had made a covenant of peace with them. Then the people of Israel complained to the elders. The elders explained that they had already sworn to these people by the God of Israel that the Israelites would not attack them. Therefore, the Israelites did not kill them but enslaved them. The Gibeonites were made to gather wood and carry water for the congregation of Israel.

Joshua had these men of Gibeon brought to him and asked, "Why did you lie to us? Why did you deceive us and tell us you lived far away? Instead, here you are living in the midst of us. Therefore, you are cursed, and you and your descendants will be our slaves forever. You will collect wood and water for the house of my God."

In verse 24, the Gibeonites told Joshua why they had deceived him. They knew that the Lord, his God, the God of Moses, had told Moses to take the entire land. They believed that the Israelites would take the entire land. Therefore, the only way they could stay alive was to lie and deceive the Israelites. The only way they could have this covenant of peace was through deception. Then they told Joshua to do as he wished to his servants. So Joshua saved them from the hand of the Israelites, and he did not kill them. They then served and lived among the Israelites in the Promised Land.

What was the reaction of this peace treaty between Israel and Gibeon among the other kings in the land? How did Adoni-Zedek the king of

Jerusalem, Hoham the king of Hebron, Piram the king of Jarmuth, Japhia the king of Lachish, and Debir the king of Eglon react?

In Joshua 10:1-5 we read that King Adoni-Zedek became afraid and sent for the other four kings, Hoham, Piram, Japhia, and Debir, to join him so they could attack and kill the people of Gibeon. Why did they unite? It was in revenge against the Gibeonites because they had made a peace covenant with Israel. We read in verse 4 that King Adoni-Zedek told the other four kings: **"Come up to me and help me, that we may attack Gibeon, for it has made peace with Joshua and with the children of Israel."**

These five kings united together to engage in war with Gibeon, but in verse 6 we see that the Gibeonites sent to Joshua at Gilgal and said: **"Do not forsake your servants; come up to us quickly, save us and help us, for all the kings of the Amorites who dwell in the mountains have gathered together against us."** Here we see the relationship between the servants and the masters. The masters were willing to fight to save their servants from being destroyed by these five kings.

It is amazing to see that when Muslims read a passage in the Bible which states that some Jews had slaves/servants, they immediately jump to the conclusion that the Bible *promotes* slavery. They say, "See, the Bible says that the Jewish people had slaves, the Gibeonites."

The same thing that is done by Muslims in the West is also done by atheists. They say, "See, the Bible teaches slavery. Joshua and his people took the Gibeonites as slaves. The Bible promotes slavery." No, the Bible never promotes slavery. The Bible never condones slavery. In fact, the punishment of slavery in the Bible is very clear.

Someone may think that I am making this up. No, my friend, I am not making this up. This is the teaching in the Bible. When we go to Exodus 21:16, which was written by Moses, we read: **"He who kidnaps a man and sells him, or if he is found in his hand, shall surely be put to death."** The punishment according to the Torah, according to the writing of Moses, and according to the Jewish faith for a man who stole or sold a person as a slave was to be put to death. When we look at what happened over the last few hundred years, as millions of Africans were kidnapped and sold to masters in the New World, we see a practice that is condemned in the Bible.

It says that kidnapping is a sin and punishable by death, and engaging in this type of kidnap-slavery is also a sin punishable by death.

For those who make fun of the Bible, saying the Bible was wrong about slavery and now maybe the Bible is wrong about homosexuality and that there are so many things in the Bible we should not believe in or practice, they need to read the Bible correctly. The Old Testament punishment for men who kidnapped and sold slaves was death.

What about the New Testament teaching about slavery? We read in Timothy 1:9-10: **⁹that the law is not made for a righteous person, but for the lawless...**¹⁰ **for fornicators, for sodomites, for kidnappers** (menstealers in KJV)**, for liars, for perjurers, and if there is any other thing that is contrary to sound doctrine...** What about all these people? If they do not repent and receive God's salvation, they will burn in Hell. That was the punishment for this sinful way of life. Stealing men was punished in the Old Testament with physical death and in the New Testament by eternal death. So those who claim that the Bible promotes slavery are 100 percent dead wrong. The Bible never promotes slavery, not in the Old Testament and not in the New Testament.

However, it is important to remember that the Scripture does speak of slavery/servanthood, and almost all of those passages are referencing *VOLUNTARY* slavery. Voluntary slavery? Yes. This was a very common practice, in which a person owed a large sum of money, and so they would offer themselves as servants in order to pay their debt or to get money upfront to pay their debt. There are several forms of slavery, and most people reading this right now are probably involved in a master-servant relationship without even realizing it.

If you go to a job, work there for a certain time period, in order to get something (usually money), then that is a form of servanthood/slavery. The employer-employee relationship would be recognized as a form of slavery in the Bible. This would also be considered voluntary slavery. You utilize your services for a certain period of time (40 hours per week) for a certain amount of money.

Now, after the conquest of Canaan, the Jews were allowed to purchase slaves of the nations around them. Most of these slaves were captives of war. No doubt the reason the Lord allowed this was so that these strangers could be brought into Israel and see the reality and goodness of the God of Israel. Throughout the Bible, we see many examples of foreigners and strangers coming into the land and entering into a relationship with the God of Israel.

Getting back to the Gibeonites, because of their peace treaty with Israel, they were able to stay alive. Notice, they **VOLUNTARILY** offered themselves as servants/slaves to Israel; and now, because of the treaty, they are in trouble with these five kings who see them as traitors.

They are slaves to the Hebrews and have benefits by being slaves to them. Not only would they live but they would also be protected by the Hebrews, their masters. For here we see that the Israelites will fight for them and will even die for them. Would masters normally die for their slaves?

When the Gibeonites wrote to Joshua, they asked him and the Israelites to come and help them quickly. They told Joshua that there were five kings united together intending to destroy them. These kings wanted to remove them from the face of the earth. If Joshua goes to help them, he would save the lives of the Gibeonites but lose some of the Israelites.

We are not talking about a simple fight here. These were five strong kings united by their desire to annihilate the Gibeonites and Joshua and the Israelites. As a matter of fact, the main reason why these five kings went to war with the Gibeonites was because of the peace treaty they had made with the Israelites and to establish the standard that no one else should ever make a peace treaty with Israel. So these kings were going to force the Gibeonites to take back the treaty and get rid of Joshua and his people.

We read in verses 7-8: **⁷So Joshua ascended from Gilgal, he and all the people of war with him, and all the mighty men of valor. ⁸And the Lord said to Joshua, "Do not fear them, for I have delivered them into your hand; not a man of them shall stand before you."**

Then we learn from the rest of the account starting in verse 9 that Joshua came to them suddenly. He actually traveled all night from Gilgal. Before this battle, we always read that *early in the morning Joshua began the fight* or *early in the morning Joshua took his people and went*, but in this case, we see that Joshua traveled all night. He did not wait until morning because it was urgent. People with whom he had made a covenant were in danger, and he would honor that treaty.

Here we see that another battle will be won for the Lord because it was a holy war. How do we know it was a holy war? Because the Lord, the God of Israel, Himself was involved miraculously to bring victory to the Israelites and the Gibeonites.

In verse 10, the Lord routed these five kings and their soldiers before Israel, and Israel struck them with a great slaughter and drove them out of the land. They fled before Israel, but that was not the end of the war because the Lord had another way to fight and bring victory. These five kings and their people could run from Israel, but they could not hide from the Lord God. He fought them from heaven. How? He fought them with hailstones according to verse 11.

Look back in history. How many times, in all of the battles which Mohammed led and all the invasions which Mohammed and his people performed, did any similar miraculous experience like this happen? In Joshua's time, God sent stones of ice, large ones from heaven, to kill the enemies of God fleeing from the Hebrews. More people were killed that day by stones of ice from heaven than those who were killed by the Israelites' swords. What a mighty God the people of Israel served. What a mighty God who would defend his people and kill the enemies of Israel.

Don't forget that these five kings were the ones who started this fight. It was not Israel who went out to find them to fight. These kings left their homes, mountains, and cities to fight the Gibeonites, and God gave these kings over to the Israelites. Some were killed by the sword, but many more were killed by the stones of ice from heaven.

However, it wasn't just the miraculous hail. We also read of another supernatural event which has happened only one time in the history of mankind. From the days of Adam until Christ comes back, this type of supernatural event will never happen again.

We read in verses 12-13: **¹²Then Joshua spoke to the Lord in the day when the Lord delivered up the Amorites before the children of Israel, and he said in the sight of Israel: "Sun, stand still over Gibeon; and**

Moon, in the Valley of Aijalon." ¹³**So the sun stood still, and the moon stopped, till the people had revenge upon their enemies.**

What a great supernatural move of God so that even the sun would not go down. The day was lengthened. It was the Lord's war. It was the Day of the Lord. It must be accomplished on that day, on one day, so that the victory was given to the children of Israel against these five strong kings and their soldiers. The Lord fought for Israel.

Then we read in verse 14: **And there has been no day like that, before it or after it, that the Lord heeded the voice of a man; for the Lord fought for Israel.**

Joshua returned with all the people of Israel to their camp at Gilgal. However, the five kings escaped and as cowards hid in a cave at Makkedah. According to verse 17, Joshua was told that these five cowards were hiding in the cave. So Joshua commanded some men to guard the entry of the cave so these kings would not escape while other men put large stones over the entry of the cave.

Joshua did not desire to waste his time with these kings and let their armies escape. He followed his enemies so they could not escape back to their own cities. Joshua commanded the Israelites to pursue their enemies because the Lord God had given them into their hands. After the fight was ended and Joshua and the Israelites killed all they could kill of the enemy, except those enemies who escaped to their fortified cities, they returned to their camp in peace.

Then Joshua, in verse 22, commanded that the cave be opened and the five kings be brought out. When the kings came out, Joshua called all the men of Israel and had the leaders of the men who fought with him to put their feet on the necks of these kings. The king of Jerusalem, the king of Hebron, the king of Jarmuth, the king of Lachish, and the king of Eglon were on the ground with the feet of these leaders on their necks.

Joshua told the people in verse 25: **"Do not be afraid, nor be dismayed; be strong and of good courage, for thus the Lord will do to all your enemies against whom you fight."**

Here Joshua acknowledged that it was not the strength of himself and his army or of his men, but it was the Lord God who gave the entire enemy to the children of Israel. As for all those the Israelites would engage with in jihad (holy war), they would be in the same condition and be defeated. All the enemies of Israel, all the original inhabitants of the Promised Land, would be defeated, and Israel would have all their lands.

Then in verse 26, Joshua killed these five kings and hung them on five trees until evening. Joshua told his men to take the kings down, put them back into the cave, and roll stones over the entry of the cave. As we continue on with what happened to Joshua and the people of Israel in verses 28-30, we read that Joshua took the city of Makkedah. He utterly destroyed all the people in it and did to the king of Makkedah what he did to the king of Jericho. Then Joshua left Makkedah and all of Israel went with him to fight the city of Libnah. The Lord delivered Libnah and its king and people into the hands of Israel by the edge of the sword.

In verses 31-39, Joshua and Israel passed on to the cities of Lachish, Gezer, Eglon, Hebron, and Debir and fought against them. The Lord delivered these cities to Israel, and Israel struck the people of these cities with the edge of the sword, just as in Libnah. Everyone was killed in these cities.

According to Joshua 10:40: **So Joshua conquered all the land: the mountain country and the South and the lowland and the wilderness slopes, and all their kings; he left none remaining, but utterly destroyed all that breathed, as the Lord God of Israel had commanded.** Joshua conquered all these lands because the Lord God of Israel fought for them. That was how Joshua won all these battles. It was God who fought for Israel. It was God who gave the victory to Israel. After Joshua conquered the land with God's leadership, he and all of Israel returned to the camp at Gilgal.

A Continuation through the Conclusion of Joshua's Holy Wars: Joshua 11-23

Joshua continued to fight many battles, and he won all of these battles because the Lord God of Israel was with him. The Lord fought the battles for Joshua. The news spread all over the land to the surrounding kings of the Promised Land.

We read about this in Joshua 11. The Bible states that Jabin king of Hazor sent for Jobab king of Madon, for the king of Shimron, for the king of Achshaph, and for the kings from the north and in the west, the Canaanites, the Amorites, the Hittites, the Perizzites, the Jebusites, and the Hivites. There were so many that these kings with all their armies and horses and chariots looked as numerous as the sand on the seashore. All of these kings gathered together to have war with Israel.

However, the Lord told Joshua in verse 6: **"Do not be afraid because of them, for tomorrow about this time I will deliver all of them slain before Israel..."**

Did you read what the Lord said? It would not be next week, it would not be next month after lots of additional military training, and it would not be sometime in the future year after they had time to craft more and better weapons. It would be tomorrow, the Day of the Lord.

Remember how we recognize that jihad in the Old Testament was a holy war? It is a war that was won in one day. It was the Day of the Lord. It was not about how many people were on the other side or how strong or weak they were. It was about the Lord being with them. If the Lord was with Israel, then they had already won the war without even going into battle.

Did God tell Joshua that tomorrow about this time He would deliver *some of the enemies of Israel*? No, no, no. God said He would deliver *all* of them slain before Israel about this time tomorrow, and God told Joshua to **hamstring the enemies' horses and burn their chariots with fire. That was** the word of the Lord.

In the Bible we read in verses 8 and 9 that the Lord gave them into the hands of the Israelites. So the Israelites attacked them and chased them into Greater Sidon and into many other places. The Israelites smote them down until none of them remained. Joshua did as the Lord instructed him, **hamstringing the horses and burning their chariots with fire.** Don't forget that all these kings came to attack Israel. They made the first move, and murder and destruction were in their hearts.

Then Joshua returned and took Hazor and killed its king with the edge of the sword. Hazor had been the head of all of these kingdoms that had come to fight Israel. The Israelites struck the people in the battle with the edge of the sword until none was left alive. Then Joshua burned Hazor with fire.

According to verses 12-15, Joshua took all the cities and all the kings of these cities and all the people of the land, and he smote all of them. Just as Moses, the servant of the Lord, had commanded, and Joshua utterly destroyed them. As for the cities, Joshua did not burn any of them except for Hazor. Then the children of Israel took all the spoils of the cities and the livestock. As for the men whom they found in the cities, the Israelites smote them with the edge of the sword and did not leave any of them alive. Just as the Lord had commanded Moses and Moses had commanded Joshua, so Joshua and the children of Israel obeyed. They did exactly what the Lord had commanded Moses to do.

Joshua took all this land and divided it for the children of Israel. The promise and covenant God had made with Abraham had been fulfilled. All the cities were taken by war except for Gibeon because it had made a covenant of peace with the Israelites.

Joshua and his people won many battles simply because the Lord, the God of Israel, had fought the battles for them. Joshua took all the land just as the Lord had told Moses and gave it to the children of Israel according to their tribes and divisions.

Then we read at the close of chapter 11 that the land rested from war. That does not mean the land was tired and needed rest. No, it is an expression in the Bible which means there was peace. War had ended, and there was peace on this part of the earth. That was obviously during the days of Joshua, but that was not the end of jihad (holy war) in the Bible.

In Joshua 13, the Bible states that the Lord spoke to Joshua and told him that, even though Joshua was an old man now, there remained plenty of land to be possessed. The Bible named the many parcels of land that the Hebrew people had not yet rightfully taken. God told Joshua in verse 6 that He Himself would drive out the inhabitants of the land before the Israelites. All Joshua had to do was to divide the land as an inheritance for the children of Israel.

In verse 7, God told Joshua to divide these lands among the nine tribes and the half tribe of Manasseh. Why? Because from verse 8 and an earlier reading in Number 32, we know that the tribe of Rueben and the tribe of Gad and half of the tribe of Manasseh had already received their inheritance of land on the east side of the Jordan River. Before Moses died, he had given this land to them himself. This was done before they crossed the Jordan River with their new leader, Joshua. As for the tribe of Levi, they did not receive any land inheritance as we read in Joshua 13:33, Moses had not given them any inheritance of land because the God of Israel was to be their inheritance. What an inheritance and what a privilege for them! Their service was in the Temple offering sacrifices. In return they got a share of what was offered to the Lord. All this land was divided as the Lord commanded his servant Moses for the nine tribes and the half tribe by casting lots.

As for Caleb, the son of Jephunneh (who was one of the twelve spies sent earlier by Moses to check out the Promised Land), he had believed that God would give the Promised Land to the Israelites. Out of all of the spies, he and Joshua were the only two who believed that God would give them this land.

Caleb made a request as recorded in Joshua 14:10-12, as I paraphrase his words: "I was forty years old when I came to this land with you. I am eighty-five years old now and am as strong today as I was forty-five years ago. I fought and I went in and I went out all these years, so give me this mountain that Moses told me that he would give to me, and you heard this yourself." Caleb continued. "You know that the Anakim are there, and they have a great city there. So give it to me. Perhaps the Lord will be with me, and I will drive them out and take the mountain as my inheritance."

So Joshua blessed Caleb and gave him Hebron as an inheritance. Once again, the Bible states at the end of chapter 14 that the land rested from war. There was peace and no more fighting.

However, some of the original people in the land were strong, and the people of Israel could not remove them from the land. That was why the Israelites let them live there with them. For example, we read in Joshua 15:63: **As for the Jebusites, the inhabitants of Jerusalem, the children of Judah could not drive them out; but the Jebusites dwell with the children of Judah at Jerusalem to this day.** There were many groups like the Jebusites who lived and dwelled among the Israelites. They did not cast all of the inhabitants completely out of the land.

A similar example is in Joshua 16:10 where we read that the Canaanites still lived in the land of Gezer among the Ephraimites. They were living as servants and paid tribute to the Ephraimites. Another example is found in Joshua 17:12-13. The children of Manasseh could not drive the Canaanites out of the land, so they allowed the Canaanites to live with them and pay tribute to the children of Manasseh.

In chapter 18:1, we read that the entire congregation of the children of Israel assembled together and set up the tabernacle. Then the Bible states that the land was subdued before them. Joshua continued to divide the rest of the land among the children of Israel as we read in chapters 18 and 19.

We learn about the six cities of refuge in chapter 20. According to the command of the Lord, these were cities which were put aside for people to flee to when they had accidentally killed someone. A person could go to one of these cities to live and could not be harmed by the slain person's family. The elders could not give the man over to the dead man's family if there was enough evidence that he had not killed on purpose (murder).

In Joshua 21:43-45, the Bible stated that the Lord gave Israel all the land which He had sworn to their fathers. Then the Lord gave them rest, and none of their enemies were able to stand against them for the Lord had given all their enemies into their hands.

In chapter 22, Joshua brought the tribe of Rueben, the tribe of Gad, and half of the tribe of Manasseh to him and thanked them for all they had done. They had kept their word to help their brothers across the Jordan River. They had left their families and their cattle behind on the east side of the river to help the rest of the tribes take the Promised Land on the west side of the Jordan River. Now, since the rest of the tribes had inherited their land and rested from war, Joshua gave the two and a half tribes permission to return to their families across the Jordan River after he blessed them.

After the children of Rueben, the children of Gad, and half of the children of Manasseh crossed back over the Jordan River to their places, they built an impressive altar. Now when the children of Israel on the west side of the Jordan River heard that these two and a half tribes had built this great altar, they thought that these tribes were going to worship a false god. They gathered and decided to go to war against the two and a half tribes.

The congregation said that these tribes had trespassed against the God of Israel by doing whatever they were doing and asked them, "Why are you rebelling against the Lord your God?" In verse 17, they reminded these tribes of the sin of Peor and the many thousands of Israelites who died of plagues which God had brought upon them because of their sin to worship the god of Baal. They also reminded the tribes about Achan who had stolen spoils from the city of Jericho and how the Lord was angry with the entire nation of Israel. Because of Achan, the Israelites lost the war with Ai even though it was the sin of one man.

However, the sons of Rueben and the sons of Gad and the sons of the half tribe of Manasseh said to the elders and leaders in Joshua 22:22-23: [22]**"The Lord God of gods, the Lord God of gods, He knows, and let Israel itself know - if it is in rebellion, or if in treachery against the Lord, do not save us this day.** [23]**If we have built ourselves an altar to turn from following the Lord, or if to offer on it burnt offerings or grain offerings, or if to offer peace offerings on it, let the Lord Himself require an account."**

Then these two and a half tribes explained to the rest of the tribes of Israel that they had not sinned against God. They explained that this altar was built as a testimony so that their children and grandchildren would know that they were true believers in the Lord God. They continued to explain that they had built this altar only as a witness between them so that the children of the tribes on the west side of the Jordan River could not say that the children on the east side of the Jordan River had no part of the Lord God of Israel.

Here we see a very important part in the history of Israel. The leaders of the nine and a half tribes crossed the Jordan River to investigate this magnificent altar to determine if the two and a half tribes were building an altar to offer sacrifices to the false gods of the people of the land. If they were, then they all would perish by the edge of the sword. They did not want the God of Israel to destroy the entire nation of Israel. Muslims and others will not quote passages like this because it will not agree with their understanding of the reality of jihad (holy war) in the Old Testament. They will only quote passages where the children of Israel fight the original people of the land, but the children of Israel performing jihad with each other because of sin in the camp - that is not reported.

If the two and a half tribes were sinning against God by offering sacrifices and worshiping false gods on this altar, the other tribes would destroy them as the entire congregation had destroyed the original people of the land. Holy war meant to get rid of evil and the false worship of false gods, no matter who had sinned, Gentiles or Hebrews.

In Joshua 23, Joshua brought together all the children of Israel along with their elders, judges, and officers. He reminded them of what the Lord had done for them with the original people of the land and how God had fought for them.

Now, the children of Israel had inherited all the land. Joshua told them to keep what was written in the law of Moses and to not turn away from it, to the right or to the left. They were to separate themselves from the original people of the land, especially those whom they had not destroyed completely. The children of Israel were not to mention or swear by the names of the gods of those people or to serve or worship those gods, but they were to cling to Jehovah God. They were to love the Lord their God.

So what would happen if the Hebrews did not obey the command of Joshua which was the command of the Lord their God? What would happen if they married the people of the land? The answer is found in Joshua 23:13: **Know for certain that the Lord your God will no longer drive out these nations from before you. But they shall be snares and traps to you, and scourges on your sides and thorns in your eyes, until you perish from this good land which the Lord your God has given you.**

Remember the statement I have shared with you so many times in the past: God is no respecter of persons. That is the message of the Old Testament. If the Hebrews sinned, they would perish just as they had destroyed the original inhabitants of the land. They performed jihad (holy war) for God to get rid of the original people of the land because of their sin. If the Hebrews themselves sinned against God, God Himself would destroy them by the wicked people of the land.

Chapter 4: The Saga Continues

That is the theme of our study as we move on into the book of Judges. We see that jihad is a continuing lifestyle for the Hebrews. It is actually a circle. When the Hebrews sinned, God would send a thorn in the flesh, their enemy, and they would be harassed and persecuted by their enemy. Then the Hebrew people would repent and cry out to God, He would send a judge to deliver them, and the land would be in peace for a time. This cycle was repeated over and over. **In Joshua's last speech to the Hebrews before he died**, he told them to stay in the word of the law and to love the Lord their God, the One who fought their battles for them, drove their enemies away, and gave them the land full of honey and milk. This was the end of the holy wars led by Joshua.

The Art of War

Othniel the First Judge - Judges 1-3

As we continue to study the subject of holy war in the book of Judges, we will see whether the Hebrews obeyed the command of Joshua and the law of the Lord God given through Moses.

Now it is time for the Hebrews to do what is right so they can continue to inherit and enjoy this land filled with milk and honey. However, if the Hebrews disobeyed the law of the Lord and intermarried with the people of the land and worshiped and swore by the name of the false gods of the people of the land, then God would destroy them. God would use the people the Israelites had left in the Promised Land to destroy the Israelites. That is the justice of God and the reality of God concerning holy war in the Old Testament. Again, as I have stated before, no matter who sinned, that person must perish for his sin, whether that person was a Hebrew or a Gentile. The wages of sin is death.

When we study the book of Judges, we see the cycle of sin, judgment, repentance, and obedience repeated over and over. The judges were deliverers. They were the people God appointed to help the Israelites get out of the crisis which they had caused by their sin against God.

So the cycle goes like this: the Hebrew people did what was right in their *own* eyes, which means they sinned against God by not following what was written in His law. They intermarried with the people of the land, and the Hebrews would worship false gods. God became very displeased with the Hebrews because of their sins. Then God punished the Hebrews by the hands of the inhabitants of the land and allowed them to enslave and abuse the Hebrews. Then the Hebrew would cry out to God.

After the Hebrews repented and stopped worshiping the false gods, God would raise up a judge from among them who would help them fight against their enemy. They would have victory, and the land would have rest from war. They would live in peace for some years, and then they would sin against God again because a new generation would arise who would not know God or worship God. The cycle continued on and on.

The Bible gives us varying detailed information about the judges. Therefore, we know very little about some judges while we know far more about others. All the judges were male except for one, Deborah.

The book of Judges begins with the children of Israel asking the Lord which tribe would be the first to fight against the wicked Canaanites. In verses 2-3, the Lord answered that it would be Judah, but the tribe of Judah asked the tribe of Simeon to help them fight the Canaanites. The tribe of Judah told the tribe of Simeon that if they helped them today, the tribe of Judah would help them when their day came. The tribe of Simeon agreed. We read, beginning in Judges 1:4, that they fought the Canaanites and killed ten thousand men at Bezek. Many battles took place in chapter 1, and the tribe of Judah won all of them.

Judah went with Simeon and fought the Canaanites according to verse 17. Judah won the cities of Gaza, Ashkelon, and Ekron. However, we read in verse 19 that even though the Lord was with Judah and Judah took the mountain, they did not drive out the inhabitants of the valley.

In verses 21-22, the children of Benjamin did not drive out the inhabitants of Jerusalem, the Jebusites. The children of Joseph fought the people of the city of Bethel, formally named Luz, and struck them with the edge of the sword. In verse 27, the children of Manasseh did not drive out the inhabitants of Beth Shean, Taanach, Dor, Ibleam, Meggiddo, or their villages. The Canaanites still lived in the land.

In these verses, we see the Israelites winning battles but then leaving some of the inhabitants in the land to live among them. That is not what God had commanded the children of Israel to do. The Israelites had many of the Canaanites pay tribute, but they did not drive the Canaanites out of the land.

We see this repeated with every one of the tribes of the Israelites. They disobeyed the command of God, the command of Moses. They were to drive out or kill the inhabitants of the land, but they did not do what they had been commanded. They chose to sin against God and allow the people of the land to live among the Israelites. These people became a snare to them, just as they had been warned.

So how did the Lord God react to this wickedness and direct disobedience to His command? In chapter 2, beginning with verse 1, we read the reaction of the Lord: **Then the Angel of the Lord came up from Gilgal to Bochim, and said, "I led you up from Egypt and brought you to the land of which I swore to your fathers; and I said, 'I will never break My covenant with you. ²And you shall make no covenant with the inhabitants of this land; you shall tear down their altars.' But you have not obeyed My voice. Why have you done this? ³Therefore I also said, 'I will not drive them out before you; but they shall be thorns in your side, and their gods shall be a snare to you.'"**

When the Angel of the Lord said this to the children of Israel in verse 4, they lifted up their voices and wept. They called that place Bochim, which means the place of weeping. We read in verse 10: **When all that generation had been gathered to their fathers, another generation arose after them who did not know the Lord nor the work which He had done for Israel.**

What did the new generation do who were unaware of Israel's rich history of God's goodness and God's laws? We find the answer in Judges 2:11-14. The children of Israel sinned against God by serving the false gods, the Baals of the people of the land who lived all around the Israelites. They worshiped these false gods and forsook the Lord God of Israel. The Lord became angry with them and delivered the Israelites into the hands of their enemies.

That is exactly what Joshua told them before he died. That is exactly what was written in the Torah. If the Israelites had stayed in and lived by the words of the law, then they would not have sinned against God. They would not have left the true worship of the God of Israel. They would not have left any of the inhabitants of the land live among them and lead them astray, but instead they did evil in the sight of the Lord. That is why the God of Israel punished them by their enemies, the ones God said He would drive away from them if the Israelites remained faithful to Him.

Because they turned from God and served and worshiped the false gods of the land and intermarried with the people of the land, God punished the Israelites. Once again, this was a justified punishment, for the wages of sin is death.

When the persecution became so severe and the Israelites could not take the distress from their enemies any longer, then they cried out to the Lord. Then God raised up judges among them, and these judges delivered them from the hand of their enemies as we read in verse 16. However, in verses 17-18 we find out that they would not listen to their judges and sinned by worshiping other gods yet again. They did not obey the commandments of the Lord. However, the Lord raised up judges for them, and the Lord was with the judge. While the judge lived, the Lord delivered them from their enemies for the Lord had pity on them because of their groaning caused by their enemies who oppressed the children of Israel. God had made promises to Abraham, and most of those promises involved the children of Israel. God would honor His promises.

In verse 19, we read that after the judge died, they quickly turned back to their wicked ways. They worshiped false gods and did everything to disobey and enrage God. So God's anger would fall upon them once again. We read this in verse 20 and throughout the remainder of the book of Judges.

When the Hebrews disobeyed God, God delivered His people into the hands of the inhabitants of the land in order that He may discipline them. We read in the last verse of chapter 2: [23]**Therefore the Lord left those nations, without driving them out immediately; nor did He deliver them into the hand of Joshua.** God knew that the Hebrews would not obey His word. They would not serve him faithfully. They would not obey the law of the Lord which was given to Moses.

These nations were left so that the Lord could use them to test Israel, to prove if they would be faithful of loving Him, of worshiping Him, and of serving Him alone. Joshua had told the Hebrews that the Lord God desired faithfulness and that it would not be easy for them to serve and worship Him alone. He would punish them for their sins, even though the Hebrews had told Joshua that they would serve and obey the Lord's command according to Joshua 24:19. That is why Joshua said that they were a witness against themselves and if they broke the law of the Lord, they would be punished by the law of the Lord.

We then read in Judges 3:1: **Now these are the nations which the Lord left, that He might test Israel by them, that is, all who had not known any of the wars in Canaan.**

Who are the people being talked about here? These are the five lords of the Philistines. Now, when we say the five lords of the Philistines, we are not taking about the Palestinians who live in the Middle East right now. The Palestinians were people who emigrated from the Aegean Islands located in the Aegean Sea. The Aegean Islands are groups of islands located between Turkey and Greece, north of Crete.

We read about the Philistines in verses 3-4 along with: [3]**... the Canaanites, the Sidonians, and the Hivites who dwelt in Mount Lebanon, from Mount Baal Hermon to the entrance of Hamath.** [4]**And they were left, that He might test Israel by them, to know whether they would obey the commandments of the Lord, which He had commanded their fathers by the hand of Moses.**

Well, surprise, surprise! In verses 5-6, once again we read that the Israelites lived among the original inhabitants of the land and intermarried with them. The Israelites served the gods of the inhabitants of the land. They did evil in the eyes of the Lord, and they forgot the Lord their God and served other gods.

What was the reaction of the Lord God? In verses 8-11, we read that the Lord was angry with Israel. He sold them into the hand of the king of Mesopotamia, and they served him. They were slaves of Cushan-Rishathaim for eight years. Then the Hebrews cried out to the Lord their God, and He provided a deliverer. The Lord raised up Othniel, Caleb's younger brother's son, to deliver the people of Israel. He judged the Hebrews because the Spirit of the Lord was upon him. He defeated Cushan-Rishathaim, and as we read in verse 11, the land rested for forty years, meaning there was no major war or widespread fighting during that time. Then Othniel died.

Judges Ehud, Deborah, and Gideon: Judges 3-6

After Othniel died, the children of Israel did not live faithfully toward God. This was the end of one cycle and the beginning of a new cycle. The cycle of sin, repentance, and delivery continued.

Chapter 5: The Art of War

In Judges 3, beginning in verse 12 and continuing through verse 30, we read that the children of Israel sinned and did evil in the sight of the Lord. Because of their sin, the Lord strengthened Eglon, the king of Moab, against the children of Israel.

There was a war between the children of Ammon and Amalek and the children of Israel. Eglon defeated Israel, and the children of Israel served Eglon for eighteen years.

Once again, the Israelites were back in slavery, so they cried out to the Lord to save them. This time the Lord sent another judge, Ehud, to be their deliverer. Ehud was the son of Gera. He was from the tribe of Benjamin. The Israelites sent him to take their tribute to Eglon. So Ehud planned to assassinate Eglon while he was presenting the tribute gift to the king.

Ehud took his double-edged dagger and fastened it on his right thigh under his clothes. Ehud had made this double-edged dagger himself. So after Ehud had met with Eglon and presented the gift, he told the king that he had a secret word to give to him. Therefore, the people who attended the king were sent out from them. Ehud told Eglon that the message he had for him was from God. Then Ehud took out his dagger with his left hand and **plunged it into Eglon's belly.**

Then Ehud left by the porch. He closed and locked the doors behind him. **When he had gone, the king's attendants came and saw that the doors were** locked. After waiting for some time, they finally opened the door with a key and found their king dead.

While the king's attendants were delaying in waiting for the king to open the door, Ehud had returned to the children of Israel. The trumpet was blown, and Ehud told the children of Israel to follow him because the Lord had given their enemies, the Moabites, into their hands. So the Israelites went with him to fight the Moabites, and the Israelites slew about ten thousand of the Moabite men. Not one escaped, and Moab was subdued. The land was at rest for about eighty years. That was the end of yet another cycle.

As we look at the next chapter in the book of Judges, chapter 4, we read of the beginning of another new cycle with another judge. The children of Israel again did evil in the sight of the Lord after Ehud died (imagine that!).

All it took was for the judge to die, the children of Israel would go back to sinning against God, and then the Lord would give them into the hands of their enemy.

Who was the new enemy now? It was Jabin, king of Canaan. Jabin ruled Hazor, and the leader of his army was Sisera. They took over the children of Israel. We read in verse 3 that the children of Israel cried out once again to the Lord because they had been oppressed and treated harshly by Jabin for twenty years.

Now the Lord sent to them their only female judge, Deborah. She was the wife of Lapidoth and a prophetess. We read in verses 6-7 that she sent for Barak and reminded him that the Lord had commanded him to take ten thousand men from the tribes of Naphtali and Zebulun into battle with Sisera, who was the commander of Jabin's army, along with his chariots and men at the Kishon River. There the Lord would deliver Sisera into Barak's hand.

That was the word of God through His judge, Deborah, to Barak. However, Barak told her that if she did not go with him, he would not go. She replied that if she went with him, he would not receive the honor. What would the people say - that a woman led the fight against Sisera? That is exactly what happened. Deborah, the female judge, delivered Israel from the hand of Sisera and his army.

Barak called ten thousand men. Deborah went with him. Sisera took nine hundred iron chariots and the people with him to the Kishon River.

Deborah told Barak to rise up because the Lord had given Sisera into his hands. So Barak got up, and the Lord routed Sisera and his army. Sisera ran away on foot, but his entire army fell by the edge of the sword. Not one of them was left alive.

So what happened to the mighty Sisera? After running away, he came to the tent of Jael. She was the wife of a Kenite man named Heber. Now there was peace between Heber and Jabin the king. Jael told Sisera to not be afraid, so he went into the tent. He was tired and thirsty. She covered him with a blanket, and she gave him some milk. Then he told her that if anyone came to her tent and asked if they had seen him, she was to say "no." Then Sisera fell asleep. As he slept, Jael quietly took a tent peg and a hammer and then drove the peg through Sisera's temple into the ground, and he died.

Barak was in pursuit of Sisera when Jael came out to him. She told Barak in verse 22: **"Come, I will show you the man whom you seek."** Then Barak saw that Sisera was dead by the hand of Jael.

So on that day, God subdued Jabin, the king of Canaan, before the children of Israel. The children of Israel became stronger and stronger against Canaan until they destroyed Jabin. We read the conclusion of this cycle in Judges 5:31, where the land now rested for forty years.

Only *forty years* of rest and then back to slavery? Why? It was because the children of Israel again sinned against God, and God punished them again by their enemies. Judges 6:1 begins with the same statement of the cycle: **Then the children of Israel did evil in the sight of the Lord. So the Lord delivered them into the hand of Midian for seven years.**

The Midianites prevailed against the Israelites to the point that they even had to live in caves of the mountains. When the Israelites were harvesting their crops, the Midianites, the Amalekites, and the people of the East, would come and take all that was in the land. They took the harvest of the fields along with the cattle, sheep, and donkeys. The Bible describes these enemies of Israel as having such great numbers that they seemed like locust, and every time they came to the land of the children of Israel, they came to destroy the land completely.

In Judges 6:6, we read that, because of these raids, the children of Israel were living in poverty. The children of Israel once again cried out to the Lord, and the Lord sent them a prophet. This prophet reminded them of the history of their ancestors. He reminded them that the Lord was the One who had delivered them out of slavery in Egypt and from all those who had oppressed them and that He had given them the Promised Land as an inheritance. We read in verse 10: **Also I said to you, "I am the Lord your God; do not fear the gods of the Amorites, in whose land you dwell." But you have not obeyed My voice.'"**

In verse 11, we read that the Angel of the Lord came and met with a new judge, Gideon. Gideon was threshing wheat in a winepress. As an Egyptian man myself, I have seen how the Egyptian farmers harvest and thresh wheat. No one threshes wheat indoors. It is done outside in the fresh air so that as the crushed wheat is tossed into the air, the wind blows the lighter chaff away, and the good kernels of wheat fall to the ground. Here we see Gideon doing this inside a winepress in order to keep from being seen by the Midianites. This is his own wheat from his own farm on his own land, and here he is threshing wheat inside a winepress to avoid being seen by their enemies instead of out in the open.

The Angel of the Lord said to Gideon in verse 12: **"The Lord is with you, you mighty man of valor!"** What a strange greeting. This shows a sense of humor in the Angel of the Lord calling Gideon a mighty man of valor since he was hiding in a winepress! However, the reality is that we see how Gideon, as a mighty man of valor, will deliver the children of Israel.

It was not about how strong the Israelites were, and it was not about how many Israelites there were. God can use the weak and the coward. God can use just a few of His own faithful people to destroy a large enemy in a very miraculous way.

The account of Gideon is a great example to show the difference between jihad in the Bible and jihad in the Qur'an. Here we see that, in the Bible, a holy war has nothing to do with the battles or with the rules of battle because this is the war of the Lord. God can deliver Israel from their enemy even without a fight, as we will see in this account. That is not how wars are won in Islam. There are no miraculous victories in Islam. Every victory in Islam was due to the human sword and blood.

In verse 15, Gideon acknowledged that he was not from a mighty tribe and that he did not come from a big family. He said: **"O my Lord, how can I save Israel? Indeed my clan is the weakest in Manasseh, and I am the least in my father's house."**

Here we see that Gideon was a humble man, broken before the Angel of the Lord and explaining that he does not qualify to be the judge or the deliverer of Israel. However, that is exactly why God *could* use Gideon, and that is when God can use us today. If we think highly of ourselves and our abilities, our trust is not in the Lord.

In verse 16, we read that the Lord told Gideon: **"Surely I will be with you, and you shall defeat the Midianites as one man."** Gideon asked the

Chapter 5: The Art of War

Angel of the Lord to stay there under the oak tree while he went to prepare a meal. When Gideon returned with the meal, the Angel of the Lord stretched out his staff and touched the meat and the bread. Fire came out of the rock which the meal had been placed upon and consumed the meal. Then the Angel of the Lord vanished.

Gideon was afraid because he had seen the Angel of the Lord face to face. In verse 23, the Lord told Gideon to not be afraid but to be at peace for he would not die. Then Gideon built an altar to the Lord and named it Jehovah Shalom. We see here that Gideon went back to the true worship of the God of Israel.

However, Gideon had to do one more thing. He had to get rid of the altar to the false god, Baal, which belonged to **Joash, Gideon's father. In verse 25,** Gideon destroyed the altar to Baal and then built an altar to the Lord the God of Israel on top of it with the help of ten men and then offered a sacrifice to the Lord on this altar. Since he feared his father's household and the people of the city, he did this at night.

In verse 28, the people arose the next morning and discovered the altar to Baal had been destroyed and a bull had been offered on the altar to the Lord God. They questioned one another asking who had done this thing. When they discovered it was Gideon who had done this, they threatened to kill him.

The people asked Joash to bring Gideon out so they could kill him, but as we read in verses 31-32, Joash told them: [31]... **"Would you plead for Baal? Would you save him? Let the one who would plead for him be put to death by morning! If he is a god, let him plead for himself, because his altar has been torn down!"** [32]**Therefore on that day he called him Jerubbaal, saying, "Let Baal plead against him, because he has torn down his altar."**

What a great lesson we can learn from this even today as we talk to Muslims. When someone burns a copy of the Qur'an or someone insults Mohammed, the self-proclaimed prophet of Islam, or someone insults Allah, the god of Islam, Muslims all over the world become very angry, riot, destroy, and kill. They do everything they can to defend Allah, to defend Mohammed, or to defend the Qur'an.

If Allah is god, if Mohammed is a true prophet, and if the Qur'an is the true word of god, then why doesn't Allah defend himself? Why doesn't Allah defend his own prophet, Mohammed? Burning churches or killing Christians in the Middle East is not a way to prove that Allah is a true god or Mohammed is a true prophet or the Qur'an is the true word of god. Their intolerance and murderous ways expose the truth of their cult.

After Gideon had destroyed the altar of Baal, built an altar to the Lord God, and offered a true sacrifice to the Lord, the enemies of Israel gathered. These were the Midianites, the Amalekites, and the people from the East. We read in chapter 6:34-35: **[34]But the Spirit of the Lord came upon Gideon; then he blew the trumpet, and the Abiezrites gathered behind him. [35]And he sent messengers throughout all Manasseh, who also gathered behind him. He also sent messengers to Asher, Zebulun, and Naphtali; and they came up to meet them.**

Here we see the Spirit of the Lord leading Gideon to gather the children of Israel to perform jihad against the Midianites. However, we see another side of Gideon. Because he doubted that the Lord would use him to deliver Israel, he tested the Lord, not once but actually twice.

Gideon said, "I will put fleece on the ground, and if there is water on the fleece alone and the earth around it is dry, then I will know for sure that You will deliver Israel by my hand." That was his first test. When Gideon woke up early in the morning, he found that the fleece was wet and that everything around it was dry.

However, Gideon spoke to the Lord again. "Don't be angry with me, but I would like to do one more test. The test is that I will put the fleece of wool on the ground outside again and if the fleece is dry and all the ground around it is wet, then I will know for sure that you will deliver the children of Israel by my hand." The Bible said that God did exactly that night what Gideon asked because the next morning the fleece was dry and all the earth around it was wet.

Then Gideon and thirty-two thousand Israelites gathered at the well of Harod, and the Midianites were on the north. As we read in chapter 7 of the book of Judges, the Lord spoke to Gideon in verse 2. The Lord told Gideon that he would not give the Midianites into the hands of the children of Israel because the number of Israelites who came to fight was too large.

The Lord told Gideon that the Israelites could then brag of their victory and claim that they had saved themselves by their own strength. So the Lord told Gideon to send home any of the men who were afraid. Twenty-two thousand men left. Only ten thousand Israelites were left to do battle with Gideon.

Let's think about this for a minute. When we compare the wars in the Bible to the wars in the Qur'an, the larger the number of men who went with Mohammed to fight a battle, the more assurance he had that they would have victory over the Christians or Jews, the people Mohammed was fighting against. I have never seen in the Qur'an or in the interpretations of Muslim scholars of the verses of Allah in the Qur'an that Mohammed ever asked his men, the good Muslim believers, to leave a battle and go home.

As we have studied together throughout the teachings of Allah in the Qur'an, Mohammed convinced every man to go and fight. Mohammed taught Muslims in the Qur'an that those who did not go and fight were hypocrites. Mohammed scared the daylights out of these Muslims by telling them, throughout the Qur'an, that if they did not fight in battle to kill Christians or Jews, they would burn in Hell, as we will see in Volume 2.

The teaching of the Bible is the opposite of the teaching in the Qur'an. Comparing the number of people who went out with Mohammed to do battle to the number of people who went out with Gideon to do battle, we see in Gideon's case the number of men dropped from thirty-two thousand to ten thousand. Then once again, the Lord told Gideon in verse 4 that there were still too many Israelites. The Lord instructed Gideon to take the men to the water and have them drink. God would tell Gideon which men to keep to do battle and which men to send home.

Now, I would like to read to you the same story of Gideon as written in the pages of the Qur'an. This is a great place where we can compare the true account of the Bible to the phony, unclear, messed-up, mixed-up, and counterfeit story of Gideon in the Qur'an written in the book of "The Cow." Beginning in Qur'an 2:246, we read that Allah is speaking to Mohammed through Angel Gabreel. Mohammed was telling the story of the children of Israel after Moses. Allah said: [246]***Have you not seen the gathering of the children of Israel after Moses?*** That is like asking *when*.

You cannot ask the question of *when* in the Qur'an because Allah does not know, Gabreel does not know, and Mohammed does not know. All we know is that it just happened sometime after Moses. It could have been a month, a year, or a hundred years because Allah only knows.

So what happened here? **When they said to a prophet for them…Which prophet?** The children of Israel are speaking to a prophet. *What was his name?* We do not know. All we know is that he was a prophet.

The children of Israel said: **"Send to us a king, we will engage in war for the sake of Allah."** They needed a king to lead them so that they could go to war for the sake of Allah. That is what the children of Israel told this prophet. We do not know who he was, and we do not know when this actually happened after Moses. Here is what the prophet said to them: **He said, "Will it be that you would not go to war if engaging in war is decreed for you?"**

Here is a good excuse from the prophet. They were asking for a king to lead them in war, but then the prophet was telling them what if engaging in war was required of them but they choose not to engage in war. When I read about a passage like this in the Qur'an, I cannot help but laugh at the ignorance of Allah, Mohammed, Gabreel, and the Muslims who believe in this lie today.

Up to this point, as you read the Qur'an, you come to the assumption that the children of Israel had never fought any battles. However, as we have been reading in our study, *Jihad in the Old Testament*, the Israelites had already been involved in many wars led by Moses, Joshua, and other judges.

Continuing in verse 246, the response of the children of Israel to the prophet was: **They said, "And why should we not engage in war for the sake of Allah, and indeed, we and our children are driven forth from our homes?"**

What homes? The children of Israel are telling their prophet why should they go and fight when they had been kicked out of their homes. What homes is Allah talking about here?

The children of Israel left Egypt, which was not their home. They were not driven out with Moses, but they literally escaped out of Egypt. The Egyptians never drove the Hebrews out of Egypt, and when the Hebrews went to the Promised Land, no one drove them out of their homes.

Chapter 5: The Art of War

The opposite is true. The Israelites drove the inhabitants out of their homes and their lands and took their possessions. This happened a long time before Moses died, before Joshua died, and before the story which we are studying in the book of Judges about Gideon occurred.

Now, let's see the reaction of the children of Israel after war was required from them in the Qur'an. ***So when the engaging in war was decreed to them, they turned back except for a few of them. And Allah knows the unjust.***

Here is another mistake in the Qur'an. There is no truth about what the Qur'an said here because the children of Israel had already fought many battles. Unless Allah was thinking about the time when the Hebrew spies were sent to check out the land of Canaan, the Promised Land, and the people refused to fight. If this was true, then this took place during the life of Moses, not after the life of Moses. During the life of Moses in the early days, they did not fight. However, the children of Israel fought many battles with Joshua as we have seen in this study. Before Gideon came into the picture, many battles were won and the children of Israel had already taken much of the Promised Land.

Continuing with Qur'an 2:247 we read that Allah said to them: *[247]And their prophet said to them, "Surely Allah has sent Tālūt (Saul) as a king to you."* Maybe from this verse we can assume that the prophet Mohammed is talking about his Prophet Samuel. If this was the case, then what does Prophet Samuel have to do with Gideon? There is a huge gap between Moses and Samuel and between Gideon and King Saul.

Here is the reaction of the children of Israel when their prophet told them that Saul would be the king over them: ***They said, "How can the kingdom be to him over us when we are more worthy of the kingdom than him...*** Excuse me, what? The children of Israel refused Saul to be a king over them? Where do we find this in the Bible? Is there any truth in such a claim? Of course, this was a false reaction. According to the Bible most of the Israelites were happy and rejoiced to have Saul as their king.

They continued by stating: ***and he has no abundance of money?"*** Where in the world can we find in the Bible that Saul was poor or came from a poor family? There is no truth in this because Saul came from a rich family.

Then we read, ***He said.*** Who is he? He is the prophet, who, according to the Qur'an, we do not know who he was. From the context in the Bible, we assume him to be Samuel. *He said, "Surely Allah has chosen him over you and has given him increase in knowledge and stature. And Allah gives his kingdom to whom he wills. And Allah is large, knowing."*

Allah chose Saul to be the king. He is smart. He's big, and Allah knows everything.

Then in verse 248 of chapter 2 in the Qur'an: [248]*And their prophet said to them, "Surely the sign of his kingdom will be that the tābūt (ark) will come to you. In it is tranquility from your lord and the relics left by the family of Moses and the family of Aaron.*

Then their prophet ended this verse by stating: *The angels will carry it. Surely in this is a sign to you if you were believers."* The angels will carry the Ark of the Covenant? I don't think so.

Now we come to the important part of why I am giving you this ridiculous story from the verses of Allah in the Qur'an. [249]*So when Tālūt (Saul) marched forth with his jund, (troops), he said, "Surely Allah will test you by a river. So whoever drinks of it so is not of me, but he who does not taste it, so surely he is of me except who scoops a scoop by his hand so they drink from it, except a few of them." So when they had passed it, he and those who believed with him, they said, "We have no strength this day with Jālūt (Goliath) and his troops." Those among them who thought that they would meet Allah said, "How many a small group have victory over a large group, by Allah's permission? And Allah is with the patient."*

What in the world are we talking about here? King Saul took his army to the river, and he told them upfront that anyone who drinks of the river is not of him and all those who do not taste it are of him except those who scoop it by their hand and drink from it.

What in the world does King Saul have to do with the river and drinking of water from the river by hand? What a wonderful test! *Do you see what is happening here?* Mohammed took three stories from the Bible and put them all together in the Qur'an as one story. All this took place after Moses. We do not even know who the prophet was about whom Mohammed was talking.

Was King Saul the one who took the soldiers by the river to test them? What kind of test is it when you tell the people what to do ahead of time? Where is the true information about this story except in the Bible?

Chapter 5: The Art of War

To make the story even worse, let us read the words of Allah, the all-knowing, in the next verse. Allah said that the children of Israel are praying to Allah here in this verse. [250]... ***"Our lord, pour out patience on us and set our feet firm and give us victory against the infidel people."***

So what happened after they prayed this wonderful prayer? We read in the next verse: **[251]So they defeated them by Allah's permission. And Dāwūd (David) killed Goliath...**

What a great salad mix. We start with Moses, then a prophet who we do not even know who he was, then the children of Israel gave excuses to this prophet asking for a king, then we get King Saul who is confused with Gideon, and then David showed up and killed Goliath! All this is in one passage in the Qur'an. Within these six verses, there is one error after another. The important part for our study here is that we discovered that King Saul is the one who led the soldiers to the river, not Gideon. What a wonderful fabrication of Angel Gabreel, Mohammed, and his false god, Allah. So where can we find the truth about this story? As I said before, the true account can be found in the Bible.

In the Bible, in the book of Judges we read about the true test the Lord used to reduce the number of ten thousand men down to a smaller number for Gideon to take into battle to fight the Midianites. In Judges 7:4 we read that God told Gideon to take the men down to the water, and God would tell Gideon who would go to fight and who would stay behind. So God told Gideon to watch the men to see how they drank the water. Up until this point, Gideon did not know the test of who would be chosen by God to fight the Midianites. Some of the men got on their knees to drink while others lapped the water as a dog. In verse 5, God told Gideon to separate the men apart by those who got on their knees and those who lapped the water with his tongue. Gideon did so, but he still did not know which ones God would use in the battle. We read in verses 6 and 7: **[6]And the number of those who lapped, putting their hand to their mouth, was three hundred men; but all the rest of the people got down on their knees to drink water. [7]Then the Lord said to Gideon, "By the three hundred men who lapped I will save you, and deliver the Midianites into your hand. Let all the other people go, every man to his place."**

This is the true account. First of all, it was Gideon, not King Saul, who took the men to the water to test them. The enemy of the Israelites at the time of Gideon was the Midianites, not Goliath and his Philistine army. The war with Goliath and his people was in David's time, not in Gideon's time.

There was a few hundred years between the days of King David and the days of Gideon. It was not in David's days or King Saul's days at all.

Not only did Mohammed confuse the story of King Saul with Gideon, Mohammed did not give any details. The Qur'an said that King Saul took the men to the river, and he performed some ridiculous test. However, Mohammed, or Allah, never told us how many people King Saul ended up with to go and fight the enemy. We do not have any information after the test.

Did King Saul lose half of the people or a quarter of the people after the test? How many people stayed with Saul after the test to perform their jihad? There is no mention whatsoever in the Qur'an that told the number of men who went to fight with Saul. There are only a few places in the Qur'an that mention numbers. When Mohammed mentioned numbers, they were usually wrong. According to the Bible, we know for sure that it was three hundred men, and the nine thousand seven hundred other men went home. What a great way to fight a battle against the Midianites. Gideon went from thirty-two thousand men to ten thousand men to three hundred men to fight a battle.

Can we find any other story like this written in the history of mankind from the days of Adam until today? If you tell this story to anyone today, unless he is a true Christian believer, who believes the true word of God and the true account in the Bible, he may think you are drunk or out of your mind.

This is the difference between holy war in the Bible and unholy war in the Qur'an, and this is the difference between jihad in the Bible and jihad in the Qur'an. It is not about numbers, and it is not about strength. It is not even about the tools of war.

I wonder what was going on in the mind of Gideon with all the things he had been through. He was called to deliver the children of Israel from the hand of the Midianites. He tested the Lord with the fleece, and the Lord answered his test. Now he has thirty-two thousand men to go and fight the battle, but the number of men was too large. Then the number dropped to ten thousand and finally to three hundred men.

What weapons do they have to fight the battle? No weapons at all! I wonder if Gideon thought this was a dream or some big mistake. That was why the Lord wanted to encourage Gideon one more time before the battle. We read about this in Judges 7:9-15. The Lord wanted Gideon to see how the

Midianites, the Amalekites, and the children of the East thought of Gideon, so the Lord told Gideon to go down to the enemy's camp because the Lord had given them into his hand. The Lord encouraged Gideon by the words of the enemy and what they said about him.

Now the enemy had a large army. They appeared as numerous as locust, but Gideon went down to their camp and heard two men talking. We read in verses 13-15: **[13]And when Gideon had come, there was a man telling a dream to his companion. He said, "I have had a dream: To my surprise, a loaf of barley bread tumbled into the camp of Midian; it came to a tent and struck it so that it fell and overturned, and the tent collapsed." [14]Then his companion answered and said, "This is nothing else but the sword of Gideon the son of Joash, a man of Israel! Into his hand God has delivered Midian and the whole camp." [15]And so it was, when Gideon heard the telling of the dream and its interpretation, that he worshiped. He returned to the camp of Israel, and said, "Arise, for the Lord has delivered the camp of Midian into your hand."**

Then we read in verse 16 that Gideon divided the three hundred men into three companies of one hundred each. The only things Gideon gave to them were trumpets and empty pitchers with torches. Have you ever heard of this kind of weaponry of war in the history of mankind? Was this how Mohammed fought his battles - with trumpets, empty pitchers, and torches? What kind of nuclear weapon or bomb did the three hundred men have? This was not a war or a battle. You cannot kill someone with a trumpet. You cannot scare someone with an empty pitcher. This was the hand of the Lord. This was how the war was won in the Old Testament.

It was not about how many children of Israel there were fighting in the battle. It was not about how strong their weapons were. It was not about how many swords or spears they had because here is another battle that was won without even a sword. Remember how many times we read in the Old Testament that jihad was performed by the mighty hand of God? Do you remember how Jericho fell? What the children of Israel did was very simple. They walked about the city one time for six days quietly. Then on the seventh day they walked around the city seven times and shouted on the seventh time. They shouted with a loud voice, and the wall fell down.

Remember when the Lord killed more people by hail from heaven than the children of Israel did by the edge of the sword? That is how we know it was a holy war. It had nothing to do with the strength of the children of Israel or their weapons. It was a holy war against evil people for their sins, and God chose to get rid of the evil people by the hand of the Israelites.

In this case with Gideon, there were only three hundred men, and they were without any weapons of war. Gideon told his three hundred men to watch and do whatever he did. In verse 18 Gideon told his men that whenever he blew his trumpet, they were to blow their trumpets and say: **"The sword of the Lord and of Gideon!"** This was the shout the three hundred men were to cry out, and that is how they would win the battle against this huge number of Midianites, Amalekites, and people of the East.

Continuing with the account in verses 19-20, we read that it was at the beginning of the middle watch in the Midian camp when Gideon and his men blew their trumpets and broke their pitchers. When they broke their pitchers, they held up their torches in their left hands and held their trumpets in their right hands. Then they blew their trumpets and shouted, "The sword of the Lord and of Gideon!"

Obviously, we do not see that the three hundred men with Gideon had a third hand to carry a sword or a spear or a weapon of war. They just shouted with their mouths after they blew the trumpets and carried their torches in their left hands. It was the men who blew the trumpets, but it was the Lord who fought the battle for them. It was a holy jihad.

How do we know this? **It was the Lord's war because when the Midianites** in the camp heard the trumpets and the shout of Gideon and his men, they began to fight each other throughout the entire camp. That is what we read in verses 21-22. So how were these people killed? It was the Midianites, the Amalekites, and the people of the East who had the swords, and the Lord set their swords against each other. Then what remained of the army fled. That is how this holy war was won.

It was a holy war to get rid of these evil men as they killed each other and left the land. They had persecuted the Israelites for seven years. Because of the Midianites, the Israelites had lived in caves. They had worked hard to plant their fields only to have the Midianites come and take their harvest. They had lived in fear, but it was the Israelites who had brought this upon themselves. *Why?* They had sinned against God.

Yes, the Lord had delivered the Israelites into the hands of the Midianites for seven years. However, this was not because God was cruel to his people. It was because they had done evil in the sight of the Lord. Because they had sinned against God, they were delivered into the hands of their enemies. Then the children of Israel cried out to God, and God delivered them by His mighty hand.

In verses 23-24: **And the men of Israel gathered together from Naphtali, Asher, and all Manasseh, and pursued the Midianites. [24]Then Gideon sent messengers throughout all the mountains of Ephraim, saying, "Come down against the Midianites, and seize from them the watering places as far as Beth Barah and the Jordan."** That is what the men of Ephraim did. They took the watering places and the Jordan River. We read that in verse 25 that the men from Ephraim captured Oreb and Zeeb, two princes of the Midianites. They killed Oreb at the rock of Oreb and Zeeb at the winepress of Zeeb and brought their heads to Gideon.

We read in chapter 8 of the book of Judges that the men of Ephraim were upset with Gideon because he had not called them to fight the Midianites with him. However, Gideon was a wise man and told them the Lord had blessed them and had delivered the two princes, Oreb and Zeeb, into their hands. What had he done compared to that? When they heard these words, their anger was subdued.

We read, in Judges 8:28, the earth rested for forty years, during the days of Gideon, and there was peace in the land. However, in verse 32, we read that Gideon died. So what happened immediately after his death? Verse 33 states: **So it was, as soon as Gideon was dead, that the children of Israel again played the harlot with the Baals, and made Baal-Berith their god.** This was the end of the cycle of Judge Gideon.

The Story of Abimelech

Again, the children of Israel fell away from the Lord their God, as we read in Judges 8:33, where they are again worshiping a false god. Here we see the cycle repeat itself. They forgot the Lord and all the good that Gideon had done as we read in verses 34 and 35: **[34]Thus the children of Israel did not remember the Lord their God, who had delivered them from the hands of all their enemies on every side; [35]nor did they show kindness to the house of Jerubbaal (Gideon) in accordance with the good he had done for Israel.**

Before Gideon's death, he was not living quite right with the Lord. He had many wives and seventy sons by them. He also had a son, Abimelech by a concubine. We read in the Bible, starting in Judges chapter 9, that

Abimelech was able to convince his mother's relatives to speak to the people in Shechem of his desire to be the new leader, the new ruler of Israel. Now Abimelech desired to kill his own brothers. The people of Shechem gave him some silver which he used to hire some worthless men to follow him and do the dirty work for him.

So Abimelech went to his father's house and killed all of them except for one, the youngest brother, Jotham, because he had hid himself. Jotham spoke to the children of Israel using sarcasm in an analogy about some trees seeking a tree to be the ruler over them. Jotham was making fun of the people of Shechem for making Abimelech their ruler. In this analogy, the trees wanted a king, so they asked an olive tree, then a fig tree, and then a grapevine to rule over them. However, each one turned down the offer to be king. Then the trees asked a bramble to be their king. Jotham told the men of Shechem that Abimelech was the bramble.

The bramble in the analogy told the trees in verse 15: **"If in truth you anoint me as king over you, then come and take shelter in my shade; but if not, let fire come out of the bramble and devour the cedars of Lebanon."**

Jotham was describing Abimelech not as a strong tree but as a useless thorn bush. Jotham rebuked Shechem for what they had done. They had forgotten that Gideon had fought for them, risked his life for them, and delivered them out of the hand of their enemy, the Midianites. Now, instead of being grateful to Gideon, they had killed the sons of Gideon and made the son of Gideon's servant to be king just because he was a relative of Shechem.

Jotham went on to ask the people of Shechem if they had done right by Gideon in making Abimelech king, then they could rejoice in Abimelech. However, if they had done Gideon wrong by making Abimelech king, then may fire from Abimelech devour them and may fire from them devour Abimelech. After Jotham gave this rebuke to them, he fled because he was fearful of Abimelech.

Abimelech ruled for three years when we read in Judges in verses 23-24: **^{23}God sent a spirit of ill will between Abimelech and the men of Shechem; and the men of Shechem dealt treacherously with Abimelech, ^{24}that the crime done to the seventy sons of Jerubbaal might be settled and their blood be laid on Abimelech their brother, who killed them, and on the men of Shechem, who aided him in the killing of his brothers.**

Here, once again we see that the wages of sin is death because Abimelech had sinned against God and against the sons of his father, Gideon, who had been born from Gideon's many wives. Abimelech killed them unjustly. God would bring judgement on Abimelech, and justice would be served. Abimelech killed many of the people of Shechem as a judgment of their work for aiding him in the killing of his own brothers.

We can read about the end of Abimelech in Judges 9:52-54 as he was attacking the tower in Thebez. **52So Abimelech came as far as the tower and fought against it; and he drew near the door of the tower to burn it with fire. 53But a certain woman dropped an upper millstone on Abimelech's head and crushed his skull. 54Then he called quickly to the young man, his armor bearer, and said to him, "Draw your sword and kill me, lest men say of me, 'A woman killed him.'" So his young man thrust him through, and he died.**

In simple words, Abimelech was ashamed to die by the hand of a woman. The truth is that he was killed by a woman even though his armor bearer killed him with his sword.

The story of Abimelech, the son of Gideon, ends in verses 56 and 57. We read that: **56Thus God repaid the wickedness of Abimelech, which he had done to his father by killing his seventy brothers. 57And all the evil of the men of Shechem God returned on their own heads, and on them came the curse of Jotham the son of Jerubbaal.**

The Cycle Continues

We read in verse 6: **Then the children of Israel again did evil in the sight of the Lord, and served the Baals and the Ashtoreths, the gods of Syria, the gods of Sidon, the gods of Moab, the gods of the people of Ammon, and the gods of the Philistines; and they forsook the Lord and did not serve Him.** Obviously, this was the beginning of a new cycle of the fall of the children of Israel as they worshiped these false gods. Here we see again the children of Israel sinning against God.

So what happened after they sinned against God? We read in verse 7: **So the anger of the Lord was hot against Israel; and He sold them into the hands of the Philistines and into the hands of the people of Ammon.** The Bible states that for eighteen years, they oppressed and harassed the Israelites. We read the details of this account in Judges 10:8-10. The Israelites were very distressed, and they cried out to the Lord to save them.

They acknowledged to the Lord that they had sinned against Him and had forsaken Him.

In verses 11-13, beginning with the Egyptians, the Lord went through the history of the people from whom He had delivered the Israelites. He reminded the Israelites that after He delivered them each time, they would again forsake Him and serve other gods.

Remember, from the beginning of Moses' days, after the children of Israel had been delivered from the hand of Pharaoh, God told them to not worship the gods of the people of the land. They were not to serve these gods, they were not to mention these gods' names, and they were not to swear by these gods' names, because if they did, God would punish the Israelites. Here we see the Israelites sinning against God again. As has been mentioned so many times previously, the God of the Bible is no respecter of persons. If the Israelites sinned, He punished them. If the Gentiles sinned, He punished them.

We see God, in verse 14, mocking the Israelites. God told them to call upon these false gods to deliver them since the Israelites had chosen to worship these gods. God told the Israelites to let these false gods deliver them, if they can.

The children of Israel cried out to God to deliver them. They knew they had sinned. They told God to do to them whatever He wished but only deliver them. The Israelites removed the false gods, and the Lord saw their misery because they had disobeyed His law, His word, and because they had served the foreign gods of the wicked people of the land.

In verses 17 and 18, we read that the children of Ammon assembled to start a fight with the Israelites. The children of Israel and the leaders of Gilead asked among themselves who would be their leader. Whoever would lead the fight against the Ammonites would be the leader of Gilead.

The Story of Jephthah

In chapter 11, verse one of the book of Judges we read about Jephthah. He was a mighty man. His father was Gilead, and his mother was a prostitute. Now, Gilead had many sons by his wife, and when they grew up, they told Jephthah that they did not want him to share any inheritance of their father with them. So they drove Jephthah away.

Chapter 5: The Art of War

So when the sons of Ammon came to fight the children of Israel, the elders of Gilead went to Jephthah and asked him to be their leader to fight the sons of Ammon. Then Jephthah said to them, "Don't you hate me? Didn't you expel me from your house? Why are you coming to me now? Is it because you are in distress?" They said, "Yes, that is why we are here. We want you to be the head of us, to all the people of Gilead."

Then Jephthah said a very wonderful statement which shows us that this was a holy war. He said in verse 9: **"If you take me back home to fight against the people of Ammon, and the Lord delivers them to me, shall I be your head?"** Here we see that Jephthah is not talking about his might or the might of his men to fight the battle. He is talking about the might of the Lord, the God of Israel, the one who can deliver Ammon into his hand. So they made a deal with Jephthah. If the Lord their God delivered the children of Ammon into Jephthah's hand, he would be their leader.

Jephthah tried to negotiate a peace treaty with the king of Ammon. He asked the king, "Why have you come to fight me in our land?" The king of Ammon gave him an excuse, "Because you and your people took our land when you left Egypt." Jephthah responded, "No, that is not what happened."

When we started our study of the history of the children of Israel under the leadership of Moses, we saw how they tried to pass through the land of Ammon without eating or drinking anything from the land of Ammon. They just wanted to pass through the land to get to the Promised Land, but the children of Ammon are the ones who refused them passage and started the fight against Moses and the Israelites. Moses did not want to fight. All he wanted to do was to travel through their land. That is why the Lord delivered them into the hand of Moses and the children of Israel. That is exactly what Jephthah explained to the children of Ammon, but they were stubborn and refused to go in peace. Therefore, Jephthah fought the children of Ammon, and the Lord delivered them into the hand of Jephthah and the children of Israel.

Jephthah made a vow to the Lord that if the Lord delivered the sons of Ammon into his hand and he won the battle, then he would sacrifice to the Lord the first thing that came out of his house. Sadly, his only daughter came out of his house, and he sacrificed her to the Lord. He fulfilled his vow because the Lord had delivered the sons of Ammon into his hand.

Some may look at this passage in the Bible and say that the Jewish faith teaches human sacrifice, as many Muslims claim. This is a 100 percent false assumption. The Lord God never commanded anyone to offer human sacrifices, except in the case of the test of Abraham when God asked him to offer his son Isaac as a sacrifice. We know from the Scripture that God did not allow him to do so because God was only testing Abraham.

What we see here in the account of Jephthah is a foolish vow made by Jephthah, which he fulfilled. This is like any other sin committed by any other godly man, king, or prophet throughout the pages of the Bible. Peter denied Jesus, but that does not teach Christians to deny Jesus. David committed the sin of adultery, but that does not teach Christians to commit adultery. This is simply a recording of history which cannot be denied. People commit sin.

This is actually proof that the Bible is still the Word of God, has never been corrupted, and has never been changed. If the Bible had been corrupted or changed, then the Jewish people and Christians would have removed all the sins from the pages of the Bible.

As Christians, we have no problem in opening the pages of the Bible to study war or killing, because holy war in the Bible is true. It is about justice. It is about killing those who commit sin and those who live in sin. It doesn't matter if the person is a Jew or Gentile. God will not let one sin go without being punished.

The Story of Samson

In chapters 13-16 of Judges, we will look at the life of Judge Samson. He was not just some character who fell in love with Delilah. No, there is more to Samson than just his romantic story.

The Scripture gives more small details about this judge than any other judge. God used Samson to bring a holy war against the Philistines. God orchestrated all that happened in Samson's life to accomplish His justice for the sins of the Philistines as well as the sins of the Israelites. For they must be punished for their sin. God is a just God and will not punish anyone unless that person sins against Him. Remember, the God of the Bible is no respecter of persons. He will punish those who sin against Him because the wages of sin is physical death, spiritual death, and eternal death.

In Judges 13:1 we read: **Again the children of Israel did evil in the sight of the Lord, and the Lord delivered them into the hand of the Philistines for forty years.** Yes, indeed. God delivered His own people

Chapter 5: The Art of War

into the hand of the enemy, the Philistines, because the children of Israel did evil in the sight of the Lord. They sinned against God; therefore, He punished them by delivering them to their enemy.

Notice that the Philistines were not a godly people. They were a very wicked people. They worshiped many false gods as we will see in our study.

The story of Samson begins with his mother and his father. Scripture reveals to us that the Lord has anointed them to raise up the new judge who will deliver the children of Israel when they cry out to God for deliverance from the hands of the Philistines. **What do we know about Samson's father and mother?** The Bible states in Judges 13:2 **that Samson's father was Manoah and that his mother was barren.** Then in verse 3, the Angel of the Lord told her that she would have a son, but she was not to drink any wine or eat anything unclean because even before she conceived, her son would be set apart for God. He would be a Nazarite (a person set apart to fulfill a special vow to the Lord God) from the womb; therefore, no razor was to touch the hairs on his head. This son would grow up and deliver the children of Israel from the Philistines. Here we see that God chose this child through these specific parents. This child would be set apart and not grow up like any of the other children in the camp of Israel.

According to verses 6-8, **Samson's mother told her husband that the Angel** of the Lord had come to her and announced that she would have a son and that she was not to drink any alcoholic drink or eat any unclean food for this boy would be a Nazarite from conception until the day he dies. Then Manoah prayed and asked the Lord to let the Man of God that He had sent before come back and teach Manoah and his wife what to do for this child. Manoah was concerned about everything about this Nazarite, this deliverer, who God was sending to free the Israelites from the Philistines.

In verses 9-14 we read that the Lord heard the prayer of Manoah. The Angel of God came to his wife once again while she was in a field. However, Manoah was not with her, so she ran and found Manoah and told him that the same Angel of the Lord had appeared to her again. Quickly Manoah and his wife went to meet with the Angel of God. Manoah questioned him about how they were to raise the boy and what would be his mission. However, the Angel of the Lord just repeated the instructions for the mother to not drink anything alcoholic or eat anything unclean. She must observe everything that He had commanded her to do.

The rest of chapter 13 describes the conversation that took place between Manoah and the Angel of the Lord and the wonderful event that took place at the end of their conversation. Manoah wanted to prepare a young goat for the Angel of the Lord, but He told Manoah that He would not eat the food. Instead, the Angel of the Lord told Manoah that if he offered a burnt offering that he should offer it to the Lord. It is interesting to note that at the end of verse 16 we find that even though Manoah was speaking to the Angel of the Lord, he did not know it was the Angel of the Lord.

Then Manoah asked the Angel of the Lord what His name was so that they could give Him honor when His words were fulfilled. However, the Angel of the Lord did not tell him since it was so wonderful. So Manoah offered the young goat with a grain offering. Then Manoah and his wife witnessed an amazing thing. When the flame of the altar from the offering went up to heaven, they saw the Angel of the Lord ascend in the flame! When they saw this, Manoah and his wife fell on their faces.

Then Manoah understood that he had seen the Angel of the Lord because in verse 22 we read: **And Manoah said to his wife, "We shall surely die, because we have seen God!"** However, Manoah's wife replied to his fear with these words in verse 23: **"If the Lord had desired to kill us, He would not have accepted a burnt offering and a grain offering from our hands, nor would He have shown us all these things, nor would He have told us such things as these at this time."** Then Manoah's wife became pregnant and had a son, and she named him Samson. The Lord blessed Samson, and the Spirit of the Lord was upon him.

Here we see that God has chosen Samson to deliver the children of Israel. Remember, because the children of Israel had sinned against God, He delivered them into the hands of the Philistines for forty years, and now God has sent a deliverer, a new judge, to set them free. Samson would fulfill his duty as a Nazarite to free the Israelites.

In the beginning of chapter 14 in the book of Judges, we see that Samson was now a man and was getting married. We read in verses 1 and 2: [1]**Now Samson went down to Timnah, and saw a woman in Timnah of the daughters of the Philistines.** [2]**So he went up and told his father and mother, saying, "I have seen a woman in Timnah of the daughters of the Philistines; now therefore, get her for me as a wife."**

Of course, when Samson's mother and father heard this, they were very upset. They asked him if there was not a godly woman from the children of

Israel from which he could find a wife instead of from these wicked, uncircumcised Philistines. Why would he want to marry this woman from their enemy? Surely there had to be some woman from his own people he could marry. However, Samson could not be persuaded to change his mind. He insisted that the Philistine woman was the only one he wanted to marry.

However, in Judges 14:4 we understand the reason why Samson desired to marry the Philistine woman. We see the purpose of Samson's life as a judge being fulfilled. Verse 4 states: **But his father and mother did not know that it was of the Lord – that He was seeking an occasion to move against the Philistines. For at that time the Philistines had dominion over Israel.**

The Lord planted this desire in Samson to want the Philistine woman as his wife. This was God's will. The Philistines were ungodly, wicked people who worshiped many false gods and had oppressed Israel for forty years. God's plan was for Samson to take this Philistine woman as wife. God knows her family will humiliate Samson by giving her to another man as wife. In response to this, Samson would take revenge for himself, for God, and for the children of Israel.

Beginning in Judges 14:5 and throughout the rest of chapter 14, we see how the marriage to the Philistine woman was the beginning of bringing deliverance to Israel. Now Samson, his father, and his mother went down to Timnah. While going to Timnah, a young lion tried to attack Samson. However, the Spirit of the Lord came upon Samson, and he tore the lion apart. His mother and father did not know he had done this.

Sometime later, Samson went to get the Philistine woman. On the way, he returned to the place where he had killed the lion. Now there was only a carcass left of the lion, but a swarm of bees and honey were inside the carcass. Samson took out some of the honey to eat as he went along. He also took his mother and father some of the honey but did not tell them where he had gotten it.

As in the custom in those days, Samson gave a wedding feast which lasted seven days. The Philistines brought thirty companions to be with Samson. We read in verses 12-14 that Samson gave the men a riddle. He said that if they could give him the answer to his riddle by the end of the seven days, he would give them thirty linen garments and thirty changes of clothes. However, if they could not give the explanation of the riddle, then they would give Samson thirty garments and thirty changes of clothing. They said to him in verses 13-14: **¹³"Pose your riddle, that we may hear it." ¹⁴So he said to them: "Out of the eater came something to eat, And out of the strong came something sweet."** The thirty Philistine men tried and tried, but they could not solve the riddle. So they went to Samson's wife and threatened her. If she did not get the answer for the riddle, they would burn her and her father's house, for they did not want to lose and give Samson thirty garments and thirty pieces of clothing.

Samson's wife came to him in tears and cried that he did not love her because he would not give her the answer to the riddle. Well, Samson told her that he had not even explained the answer to his own father and mother, so why should he tell her the answer. He loved his father and his mother, and that did not mean that because he did not give her the answer he did not love her. However, she continued to implore Samson to tell her, and he finally relented and gave her the answer.

So just before the sun set on the seventh day, the Philistine men gave Samson the correct answer in verse 18: **"What is sweeter than honey? And what is stronger than a lion?"** Samson realized that his own wife had given them the answer. He told the men that they had gotten the answer by using his own wife. Now Samson had to come up with thirty garments and thirty pieces of clothing to give to these men.

Here we see the first holy jihad to be accomplished by Samson. In verse 19, the Spirit of the Lord came upon Samson in a mighty way. He killed thirty men in Ashkelon and took their apparel to give to the Philistine men who had explained the riddle. Samson was angry, and then he returned to his father's house.

So why was Samson angry? The answer is very simple. The Philistine men had threatened to burn his wife and her father, and they had forced her to get the riddle from him. Therefore, that gave him the right to kill the thirty men in Ashkelon for they were wicked people and to give their clothing to the Philistine men who had answered the riddle. This was the first jihad performed by Samson as a judge.

Will Samson have a happy life with his Philistine wife? Will Samson and his wife live happily ever after? What would the relationship be like between Samson and the Philistines? Well, we read in Judges 14:20 that Samson and his wife would not live happily ever after because his wife was given to his best man. Wow. What a best man!

Wow, this marriage did not last long at all! What will Samson do when he learns that his wife has been given to his best man? In chapter 15 of Judges, we read that during the time of the wheat harvest Samson went to visit his wife. Well, when he asked to go to her in her room, her father would not permit him to do so. Imagine Samson's surprise when his father-in-law tells him in verse 2: **"I really thought that you thoroughly hated her; therefore I gave her to your companion. Is not her younger sister better than she? Please, take her instead."** Maybe this was an easy answer for his father-in-law to give to Samson, but that is not what Samson wanted. He wanted his wife, not his sister-in-law.

This gave Samson the right to revenge. In Judges 15:3 we read: **And Samson said to them, "This time I shall be blameless regarding the Philistines if I harm them!"** Then Samson went out and caught three hundred foxes. He tied two foxes together by their tails and then put a torch between each pair's tails. He set the torches on fire and let the foxes go in the Philistines' grain fields. The grain in the field and the shocks of grain along with the olive groves and vineyards were burned up. Of course, the Philistines wanted to know who had done this terrible thing. When they learned that it was Samson and why he had done this, they took Samson's wife and his father-in-law and burned them with fire.

Now the Philistines made Samson even angrier. In verses 7 and 8: [7]**Samson said to them, "Since you would do a thing like this, I will surely take revenge on you, and after that I will cease."** [8]**So he attacked them hip and thigh with a great slaughter; then he went down and dwelt in the cleft of the rock of Etam.**

After this the Philistines camped in Judah. The men of Judah wanted to know why the Philistines had come to fight them. They replied that they had come to arrest Samson in revenge for what he had done to them. Therefore, three thousand men of Judah went to Samson and asked him in verse 11: **"Do you not know that the Philistines rule over us? What is this you have done to us?"** His reply was: **"As they did to me, so I have done to them."**

Samson had done to the Philistines just as they had done to him, but the men of Judah were afraid of the Philistines. They told Samson that they had come to arrest him and turn him over to their enemy. Samson agreed to go with them as long as the men of Judah swore not to kill him themselves. The men of Judah promised they would not kill him, but they would tie him up. So they took two new ropes and bound up Samson to turn him over to the Philistines.

We read in verse 14: **When he came to Lehi, the Philistines came shouting against him. Then the Spirit of the Lord came mightily upon him; and the ropes that were on his arms became like flax that is burned with fire, and his bonds broke loose from his hands.** When Samson broke free from the ropes, he picked up a jawbone of a donkey, and he killed a thousand Philistine men with it. This was the third revenge by Samson. The first was the thirty men he killed, the second was the Philistine's crops he destroyed using foxes and torches, and now these thousand men he killed with the jawbone of a donkey.

There is a very important point we need to note about Samson: the rule of the Spirit of the Lord in his life. We read in Judges 13:25 that the Spirit of the Lord began to move upon Samson. This same Spirit of the Lord came mightily upon Samson in Judges 14:6 when he tore the young lion apart with his bare hands. In Judges 14:19, the Spirit of the Lord came mightily upon Samson when he killed the thirty men. Now, once again, the Spirit of the Lord came mightily upon him in Judges 15:14 as he broke his bonds and killed one thousand men with the donkey's jawbone.

Continuing with the account of Judge Samson, after killing the one thousand men, he became very thirsty. In verse 18 Samson cried to the Lord: **"You have given this great deliverance by the hand of Your servant;** Notice here that Samson acknowledged that his deliverance from the hand of the Philistines was from the Lord. It was not through his own strength but by the Spirit of the Lord working in his life. Then he continued in verse 18 by saying: **and now shall I die of thirst and fall into the hand of the uncircumcised?"** Isn't it amazing that Samson who was just miraculously delivered by the Lord is now complaining about dying of thirst? Notice that the Lord answered Samson's prayer by splitting a hollow place in which water came out. When Samson drank of the water, his was revived. Chapter 15 ends with verse 20 stating that Samson judged Israel for twenty years.

In chapter 16 of Judges, we read of the familiar story of Samson and the Philistine woman named Delilah. According to verse 4, Samson loved Delilah. This knowledge was another opportunity for the Philistines to try to take Samson. The previous attempts had failed. This time the Philistine leaders approached Delilah to find out the source of Samson's strength. If she could find out the secret, then they planned to bind up Samson and afflict him. Each leader promised to pay her eleven hundred pieces of silver for the information.

Delilah pleaded in verse 6: **"Please tell me where your great strength lies, and with what you may be bound to afflict you."** What a wonderful, polite request! Please! Please tell me the secret of your strength! Please tell me how we can make you weak and kill you! This is a strange question to this mighty man.

Samson answered her in verse 7: **"If they bind me with seven fresh bowstrings, not yet dried, then I shall become weak, and be like any other man."** Well, the Philistine leaders brought seven fresh bowstrings to Delilah. While Delilah tied him with the bowstrings, the Philistines were lying in wait. Then she cried out that the Philistines are here. Instead of being weakened, Samson easily broke the bowstrings. So that was not the secret of his strength.

Then Delilah said to Samson in verse 10: **"Look, you have mocked me and told me lies. Now, please tell me what you may be bound with."** He responded to her: **"If they bind me securely with new ropes that have never been used, then I shall become weak, and be like any other man."** Delilah tied Samson with new ropes. While the Philistines again were hiding in her house, she cried out that the Philistines are here. Just as before, Samson broke the bonds.

Once again, Delilah accused him of making fun of her and lying to her. She asked him for the third time to tell her the secret of his strength. This time, in verse 13, he replied to her: **"If you weave the seven locks of my head into the web of the loom -"** So, while he was sleeping, that is what Delilah did, but the results were the same as before. This again was not the secret to Samson's strength.

Now Delilah was getting really upset with Samson. She told him in verse 15: **"How can you say, 'I love you,' when your heart is not with me? You have mocked me these three times, and have not told me where your great strength lies."** In simple words: "How can I tie you? How can I make you weak and make you like everyone else so we can kill you? Can't you see the question given to Samson? Even if the question starts with the word please, that is how Satan works in our lives. Satan wants to know where our strength is so he can take it away. Then we will become like everyone else. Then we will fall into sin, and we will die, not just spiritually but physically and eternally. That is the desire of Satan. Every one of us has a Delilah. She is talking in our ears. She is talking to our hearts. She wants to know where our strength is so she can to make us weak, and then we will die.

Samson, the mighty man who delivered the children of Israel from the Philistines and judged Israel for twenty years, also had his Delilah. Delilah and the Philistines wanted to take him out, so she kept on nagging him about revealing his source of strength so that he would become like everyone else. That was the beginning of the end of the great judge, Samson. After Delilah wore him down, he finally relented and told her the truth about the source of his strength in verse 17: **"No razor has ever come upon my head, for I have been a Nazarite to God from my mother's womb. If I am shaven, then my strength will leave me, and I shall become weak, and be like any other man."** Delilah realized that he had told her the truth. She sent for the leaders of the Philistines who came with the silver to pay her. While Samson slept on Delilah's lap, she had a man come and shave Samson. This was the woman who claimed to love Samson, yet she helped to cause his downfall. Then, just as she had done before, she cried out to Samson that the Philistines were here.

Samson woke up and got up to leave as before, but he did not know that the Lord had departed from him. The Philistines captured Samson. They put out his eyes and took him to Gaza. There they put chains on him and bound him and put him to work grinding grain in the prison.

This one judge stood against the Philistine nation. This one man fought holy war against the Philistines as the Spirit of the Lord was upon him, and this one man was able to kill so many of the Philistine men. This one man alone fought a nation. We know that God had anointed Samson to be set apart even before his birth. He was to live right before God. He was a Nazarite. He was not to taste strong drink or have any hair on his head shaved. He was not to touch anything unclean. We see the rule of the Spirit of the Lord working in Samson's life.

Every time the Spirit of the Lord moved upon him, he was able to do great things. As mentioned before, we saw the Spirit of the Lord on Samson when he tore the young lion apart with his own bare hands. We also saw the Spirit of the Lord fill Samson when he killed the thirty men for threatening his wife and his father-in-law **to be burned if Samson's** wife did not give them the answer to the riddle. The Spirit of the Lord was upon Samson when he burned the Philistines' fields. **When the Philistines killed his wife and his** father-in-law because Samson had burned their fields, he killed many

Chapter 5: The Art of War

Philistines. He killed one thousand Philistines with the jawbone of a donkey. Then Samson met Delilah, and because he told her the secret of his strength, the Spirit of the Lord left him.

Now, we see Samson in prison with his head shaved, blinded, and working like an animal grinding grain. Then we read in verse 22 that Samson's hair began to grow. In verses 23-24, the Philistines praised their god Dagon for giving them victory over Samson and offered sacrifices.

In their rejoicing of the victory over Samson, they called for Samson to come and entertain them. They wanted him to perform for them. Samson told the lad who was leading him into their temple to put him between the support pillars of the temple, which was full of people, including the leaders of the Philistines. There were about three thousand people there to watch Samson perform.

At the end of chapter 16 in verses 28 through 31 we read that Samson called upon the Lord and asked the Lord to remember him. In his prayer in verse 28, he said: **"O Lord God, remember me, I pray! Strengthen me, I pray, just this once, O God, that I may with one blow take vengeance on the Philistines for my two eyes!"** Then Samson stood between the two support pillars with his arms outstretched with his left hand on one pillar and his right hand on the other pillar. In verse 30 Samson said: **"Let me die with the Philistines!"** Then Samson pushed with all his might. The temple collapsed, and all the people in the temple died. Samson killed more people at the time of his death than the number he had killed while he was alive. Then Samson's brothers and his father's house came and took his body. They buried him in the tomb of his father Manoah. Samson had judged Israel for twenty years.

Now, let's once again compare the account of Samson's holy war in the Bible with any verses concerning jihad in the Qur'an. In the Bible the Spirit of the Lord used one man, Sampson, against an entire nation. He was able to kill thousands of Philistines. However, in Islam, there is no such thing as one man. It was hundreds or thousands of Muslims who attacked small villages and small groups of people. Muslims took advantage of their numbers, strength, and might. Many Muslims were able to kill many Christians and Jews.

I would like to share with you a verse in the Qur'an. We read that Allah, the god of Mohammed, encouraged Muslim believers to go and fight. Notice that Allah was addressing Muslim believers who were going to fight. Allah did not call them radical or extremist. They were just simply called believers. Allah said in Qur'an 8:65: *O you prophet, provoke the believers to engage in war. If there will be twenty patient (steadfast in fighting) of you, they will have victory over two hundred; and if there will be a hundred of you, they will have victory over a thousand of those who became infidels because they are people who do not understand.*

Now, let's look at the numbers. Twenty would have victory over two hundred, and if there were a hundred Muslims, then they would have victory over a thousand. That means each Muslim believer was commanded by Allah to kill ten infidels. When the believers heard this, they became scared. They got worried. They each had to kill ten infidels! They couldn't do that. So Allah gave them a big reduction in Qur'an 8:66: *Now Allah has lightened for you, and he knows that there is weakness in you. So if there will be a hundred patient ones of you, they will have victory over two hundred; and if there will be a thousand of you, they will have victory over two thousand by Allah's permission. And Allah is with the patient.* Allah made it easy for them now to fight. Why? Because they were weak! Allah lightened the number because they were not strong believers. Therefore, Allah reduced the amount so that every hundred Muslim believers now only had to kill two hundred infidels, and for every thousand Muslim believers, they had only to kill two thousand infidels. So the new number for each Muslim believer to kill was just two Christians or Jews.

Notice in the accounts of Moses, Joshua, Gideon, and Samson that it was not ever about numbers. How many times did we read about all the battles that were fought in the books of Genesis, Joshua, and Judges, and it was not about their strength, their numbers, or even their weapons. There is one more fact we need to remember about the holy war led by Samson. He killed wicked people. Why were the Philistines wicked? They were worshiping the false god Dagon and offering sacrifices to him. These were wicked people. That is why we call this a holy war. It is a just war, a holy war, to get rid of evil people who worship false gods.

The Account of Jews Killing Other Jews

This is the account of a war which, once again, Muslims will not mention, because it will not fit well with their agenda to show the hatred of God or the Jewish people toward some foreign enemy. Nevertheless, it is an obvious holy war in the Bible about killing people who have sinned. In this case, it was a war between Jews and other Jews. The children of Israel

Chapter 5: The Art of War

united to almost remove one tribe of Israel from the face of the earth because of a great sin that had been committed in this tribe.

You will not see anywhere in the history of Islam that Mohammed engaged in war with some Muslims because they had sinned against god because, in Islam, people live in sin. We have seen it so many times in the teaching of the Qur'an.

What is adultery? What is stealing? What is lying? What is killing? These are not sins for these are the commands of Allah for all Muslims to follow and to believe in and to practice as long as they live on earth.

When Muslims die and go to paradise, how do they live for eternity? They still live in sin! The sexual relationships and the lust of the eyes and all the fleshly desires are given to them in paradise as Mohammed taught them in the hadith. The sinful things of the world are exactly what Muslims are waiting for because that is their reward in their heaven.

In chapters 19, 20, and 21 of the book of Judges, we see that when a tribe of Israelites sinned against God by committing evil, the rest of the children of Israel went to war against them. The punishment was so severe that, except for six hundred men, all the people of this tribe were wiped out, including all the females and all the children, because not only did they allow sin to continue in their community, but they also fought on behalf of the sinners.

We read in Judges 19:1-4 that when there was no king in Israel, a Levite, who was staying in Ephraim in the remote mountains, went to Bethlehem in Judah to take for himself a concubine. This woman committed adultery and went back to Bethlehem to her father's house. She had been there for four months when her husband, along with his servant, went to her father's house to reconcile with her and bring her back. So she brought her husband inside, and her father was so happy to see his son-in-law that he convinced him to stay for three days.

Now on the fourth day, they got up early in the morning to leave, but the father said to his son-in-law in verse 5: **"Refresh your heart with a morsel of bread, and afterward go your way."** The father and son-in-law sat down and had a meal together. In verse 6 the father-in-law said to him: **"Please be content to stay all night, and let your heart be merry."** So the Levite stayed. Again, he was ready to leave early in the morning, but the father-in-law insisted once again that he should stay until the afternoon. So he did.

When the man started to leave with his wife and servant on the fifth day, once again the father-in-law spoke to him to delay his departure in verse 9: **"Look, the day is now drawing toward evening; please spend the night. See, the day is coming to an end; lodge here, that your heart may be merry. Tomorrow go your way early, so that you may get home."**

I grew up in this culture. I know about this culture. When I read a story like this, it reminds me of when I lived in Egypt and someone would come to visit our home. They might plan to stay a couple days, but they literally would end up spending a couple of weeks. People there have all the time in the world. They have few responsibilities, so they just visit, sit, eat, and drink. Then ten days or a couple of weeks later, they would really decide to leave.

Continuing with our story, this time the man refused to spend another night in his father-in-law's house, and they departed. Since they had left late in the day, when they came to Jebus (Jerusalem), the servant asked that they spend the night there.

The man would not turn aside to spend the night. He told his servant in verse 12: **"We will not turn aside here into a city of foreigners, who are not of the children of Israel; we will go on to Gibeah."** Because Gibeah belonged to the tribe of Benjamin, that is exactly what they did. However, they arrived after sunset, and no one would take them into their home to spend the night. This was a sin because according to Mosaic Law, God commanded the children of Israel to invite the stranger into their homes.

While the Levite was sitting in the city square, an old man, who was also from the mountains of Ephraim, came in from the fields where he had been working. He saw the man sitting in the square. In verse 17, the old man asked the Levite where he was from and where he was going.

The Levite told the old man that they were returning to the mountains of Ephraim where he lived and to the house of the Lord. He also told the old man that no one would take them in for the night even though he had provisions for himself and those with him including his donkeys. All he needed was just a place to spend the night. In verse 20 we read: **And the old man said: "Peace be with you! However, let all your needs be my responsibility; only do not spend the night in the open square."** Then the old man took him and his party in for the night and took care of all their needs.

Now we come to the sin of the Benjamite men of Gibeah. In verse 22, we read: **As they were enjoying themselves, suddenly certain men of the city, perverted men, surrounded the house and beat on the door. They spoke to the master of the house, the old man, saying, "Bring out the man who came to your house, that we may know him carnally!"**

Here is the sin that reminds us of the sin of the men in Sodom and Gomorrah who told Lot to send out the two men visitors so that they might know them, meaning to have sex with them. Now we see the same sin being committed by Israelite men from the tribe of Benjamin. What a wicked day to see the sin of the world repeated by God's chosen people.

However, the old man spoke to the men and implored them to not do such a vile, wicked thing for this man was his guest. The old man offered his virgin daughter and the man's concubine to these men, but the men would not listen. They still wanted the man to be given to them so they could have sexual relations with him, but the man gave them his concubine. These wicked men abused her all through the night until morning and then let her go. She fell at the door of the old man's house and lay there until daylight. When the man was ready to leave, he opened the door and saw her there with her hands on the door's threshold. He told her to get up so they could be on their way, but she did not answer. The man picked her up, put her on a donkey, and then left for his home.

In verses 29 and 30 we read: [29]**When he entered his house he took a knife, laid hold of his concubine, and divided her into twelve pieces, limb by limb, and sent her throughout all the territory of Israel.** [30]**And so it was that all who saw it said, "No such deed has been done or seen from the day that the children of Israel came up from the land of Egypt until this day. Consider it, confer, and speak up!"**

This man asked the children of Israel what should be done to the Benjamites for this great sin. What should be done for the sin committed against him and his wife?

We read in chapter 20 in the book of Judges what the children of Israel did in response to the Levite's question. They gathered from Dan to Beersheba as one man in Mizpah. The leaders of Israel presented four thousand soldiers before the Lord and the people. The Israelites asked how this evil, wicked deed had happened.

In Judges 20:4, the Levite told them that on the way back home, he and his wife had stopped at Gibeah to spend the night. He told them in verses 5 and 6: **And the men of Gibeah rose against me, and surrounded the house at night because of me. They intended to kill me, but instead they ravished my concubine so that she died. ⁶So I took hold of my concubine, cut her in pieces, and sent her throughout all the territory of the inheritance of Israel, because they committed lewdness and outrage in Israel."** Then the Levite asked their advice of what to do. The people of Israel stood as one man and said that none of them would go home until they dealt with the people of Gibeah. They would choose by lot the men who would repay the people of Gibeah for the evil sin they had committed.

Notice that these were Jewish men from eleven tribes of Israel who had joined together in agreement and in action to perform holy war against the people of the tribe of Benjamin in Gibeah. This was one of their own tribes. We see here eleven tribes of Israel gathering together for the purpose of performing holy war against one of their own people, the Benjamites.

In Judges 20:12 and 13 we read: ¹²**"Then the tribes of Israel sent men through all the tribe of Benjamin, saying, "What is this wickedness that has occurred among you? ¹³Now therefore, deliver up the men, the perverted men who are in Gibeah, that we may put them to death and remove the evil from Israel!"**

The Israelites did not want to kill the entire tribe of Benjamin. They only wanted the perverted men from Gibeah who had sinned. Why? It was because the children of Israel did not want to have evil in Israel for they knew, because of evil, God's judgement would come upon them all. As we have studied in the book of Judges, when the children of Israel sinned against God, God became angry and punished them as He delivered them into the hands of their enemies. When they cried out to God and repented of their sin, God delivered them through a new judge. Then the land rested, and they lived in peace until they sinned again.

We see in chapters 19 and 20 that the Benjamites had sinned against God, and the evil would bring judgment to all the children of Israel. That is why they gathered to bring justice on the perverted men who had sinned against the Levite man and his wife.

However, in the rest of verse 13, we see that the children of Benjamin did not listen to their brother Israelites and refused to turn the wicked men over to them. It would have been very simple for the tribe of Benjamin to

Chapter 5: The Art of War

investigate what happened, but they did not do that. They could have removed this evil from their land by simply giving these wicked men over to face judgement for their evil deeds, but they did not do that. If fact, they did the opposite.

According to verses 14 through 17, not only did the tribe of Benjamin refuse to turn these men over, but they gathered together more men from their cities to engage in war against the rest of the Israelites until they had a force of twenty-six thousand fighting men plus seven hundred men from Gibeah. Out of these fighting men from the tribe of Benjamin, there were seven hundred left-handed men who were excellent shots with a sling. On the other side, the other tribes together had a force of four hundred thousand men of war.

The children of Israel went to the house of God in verse 18. They asked God who would be the first to go and fight against the children of Benjamin. God told them that Judah would be the first.

In verses 19 through 47, we read about the battle that took place. Early in the morning the children of Israel went to fight the children of Benjamin. The children of Benjamin came out of Gibeah and killed twenty-two thousand Israelites. Again, the children of Israel gathered on the battle line as before, but this time they wept and asked counsel of the Lord. They did this until evening. They asked the Lord if they should go into battle against the men of Benjamin once again, and the Lord told them to go fight them.

On the second day, the children of Israel gathered as before, and the children of Benjamin came out of Gibeah and killed eighteen thousand more of the Israelites. Then all the people of the children of Israel went to the house of the Lord. They wept and fasted until evening and offered to the Lord peace offerings and burnt offerings. They again asked the Lord if they should go do battle once more against their brothers, the children of Benjamin. This time the Lord told them in verse 28: **"Go up, for tomorrow I will deliver them into your hand."**

On the third day, the children of Israel placed men in ambush around Gibeah, and then as before they went to fight the children of Benjamin. As previously, the children of Benjamin came out of Gibeah to fight. As they fought, the children of Benjamin were drawn away from Gibeah into the highways and fields. They killed about thirty Israelites and were confident that the results of this day's battle would be as before.

Now as the children of Benjamin were feeling secure of another victory, the children of Israel who were waiting in ambush rushed forward. There were ten thousand chosen men of Israel who fought a fierce battle out along the highways and in the fields. The Benjamites were defeated by the Lord before the Israelites. Twenty-five thousand one hundred Benjamites were killed that day. Since the Israelites had drawn the Benjamites away from Gibeah, the men in ambush rushed into the city to destroy those in it with the edge of the sword.

The Israelites had decided on a signal between the two groups. When the men in ambush rushed the city they would make a great flame with the smoke rising up from the city. Then the men of Israel fighting in the fields and highways would turn to fight the Benjamites.

When the children of Benjamin saw the smoke and the Israelites turning back, they panicked. What they thought was another victory for them was now a disaster, not just a defeat. The Benjamites ran. Eighteen thousand Benjamites had already fallen, and as they fled toward the wilderness, another five thousand fell on the highways. Then another two thousand were killed as the Israelites chased after them. So the total number of Benjamites that fell that day was twenty-five thousand. These men had all been strong fighters.

At the end of chapter 20, we read that only six hundred of the children of Benjamin escaped to the rock of Rimmon for four months. The Israelites turned back and struck down the Benjamites wherever they found them. They killed the Benjamites by the edge of the sword, both people and animals and set their cities on fire.

What a sad account we read in the Bible when the children of Israel wiped out almost the entire tribe of Benjamites, but that is holy war in the Bible. It was better to get rid of one tribe than for all the Israelites to be punished by the hand of God because of the sin of one tribe. All this took place simply because the Benjamites refused to surrender the perverted men and instead went to war on their behalf against the children of Israel. There was no other option for the children of Israel but to engage in war with the tribe of Benjamin. All that was left of this tribe was the six hundred men without any wives.

The account of what happened to the tribe of Benjamin continues in chapter 21 of the book of Judges. In verse 1, the men of Israel took an oath declaring: **"None of us shall give his daughter to Benjamin as a wife."**

The people of Israel were sorrowful and wept over the loss of the tribe of Benjamin. They went to the house of the Lord and in verse 3 cried to the Lord: **"O Lord God of Israel, why has this come to pass in Israel, that today there should be one tribe missing in Israel?"**

The next morning, they built an altar and offered burnt offerings and peace offerings to the Lord. They continued to grieve over the loss of the tribe of Benjamin and for the six hundred Benjamites who had fled to the rock of Rimmon. Their tribe would be wiped out for they had no wives. Then the Israelites asked among themselves if any among all the tribes of Israel had not assembled before the Lord at Mizpah. They discovered that no one from Jabesh Gilead had come to assemble with the rest of Israel. The Israelites had taken an oath that anyone who had not come to the assembly would put to death.

In verse 10, we read that twelve thousand valiant Israelite men were sent by the people assembled at Mizpah to go to Jabesh Gilead and strike the entire inhabitants with the edge of the sword. That meant all the men of Gilead plus the children and the women, those who had been intimate with men, were killed by the edge of the sword. However, the Israelite men found four hundred young virgins in Gilead and took them to Shiloh.

The Israelites sent word to the six hundred Benjamites and gave the four hundred virgins to the Benjamite men, but there were still two hundred men who did not have wives. So the people of Israel still grieved for the tribe of Benjamin and asked what they should do to provide wives for the other two hundred Benjamites.

Now there was a feast of the Lord in Shiloh. In verse 20, the Israelites instructed the two hundred Benjamites who still did not have a wife to hide in the vineyards and wait. When the daughters of Shiloh came out to dance at the feast, each Benjamite man was to run out and catch a wife for himself. When the fathers or brothers came to complain, the Israelites would ask the men of Shiloh in verse 22: **"Be kind to them for our sakes, because we did not take a wife for any of them in the war; for it is not as though you have given the women to them at this time, making yourselves guilty of your oath."** If the Benjamites kidnapped these daughters of Shiloh, this would give wives to the Benjamites while preventing the parents from breaking their oath to not give their daughters to the men of Benjamin. Therefore, the people of Shiloh would not be cursed. When the families complained about their daughters being kidnapped, the Israelites asked the people of Shiloh to have compassion on the Benjamites so that the tribe of Benjamin would not cease to exist. So the two hundred Benjamites, those who had not taken a wife earlier from Gilead, took enough of Shiloh's daughters for each man to have a wife. The Benjamites returned to their land and rebuilt their cities. The tribes of Israel also left and each returned to their own land of inheritance.

Chapter 21 ends with this statement in verse 25: **In those days there was no king in Israel; everyone did what was right in his own eyes.** So what do we learn from this holy war? The story of holy war between the Israelites is in the Bible. It was not removed. This holy war was a just war, a punishment for sin.

When the children of Israel chose to sin against God, they themselves were punished by God. When they repented of their sin, God sent to them a deliverer through the judges. They fought their enemy and had victory over the enemy, and the land rested in peace until they sinned again. When they sinned again, God's anger fell on the children of Israel, and God punished them by delivering them into the hands of their enemies. As we have seen in these three chapters of Judges, even when the children of Israel sinned against God by sinning against their own people, God punished the sin of the tribe of Benjamin by the other tribes of Israel. The sin of Benjamin led to death, for the wages of sin is death. Thousands of Benjamites and Israelites died because of the wages of sin. God demands justice be served. Spiritual death leads to physical death and then to final eternal death. God is not a respecter of persons. This story of holy war in the Old Testament was a just war.

The Jihad of King Saul

Holy War in the Book of Samuel

Even though the name of Prophet Samuel is not mentioned in the Qur'an, we can read in Qur'an 2:246 where Allah said that the children of Israel asked a prophet of them to give them a king over them after Moses. This was the Prophet Samuel. We encourage our Muslim friends to open the Bible and read the account of Samuel as written in 1 Samuel. It is a very interesting account, but Muslims do not know any information about Samuel.

Who was Samuel? Samuel was the last judge and prophet before the establishment of the monarchy began in Israel. Samuel was the prophet and judge who anointed the first king of Israel, King Saul. As we learn from chapter 1 of 1 Samuel, his father was Elkanah, an Ephraimite, and Hannah was Elkanah's wife. Because Hannah had no children, she was broken-hearted. When they went to the house of the Lord, she wept and prayed to the Lord and made a vow to Him. She asked the Lord to bless her with a male child, and she would give him back to the Lord.

After they returned home, Hannah became pregnant because the Lord had heard her prayer. She had a son and named him Samuel. When Samuel was weaned, Hannah kept her vow. She took him to the house of the Lord and presented him to the priest, Eli, who was serving at that time. Because the Lord had answered her petition, she gave Samuel to the Lord for as long as he lived.

In chapter 2 we read that Elkanah and Hannah went to the house of the Lord to offer the yearly sacrifice. Each year Hannah took Samuel a new coat. Because Hannah fulfilled her vow, the Lord blessed her. In verse 21, we see that she conceived and had three sons and two daughters. During this time, Samuel grew before the Lord serving in the house of the Lord.

Eli, the high priest, had two sons, Hophni and Phinehas, who served as priests in the tabernacle. They were not very godly men. They were sinful. We know this because 1 Samuel 2:12 states that they were very corrupt and did not know the Lord. They were sons of Belial, meaning that they were worthless and wicked men.

How do we know that they were ungodly men? The Bible describes many of their sins. These two sons of Eli did not serve the Lord but were actually serving themselves by stealing the sacrifices which were offered to the Lord. By so doing, they fattened themselves and forgot the Lord. They belittled the sacrifices offered to the God of Israel.

Another sin of Hophni and Phinehas was that they would send their servants out to bring them a portion of a sacrifice that was uncooked, meaning they were taking meat before the sacrifice had been burned. When the men who offered the sacrifice refused, the servants of the priests then took the uncooked portion of the sacrifice by force. According to the Law of Moses, the entire fat of the sacrifice had to be burned as a burnt offering to the Lord. In verse 17, the Bible describes the sin of the young priests as very great before the Lord.

Another great sin committed by Hophni and Phinehas is written in verses 22-23: **[22]Now Eli was very old; and he heard everything his sons did to all Israel, and how they lay with the women who assembled at the door of the tabernacle of meeting. [23]So he said to them, "Why do you do such things? For I hear of your evil dealings from all the people.** So here we know that they were living in sexual immorality with the women who came to serve at the entry of the tabernacle. Eli spoke to his sons and told them that they were not doing right and were causing the people to transgress against the Lord. He told them in verse 25: **"If one man sins against another, God will judge him. But if a man sins against the Lord, who will intercede for him?"** However, the sons of Eli did not listen to their father because the Lord wanted to kill them.

The description of Eli's sons, Hophni and Phinehas, showed they were very wicked, but the Bible describes Samuel as a young man who was living in righteous in the house of the Lord. He grew in favor with the Lord and with men.

The Lord was very displeased with Eli and his sons because they were living in sin. The judgement of the Lord was very clear at the end of chapter 2 in verses 33 and 34. God told Eli that none of his descendants would live to an old age and that He would give Eli a sign that this would happen to his descendants. The sign was that both his sons, Hophni and Phinehas, would die on the same day.

Chapter 6: The Jihad of King Saul

In verse 35, the Lord told Eli that He would **"raise up for Myself a faithful priest who shall do according to what is in My heart and in My mind..."** This priest would live and serve God all of his days. As for the rest of the descendants of Eli, they would come to this priest and beg him for a little silver and for food. They would beg him for any work that they could do in the priesthood so that they may have some food to live. All this took place while Samuel was a boy living in the Lord's house. **During this time, the** Lord had not given any visions.

One evening, Eli was lying down to sleep. His eyes were growing dim because of his old age. Samuel was also lying down to sleep in his own room when the Lord called to Samuel three times. Each time that the Lord called, Samuel went to Eli, and each time Eli told Samuel that it was not he calling. On the third time, Eli realized that the Lord was calling and had a message for Samuel. In verse 9, Eli told Samuel that if the Lord comes to him again and calls, to answer, **"Speak, Lord, for Your servant hears."**

The Lord told Samuel about His judgement on Eli concerning his household for the sins of Hophni and Phinehas. They deserved the curse which they brought upon themselves, and Eli had not restrained them. In verse 14 of chapter 3, the Bible clearly declares there was not any sacrifice that Hophni and Phinehas could offer to atone for their sins.

The next morning, Eli asked Samuel what the Lord had told him and not to hide anything from him. According to verse 18, Samuel did not hide anything but told him all that the Lord had said.

Samuel grew up, and the Lord was with him. All the children of Israel from Dan to Beersheba knew that the Lord established Samuel to be the prophet. This was the foundation for the next holy war, the war between the Philistines and the children of Israel as written in 1 Samuel chapter 4.

Now we understand the condition of Israel and the priests, who were the leaders of Israel. They were ungodly men who lived in sin and caused the children of Israel to sin. They were about to engage in war with the Philistines. In verse 2, the Bible states that when they joined in battle, Israel was defeated and the Philistines killed about four thousand men.

The Israelites came back to camp and asked why the Lord allowed them to be defeated that day. Then they decided to take with them the Ark of the Covenant so that when the Ark would go in the midst of the Israelites, they would have victory over the Philistines. So the people of Israel sent to

Shiloh for the Ark of the Covenant, and the sons of Eli, Hophni and Phinehas, were with the Ark of God. According to verse 5, a great commotion took place when the Ark came to the camp of the Israelites, and the children of Israel shouted so loudly that the earth shook. The Philistines heard the shout. They asked what this great noise was in the Hebrew camp. Then they understood that the Ark of the Covenant had come to the camp of the Israelites. The Philistines said: [7]…**"Woe to us! For such a thing has never happened before. [8]Woe to us! Who will deliver us from the hand of these mighty gods? These are the gods who stuck the Egyptians with all the plagues in the wilderness."**

Then in verse 9, the leaders of the Philistines told their men that they must have courage and be strong against the Israelites in order to have victory over Israel or else they would be slaves to the Israelites forever. So the Philistines engaged in war with Israel. They were able to defeat Israel by a great slaughter and killed on that day thirty thousand men, and they also took the Ark of the Covenant.

In verse 11, we see the words of the Lord concerning Eli's sons, Hophni and Phinehas, come to pass. They both died. One of the Benjamite men left the battle and ran to Shiloh. His clothes were torn and dust was upon his head. When the news of the defeat and the loss of the Ark of God into the hands of the Philistines was told, the entire city cried.

Now, Eli was ninety-eight years old at this time. His eyes were dim, and he could not see. He asked the Benjamite man to tell him what had happened. The man told Eli, who was sitting on his chair, that the children of Israel had been defeated by the Philistines and that his sons were dead. He also told Eli that the Ark of God had been taken. We read in verse 18 that when he heard that the Ark had been taken, he fell off of his chair backwards. He broke his neck and died for he was a heavy old man. He had judged Israel for forty years.

When the wife of Phinehas heard that her husband and her father-in-law were dead and the Ark of God had been taken, she went into labor and gave birth to a baby boy. As she was dying, she named her son Ichabod and saying in verse 22: **"The glory has departed from Israel, for the ark of God has been captured."** She said this because of the death of her husband and father-in-law and because the Ark of God had been captured by the Philistines.

Chapter 6: The Jihad of King Saul

The children of Israel lost the battle with the Philistines simply because of sin in their midst. Once again, we see that holy war in the Bible was a just war. When the children of Israel sinned against God, they lost the battle to the Philistines, and God brought justice to the children of Israel. That way they would know that they must repent of their sin. There was no victory as long as there was sin in the lives of the Israelites.

The children of Israel thought that if they took the Ark of God with them into the battle, they would have victory. However, the Ark of the Covenant did not help them as long as they had sin in their lives. The Ark of the Covenant was a representative of God Himself. Having the Ark in the battle judged them for their sin and caused them to be defeated by their enemy. That is what the children of Israel did not understand about the nature of God for He is holy and will not allow sin to continue among His people without being punished.

If there was sin in the Hebrews' lives, they lost the battles. When there was no sin and they were living right, they won the battles. It was the battle of the Lord. Just having the Ark of the Covenant with them did not help them. The Ark was not a good luck charm. Had the children of Israel been faithful to God, they would have had victory over the Philistines, even if they were outnumbered. So how can the ungodly Philistines have the Ark of the Covenant? We read about this in 1 Samuel chapter 5.

After defeating the Israelites, the Philistines captured the Ark of the Covenant and took it to the city of Ashdod, and they put the Ark near their god, Dagon. When the Philistines went into the house of Dagon the next morning, they discovered that Dagon was face down on the ground before the Ark.

They raised it up and put it in its place again, but on the following morning, they once again found their god, Dagon, fallen before the Ark. This time its head and hands were cut off, and only the body remained of their god.

In verse 6, we read that the hand of the Lord was very heavy on the people of Ashdod. They were all ill with tumors. When the people realized that this was the hand of God, they said they could not keep the Ark in their city for **the God of Israel's** hand was heavy upon them and upon their god.

Therefore, they decided to send the Ark of the Covenant to the city of Gath. We read in verse 9 that the Lord was also against this city. He sent great destruction upon them, and the young and the old were afflicted with tumors. Therefore, according to verse 10, they decided to send the Ark of the Covenant to the city of Ekron.

When the Ark of the Covenant entered the city of Ekron, the people cried out and asked if the other Philistines were trying to kill them by sending the Ark to their city. The Lord struck Ekron with destruction, and the Bible states in verse 12 that the people who did not die were stricken with tumors. They asked the lords of the Philistines to send the Ark back to the people of Israel so that it would not kill the people of Ekron and the people of Philistia.

In chapter 6, we see that the Ark of the Covenant stayed in the land of the Philistines for seven months. The Philistines asked their priests and their diviners what should be done to return the Ark back to Israel. The priests and diviners told them that if they returned the Ark of God back to Israel, they could not return it empty. They needed to send a gift with it so that they would be healed and the hand of the God of Israel would be removed. In verse 4, the Philistines sent gifts along with the Ark. The gifts were five golden statues of tumors and five golden statues of rats for their five Philistine lords.

They told the Philistines to not harden their hearts as the Pharaoh and the Egyptians had hardened their hearts when God did mighty things among them. They told their people to put the Ark on a cart and to put the golden tumors and rats in a chest with the Ark. The cart was to be hitched to two cows that had calves. The calves were to be taken home, and the cows pulling the cart were to be sent down the road towards Israel. If the cows continued toward Israel, then the Lord would remove His hand from the Philistines. If the cows turned around and headed home, then this evil that had come to their land was just a coincidence. They loaded the Ark with the offering of the golden statues in a box on a cart and pointed the two cows toward Israel. The cows did not turn to the left or to the right, but they headed straight down the road to Israel. To make sure that the cows continued on their way to Israel, the lords of the Philistines followed them to the border of Beth Shemesh.

In 1 Samuel chapter 6, we see in verses 13 through 15, that when the people of Beth Shemesh, who were out in their fields reaping wheat, saw the Ark coming to them, they rejoiced. There was a large stone in the field where the cart stopped, and the Levites took the Ark of God and the box with the golden articles off the cart and put them on the stone. Then the people of

Chapter 6: The Jihad of King Saul

Beth Shemesh broke the cart apart and offered the cows as a burnt offering to the Lord.

Then according to verse 19, the Lord killed over fifty thousand men of Beth Shemesh. *Why?* It was because they had looked into the Ark of the Lord. We read in verses 20 and 21: [20]**And the men of Beth Shemesh said, "Who is able to stand before this holy Lord God? And to whom shall it go up from us?"** [21]**So they sent messengers to the inhabitants of Kirjath Jearim, saying, "The Philistines have brought back the ark of the Lord; come down and take it up with you."**

The account of the Ark continues in chapter 7 where we read that the people of Kirjath Jearim came and brought the Ark of the Covenant to the house of Abinadab. They also consecrated his son, Eleazar, to keep the Ark, and it remained in Kirjath Jearim for twenty years. However, the people were sorrowful during this time.

Now we come back to the last godly judge to rule over Israel, Samuel, the prophet. He was the one God raised up to lead Israel after the death of Eli and his sons, Hophni and Phinehas. Samuel told the people of Israel that if they returned to the Lord, stopped worshiping foreign gods, the Baals and the Ashtoreths, and served only the Lord, He would deliver them from the Philistines.

So what have we learned about the children of Israel? They were not living right before God because they were serving the Baals and the Ashtoreths. That is why they had lost the war with the Philistines. It was not just their leaders, Hophni and Phinehas, who had been living in sin, but it was also the people themselves who had sinned against God by worshiping these foreign gods.

So what would they do? Would they get rid of their foreign gods and give their hearts to the Lord God of Israel and serve only Him? We read in verse 5, that is exactly what they did. Samuel fulfilled his role as a godly leader and told them what to do. They did what he said, gave up their foreign gods, and turned their hearts back to the Lord. Then the children of Israel gathered in Mizpah. They acknowledged their sin, repented before the Lord, and fasted. Samuel prayed to the Lord on their behalf.

In verse 7, the Philistines gathered to fight the children of Israel while they were at Mizpah. The children of Israel were afraid and asked Samuel to continue to pray to the Lord for them so that the Lord would save them from the Philistines. As Samuel was praying to the Lord, the Philistines came to do battle with the Israelites.

Now we see the Lord perform holy war upon the Philistines. God will prove that He is able to deliver the Israelites. The Israelites were afraid, but they had given their hearts to the Lord and had repented. Remember, holy war is a war against sin. As Samuel offered sacrifices to the Lord, the Philistines came to attack, but the Lord thundered with such a loud thunder that the Philistines became confused. Then the Israelites ran out of Mizpah and pursued the Philistines and drove them back to Beth Car. The victory was the Lord's. Then Samuel put a stone between Mizpah and Shen where they had stopped. He called the stone Ebenezer and said in verse 12: **"Thus far the Lord has helped us."** The Philistines were driven back. The Lord had delivered Israel once again. The Israelites regained some of the cities that the Philistines had captured from Ekron to Gath, and the Philistines did not invade Israel any more. So the Lord brought peace to the land, and Samuel judged Israel all the days of his life.

Samuel and King Saul: 1 Samuel 8-10

We will move on from the book of Judges and look at Samuel and his two sons. When Samuel became old, he made his sons judges over Israel. Would they follow in their father's footsteps and be godly leaders? We will find the answer in 1 Samuel chapter 8.

Samuel's sons were Joel and Abijah. They were judges in Beersheba. Sadly, they were not godly men as their father was. Judges 8:3 states: **But his sons did not walk in his ways; they turned aside after dishonest gain, took bribes, and perverted justice.** Here we see that the sons of this great judge and prophet, the one God used to replace the wicked sons of Eli, Hophni and Phinehas, were also wicked men. Samuel's sons were looking out for themselves and doing evil in the sight of the Lord and the people of Israel.

The leaders approached Samuel about his sons and told Samuel that they did not want his sons to be their leaders. They told Samuel they wanted a king to judge over them just as the other nations had. This was a great sin that the children of Israel fell into. They wanted to be like all the other ungodly nations around them. When they lived in Egypt for four hundred years, they saw that the Egyptians had a king. When they left Egypt and

Chapter 6: The Jihad of King Saul

came to the Promised Land, they discovered that all the other nations around them had kings. Therefore, they wanted to have a king like each of the other nations instead of recognizing that they had the King of kings, the Lord of lords, as their king. They refused God Almighty to be their king and wanted to have a human king to rule over them and fight their battles. This was the sad state of affairs in Israel, and it grieved the heart of God and the heart of Samuel.

Samuel was displeased with the people because of their request for a king, but the Lord told Samuel in verse 7 to listen to the people: **for they have not rejected you, but they have rejected me…** The Lord reminded Samuel that, ever since He had brought them out of Egypt, again and again the children of Israel had forsaken their Lord and worshiped other gods. The Lord also told Samuel to warn the people and show them what a king would expect from them and would do to them.

According to verses 11 through 18, the king will take their sons and appoint some of them to be charioteers and horsemen (draft them into military service). He will appoint others as captains to be over them. He will make some of their sons work in his fields plowing and reaping the harvest. Some will make equipment for his chariots and weapons for war. The king will also take their daughters as cooks, bakers, and perfumers. The king will take their best fields, vineyards, and olive groves and give them to his servants. Not only that, but he will take a tenth of their vintage, grain, and sheep (income tax). The king will also take their male and female servants, their finest young men, and their donkeys and put them to work. The people will be the servants of the king instead of the servants of the Lord. Then when they cry out because they have a king, the Lord will not hear them. He had warned them ahead of time, but the choice would be theirs.

After hearing what a king would take from them, it is amazing that they still insisted that they wanted a king. They wanted to be like all the other nations according to verses 19 and 20. So the Lord told Samuel to give them a king. This must have broken the very heart of God! This is similar to Romans 1:18 where God gives them over to their own desires.

Therefore, in chapters 9 and 10 of 1 Samuel, we read that Samuel anointed a king over the people of Israel. Samuel anointed Saul, a Benjamite and son of Kish, as king. **Chapter 9 describes the events leading to Saul's meeting** with Samuel and then Samuel giving a word of the Lord to Saul. The end of chapter 9 and continuing with chapter 10 describes Samuel anointing Saul as earthly king over the children of Israel.

In 1 Samuel 10:17, Samuel called the children of Israel to Mizpah to hear the word of the Lord. Samuel reminded the people of how the Lord had brought them out of Egypt and delivered them from the Egyptians and all the other nations who had oppressed them. However, they rejected the Lord, the God who delivered them from all their enemies and troubles. They now want an earthly king.

Then Samuel called the children of Israel together by their tribes and clans. The tribe of Benjamin was chosen. Then, from out of the tribe of Benjamin, the family of Matri was chosen, and out of Matri, Saul the son of Kish was chosen as king. When the people looked for Saul, they found him hiding. When Saul stood up, he was taller than anyone else. He was brought before the people, and Samuel said in verse 24: **"Do you see him whom the Lord has chosen, that there is no one like him among all the people?" So all the people shouted and said, "Long live the king!"**

Then Samuel sent the people away to their homes. Saul also went home accompanied by some valiant men. However, there were some people who despised Saul and asked in verse 27 how he could save them, but Saul held his peace.

King Saul and the Ammonites - 1 Samuel 11

The first war that King Saul led was against the Ammonites. This account is found in 1 Samuel 11 starting with verse 1. Nahash, the Ammonite, came to Jabesh Gilead. The men of Jabesh were afraid and asked Nahash to make a treaty with them. If he did, then they would serve him.

Nahash agreed to make a treaty with them on one condition: he would put out their right eyes. This would bring shame upon all of Israel. The leaders of Jabesh asked Nahash to wait for one week so they could send throughout all Israel for someone to come and save them. If no one came, then they would agree to Nahash's terms.

Now, beginning in verse 4, when the messengers reached Saul at Gibeah with the news, the Spirit of the Lord came upon him, and he became very

Chapter 6: The Jihad of King Saul

angry. He took oxen and cut them into pieces and sent the pieces throughout the land of Israel along with a message. If anyone did not join Samuel and Saul to fight the Ammonites, then his oxen would be cut up just as the pieces Saul had sent throughout the land. The fear of the Lord was on the people, and they all agreed to join together to fight the Ammonites. They sent the messengers back to Jabesh Gilead with the good news that help was on the way. Three hundred thousand men of Israel and thirty thousand men of Judah would arrive the next day in the afternoon, and salvation would come to them. The Lord would deliver them.

In verse 11, we read that Saul divided the men into three groups and entered the camp in the morning and killed the Ammonites until the afternoon. The Ammonites who survived ran away in such a manner that no two of them were together.

After the battle, the people asked Samuel in verse 12: **"Who is he who said, 'Shall Saul reign over us?' Bring the men, that we may put them to death."** These were the men who despised and rejected Saul as king and had made these remarks just after Saul had been anointed. However, we read Saul's response in verse 13: **But Saul said, "Not a man shall be put to death this day, for today the Lord has accomplished salvation in Israel."** So Saul did not have them put to death for the Lord had just given them a great victory over their enemy.

Then, in verse 14, Samuel told the people to go to Gilgal where they would renew the kingdom. The people went to Gilgal and officially made Saul king before the Lord. They offered sacrifices of peace to the Lord, and all the people of Israel rejoiced.

So was this first war that Saul led a just war? Absolutely. The Ammonites wanted to enslave the children of Israel. The Ammonites not only wanted to enslave them, but Nahash wanted to pluck out the right eyes of the people of Jabesh Gilead. It was a just, holy war for here we see Saul, the king of Israel, fulfilling his duty as an anointed king by fighting their battles and delivering them from the hand of Nahash, the Ammonite. As I have written so many times before, this was a just war, not like jihad in the Qur'an in which Mohammed and his savage people invaded the world by killing Christians and Jews to force people to submit to the wicked cult of Islam at the sharp edge of a sword. Search the whole world over, look for any nation or region that became followers of Islam after spending time reading, researching, and studying about whether or not Islam was true and about whether or not Allah was god and that Mohammed was a true prophet. You will not find it. Islam does not spread by love and evidence and free will. Rather, read history…it has only spread by the use of the sword and threats of death, and untold millions have died in the Middle East and in Eurasia and in Africa and across the Far East. Why have they died? Because they would not submit to the armies of Islam which invaded their lands.

Then we read in 1 Samuel chapter 12 where Samuel said to the people of Israel that he had listened to them and had appointed a king over them to walk before them. Samuel was old now. He asked the people of Israel if he had ever been unjust with anyone, if he had ever stolen anything or cheated anyone, or if he had ever oppressed anyone. The people replied that he had never done any of these things. Then he asked the Lord and Saul to witness that he had been faithful to them and that the people had not found anything against him.

Beginning in verse 6 of chapter 12, Samuel reminded the people of Israel of what the Lord had done for them when He brought them out from under the hand of Egypt into the Promised Land. He reminded them of their rejection of the Lord and then the Lord giving them into the hands of Sisera and the Philistines and the Moabites. Then, he said, when they repented and stopped serving foreign gods and served the Lord, the Lord sent the many judges to deliver them from their enemies. When Nahash the Ammonite came against Jabesh, Samuel reminded them that they had rejected the Lord as their King in order to have a man as king over them.

In verses 13 through 16, Samuel told the people that they now had chosen their king, King Saul, and the Lord had given them a king to rule over them. If they trust and serve the Lord and do not disobey His word, then both the king and the people will follow the Lord and prosper. However, if they do not trust and serve the Lord but instead disobey the Lord's word, then the Lord will be against them just as He was against their fathers when they sinned against Him.

Here, once again, we see the justice of the Old Testament. If God's chosen people do what is right, love the Lord their God, obey His commands, worship Him, and serve Him alone, they will live in peace. However, if they

Chapter 6: The Jihad of King Saul

do not obey the voice of the Lord and disobey His commands, then the Lord God of Israel will punish them as He punished the people of the earth when they sinned against Him. War and killing was a justified act by the God of Israel throughout the Old Testament.

According to verse 17, it was the time of the wheat harvest, and Samuel wanted to teach the children of Israel how great their sin was in asking for a king to rule over them instead of the Lord their God. Therefore, Samuel told them that he would call upon the Lord to send thunder and rain that day. When the people heard the thunder and saw the rain the Lord had sent, they feared the Lord and Samuel.

The people went to Samuel and asked him, in verse 19, to pray on their behalf to God that they would not die. They acknowledged that they had added to their sins this great sin of seeking for a human king and rejecting the God of Israel to rule over them. Then Samuel assured the people and told them not to fear. Even though they had done this evil thing of asking for a king, he told them to follow and serve the Lord with all their hearts. The Lord would not leave His people, not because of their sin but because of His own great name. He had made promises to Abraham. God would be true to His word, regardless of how untrue the people had become to Him.

Then Samuel said that he would continue to pray for them and that he would teach them to walk in the right way. Samuel ended his speech to them in verses 24 and 25: **24Only fear the Lord, and serve Him in truth with all your heart; for consider what great things He has done for you. 25But if you still do wickedly, you shall be swept away, both you and your king."**

Saul's Attacks on the Philistines and the Amalekites - 1 Samuel 13-15

After Saul had been king for a few years, he faced a new challenge of a new holy war with the Philistines. He chose three thousand men of Israel to go with him. He took two thousand with him to Michmash and placed one thousand with his son Jonathan in Gibeah. In chapter 13:3, we read that Jonathan attacked the Philistines' garrison in Geba. When Israel heard the call of Saul and that the Philistines' garrison had been attacked, they gathered together at Gilgal.

The Philistines were encamped at Michmash. They had thirty thousand chariots, six thousand horsemen, and such a great multitude of men that their numbers looked like the sand along the seashore. In verse 6, when the men of Israel saw the great number of Philistines, they became afraid. The people of Israel were so afraid that they hid. Some hid in caves, some in holes and pits, some in thickets, some among the rocks, and some even crossed the Jordan River.

This was the condition of the children of Israel under the leadership of King Saul. The people who followed Saul trembled because they were so fearful. King Saul waited in Gilgal seven days for Samuel to arrive at the appointed time. Because Samuel was late, the people began to scatter. Therefore, Saul commanded the burnt offering and peace offerings to be brought to him (contrary to what he had been told to do). After the burnt offering had been offered by Saul, he saw Samuel coming and went out to meet him. As soon as Samuel met Saul, he asked Saul what he had done.

Why was Samuel upset with Saul? Had Saul done something wrong? We need to understand that the command of the Lord given to Saul by Samuel was for Saul to *wait* until Samuel arrived. What Saul did was a sin. Saul was the king, not a priest. Samuel was the prophet. Samuel was the priest. He was the one to offer the sacrifice, not Saul.

Samuel asked Saul what he had done, and Saul's reply to Samuel is found in verses 11 and 12. Saul gave Samuel three excuses. First, he told Samuel that the people were scattering. Second, Samuel was late (*"It's YOUR fault, Samuel!"*). Third, the Philistines were gathered to fight. Saul was concerned that the Philistines would attack before the offering to the Lord had been made, and because Samuel was late, Saul felt compelled to offer the burnt offering himself. Saul thought that he could do the wrong thing for the right reason!

In verse 13, Samuel told Saul that he had done a foolish thing by not keeping the command the Lord had given to him. The Lord would have established Saul's kingdom forever if he had obeyed, but that would not happen now. Saul's kingdom would end, and the Lord would give it to another. The Lord would give the kingdom to someone who would follow the Lord with all his heart. So, because Saul did not obey the Lord's

Chapter 6: The Jihad of King Saul

command, his kingdom would not continue. This was the first sin of King Saul and why the Lord rejected Saul as king over Israel.

Now, in 1 Samuel 14:6, we read that Saul's son Jonathan and his armor bearer went to the Philistines to confront them. Jonathan told his armor bearer that the Lord can save by many or by a few. As we have seen in our study, entire wars had been won in which the children of Israel had great victories even though they were few in number and even when they had few weapons of war.

Jonathan revealed to his armor bearer, beginning in verse 8, that they would go to the Philistines and show themselves to them. If the Philistines told them to wait until they came to them, then Jonathan and his armor bearer would stay where they were and not go to the Philistines. However, if the Philistines told them to come up, then Jonathan and his armor bearer would go up and fight because the Lord would deliver the Philistines into their hands. That is exactly what happened in verse 12. The Philistines called to them to come up, and Jonathan and his armor bearer killed about twenty Philistines. However, King Saul did not know that Jonathan and his armor bearer had done this thing.

Then in verse 15, we see God's miraculous work. There was an earthquake, and the watchmen in Gibeah saw the Philistines running away. So Saul asked who was missing from their camp. When the roll was called, it was discovered that Jonathan and his armor bearer were missing.

King Saul asked the priest to bring the Ark of God. Verse 19 describes the event in which the noise continued to increase in the Philistines' camp (because, in their confusion, the Philistines were killing each other by the sword). When Saul saw what was happening, he and those men with him went to battle with their enemy. Then the Hebrews who had been living among the Philistines joined with the Israelites to fight the Philistines. This encouraged the Israelites who had been hiding in the mountains of Ephraim to also join in the battle, and they pursued the Philistines as they fled. This war ended with the statement in verse 23: **So the Lord saved Israel that day, and the battle shifted to Beth Aven.** Then we read in verse 52 that there was war with the Philistines all during Saul's life, and anytime Saul saw a strong man, Saul drafted that man into his service. Saul was trusting in the strength of his army rather than the strength of the Lord God.

Now we move to chapter 15 of 1 Samuel to look at the new assignment Samuel gave King Saul. Samuel reminded Saul that the Lord had sent him to anoint Saul as king over Israel because the people of Israel wanted a human king to lead them in battle. Then Samuel told Saul that the Lord had remembered what Amalek did to the children of Israel when they first came out of Egypt. So he gave Saul the command from the Lord to punish Amalek for what that wicked nation had done to Israel, His chosen people. God is not like us, He does not forget things. He remembers sin.

What was the sin of Amalek? Amalek had attacked Israel after the Israelites left Egypt and were on their way to the Promised Land. Exodus 17:8-16 describes this battle and how Moses told Joshua to choose some good men to fight the Amalekites. Moses went to the top of a hill with his rod in his hand, and as they battled, Moses raised his hands. As long as his hands stayed raised, the Israelites prevailed. However, when Moses became tired and let down his hands, the Amalekites prevailed. So Hur and Aaron held up Moses' hands until sunset, and Joshua defeated Amalek and his people with the edge of the sword.

In Exodus 17 verses 14-16, the Lord told Moses to write down in the book the evil thing that Amalek had done as a reminder that the Lord would blot any remembrance of them. The Lord promised that He would have war with the Amalekites down through the generations.

Another important verse about Amalek is found in Numbers 24:20. This verse states: **Then he looked on Amalek, and he took up his oracle and said: "Amalek was first among the nations, but shall be last until he perishes."** Here we see a prophecy written by Moses concerning the future of Amalek and the Amalekites and that they must perish.

Another passage is Deuteronomy 25:17-19 in which Moses spoke to the Israelites. He told them: [17]**"Remember what Amalek did to you on the way as you were coming out of Egypt,** [18]**how he met you on the way and attacked your rear ranks, all the stragglers at your rear, when you were tired and weary; and he did not fear God.** [19]**Therefore it shall be, when the Lord your God has given you rest from your enemies all around, in the land which the Lord your God is giving you to possess as an inheritance, that you will blot out the remembrance of Amalek from under heaven. You shall not forget.** Here we read the advice of Moses to

Chapter 6: The Jihad of King Saul

the Israelites for future years to come. Moses knew that they would take all of the Promised Land, and after the Israelites accomplished that, they needed to remove the memory of Amalek from the face of the earth. Why? Because the Amalekites were wicked people. They sinned against God and the children of Israel. They did not fear God as they attacked the children of Israel from behind. So now is the time for the sins of Amalek to be punished.

Someone may ask why the new generation of Amalekites had to pay for the sins of their ancestors. My dear friends, it was not about paying for the sins of their fathers or their ancestors. It was actually for their own sins. These people were not a righteous people. They did not worship the God of Israel. Not only did God remember the sins of their ancestors, but He also punished them for their own sins. They had continued to do what their ancestors had done.

We read in 1 Samuel 15 in verses 1-3 that it was now time for their punishment, and Saul was chosen to administer their punishment. The Lord spoke through Samuel and told Saul that he was to attack them, destroy all that they owned and that he was not to spare any of them. He was to kill all the men, women, babies, and even all the sheep, oxen, camels, and donkeys.

When Muslims read a passage such as this, they immediately come to the conclusion that the god of Mohammed is the God of Samuel and of King Saul because the Bible teaches that Prophet Samuel commanded King Saul to kill all the people of Amalek. Amazingly, some Muslims will even go further than this by stating that the god of Mohammed is more merciful than the God of Moses, Prophet Samuel, and King Saul. Why? Because in the **Qur'an, the teaching of Allah, the god of Mohammed, never commanded** Mohammed to kill women and children or to kill oxen, sheep, camels, or donkeys (which is not true). So, according to these Muslims, the god of Mohammed, Allah, is more merciful than the God of the Bible.

No, my dear readers. No, dear Muslims. That is not true. The reason Mohammed did not kill women and children was because they were the spoils of war and were actually the reward Allah gave to Mohammed and his followers. They killed the Jewish men and the Christian men, and they took the women and children as concubines and slaves. That was their income. It was their profit. That is why Mohammed did not command his believers to kill women or children. Those people were their reward. That does not mean Muslims were forbidden to kill women and children in war. We know from the hadith and the Sunnah that Mohammed allowed the killing of women and children when Muslims engaged in war at night and when Muslims fought battles against fortified cities when they used catapults. The rocks and the fire which flew from the catapults did not distinguish between men, women, and children.

You will never see anywhere in the Qur'an (or in the history of Islam) that Mohammed purposely commanded his people to kill women and children or the oxen, sheep, camels, or donkeys in their battles, but sometimes Mohammed gave orders for killing specific women who insulted him in their words or in their writings. We will go into this in more detail in volume 2 of this series. Once again, this was their reward, the spoil of war. That was why Muslim men went to fight in the first place. It was to get women and slaves and riches through the spoils of war, not to purify their land.

This draws a line between holy war in the Bible and unholy war in the Qur'an. The Bible did not teach Jewish people in the Old Testament to engage in war for the purpose of gaining women and children or for the purpose of gaining animals or metals such as silver and gold, even though in some wars God did allow the taking of spoil. The entire purpose in performing holy war in the Bible was to punish the people who had sinned against God. They must receive their wages for sin which is death, not only physical death, but also eternal death in Hell.

These Amalekites had sinned against God by living ungodly lives and by attacking the Jews in the early days when they left Egypt and were on their way to the Promised Land. The Amalekites had sinned by not worshiping the God of the Bible. Instead, they worshiped many false gods. As we stated before, justice in the Old Testament was the whole purpose of holy war. We have read this so many times in the Bible, starting with the Flood of Noah, the fire of Sodom and Gomorrah, and in all of the battles that the children of Israel fought.

Every time God commanded the utter destruction of a city, every living thing in the city was to be destroyed. The children of Israel were commanded to kill everything that had breath, humans and animals. God told the Prophet Samuel to tell King Saul to listen to the word of the Lord: go attack and destroy all the Amalekites. As it was in the time of the Flood, as it was in Sodom and Gomorrah, and as it was in the time of many of the early battles, everything had to be utterly destroyed.

Then we read in 1 Samuel 15:4-5 that Saul gathered the Israelites together and counted the men. There were two hundred thousand soldiers from Israel and ten thousand from Judah. Then Saul led them to the city of Amalek, and they laid in wait. Before Saul attacked, according to verse 6, he told the Kenites who were among the Amalekites to leave so they would not be destroyed along with the Amalekites. Why did Saul warn the Kenites? He warned them because the Kenites had shown kindness to the Israelites after they had left Egypt. Then King Saul attacked the Amalekites.

King Saul Rejected and King David Anointed – 1 Samuel 15-16

According to the command of the Lord, King Saul was to utterly destroy the Amalekites. In 1 Samuel 15:8-9, we find that Saul once again disobeyed the command of the Lord. Saul destroyed all the Amalekites with the edge of the sword except the Amalekite king, Agag. By taking Agag alive, King Saul directly disobeyed the Lord. In addition to sparing the king, Saul and the Israelites kept the best of the oxen, sheep, and all the good things of the Amalekites. So here we see Saul and the Israelites failing to utterly destroy every person and all the animals of the Amalekites.

Why did the Israelites continue to live in disobedience? Had they not learned anything from all the sins of their fathers and early ancestors? Did they forget about the sin of Achan when he stole the forbidden spoil from the city of Jericho and how they lost the war against Ai because of one man's sin? Here we see all the people sinning against God and disobeying His command by sparing Agag and the best of the animals and things of the city. Then we read at the end of verse 9 that the only things that Saul and the Israelites destroyed were the "worthless things."

As we continue reading in 1 Samuel in chapter 15, we see that in verses 10-13, the Lord told Samuel that He had sorrow that He had made Saul king over Israel. Why? The Lord declared that Saul had stopped serving Him and stopped obeying His commandments. When the Lord told this to Samuel, Samuel was brokenhearted over the sin of Saul and cried all that night to the

Lord. The next morning, Samuel went to meet Saul at a place called Carmel. When Saul saw Samuel, he greeted him by saying in verse 13: **"Blessed are you of the Lord! I have performed the commandment of the Lord."** Was this a true statement? Did the Lord tell Saul to keep Agag alive? Did the Lord tell Saul to keep the best of the animals? No. Saul had *not performed* the commandment of the Lord.

Samuel's response to Saul's greeting in verse 14 was: **"What then is this bleating of the sheep in my ears, and the lowing of the oxen which I hear?"** Samuel had already been told by God what Saul had done. Did Saul think he could hide this sin from the Lord and Samuel? Then Saul tried to condone what he had done by saying that the people had brought the best of the animals to offer as sacrifices to the Lord. *They?* The command was given directly to Saul, not the Israelites, to utterly destroy all the Amalekites and all their animals. Is this what the Lord wanted? Did the Lord want a sacrifice? No, the Lord wanted obedience from Saul and the Israelites. Instead of repenting, Saul tried to spread the blame around (just as humanity's first parents had done thousands of years before).

According to 1 Samuel 15:16: **Then Samuel said to Saul, "Be quiet! And I will tell you what the Lord said to me last night."** Samuel continued in verse 17: **"When you were little in your own eyes, were you not head of the tribes of Israel? And did not the Lord anoint you king over Israel? [18]Now the Lord sent you on a mission, and said, 'Go, and utterly destroy the sinners, the Amalekites, and fight against them until they are consumed.' [19]Why then did you not obey the voice of the Lord? Why did you swoop down on the spoil, and do evil in the sight of the Lord?"** You see, King Saul did not obey the command of God. He did not understand that this was a holy war to destroy the Amalekites. He was not to keep anyone alive or any of the animals alive.

Saul argued with Samuel in verses 20 and 21 and told Samuel that he had obeyed the voice of the Lord. He had gone on the mission and utterly destroyed the Amalekites, except for Agag, their king. It was the people who took the spoil of sheep, oxen, and the best of the things to sacrifice to the Lord, Samuel's God, in Gilgal.

Then Samuel responded in verses 22 and 23: [22]**"Has the Lord as great delight in burnt offerings and sacrifices, as in obeying the voice of the**

Lord? Behold, to obey is better than sacrifice, and to heed than the fat of rams. ^{23}**For rebellion is as the sin of witchcraft, and stubbornness is as iniquity and idolatry. Because you have rejected the word of the Lord, He also has rejected you from being king."**

Samuel announced the punishment for King Saul because he refused to obey the word of the Lord. The truth of the word of God is that God is not a respecter of persons. Saul was commanded to go kill the sinners, and when Saul himself sinned against God, then he was not worthy to be the king over the children of Israel.

That is why God rejected Saul as king over Israel, even though Saul confessed his sin in verses 24 and 25. In his confession, Saul told Samuel that he had disobeyed the command of the Lord because he feared the people and listened to them. Then Saul asked the Lord to pardon him and for Samuel to return with him. So here we see that Saul feared his people, but he did not fear God, the God of his people. What a shameful sin! To fear the creature and not fear the Creator. To crave the praise of people, and yet to despise the approval of God. If King Saul had instead commanded the people to obey the word of the Lord, he would have had the respect of his people and been blessed with a kingdom that could have lasted forever.

Then Samuel told Saul in verse 26: **"I will not return with you, for you have rejected the word of the Lord, and the Lord has rejected you from being king over Israel."**

As Samuel turned to leave, King Saul grabbed the edge of Samuel's robe and it tore. Samuel told Saul in verses 28 and 29: **"The Lord has torn the kingdom of Israel from you today, and has given it to a neighbor of yours, who is better than you.** ^{29}**And also the Strength of Israel will not lie nor relent. For He is not a man, that He should relent."**

Once again, King Saul told the Prophet Samuel that he had sinned but asked Samuel to honor him before the elders and Israel. He asked Samuel to go with him so they could worship the Lord together. So the Prophet Samuel returned with Saul, and Saul worshiped the Lord.

In verses 32 and 33, Samuel sent for the Amalekite king, Agag, to be brought before him. Now Agag thought that he would not be killed at this point. However, Samuel told Agag that as his sword had made women childless, Agag's own mother would now be childless. With that being said, Samuel hacked Agag into pieces.

Perhaps when Muslims read this passage in the Bible, they may come to the conclusion: "Hey, Prophet Samuel was as good as Prophet Mohammed. They both killed people, and here we do not see any mercy in the Bible." However, here is the fact: when God commanded a killing in the Bible or a prophet performed a killing according to the command of God in the Bible, it was always a justified killing due to specific sin and rebellion.

The Prophet Samuel did not kill King Agag for a personal reason or for revenge or for spoil (as in many cases in the life of Mohammed). Samuel did not kill Agag because he did not believe in the Prophet Samuel or because he did not believe in the God of Israel. Samuel killed him because he was a sinful man as we read in the passage. King Agag was a killer and killed many, many *children*.

Therefore, it was sin for Saul to keep Agag alive. Saul disobeyed the command of God. The entire Amalekite people were sinners and deserved to die physically, and all those who commit sin must also die eternally in Hell. It was justice for the Prophet Samuel to kill King Agag because he was a sinful man. The wages of sin is death.

Then we read at the end of chapter 15 that Saul went to his home in Gibeah, and Samuel went to Ramah. Samuel did not see Saul again until Saul's death. Nevertheless, Samuel mourned for Saul, and the Lord had sorrow that He had made Saul king (according to the stubborn desire of His people).

It's very important to highlight that there was not any hate or bitterness on the part of Samuel or God towards Saul for anything personal. The rejection of Saul as king was a result of King Saul's sin. He disobeyed God over and over. Samuel mourned over the tragic outcome of the life of the first king of Israel.

We see this clearly in the beginning of chapter 16 in 1 Samuel. In verse 1, the Lord asked Samuel how long he would mourn over Saul since the Lord had rejected Saul as king. That was great evidence that Samuel loved Saul. He was mourning over Saul because of Saul's sin and God's rejection of Saul. Then the Lord told Samuel to take some oil and go see a man by the name of Jesse, a Bethlehemite. The Lord continued by telling Samuel that He would provide a king from among Jesse's sons.

Now since Saul was still alive, Samuel asked the Lord in verse 2: **"How can I go? If Saul hears it, he will kill me."** However, the Lord told Samuel to take a heifer with him and to say that he had come to offer a sacrifice to the Lord. Samuel was to invite Jesse to go with him, and the Lord would show Samuel what he was to do and which one of the sons of Jesse to anoint as the new king.

Samuel obeyed the Lord's directions. He went to Bethlehem, consecrated Jesse and his sons, and invited them to come with him to offer the sacrifice to the Lord. When they came, Samuel looked at Jesse's son Eliab. Samuel thought that he must be the one the Lord had chosen, but the Lord told Samuel in verse 7: **"Do not look at his appearance or at his physical stature, because I have refused him. For the Lord does not see as man sees; for man looks at the outward appearance, but the Lord looks at the heart."**

Therefore, the Lord did not choose Eliab. Then Jesse brought forth his sons Abinadab and Shammah. The Lord did not choose these either. Seven of Jesse's sons quickly passed before Samuel, but none of them were the one chosen by the Lord. So Samuel asked Jesse if he had any other sons. Jesse said there was one more, the youngest, who was out tending the sheep. In verses 11 through 13, Samuel told them to send for the youngest son. This son of Jesse was good-looking with bright eyes and a ruddy appearance. This son's name was David. When he arrived, Samuel took the oil and anointed him in the presence of his brothers because the Lord had chosen David, and the Spirit of the Lord came upon him. Then Samuel left and returned to Ramah.

A Kingdom with Two Kings: Saul and David – 1 Samuel 16:15-17

How can this be? Who will rule over Israel? King Saul or King David? Obviously, the answer is written in 1 Samuel. King Saul continued to rule until his death, and then King David ruled over Israel. However, that is not what Muslim scholars teach. In Ibn Kathir's book, *The Beginning and the End, The Stories of the Prophets*, we read that when Goliath challenged the

Israelites to fight, King Saul asked for someone to volunteer to fight the giant. David volunteered, and he killed Goliath.

Then Ibn Kathir stated that it was said that all the people removed Saul from power and made David king over them. Ibn Kathir also stated that it was said that it was the command of Samuel, and some said Samuel appointed him (David) as king before this incident (meaning the killing of Goliath). Obviously, as Muslim scholars always do, they ended their historical fabrication by the statement "and Allah knows best."

Continuing with our study, we see that it was by the wisdom of God that David would be loved by all the people of Israel, even by the servants of King Saul. David was even very close to King Saul during Saul's reign.

In 1 Samuel 16:13-18, after the Prophet Samuel anointed David with oil, the Spirit of the Lord came upon David at the same time that the Spirit of the Lord left King Saul, and Saul became troubled by a wicked spirit by the permission of the Lord. The servants of Saul asked him if he would allow them to search for a man who could play a musical instrument and thus ease his troubled thoughts. Saul agreed. Then one of the servants told Saul about David, the son of Jesse, who could play the harp very skillfully. Not only that, but David was a valiant man, and the Lord was with him.

According to verses 19 through 23, Saul sent for David. When the troubling spirit came upon Saul, David played the harp. Then Saul became calm, and the wicked spirit departed from him. King Saul loved David like a son and was well pleased with him. Saul even made David his armor bearer. Now we see the relationship between King Saul and David and how David was brought into the kingdom of Saul.

In the Bible, no two kings served at the same time in Israel until the kingdom split between the Northern Kingdom and the Southern Kingdom. The Northern Kingdom had its own king, and the Southern Kingdom had its own king. From the reading of the Bible, we know that King Saul served all his term as one king until his death. King David also served as one king over Israel until his son, Solomon, became king over all the kingdom of Israel as one king. During the reign of each of these three kings, Israel was one kingdom.

Chapter 6: The Jihad of King Saul

However, this was not what was written in the Qur'an. In Qur'an 21:78-80, Mohammed claimed that both King Solomon and King David ruled over Israel as king at the same time. *⁷⁸And David and Solomon, when they judged concerning the crop when the sheep of the people pastured in it, and we were to their judgment a witness. ⁷⁹So we caused Solomon to understand it, and to each of them we gave wisdom and knowledge. And we made subservient with David the mountains and the birds to praise, and we were the doers.*

Here is the last of these three verses of Allah in Qur'an 21 concerning King David for Allah said: *⁸⁰And we taught him the making of clothes for you to protect you from your violence. So are you thankful?* Once again, we see a very strange teaching of Allah in the Qur'an because here we read that David was a tailor, not to make some simple clothes but to make armor for war. It is a very strange passage and quite full of blatant errors. The simple conclusion from these three verses is that the Qur'an teaches that King David and King Solomon ruled together at the same time.

The Jihad of King David

David's First Holy War and the Killing of Goliath – 1 Samuel 17

Now we will move on in our study to 1 Samuel 17 about a holy war between the Philistines and King Saul and the Israelites near Sochoh. The Philistines and the Israelites faced each other with a big valley between them. In verse 4, there was a champion of the Philistines by the name of Goliath from Gath. He was over nine feet tall. He came out and challenged the Israelites over and over again. The challenge was that he would fight with one man from Israel. If Goliath won, then Israel would be the servants of the Philistines, and if the Israelite won, the Philistines would be their servants. Goliath defied the Israelites and taunted them to give him someone to fight. In verse 11, we read that when Saul and his army heard the words of Goliath, they were discouraged and very afraid.

At that time, David's father Jesse sent him with some food supplies to take to his brothers who were with King Saul's army in the Valley of Elah. When David arrived at the Israelite camp, he heard Goliath challenge the Israelites and saw how afraid they were of him. In verse 26, David asked the men near him: **"What shall be done for the man who kills this Philistine and takes away the reproach from Israel? For who is this uncircumcised Philistine, that he should defy the armies of the living God?"**

The answer to his question was given in verse 25. The king would give to the man who killed Goliath great riches, the king's daughter, and his father's house would be exempt from taxes. Wow! The man who killed Goliath would be wealthy, be the son-in-law of the king, and never have to pay taxes again.

When Saul was told of David's brave words, he sent for the young man. In verses 32 through 37, David encouraged Saul by saying: **"Let no man's heart fail because of him; your servant will go and fight with this Philistine."** Then Saul told David that he was just a youth while Goliath was a man of war, so how could he fight such a warrior? However, David

Chapter 7: The Jihad of King David

told Saul about his background as a shepherd. When a lion or a bear attacked his father's sheep, David went after the attacker, rescued the lamb, and fought and killed the lion and the bear. This uncircumcised Philistine would be like the lion or bear. The most powerful reason David gave was: **"The Lord, who delivered me from the paw of the lion and from the paw of the bear, He will deliver me from the hand of this Philistine."** Then Saul told David to go and may the Lord be with him.

According to verses 38 and 39, Saul put his armor and helmet on David, but David was not used to wearing big, bulky armor. David added Saul's sword to the armor, but then he could not even walk. Therefore, he took them off.

Then David took his staff and five smooth stones from a creek which he put in a bag. He also took his sling. When David approached Goliath, Goliath was insulted to see that only a young man was coming to fight him instead of an older, experienced warrior. Goliath told David in verse 43: **"Am I a dog, that you come to me with sticks?"** Then Goliath cursed David. Goliath continued in verse 44 and said to David: **"Come to me, and I will give your flesh to the birds of the air and the beasts of the field!"**

David replied in verses 45 through 47: **^{45}"You come to me with a sword, with a spear, and with a javelin. But I come to you in the name of the Lord of hosts, the God of the armies of Israel, whom you have defied. ^{46}This day the Lord will deliver you into my hand, and I will strike you and take your head from you. And this day I will give the carcasses of the camp of the Philistines to the birds of the air and the wild beasts of the earth, that all the earth may know that there is a God in Israel. ^{47}Then all this assembly shall know that the Lord does not save with sword and spear; for the battle is the Lord's, and He will give you into our hands."** Notice that in verse 46, David said it was the Lord, not David, who would deliver Goliath into his hand.

Once again, I must emphasize the difference between holy war in the Bible and unholy war in the Qur'an. According to the teaching of the Word of God, holy war in the Bible does not depend upon the number of men or the weapons of war. We see all throughout the Bible that the Lord won all His battles without the help of weapons or the help of men. However, in Islam, Mohammed *always* won his battles by the number of his soldiers and with the strength of his weapons…never any miraculous aid. Mohammed always took the side of peace and did not engage in war when he did not have large numbers of men to fight or enough weapons to win a battle. It was the mighty hand of Muslim men, not the hand of God as we see throughout the Bible.

We know from the rest of the story that the Philistine Goliath stood up, and David ran toward the army of the enemy to engage the Philistine. In the great Muslim scholar Al Sadi's interpretation to this portion of this story in the Qur'an, we see even more errors. He stated that David had another twelve brothers, and when he heard that the king of Israel was provoking his soldiers to find someone to kill Goliath that King Saul said that whoever killed Goliath, Saul would give him his daughter as wife and make him a partner in Saul's kingdom.

According to the Qur'an, because David was good with a sling, a stone "called" to him and said: "If you will take me and throw me on Goliath, I will kill him." So David took this rock that spoke to him and put it in his bag. While he was doing that, another rock said the same thing, and then a third rock said the same thing. Now David had three "talking rocks" in his bag. He put the three rocks in the sling. Al Sadi stated that miraculously these three rocks became one rock, and David used it to kill Goliath. The rest of the army fled as losers.

However, the true, historical account in the Bible, in verses 48 through 51, is quite different. David put his hand in his bag, took out just one stone, slung the stone deep into the Philistine's forehead, and Goliath fell on his face on the ground. So David prevailed with a single stone and his sling. Because David had no sword, he ran over and took Goliath's own sword and cut off the Philistine's head.

When the Philistines saw that their champion was dead, they fled. Then the Israelites rose up, shouted and pursued them as far as Ekron. As the Israelites returned from chasing the Philistines, they took the plunder from the Philistines' camp, and David took the head of Goliath with him to Jerusalem.

Relationship Between King Saul and David - 1 Samuel 18-23

What was the relationship between King Saul and David? The answer is found in 1 Samuel chapter 18. What started out as a good relationship changed after King Saul and David returned from fighting the Philistines. As we read in verse 7, the women greeted their return home by singing: **"Saul has slain his thousands, and David his ten thousands."** When Saul heard this, he became very angry and jealous. Saul thought: "What else could David now have than my kingdom?" Saul remained suspicious of David from that day forward. On the other hand, King Saul's son, Jonathan, loved David as he loved his own soul with brotherly love.

In 1 Samuel 18:12-16, Saul was so afraid of David because the Lord was with David and not with him that he sent the young warrior away to serve as a captain in his army. Because the Lord was with David, he served and behaved wisely which caused Saul to continue to be afraid of David. It did not help matters when Saul saw how much the people loved David.

Remember how King Saul had offered the man who killed Goliath his daughter Merab as wife? In an act of humility, in verse 18, David told Saul that he was not worthy to be a son-in-law to the king. When the time came when Merab should have been given to David as his wife, she was instead given to another man, Adriel.

However, when Saul learned that another one of his daughters, Michal, loved David, he thought to give her to David as a wife in hopes that she might be a snare to David. So Saul offered David a second chance to become his son-in-law. Again, David said he was not worthy to be the king's son-in-law because he was poor and from a poor family. In verse 25, Saul used this as an opportunity to get rid of David. Saul told David that he did not want a dowry of gold or silver but for David to kill one hundred Philistines for the dowry. David accepted and went out that very day and killed not just one hundred but *two* hundred Philistines.

In verses 28 and 29, Saul now knew for sure that the Lord was with David. In addition, his own daughter loved David. So Saul feared David even more and was now David's enemy. We see here that the enemy relationship did not start on David's part but rather it started with Saul. We read in the Scripture that Saul made many attempts to kill David, but David was able to escape each time. On the other hand, David had many opportunities to kill King Saul, but he chose not to touch the anointed one, the king of Israel.

We read in the last verse of chapter 18 that many times the Philistines engaged in war with David. When they fought, David was always successful and had many victories. That was why his name was greatly respected and honored throughout Israel.

As we look at chapter 19 in 1 Samuel, we see another attempt by King Saul to kill David. In this attempt, Saul wanted his servants (and even his own son Jonathan) to go out and kill David, but Jonathan was able to convince his father not to kill David. Jonathan reminded his father that the Lord had delivered the Philistines into the hand of David. He had killed many of them, and he brought salvation to the children of Israel. Jonathan asked his father why he wanted to shed innocent blood without any reason. Then Saul swore to Jonathan in verse 6: **"As the Lord lives, he shall not be killed."** Then Jonathan brought David back to the house of Saul.

We read in verse 8 that there was a continuing war between the Philistines and Israel, and David was able to go out and engage in war with them. Because David killed many of them, they fled from him. Over time, Saul could not contain his jealousy and anger towards David, and finally, David had to flee from him.

David's Second Holy War with the Philistines - 1 Samuel 23

As we move to 1 Samuel chapter 23, we read about another holy war between David and the Philistines. David was told that the Philistines were stealing the grain from the threshing floors of Keilah. David asked the Lord in verse 2 if he should attack the Philistines and save Keilah. The Lord assured David in verse 4 that He would deliver the Philistines into the hand of David. So David and his men defeated the Philistines and saved the people of Keilah.

Once again, we must emphasize that this war between Israel, under the leadership of David, and these ungodly Philistines, who were stealing the grain of Israel, was a holy war because David was not fighting for himself. After he sought the Lord, he asked the Lord if he should go and fight even though he only had a few hundred men. God gave him the strength to have victory over these wicked, ungodly Philistines who came to fight the children of Israel.

Then we read in verse 7 that Saul found out that David was in the city of Keilah. This city was secure with gates and bars. King Saul thought that God had delivered David into his hand. This was a shameful thought! Saul was more concerned about killing David than about killing the enemy who was stealing food from the Israelites. This is the tragedy and insanity of sin. Often it causes us to harm those we should love the most.

In verse 8, Saul called his people to go to war against David and besiege him and his men. Once again, in verse 10, David asked the Lord if he should stay in Keilah or escape from the city for he did not know if the people of Keilah would give him and his men over to Saul. The Lord told David that the people of Keilah would give him up to Saul.

David and his six hundred men left Keilah and escaped before Saul surrounded the city with his men. Then he and those with him had to live in the mountains of the Wilderness of Ziph.

David Shows Mercy and Spares Saul's Life – 1 Samuel 24-26

As I stated earlier, Saul continued his attempts to kill David, but David escaped every time. The opposite was true of David. He had several opportunities to kill King Saul, but David would not touch the anointed one of the Lord, the king of Israel.

Remember, as I have mentioned so many times, God is no respecter of persons and the wages of sin is death. There are three deaths, *spiritual* death which leads to *physical* death and *eternal* death. Because Saul had sinned against God, he must be put to death.

We will look at one of the times that David had an opportunity to kill Saul. **Even David's men encouraged him to do so, as we read in 1 Samuel 24.** Saul returned from chasing the Philistines. He was told David was now in the Wilderness of En Gedi. Saul took three thousand men with him to hunt down David. Now these were not just three thousand ordinary men. These men were chosen men from all of Israel...Saul's best warriors.

In verse 3, Saul went into a cave to take care of his personal needs. He did not know that the cave he had just entered was the same cave where David **and his men were hiding. In verse 4, David's men told David that the Lord** had delivered Saul into his hand. It would have been an easy matter for

David to kill King Saul, but David only cut off a corner of the king's robe. However, after he had cut off the corner, David was troubled because he had stretched out his hand against Saul, the anointed one of the Lord. David refused to kill King Saul or to let his men kill Saul. In fact, in verse 7, Saul did not even know how close he had come to being killed by David's men. Then Saul left the cave, unaware of the threat to his life.

In verse 8 through 10, when David came out of the cave, he called to Saul and said, [8]…**"My lord the king!...** [9]**…Why do you listen to the words of men who say, 'Indeed David seeks your harm'?** [10]**Look, this day your eyes have seen that the Lord delivered you today into my hand in the cave, and someone urged me to kill you. But my eye spared you, and I said, 'I will not stretch out my hand against my lord, for he is the Lord's anointed.'"** David revealed to King Saul the opportunity he had to kill him in the cave by holding up the corner of Saul's robe. In verse 11, David told Saul that there was no evil or hate in his heart and that he had not sinned against Saul. Saul was continually seeking to kill David. However, David requested that the Lord be the judge between them. Again, David told King Saul that his hand would not be against the king.

In verses 16 through 21, Saul wept after hearing the words of David. He acknowledged that David was more righteous than he was because David did not seek to retaliate towards the king even though the king had already tried several times to kill David. David had returned good for the evil the king had done towards him. Then Saul responded in verses 20 and 21: [20]**"And now I know indeed that you shall surely be king, and that the kingdom of Israel shall be established in your hand.** [21]**Therefore swear now to me by the Lord that you will not cut off my descendants after me, and that you will not destroy my name from my father's house."** That is exactly what David did. He swore to Saul that he would not cut off Saul's descendants. Then Saul went home, and David and his men went to a stronghold.

I remember as a child reading the story of King Saul and David. When I got to this point in chapter 24, I thought that's it. It is all over. Saul confessed he was not a good man. David proved he was a righteous man when he had the opportunity to kill King Saul but did not. Even Saul confessed that David was a righteous man compared to himself. King Saul knew for sure that David would be king over Israel and his kingdom would be established forever. David had sworn that he would not destroy Saul's household. Therefore, that is it. David will be the new king of Israel after Saul, and Saul would no longer desire to seek or kill David. However, that is not how the story ended. Why is that? Saul listened to the evil people, and he still desired to kill David. How do we know that? We read the answer in the Bible in 1 Samuel chapter 26.

In chapter 26:1-4, Saul was at home in Gibeah when the Ziphites came to him with news of David's whereabouts. In response, Saul once again took three thousand chosen men with him to the Wilderness of Ziph. David heard that King Saul was in the wilderness and sent out spies to find out if that was true.

Continuing on in chapter 26, David went to where Saul was encamped. He saw Saul in the center of the camp with all his men around him, including the commander of his army, Abner. As Saul and his men were sleeping, David took Abishai with him, and they entered the camp and came to Saul. Abishai told David that the Lord had delivered Saul into his hand, and then he pleaded with David to let him take Saul's own spear, which was near Saul's head, and kill him.

However, David told Abishai in verses 9-10: [9]**..."Do not destroy him; for who can stretch out his hand against the Lord's anointed, and be guiltless?"** [10]**David said furthermore, "As the Lord lives, the Lord shall strike him, or his day shall come to die, or he shall go out to battle and perish."** Here we see another opportunity for David to kill Saul, but once again he refused. David told Abishai, just as he said earlier at the cave, that he would not stretch out his hand against the Lord's anointed. However, they took Saul's spear and a water jug and left. Because the Lord had caused the men in the camp to be in a deep sleep, they did not hear or know that David and Abishai had been in their camp.

When David had gone and stood on a hill a great distance from Saul's camp, he called out to the camp and specifically to Abner, the commander of Saul's army. David embarrassed Abner in verses 15 and 16 when David asked Abner: [15]... **"Are you not a man? And who is like you in Israel? Why then have you not guarded your lord the king? For one of the people came in to destroy your lord the king.** [16]**This thing that you have done is not good. As the Lord lives, you deserve to die, because you**

have not guarded your master, the Lord's anointed. And now see where the king's spear is, and the jug of water that was by his head." Abner was the commander of Saul's army, yet David rebuked him for not protecting and guarding his king and for allowing someone to approach the king who could have easily harmed or killed him. That was not a good thing for the commander of the army to hear about himself.

Then David addressed Saul and asked him what he had done that Saul was again seeking him. In verse 21, Saul told David that Saul had sinned and was a fool to do what he had done. He acknowledged that David had spared his life once again; therefore, he would not harm David. David told Saul to send one of his young men over to retrieve Saul's spear. Then David reminded Saul that he would not stretch out his hand against the Lord's anointed. You see, David did what was right and honorable. Saul was the king. He had been anointed to be king, and David would honor Saul as king, the Lord's anointed. Then Saul blessed David and even called David his son. After that, Saul went home, and David went his way in safety.

David Lives Among the Enemy While Performing Many Holy Wars – 1 Samuel 27

What an amazing biblical account where we see that King Saul still wanted to pursue David even after David had spared his life in chapter 24 and then again in chapter 26. Because David sensed his life was no longer secure, he decided to leave Israel and go live in the land of the Philistines as we read in chapter 27. David thought Saul might become tired of seeking him and give up the hunt if he left Israel. Six hundred men went with David to Gath. The king of Gath, Achish, allowed David, his men, and their families to live in Gath. Verse 4 states that when Saul heard that David was in Gath, he did not search for David any more.

One day, David asked Achish that if he had found favor with the king to give David and his men a town in the country where they could live instead of in the royal city of Gath. Achish agreed and gave David the town of Ziklag, and David lived there for over a year.

While David lived in Ziklag, he and his men raided nations, such as the Amalekites, to the south as far as Egypt. According to verse 9 of chapter 27, he left no man or woman alive for them to report back to King Achish about what he had done in these lands. However, at times, David brought back animals and other spoil to Achish.

Some Muslims, when they read these passages in the Bible, come to the assumption that the God of the Bible is the same god of Mohammed, Allah. As Mohammed attacked and killed Christians and Jews and as Muslims invaded the world by the sword, so it was the same action David took here as he killed people and took all the camels, oxen, sheep, and their spoils of war. So what is the difference? **These Muslims say: "The Bible teaches killing and the Qur'an teaches killing."** Once again, let me remind you, my dear Muslim readers, killing in the Bible is justifiable. **Killing in the Qur'an is not.** Why? David was not killing a godly people. He was killing a sinful people whom **God had already commanded David's ancestors, hundreds of** years earlier, to kill, for the wages of sin is death. Physical death is one universal proof of the curse of sin on humanity.

When the Jewish people sinned, God killed them. So when the people of the land were living ungodly lives, God commanded David or Saul or many of the other Jewish leaders, as we have seen previously, to kill them as punishment for their sins.

In the Qur'an, Mohammed was not sent by God but by Satan to kill the infidels of the earth. Who were the infidels that the Muslims killed? They were the Christians, Jews, and any other people who refused to submit to Mohammed as a true prophet. That is the great difference between jihad in **the Bible and jihad in the Qur'an.** Mohammed was getting rid of the godly ones (the Christians) simply because they believed in Jesus Christ as their Lord and Savior, simply because they believed that Jesus is God Almighty who became flesh, and simply because they believed that Jesus died on the cross for their sins, was buried, and then arose from the grave. All of these fundamental Christian beliefs warrant execution according to Mohammed.

David and all the other men in leadership were commanded by God, the God of the Bible, to kill the wicked people of the land, such as those who worshiped false gods. That is the great difference between jihad in the Bible and jihad in the Qur'an.

Last War of King Saul with the Philistines - 1 Samuel 28-29

Now we continue in 1 Samuel chapter 28 in verses 1 and 2: **¹Now it happened in those days that the Philistines gathered their armies together for war, to fight with Israel. And Achish said to David, "You assuredly know that you will go out with me to battle, you and your men." ²So David said to Achish, "Surely you know what your servant can do." And Achish said to David, "Therefore I will make you one of my chief guardians forever."**

Here we see that the Philistines had gathered to engage in war with the Israelites. King Achish assumed that David would go with him to fight the Israelites. David had been living in the land of the Philistines because King Saul had been seeking to kill him. King Achish thought that David was fighting in the southern Judah and the Kenite areas. He did not know that David had actually been fighting against the Philistines and other wicked people (such as the Amalekites) for over a year. King Achish assumed that David was no longer in love with Israel and would surely join the Philistines to fight Israel. Will David join King Achish to fight his own people, the Israelites?

In verse 3 of chapter 28, Samuel died and was buried in Ramah. The entire nation of Israel wept for him. Also, at this time, Saul had put the mediums out of the land of Israel. Continuing with verses 4 through 19, Saul gathered his army at Gilboa to fight the Philistines. Now when he saw the army of the Philistines, he was terrified and called upon the Lord. However, the Lord did not answer him. So Saul told his servants to seek out a medium (one who attempts to speak with the dead) so he could inquire of her about the war.

This was yet another sin of Saul because the Lord's command to the children of Israel was very clear. They were not to seek such people for knowledge according to Deuteronomy 18:9-11: **⁹"When you come into the land which the Lord your God is giving you, you shall not learn to follow the abominations of those nations. ¹⁰There shall not be found among you anyone who makes his son or his daughter pass through the fire, or one who practices witchcraft, or a soothsayer, or one who interprets omens, or a sorcerer, ¹¹or one who conjures spells, or a medium, or a spiritist, or one who calls up the dead."** Here we see that

King Saul forgot the word of the Lord and searched for a woman to bring the Prophet Samuel up from the dead so Saul could speak with him and learn from Samuel what would take place with the Philistines.

Saul's servants found a medium in En Dor. So he disguised himself and took two men with him, and they went to the medium at night. Saul told the woman to seek through a familiar spirit (demonic spirit) the spirit of a particular person so that he might learn what would take place in his battle with the Philistines.

Since Saul had put all the mediums out of Israel, the woman was afraid and asked why he was trying to get her in trouble and cause her death. Therefore, Saul promised her by the name of the Lord that nothing would happen to her. So the women asked who he wanted her to bring up, and Saul responded that he wanted Samuel brought up. When the woman saw Samuel, she cried out and asked Saul in verse 12: **"Why have you deceived me? For you are Saul!"** Saul told her not to be afraid and told her to describe what she saw. Then Samuel asked Saul why he had disturbed him. Saul proceeded to tell Samuel that he was greatly disturbed because the army of the Philistines was set to fight Israel and because the Lord had departed from Saul and would not answer him through dreams or by the prophets. Therefore, Saul had summoned Samuel because he did not know what to do.

In verses 16-19, Samuel told Saul the bad news: **[16]"So why do you ask me, seeing the Lord has departed from you and has become your enemy? [17]And the Lord has done for Himself as He spoke by me. For the Lord has torn the kingdom out of your hand and given it to your neighbor, David. [18]Because you did not obey the voice of the Lord nor execute His fierce wrath upon Amalek, therefore the Lord has done this thing to you this day. [19]Moreover the Lord will also deliver Israel with you into the hand of the Philistines. And tomorrow you and your sons will be with me. The Lord will also deliver the army of Israel into the hand of the Philistines."**

The consequences of Saul's sin affected him, his family, and the entire nation of Israel. The Lord was no longer with Saul, and on the following day, Saul would not only lose the right to rule the kingdom, but he, his sons, and the nation of Israel would be delivered into the hand of the Philistines.

In chapter 29, the Israelites and the Philistines were assembled for battle. The Israelites were at Jezreel and the Philistines were at Aphek. The lords and princes of the Philistines passed by in review of their troops. When they got to the rear where Achish was, they saw the Israelites with him. They asked Achish what these Israelites were doing with their army. Achish gave a high report and recommendation of David and his men and how they had served Achish well and were the enemy of Saul. However, the lords of the Philistines were angry with Achish and told him that they did not trust having Israelites behind them during a battle. Besides, was this not the **David who had killed "his ten thousands" according to the** song of the Hebrews? Perhaps these Israelites would betray them and decide to attack the Philistines from the rear. They would not take that chance.

Achish continued to give a good report about David and his men, but the lords of the Philistines still did not trust David. Therefore, they told Achish to send David and his men back to their homes in the land of the Philistines early in the morning. Achish reported to David what the lords of the Philistines had decided. So David and his men left early in the morning, and the Philistines headed toward Jezreel where the Israelites were encamped.

This is how the Lord delivered David from fighting his own people. For how could David fight the Israelites since he had been anointed by the Lord through Samuel to be the king over all of Israel?

Amalekites Invasion of Ziklag and the Victory of David – 1 Samuel 30

In chapter 30, when David and his men returned to Ziklag, they discovered that the Amalekites had invaded their city. The Amalekites had burned Ziklag and taken the women, the children, and all the rest of the people as **captives and carried them away. David's two wives, Ahinoam and Abigail** were also taken. The men wept until they had no strength left to weep and were so distressed that they even talked of stoning David. However, David trusted and gained strength through the Lord.

David asked Abiathar, the priest, to bring him the ephod in order to inquire of the Lord if they should pursue the Amalekites. The Lord revealed to him that they should pursue the Amalekites and they would recover all their wives, children, and everyone taken captive.

Here we see the difference between David and Saul. When Saul sought the guidance of the Lord, the Lord did not answer him. That was why Saul turned to a medium in disobedience to God's direct command. When David sought the Lord, the Lord responded to him. If the Lord was with David, then who could be against him?

In verse 9 of chapter 30, David and his six hundred men arrived at the Brook Besor. Two hundred of his men stayed there because they were very weary. However, the other four hundred men continued with David to pursue the Amalekites.

David's men found an Egyptian in a field and brought him to David. The man was very weak because he had not eaten or had anything to drink for three days. After he ate and drank some water, David asked him who his master was and where he was from. The young Egyptian told David that he was a servant of an Amalekite. His master had left him behind because he had become sick. He also told David that these were the Amalekites who had burned Ziklag.

David, in verses 15 through 20, asked the young man if he would lead them to the Amalekites. The young man said that he would if David promised not to kill him or return him to his master. When David and his men came to the camp of the Amalekites, they found the Amalekites eating, drinking, and dancing because of all the great spoil they had taken from Judah and the Philistines. David and his men attacked and fought the Amalekites until none were left except four hundred young men who escaped. So David and his men recovered all that the Amalekites had taken from them. Nothing was missing that had been taken. David also took all the flocks and herds.

Death of Saul - 1 Samuel 31

As we read in 1 Samuel 31, in the battle between the Philistines and Israel, the Israelites with Saul ran from the Philistines and were defeated on Mount Gilboa. The Philistines pursued Saul and killed his sons, Jonathan, Abinadab, and Malchishua. Saul was pierced with an arrow and severely wounded. Saul instructed his armor bearer to take his sword and kill Saul. However, the armor bearer was afraid of killing the king, so Saul took his own sword and fell upon it. When the armor bearer saw what Saul had done, he too fell upon his sword and died. Verse 6 states that Saul, his three sons, his armor bearer, and his men died on that same day, as Samuel had predicted.

When the Israelites who were on the west side of the valley and the Israelites on the east side of the Jordan saw that the other Israelites had fled and that Saul and his sons were dead, they abandoned their cities and fled. Then the Philistines took over these cities to live in them. The Philistines came the next day to strip the bodies of the dead. When they found the bodies of Saul and his three sons on Mount Gilboa, they stripped off Saul's armor and cut off his head. Saul's armor was put in the temple of their idols, the Ashtoreths, and Saul's body was hung upon the wall at Beth Shan.

We read in verses 11 through 13 that when the people of Jabesh Gilead heard what had happened to the bodies of Saul and his sons, the valiant men of Jabesh went to Beth Shan at night and took their bodies down off the wall. The men brought the bodies of Saul and his three sons back to Jabesh. They burned their bodies, buried their bones under a tree, and then fasted for seven days.

One of the important things we must emphasize here is that most Muslims have very little information concerning the accounts of events found in the Bible. Yes, Muslims believe in David, they believe that he was a king over Israel, and they believe that he was a prophet. However, they do not know how David became a king or when he became a king. All they know is found only in a few verses in the Qur'an. In the Zabor (the book of Psalms), they learn about David killing Goliath. Virtually none of this information which we are sharing in this book concerning King Saul, David, or Samuel is known to the Muslims. Therefore, I believe it is very important for Muslims to read the Bible, for there alone will they discover how much important information has been left out of Mohammed's stories in the Qur'an.

Getting back to the tragedy at the hand of the Philistines...what is the reaction of David when he hears about the death of King Saul and his sons? When will David become king over Israel? The answers to these questions and many more are found in 2 Samuel.

Chapter 7: The Jihad of King David

David Becomes King and Fights Many Battles with the Philistines - 2 Samuel 1-8

On the third day after David and his men returned to Ziklag from recovering all that the Amalekites had taken, a man came from Saul's camp. His clothes were torn, and his head had dust on it. This was the sign of sorrow. David asked him how the battle had gone. The man told David that the Israelites had fled and that King Saul and three of his sons were dead. David then asked the young man how he knew for sure that Saul and Jonathan were dead.

In verses 6 through 10, we read of this young man's account of how the death of Saul occurred. The young man, an Amalekite, told David that he happened to be on Mount Gilboa and saw Saul leaning on his spear. The Philistines were following him. When Saul saw the young man, he called him to come and kill him because he was mortally wounded and in anguish. So, according to the young man's story, that is what he did. He stood over Saul, killed him, and then took Saul's crown and bracelet. He brought the crown and bracelet with him to give to David.

We know from 1 Samuel 31:4 that Saul killed himself by falling on his own sword. So why did this young Amalekite tell such a lie about killing the king? Did he think that David would make him a hero or maybe reward him for such an act? Surely David would be happy to hear that Saul was dead. After all, Saul had been trying to kill David for years.

Upon hearing this report, David and his men tore their clothes, mourned, wept, and fasted until evening because of the death of Saul and Jonathan. Then David asked the Amalekite why he was not afraid to kill the king, the Lord's anointed. We read David's reaction to what the Amalekite claimed he had done in verses 15 and 16: **[15]Then David called one of the young men and said, "Go near, and execute him!" And he struck him so that he died.** **[16]So David said to him, "Your blood is on your own head, for your own mouth has testified against you, saying, 'I have killed the Lord's anointed.'"** This was a justified killing of this Amalekite because he claimed to have killed the Lord's anointed, and now his own mouth condemned him. So instead of being a hero or gaining a reward, the man was rightfully stuck down.

Next, we move our study to 2 Samuel 2. David asked of the Lord if he should go to any of the cities in Judah. What a wonderful way for the new king to begin his rule, by humbly asking the Lord what to do. Saul had acted in self-will and reckless disobedience, but not David, the new king. The Lord told him to go to Hebron in Judah. So David, his two wives, his men and their families lived in the city of Hebron. Then the men of Judah anointed David king over all the house of Judah. When David was told that the men of Jabesh Gilead had buried Saul and his sons, he blessed them for showing kindness to Saul and asked the Lord to bless them.

In verses 8 through 11, Abner, the commander of Saul's army, made Saul's son, Ishbosheth, king over Gilead and all Israel. Only the house of Judah followed David. Ishbosheth was forty years old and reigned for two years while David was king over the house of Judah for seven years and six months.

There are so many events that took place in 2 Samuel that we could cover, but I will just emphasize some of the major wars David fought. I encourage you to read all of 2 Samuel to get the full picture of what took place.

There was a civil war between Ishbosheth, ruling as king of *Israel*, and David, the king of *Judah*. This was the first war between Israel and Judah during the two years that Ishbosheth lead Israel. **Abner and Ishbosheth's army met Joab, the commander of David's army, to fight at Gibeon. Then the two armies fought, and David's army defeated Abner and Israel.**

During this battle, David lost nineteen men and Asahel. However, David's men killed three hundred and sixty of Abner's men. In 2 Samuel 3, we read that there was a long war between the house of Saul and the house of David, and Saul's house became weaker and weaker while David's house became stronger and stronger. However in verse 6, Abner became strong within the house of Saul. Finally Ishbosheth accused Abner, in verse 7, of taking one of his father's concubines. Abner became very angry and reminded Ishbosheth of his loyalty and all that he had done for him. Abner had not turned him over to David, and now Ishbosheth accused him of such a thing. Abner told him in verses 9 and 10: [9]**"May God do so to Abner, and more also, if I do not do for David as the Lord has sworn to him –** [10]**to transfer the kingdom from the house of Saul, and set up the throne of**

Chapter 7: The Jihad of King David

David over Israel and over Judah, from Dan to Beersheba." Then Ishbosheth feared Abner.

As we read in chapter 3 in verses 12 through 26, Abner sent messengers to King David asking David to make a covenant with him, and Abner would bring all of Israel to him. David agreed to make a covenant with Abner, but with a condition. David would not see Abner unless Abner brought David's wife Michal (Saul's daughter who had been David's reward after killing Goliath) to him. David also sent messengers to Ishbosheth, Saul's son, that he wanted his wife, Michal, returned to him.

Abner spoke with the elders of Israel. He reminded them that in the past they had wanted David to be the king over Israel. This was the time to do it because the Lord was with David and the Lord would save Israel from the hand of the Philistines through David.

Abner then went to Hebron and took twenty men with him. David gave a feast for them, and Abner told David that he would gather Israel to David to make a covenant with him. David would rule over Judah and Israel. Then David sent Abner and his men home in peace.

Now Joab came to David in verse 24 and asked David what he had done. He declared that surely Abner had only come to spy on David to find out what David's plans were. So Joab left David and sent messengers, without David's knowledge, to Abner to ask him to come back. We read in verse 27: **Now when Abner had returned to Hebron, Joab took him aside in the gate to speak with him privately, and there stabbed him in the stomach, so that he died for the blood of Asahel his brother**.

In verse 31, when David learned that Abner had been killed, he told Joab and all the people with him to tear their clothes, put on sackcloth, and mourn for Abner. They buried him in Hebron, and David and the people wept for Abner.

When Ishbosheth heard that Abner had been killed, in 2 Samuel 4:1, he lost heart. In verse 7, two captains of Israel went to Ishbosheth's house and killed him as he was sleeping in his bed. They beheaded him and took his head to David in Hebron. They said in verse 8: **"Here is the head of Ishbosheth, the son of Saul your enemy, who sought your life; and the**

Lord has avenged my lord the king this day of Saul and his descendants."

Instead of being happy, David was angry with them. In verse 12, David ordered them executed, had their hands and feet cut off, and then hanged them in Hebron. Then the men of Hebron took Ishbosheth's head and buried it in Abner's tomb.

One thing we must emphasize here is the decency of David as a man after God's own heart. David did not live just for revenge. Many times David forgave and pardoned people, no matter how big their crime against him had been. King Saul tried to kill David many times while David ran for his life. On the other hand, David had many opportunities to kill King Saul, but he refused to do so.

Just as it was with the Amalekite man who lied and claimed that he had killed King Saul and David gave the order for him to be killed, now David commanded that these two captains be killed because they committed the crime of murdering a man in his bed, not in a battle. David did not hate Saul, and he did not hate Saul's descendant, Ishbosheth, the king over Israel. King David, as he had promised King Saul, would not retaliate against the family of Saul. In fact, the opposite was true. David avenged the murder of King Saul's family.

Then we read in 2 Samuel 5:1 that the tribes of Israel gathered in Hebron before David. They spoke to King David and said: **"Indeed we are your bone and your flesh. ²Also, in time past, when Saul was king over us, you were the one who led Israel out and brought them in; and the Lord said to you, 'You shall shepherd My people Israel, and be ruler over Israel.'"** So all the elders of Israel made a covenant with David, and they anointed David king over Israel. According to verse 4 of chapter 5, David began his reign when he was thirty years old and reigned for forty years.

As we continue to read in 2 Samuel, we see that David led many battles against the enemies of Israel and against the Philistines to free the Jewish lands from their control. In verses 6 through 8, David engaged in war with the Jebusites, he took over their city, and it became the City of David, also known as Jerusalem. In verse 11, a nearby ruler, King Hiram, sent David cedar trees, masons, and carpenters in order to build David a magnificent house in Jerusalem. Then David knew that the Lord had established his kingdom forever over Israel.

In verses 17 through 21, a battle between David and the Philistines occurred when the Philistines learned that David was king over all of Israel. They gathered to go to war against Israel at the Valley of Rephaim. Notice here that the Philistines are the ones who started the war. So David sought the Lord and asked the Lord if He would deliver the Philistines into his hand, and the Lord told him to go and fight. David fought and defeated the Philistines. David gave the credit to the Lord, the God of Israel, for his victory against the Philistines.

Once again, in verses 22 through 25, the Philistines came to fight Israel in the Valley of Rephaim. As he had done in the past, David asked the Lord if he should go and fight them. This time the Lord told him no but to go and surround the Philistines among the mulberry trees and when David heard the sound of marching in the tops of the mulberry trees, he was to run out quickly and strike the Philistines. David did what the Lord commanded and drove back the Philistines as far as Gezer.

Then we read in 2 Samuel 8, that David engaged in war against the Philistines and subdued them. David also defeated the Moabites. He divided the Moabites into three lines. Two lines David put to death and the third line **became David's servants (a mercy for sure).** Next, David defeated the king of Zobah and recovered that territory. David captured a thousand chariots, seven hundred horsemen, and twenty thousand soldiers. David also hamstrung most of the chariot horses. The Syrians came to help the king of Zobah, and David killed twenty-two thousand of the Syrians. Then the Syrians became the servants (spoils of war) of David.

David took gold, silver, and bronze from the countries he had subdued and dedicated them to the Lord. Everywhere he went, the Lord protected David. Chapter 8 ended with: **So David reigned over all Israel; and David administered judgment and justice to all his people.** .

Jihad in Transition

David's Desire to Build the House for the Lord - 2 Samuel 7, 9-10

In this part of our study, we will look at David's desire to build a house for the Lord. In the beginning of 2 Samuel 7, we read that King David was concerned about living in a beautiful house built of cedar while the Lord's house was little more than a big tent (the tabernacle). When David spoke of this to the Prophet Nathan, he told David to go ahead and build a house for the Lord. However, Nathan forgot to inquire of the Lord first. Nathan probably fell into the same trap that many of us fall into…we hear about some idea that seems spiritual and right, and we go along with it, rather than taking the time to seek God's guidance.

In chapter 7:4-7, that very night the Lord spoke to Nathan and told him to tell David that he could *not* build the Lord a house. Nathan was to remind David that the Lord had lived in a tent ever since the Israelites had left Egypt. God "lived in a tent" so that His presence would be with His people as they journeyed to the Promised Land. The Lord had never asked to have a house built of cedar or stone.

Now our study will move to chapter 10 to look at more battles that David fought. Then we will come back to chapter 7 to study why David was forbidden to build a house for the Lord. The timeline of chapter 7 actually took place after chapters 8 and 9.

Let us look at chapter 10:1-19. Nahash, the king of Ammon, died. David wanted to show kindness to Nahash's son, Hanun, who was now the new king. So David sent his servants to comfort Hanun. The leaders of Ammon questioned their king and asked if David truly wanted to comfort him or were David's servants there to spy on their city and then overthrow them. Perhaps it was prudent for them to be skeptical, but Hanun took it too far.

Hanun took David's servants and did things to humiliate them. He shaved off half of their beards, cut their garments off below the waist to shame them, and sent them home. When David heard what had happened to his servants, he met them before they arrived home. Because they were so embarrassed, he told them to wait at Jericho until their beards grew back.

When the Ammonites learned that they had wronged these men and that David actually just wanted to comfort them and their new king at the loss of his father, they hired soldiers from Syria and from some other cities (instead of repentance he brought reinforcements). Upon hearing this, David sent Joab and his army of mighty men to fight the Ammonites and the Syrians. Instead of comforting King Hanun, as was his original intent, David now had to fight the Ammonites and the Syrians.

Joab defeated the Syrians. When the Ammonites saw the Syrians fleeing, they also ran. Joab and his army returned to Jerusalem. Now, this was not the end of the battle. Once again, as we read in verses 15 through 19, the Syrians gathered with more Syrian soldiers from towns across the river to fight against the Israelites. As in the past, David and the people of Israel had to defend their homes and their land from these wicked people. Holy wars during the life of David were mainly battles in which David fought to defeat ungodly people who were attacking him and Israel. As before, the Israelites defeated the Syrians, and because of this, they made peace with Israel and served them. Therefore, the Syrians feared to help the Ammonites any more.

We have no problem as we read in the Bible about the wars in which Israel was involved. All of this goes back to one simple fact. War is history in the Old Testament. War is reality. Because of greed and evil, war has always plagued mankind.

When the God of Israel commanded the Jewish people to engage in war to kill some wicked people, it was a justifiable war. Why? Once again, because, according to the teaching of the Bible, the wages of sin is death. Spiritual death leads to physical death. This does not stop there because it also leads to eternal death if the people don't repent of their evil ways and turn to the Lord. That is the greatest and final punishment.

All of us are going to die. Some of us will die as a result of our own negligence. Some of us will die as a result of someone else's negligence.

Some of us will die due to illness or old age. Some of us will die a sudden death, such as a car accident. However, the true problem is not our *physical* death but our *eternal* death. For if we die physically without knowing Jesus Christ as Lord and Savior, this will lead to the third death, the eternal death, which is to burn in Hell forever.

Dear reader, if you do not know Jesus Christ as your Lord and Savior, and you understand the seriousness of your situation…why not turn from your sins and trust in Him this very moment? He is waiting. In the book of Revelation in the New Testament, we see Jesus standing outside the door of your heart. He says: **"Behold, I stand at the door and knock. If anyone hears My voice and opens the door, I will come in to him and dine with him, and he with Me."** (Rev. 3:20) Please do not hesitate. None of us is promised even one more minute of physical life in this world. If you die physically without Jesus Christ, you will die the eternal death in hell fire. That is God's warning, not merely my warning. He loves you and doesn't want you to be separated from Him forever. However, it is *your* choice.

Getting back to the historical facts in the Scripture, another simple fact we see throughout the Old Testament is that when the Israelites sinned, God punished them in many different ways. Sometimes God used the enticement of the Israelites by the enemies of the land or by a plague or by killing each other by the sword or by the angel of the Lord or by the poison of serpents. While there were many ways to die, the real reason why physical death took place in the Bible was because of sin. If it was not for the sin of Adam and Eve at the beginning of Creation, they and all their children would be alive today. It is a spiritual law. Sin brings death.

God brought His just judgment upon sin which is death, and this killing is justifiable throughout the Bible. However, killing in the Qur'an is not justifiable. Why?

The verses in the Qur'an (about engaging in war or performing jihad) were not ordered by God but by Allah (Satan) and were aimed toward the infidel Christians and Jews, those who did not submit to Mohammed. This was their right to do because Mohammed was not a true prophet. Mohammed did not prophesy, and he did not speak for the God of Israel. Mohammed condemned the actual teachings of Jesus, who is the unique Son of God,

Chapter 8: Jihad in Transition

God in the flesh, who came to die for our sins and then be resurrected from the dead. Mohammed taught many, many things that are in direct contradiction to the history and the theology of the Bible, which obviously disqualifies him from being an actual prophet of the true God. Islam is not "another faith stemming from Abraham," rather, Islam is a savage cult, and the evidence is found in the writing of the Qur'an and the teachings of Mohammed in the hadith as we will see in detail in volume 2.

So why did God forbid David from building the house of the Lord? The answer is found in 2 Samuel 7 and in 1 Chronicles 22:7-10. We will look at 1 Chronicles first as David called for Solomon and said to him: [7]**"My son, as for me, it was in my mind to build a house to the name of the Lord my God;** [8]**but the word of the Lord came to me, saying, 'You have shed much blood and have made great wars; you shall not build a house for My name, because you have shed much blood on the earth in My sight.** [9]**Behold, a son shall be born to you, who shall be a man of rest; and I will give him rest from all his enemies all around. His name shall be Solomon, for I will give peace and quietness to Israel in his days.** [10]**He shall build a house for My name, and he shall be My son, and I will be his Father; and I will establish the throne of his kingdom over Israel forever.'"**

David made all the preparations for the house of the Lord, but he was not allowed by God to build it. His son, Solomon, would be the one to fulfill this task. Why? The Lord said that David was a man of war and had too much blood on his hands in order to secure the kingdom. A life of violence, even in serving the Lord, disqualified David. However, this enabled Solomon to live in a time of peace and allowed him the time to build instead of fighting to secure the kingdom. He would be a man of peace, and the house of the Lord must be built by a man of peace.

The other reason King David was not allowed to build the house of the Lord was a spiritual one. As we read in 2 Samuel 7:5-7, on the same night that Nathan told David earlier that he could build the house of the Lord the word of the Lord came to Nathan. The Lord told Nathan to tell David: [5]**"...'Thus says the Lord: "Would you build a house for Me to dwell in?** [6]**For I have not dwelt in a house since the time that I brought the children of Israel up from Egypt, even to this day, but have moved about in a tent** and in a tabernacle. ⁷Wherever I have moved about with all the children of Israel, have I ever spoken a word to anyone from the tribes of Israel, whom I commanded to shepherd My people Israel, saying, 'Why have you not built Me a house of cedar?'"

The Lord continued with his message for David in verse 11: **since the time that I commanded judges to be over My people Israel, and have caused you to rest from all your enemies. Also the Lord tells you that He will make you a house."'**

God is omnipresent and cannot be limited to a specific place or a specific time. God is all over the universe. He is not limited to any location.

In Acts 7:44, Stephen, the first martyr of the church, made a speech. He was speaking to the Jewish people, explaining to them how the Hebrews traveled in the wilderness and how the Lord traveled with them because His presence was with them in the tabernacle. God gave Moses the exact measurements for the tabernacle. In verse 45, we read that God continued to dwell with the children of Israel in the tabernacle from the days of Joshua to the days of David. Because of the presence of the Lord, the children of Israel were able to have rest from all their enemies who lived in the Promised Land until the days of David. Then Stephen said, in verses 46 and 47, that David was the one who thought to make a place for God in which to dwell, but Solomon was the one who built the house.

The most important part of Stephen's speech is found in verses 48 through 50 as Stephen said: ⁴⁸**"However, the Most High does not dwell in temples made with hands, as the prophet says:** ⁴⁹**'Heaven is My throne, And earth is My footstool. What house will you build for Me? says the Lord, Or what is the place of My rest?** ⁵⁰**Has My hand not made all of these things?'** There is no way that a man can build a place of rest for the God of rest. God created the entire universe by His hands. How can *we* build God a house in which to rest? The truth is that God will make Himself a Temple, and all who believe in Him will have the true rest. 1 Peter 2:5 explains that we are the living stones. We, the church, each person, is now the temple of God. God now resides in our hearts.

Another important event found in 2 Samuel 24 added to the list of reasons that David was not allowed to build the temple. It was at the end of the holy wars which David fought that he decided to make a census of the people of Israel. Why was this a sin? Because this was not God's will since the holy wars were over for David. There was peace. There was to be no more killing, and any killing coming after this, was not of God.

Why did David decide to count the number of men? It was to see the strength of Israel and Judah so they could invade other counties that were not part of the Promised Land. Counting the people was a way of trusting in his numbers and strength, rather than in the protection and provision of the Lord.

When the count of men was determined and given to David, he then realized that he had greatly sinned against God. He asked the Lord to take away his iniquity. In 2 Samuel 24:11-17, God sent the Prophet Gad to David to tell him that the Lord was offering him three choices of punishments because of his sin in numbering the people. According to verse 13, David was to choose one of the following: **"Shall seven years of famine come to you in your land? Or shall you flee three months before your enemies, while they pursue you? Or shall there be three days' plague in your land?"**

In verse 14 David chose to: **Please let us fall into the hand of the Lord, for His mercies are great; but do not let me fall into the hand of man."** Therefore, the Lord sent a plague on Israel in which seventy thousand men died. The Lord stopped the hand of the angel of the Lord who was destroying the people in Jerusalem by the threshing floor of Araunah the Jebusite. David saw that the angel of the Lord stopped at the threshing floor. So he purchased it and the oxen from Araunah, built an altar there, and sacrificed the oxen as a burnt offering to the Lord, and the Lord stopped the plague. So David finished the holy wars, and now Solomon would have forty years of peace.

Solomon Builds the Temple – 2 Samuel 7 (Short Term Prophecy Fulfillment-Jesus the True Fulfillment)

The promise of God to David concerning his seed was that there would be a son to come out of David who would be the one to build the house of the Lord. The prophecy given to David through Prophet Nathan had a two-fold (dual) fulfillment.

Many of the prophecies given in the Old Testament have a short-term fulfillment and a long-term fulfillment. In the short-term fulfillment, David would have a son, Solomon. Solomon's name comes from the word *peace*, for in his days there would be peace on earth. The holy wars in the Old Testament ended when David established the kingdom of Israel on earth. Now there would be no more jihad in the Old Testament because the children of Israel would dwell in the Promised Land permanently. None of the sinful people would harass them anymore, and there would be rest from war.

King Solomon ruled over Israel for forty years, and during that time, there was no war. It was the longest period of peace in the history of Israel. That is why God told David that his son Solomon would build His house. Here is also a greater picture for the true understating of the dwelling of God with men: not in a house built of rocks, gold, and silver, but the true house of peace. It was the fulfillment of God's promise to David that through his son, one seed, the son of David, they would have peace and rest. In the short-term fulfillment of God's promise, King Solomon built the Temple of Solomon, but in the long-term fulfillment, Jesus Christ provided the true dwelling between God and man. Jesus (called the "Son of David") gave His life and died for our sins so that we could have true and eternal peace with our Creator God.

We read in 2 Samuel 7:12-17 that God spoke to David through Prophet Nathan. God told David: **[12]"When your days are fulfilled and you rest with your fathers, I will set up your seed after you, who will come from your body, and I will establish his kingdom. [13]He shall build a house for My name, and I will establish the throne of his kingdom forever. [14]I will be his Father, and he shall be My son. If he commits iniquity, I will chasten him with the rod of men and with the blows of the sons of men.**

Chapter 8: Jihad in Transition

¹⁵**But My mercy shall not depart from him, as I took it from Saul, whom I removed from before you.** ¹⁶**And your house and your kingdom shall be established forever before you. Your throne shall be established forever."** ¹⁷**According to all these words and according to all this vision, so Nathan spoke to David.**

As we read in verse 12, God told David that when he dies, God would set up his seed after him who would come from David's body. How can his seed not come from his body? That is very important because in the long-term fulfillment of the true rest, the coming of our Lord and Savior Jesus Christ, He must be from the seed of King David, from his body according to the flesh. According to verse 14, **I will be his Father, and he shall be My son.** Will he be called the son of David or the Son of God? This is actually referring to both, because according to the flesh, he will be the son of David, but according to the Spirit, He is the Son of God. **If he commits iniquity** refers to Solomon (short-term fulfillment), not Jesus Christ (long-term fulfillment) because Jesus was without sin.

Here we see two buildings, the physical building of the Temple of Solomon and the spiritual building brought about by our Lord and Savior Jesus Christ. Solomon built a temple made out of rocks and silver and gold, but the true Temple of God is when Jesus Christ, our Lord and Savior, came to save and establish His church.

To understand the full fulfillment of God's promises given to King David through Nathan, we will look at seven facts. This information comes from *The New American Commentary* of 2 Samuel 7 by Bergen. The commentary states: "The Lord's words recorded here arguably play the single most significant rule of any Scripture found in the Old Testament in shaping the Christian understanding of Jesus. The divine declaration proclaimed here through Prophet Nathan is foundational for seven major New Testament teachings about Jesus." (1, 2 Samuel: An Exegetical and Theological Exposition of Holy Scripture (*The New American Commentary*) Bergen, 1996, page 337).

The first fact is that Jesus is the son of David. As we go through many passages in the New Testament, we see this to be factual. In Matthew 1:1 we read that this is: **The book of the genealogy of Jesus Christ, the Son of David, the Son of Abraham.** Who is Jesus? He was the son of David.

In the book of Acts 13:22-23, we read: [22]**And when He had removed him, He raised up for them David as king, to whom also He gave testimony and said, "I have found David the son of Jesse, a man after My own heart, who will do all My will."** [23]**From this man's seed, according to the promise, God raised up for Israel a Savior – Jesus.** Here God removed Saul, and He brought in a king after God's own heart. Verse 23 is very important for from this man's seed God raised up a Savior. Who is this Savior? It is Jesus Christ, our Lord and Savior.

Romans 1:3 states: **Concerning His Son Jesus Christ our Lord, who was born of the seed of David according to the flesh.** In 2 Timothy 2:8, the Scripture states: **Remember that Jesus Christ, of the seed of David, was raised from the dead according to my gospel.** Finally, in Revelation 22:16: **"I, Jesus, have sent My angel to testify to you these things in the churches. I am the Root and the Offspring of David, the Bright and Morning Star."**

These are some of the verses we find throughout the Scripture emphasizing that Jesus Christ is the son of David and that the promise and the vision which God gave to David through Prophet Nathan has been fulfilled as written: from the seed of David salvation would come to Israel.

Now the second fact about Jesus Christ is that He would be raised from the dead. We see this in Acts 2:30 as the Scripture states: **Therefore, being a prophet, and knowing that God had sworn with an oath to him that the fruit of his body, according to the flesh, He would raise up the Christ to sit on his throne.** Also, in Acts 13:23 we read: **From this man's seed, according to the promise, God raised up for Israel a Savior – Jesus.** Who are we talking about here? The risen Lord Jesus Christ.

The third fact about Jesus Christ is that He will be the builder for the house of God. We read in John 2:19-22: [19]**Jesus answered and said to them, "Destroy this temple, and in three days I will raise it up."** [20]**Then the Jews said, "It has taken forty-six years to build this temple, and will You raise it up in three days?"** [21]**But He was speaking of the temple of**

His body. [22]**Therefore, when He had risen from the dead, His disciples remembered that He had said this to them: and they believed the Scripture and the word which Jesus had said.** The response of the Jews in verse 20, obviously, showed that the Jewish leaders, the educated ones, the most learned ones, did not understand that Jesus was not talking about the temple made of stone. Jesus was talking about Himself. He was speaking of the temple of his body. To what Scripture was verse 22 referring? The only Scripture used in those days was the Old Testament writings.

The fourth fact about Christ is that He will be the possessor of the throne. Hebrews 1:8 states: **But to the Son He says: "Your throne, O God, is forever and ever; a scepter of righteousness is the scepter of Your kingdom."** We also read about the possessor of the throne in Revelation 3:21: **To him who overcomes I will grant to sit with Me on My throne, as I also overcame and sat down with My Father on His throne.** There are several other verses that address this throughout the Bible.

The fifth fact about Christ is that He will be the possessor of an eternal kingdom. We read about this in 1 Corinthians 15:24-25: [24]**Then comes the end, when He delivers the kingdom to God the Father, when He puts an end to all rule and all authority and power.** [25]**For He must reign till He has put all enemies under His feet.** Also, in Ephesians 5:5: **For this you know, that no fornicator, unclean person, nor covetous man, who is an idolater, has any inheritance in the kingdom of Christ and God.** Hebrews 1:8 states: **But to the Son He says: "Your throne, O God, is forever and ever; a scepter of righteousness is the scepter of Your kingdom."** Finally, in 2 Peter 1:11: **For so an entrance will be supplied to you abundantly into the everlasting kingdom of our Lord and Savior Jesus Christ.**

The sixth fact about Jesus Christ is that He is the Son of God. It is amazing that when I meet with Muslims, they often ask me where does the Bible say that Jesus is the Son of God. They ask me to show them just one verse. Well, here we go. Mark 1:1, along with several passages such as Matthew 3:1-11, Luke 3:3-16, and John 1:19-34, points to the gospel of Jesus who is the Son of God. We read in Mark 1:1: **The beginning of the gospel of Jesus Christ, the Son of God.** John 20:31 states: **But these are written**

that you may believe that Jesus is the Christ, the Son of God, and that believing you may have life in His name. We continue with Acts 9:20 which states: **Immediately he preached the Christ in the synagogues, that He is the Son of God.** Then in Hebrews 4:14: **Seeing then that we have a great High Priest who has passed through the heavens, Jesus the Son of God, let us hold fast our confession.** Also, we read in Revelation 2:18: **"And to the angel of the church in Thyatira write, 'These things says the Son of God, who has eyes like a flame of fire, and His feet like fine brass.'"**

Now we come to the seventh fact of the description of Jesus Christ, the descendant of David, that He will be the product of Immaculate Conception since God is His Father. We read that Jesus will be great and called the Son of God in Luke 1:32-35: **[32]He will be great, and will be called the Son of the Highest; and the Lord God will give Him the throne of His father David. [33]And he will reign over the house of Jacob forever, and of his kingdom there will be no end." [34]Then Mary said to the angel, "How can this be, since I do not know a man?" [35]And the angel answered and said to her, "The Holy Spirit will come upon you, and the power of the Highest will overshadow you; therefore, also, that Holy One who is to be born will be called the Son of God.**

In verses 34 and 35, Mary miraculously conceived the Holy One, and He will be called who? He will be called the Son of God. This is the true fulfillment for the vision God gave to David through the Prophet Nathan.

King David was not allowed to build a house for the Lord, but his son Solomon would build the temple. This was the short-term fulfillment to this fascinating prophecy of God given through Nathan. However, the true fulfillment, Jesus Christ, God's Son Himself, will dwell in the flesh from the seed of David. In Him the entire world will have peace and rest.

Believe it or not, about 25 percent of the Bible is prophetic! There are about 32,000 verses in the Bible, which means that about 8,000 of those verses are prophetic. Think about that…8,000 verses are speaking of people and events and details that were still in the future! There is no other "holy" or "sacred" book in all the world like the Bible when it comes to precise, exact

Chapter 8: Jihad in Transition

prophecies. Why? Because all the other so-called "scriptures" are merely the ideas of people, not the words of the God of the Universe.

Why were all these holy wars and jihad in the Old Testament fought? As mentioned many times before in this book, it was punishment for the sin of mankind because the wages of sin is death. Having the Temple of Solomon, the house of the Lord, built in Jerusalem would not end sin. For as long as this house existed, there would be sin. That is why Solomon built the house for worship, for the offering of sacrifices.

Why did the Jewish people offer sacrifices? It was because they wanted to cover their sins and transgressions. We see this throughout the Old Testament. Even in the Garden of Eden, we see an animal sacrificed and blood shed. From the days of Adam to the days of David and Solomon and to the days of the coming of our Lord and Savior Jesus Christ, we see that those who sought after the Lord did so in sacrifice. That was the one way a holy God could continue to communicate with His sinful people.

The Jewish people were separated from God spiritually because of their sin. Offering an animal sacrifice did not completely resolve the problem of sin because man is dead spiritually which brings the physical death and then the final death, eternal death in the fires of Hell. Animal sacrifices were only a temporary covering until the ultimate payment could be made through the once-for-all **sacrifice of God's lamb…the Lord Jesus Christ. The Old** Testament animal sacrifices were only a foreshadowing, a temporary representation, of the one true sacrifice that God would make for the sin of all mankind.

Thank God for Jesus…the true fulfillment, the true and final sacrifice for sin. He came and died and was buried and then resurrected from the grave. Through Him we can have eternal life and eternal peace. Yes, under King Solomon there was peace for forty years (temporary), but there was still sin for forty years. Therefore, because of sin there was death.

Now, we will continue in our study by looking at the sacrifices in the Old Testament as a substitute for the sin of men, and that is what is missing in **the teaching of the Qur'an. Yes, the Qur'an talks about the stories of the** Bible, but Mohammed purposefully refused to mention the sacrifices, except in **one passage,** Qur'an 37:100-113 when Abraham offered the great sacrifice which Allah provided as a redemption and substitute for his son, Isaac. This leads us to jihad in the New Testament.

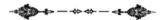

Prelude to the Final Conflict

Sacrifices in the Old Testament Leads to the New Testament

Now we will begin the study of jihad as recorded in the New Testament. I know it sounds strange to many Christians that the Bible still talks about holy war or jihad in the New Testament. It is fairly easy to see/understand jihad in the *Old* Testament (with the many wars that were fought). One might be tempted to say that holy wars only happened in the Old Testament. However, the truth is that there is also holy war mentioned in the New Testament.

Without understanding the sacrifices of the Old Testament, we cannot understand jihad in the New Testament. I remember that one time I was bidding on a job for a builder. This was my first custom painting job. I was so excited about bidding on this job. It was a $2 million, three-story home on beach front property in Venice, Florida. I knew that I would make good money painting this massive house. I had not been working for almost a month, so I was really excited about getting this job. After I met with the builder, I was very disappointed. Why? Because he gave me the blueprints of the house, and he asked me to extract all the information I needed to set the specifications of bidding on the job from that blueprint. However, I did not know how to read blueprints! Therefore, I could not really bid on the job properly. You see, I needed to understand the blueprints to be able to submit a bid and get the job. It was not an easy process, but with the help of God, I bid on the job and got it. Thankfully, I even made a good profit.

It is the same with gaining the understanding of jihad in the New Testament. You see, the Old Testament sacrifices were actually the blueprints which God used to help us understand the final jihad, the most holy war, of the New Testament. Many people will not believe in the jihad of the New Testament simply because they do not understand the sacrifices of the Old Testament. So let us study to understand the blueprint of the Old Testament, not only to know but also *to believe* in the fulfillment of the New Testament, which is the most awesome holy jihad.

The God of the Bible never changes. The God of the Old Testament is the God of the New Testament. The God of the Old Testament, a just God, punished sin no matter who the person was who had sinned. When people sinned in the Old Testament, He punished them as we saw in many places in our study of jihad. God punished people in many ways because of their sin. The initial punishment was physical death.

We saw this very clearly in the account of Noah when God covered the entire world with water. Every man, woman, and child died in the Flood except for Noah and his family. We saw it also in the fiery destruction of Sodom and Gomorrah. Then we saw jihad performed by the edge of the sword as God commanded Moses and Joshua to perform holy war to eliminate the wicked people of the Promised Land.

When the Jewish people sinned against God, God did the same thing to them. Sometimes He punished them by an angel as He killed thousands of them in one day. Sometimes He used the poison of serpents to bite the Jewish people when they grumbled against His provision and Moses in the wilderness. Sometimes He used plagues to kill hundreds of thousands of His people. Sometimes God used their enemies to kill the Jewish people for their sins. Sometimes God used His own people to kill each other by the sword as we have seen throughout the Bible and always because of their sin.

That is the nature of jihad in the Old Testament. Sin must be punished, and the wages of sin is death. Spiritual death separated man from God which led him to die physically. The final justice of God would be served to all those who did not live rightly before God. This led to the third death which is eternal death, and that is spending eternity in Hell.

We must understand that all the people in the Old Testament who were not physically killed for their sin were saved through the blood of the sacrifices thereby escaping the third death, the eternal death in the fires of Hell. Also, some of those who were physically killed would not be punished with the third death. Obviously, those who repented of their sin before their physical death would escape the third death simply because of the sacrifices of the Old Testament which was a foreshadowing of the sacrifice of our Lord and our Savior, Jesus Christ. Therefore, Solomon built the temple of God so that

Chapter 9: Prelude to the Final Conflict

the Jewish people could continue to have a relationship with God through the worship outlined in their Jewish faith. The Jewish people offered sacrifices of animals throughout their history to reconcile with and draw near to God.

We will begin with the study of the history of the Jewish faith through sacrifices beginning with Adam and Eve through the sacrifice of the last prophet who offered a sacrifice in the temple. Even after Solomon became the king and the land rested from war for forty years, this did not end the problem of sin. The temple was built so that people could continue to offer sacrifices to God because they continued to sin against God. Therefore, God provided a temporary restoration of His relationship with people through animal sacrifices. This was the only way for people to receive forgiveness and be restored to God. Through the shedding of blood and these sacrifices, people received covering for their sin. Sin brings death, and the death of an innocent substitute (a clean animal) would provide a temporary covering for their sin.

As we study the Old Testament accounts and the stories in the Qur'an (which Mohammed literally copied from the Bible and inserted in the Qur'an), we will see how Satan used Mohammed, in his cult of Islam, to give *some* of the facts of the history of the Jewish people and the history of mankind on earth. We will also see how Satan, through his deception, removed the only way which man could be drawn near to God. That was through sacrifices. Satan simply removed the blood and the portions about sacrifices found in the accounts in the Bible as Mohammed copied the stories into the Qur'an.

As Muslims in the West say: "We believe in Prophet Adam. We believe in Prophet Noah. We believe in Prophet Moses." They believe in all these stories that Mohammed copied from the **Bible and put in the Qur'an**. Now there was one element, one important fact, about the history of the Jewish faith that Mohammed, in the cult of Islam, purposefully removed. He removed the fact that the Jewish people offered sacrifices throughout the Old Testament, except in one instance. We will see that Mohammed made a mistake in the story of Abraham and Isaac. Mohammed mentioned the story of the sacrifice, but he did not give any of the wonderful details as we find in the account of the Bible.

All the Old Testament sacrifices were a picture, a temporary representation, of the coming true sacrifice in the New Testament of Christ Jesus, our Lord and Savior. In Jesus Christ we see the fulfillment to the sacrificial prophecies given throughout the Old Testament. In Him alone, the true jihad has been accomplished between God and man through Christ's sacrifice. The wages of sin is death, and Jesus, the one true sacrifice, paid that death penalty for us to make us perfect before God!

Adam and Eve and the First Sacrifice

We read Mohammed's version of the story of Adam and Eve in Qur'an 2:30-39. In verse 30, we see that Allah told the angels that he is about to place a kalefah (a successor/man) on earth. Then the angels asked Allah: ***"Will you place it in those who will vandalize in it and shed the blood...?"*** How did the angels know that Adam or his children would sin against god (Allah)? Obviously, there is no answer, especially as we read the rest of the story when Allah said to the angels: ***"Surely I know what you do not know."***

In verse 31, Allah taught Adam the names. The names of what? We do not know what these things were which Allah taught to Adam, and Muslim scholars give many different opinions on this. Then Allah said to the angels: ***"Inform me the names of these, if you are truthful."*** It is as if Allah is debating or challenging the angels to let them know that He is much smarter than they are. In verse 32, the angels said: ***"Praise be to you. We have no knowledge except what you have taught us."*** Wait a minute. How did the angels know the future of Adam if they did not know the names of whatever these things were that Allah revealed to Adam?

Then in verse 33, Allah said to Adam: ***"Inform them of their names."*** Adam told them the names of the things that Allah had taught him. What a joke. The writing of the Qur'an here is nothing but confusion and empty talk. Why? Because if Allah taught Adam the names of some animals or stars or birds or plants or whatever, then why was it so hard for Adam to say the names of these things? Where was the challenge here between Allah and the angels? If he taught it to Adam, Adam would know their names. He never taught it to the angels, so they did not know the names. This would be an unfair and unjust challenge to the angels. Nonsense!

Chapter 9: Prelude to the Final Conflict

Now let us look at the important part of our study in verse 34 as Allah told the angels: *"osjodo (worship) to Adam:" so they all worshiped except Iblis (Devil).* Satan refused to worship Adam, and the Qur'an explains why. It was because Satan was among the infidels.

Then Allah told Adam in verse 35: *"O Adam, askon (dwell) you and your wife in the garden and eat from it plentifully wherever you will, and do not come near this tree so that you will be of the unjust."* However, Satan in verse 36 caused Adam to eat from the tree, and that is why Allah told Adam in verse 36 to: *"Get down. You will be enemies to one another, and you will have on earth a dwelling place and enjoyment for a while."*

Here we know from the teaching of the Qur'an that Adam sinned by eating of the tree from which Allah told him not to eat. That is why Allah cast Adam from heaven. Mohammed taught in the Qur'an that the Garden of Eden was *not on earth* but up in heaven. Therefore Adam and his wife were sent to earth to live, and they would enjoy life on earth for just a short time.

The answer to the problem is found in verse 37: *So Adam received words from his lord, so he taba (relented) toward him. Surely he is the tawwab (relenting), the merciful.* As conveyed to us in the Qur'an, that is supposedly how the problem of sin committed by Adam and Eve was fixed. What was the answer for their sin? Allah gave Adam words. Allah gave Adam a prayer to say. So when Adam said that prayer, Allah gave Adam mercy and forgave Adam of his sin of disobedience. That is the teaching of Allah in the Qur'an in verse 37 of chapter 2. No sacrifice was involved.

What words did Adam receive from Allah whereby he could receive forgiveness of sin just by saying these words? Listen to what the great Muslim scholar Ibn Kathir tells us. He said the words were: "Our lord, we have done injustice to ourselves, and unless you forgive us and have mercy on us, we will for sure be among the losers." Is that it? Adam said this one sentence, and Allah forgave him of his sin?

In the hadith it is written that Qatadah said that Ibn Abbas said that Mojahid said in a conversation between Adam and Allah that Adam said to Allah, "Lord, my sin, the sin which I have sinned against you, did you prescribe it for me, did you ordain it for me before you created me, or did I invent it myself? Allah said, "Yes, I ordained it for you before I created you." That is when Adam said to Allah, "So, because you have ordained it for me and have prescribed it for me, then forgive me." That is when Allah said in the Qur'an that Adam received words from his lord so he relented of his punishment for him. What a strange story! What a wonderful fabrication to understand how Adam and Eve received forgiveness for their sins.

Muslim scholars have given many different interpretations. Some of the scholars have said that this is strange. For we read also that Ibn Jarir said that Ibn Abbas said: Adam said to Allah, "If I repent of my sins, will you return me back to the garden?" Allah said, "Yes."

That is how it was written by Saeed Ibn Jarir and Saeed Ibn Mabin as Abbas stated. What a wonderful fabrication that simply refutes itself. If this was a true statement, then why did Adam not go back to the garden? No Muslim scholars have been able to provide a satisfactory answer for that simple question.

So what did Mohammed do here? Mohammed, on purpose, removed one of the most important facts in all of Scripture, which is how did God allow Adam (or any sinner) to have a continuing relationship with Him? When Adam and Eve sinned and ate from the tree, which God told them not to do, they broke the command of God. They transgressed against God, and that is sin. The wages of sin is death. Adam did not simply receive words from God, like some ritual, in order for God to forgive him. No, a sacrifice had to be offered, as we see beginning in Genesis and throughout all of Scripture.

Since so much of the Bible contains instructions and examples of sacrifices, there is no doubt that Mohammed refused to mention the total truth of any of the stories on purpose. He just took bits and pieces out of the Bible and added them together to make the stories into the poetical writing of the Qur'an. However, this is not the full account as we read in the Bible.

Returning to the Bible, in Genesis 3, we read that after Adam and Eve ate from the tree and discovered they were naked (exposed in their sin), they hid from God, which is the *spiritual* death, separation between man and God.

Chapter 9: Prelude to the Final Conflict

What caused Adam and Eve to hide from God? It was their sin as we read in Genesis 3:9: **Then the Lord God called to Adam and said to him, "Where are you?"** Then Adam responded to God in verse 10: **So he said, "I heard Your voice in the garden, and I was afraid because I was naked; and I hid myself."**

Why did Adam hide from the face of God? Adam and Eve had been walking and talking with God before this. What had changed? It was because of Adam's sin. That is exactly what the Bible states in Isaiah 59:2: **But your iniquities have separated you from your God; and your sins have hidden His face from you, so that He will not hear**.

This is what we call spiritual death, the separation from God because of our sin and rebellion, and now, Adam must also die physically because the wages of sin is death. That is why God told Adam in Genesis 3:19: **"In the sweat of your face you shall eat bread till you return to the ground, for out of it you were taken; for dust you are, and to dust you shall return."** That was physical death. So how could Adam continue to live for years after he had sinned against God and at the same time have communication and a relationship with God?

The answer can be found in the true account of the sacrifice as given by the Holy Spirit in Genesis 3:21: **Also for Adam and his wife the Lord God made tunics of skin, and clothed them.** In order to have garments of skin, a sacrifice was offered. An innocent animal had to die in their place. Blood was shed. This was the first sacrifice in the Bible. Sin leads to death, and an innocent substitute died in their place at this time. Ultimately, they will have to physically die.

Genesis 3:21 is one of the portions that Mohammed purposefully omitted in his passages about Adam. Mohammed taught: rebel against God and then simply say some special words and all is well. Let me ask where is the justice, where is the repentance, where is the holiness and righteousness of God vindicated in this fabricated system of "spiritual restoration"?

The true account is found in the pages of the Bible. Adam sinned, and just as God said, he died spiritually, and now he must die physically. He was separated from God, but he could still temporarily communicate with God through the sacrifice of animals (an innocent substitute).

The "nakedness" of Adam must be covered. Adam and his wife must be clothed. Their nakedness (shame) was the result of an awareness of sin and its sure punishment…death. So instead of God killing Adam and Eve, He substituted an innocent animal to take their place. Then God used the skin of the sacrificed animal to cover their nakedness. This is the repeated solution for sin throughout the pages of the entire Old Testament. It is a beautiful and graphic picture of both our problem and God's incredible solution through His Son, our Lord Jesus Christ.

Someone may object and say, "Well, Adam and Eve had to kill some animals to eat for their meals; and therefore, logically, they could use the skins of the animals to cover their nakedness." However, that is not true at all. For neither Adam nor Eve nor their descendants, until the Flood of Noah, ate the meat of their sacrifices as the command of God was given to them that they could only eat vegetables and fruit of the trees as we read in Genesis 1:29-30: **[29]And God said, "See, I have given you every herb that yields seed which is on the face of all the earth, and every tree whose fruit yields seed; to you it shall be for food. [30]Also, to every beast of the earth, to every bird of the air, and to everything that creeps on the earth, in which there is life, I have given every green herb for food"; and it was so.** After the Flood, God gave Noah and his descendants permission to eat meat as part of their food as we read in Genesis 9:3-4: **Every moving thing that lives shall be food for you. I have given you all things, even as the green herbs. [4]But you shall not eat flesh with its life, that is, its blood.**

Cain and Abel and the Acceptable Sacrifice

It began there with Adam and Eve and continued all the way through the pages of Scripture until the New Testament. This was the temporary solution to re-establish a right relationship with Himself which God provided for man after man fell into sin. This is the way it was since the days of Adam and Eve. We see this clearly in the accounts of their sons, Cain and Abel.

Chapter 9: Prelude to the Final Conflict

Here is another story Mohammed copied from the Bible to put in the Qur'an. As usual, Mohammed removed the true teaching from the Scripture about the sacrifices offered and why God accepted one son's sacrifice and not the other son's sacrifice.

Sadly, even if you read the story of Cain and Abel in the Qur'an today, you would not be able to understand the truth behind this story. Why? Mohammed omitted certain necessary parts from the story. He gave us bits and pieces without any details. How do I know this? It is very simple. I have read the Qur'an, and I have read it in the native language in which it was written...Arabic. When Mohammed told the story of Adam's sons, Mohammed did not mention their names. He did not even know their names!

We read what Allah said in Qur'an 5:27: *"And recite to them the news with the truth of the sons of Adam when they each offered an offering..."* Now we have to ask a question here. Did both sons offer an offering? From the Qur'an we do not know what this offering was. Is this what is written in the Bible? The Qur'an continues with: *"...so it was accepted from one of them and not accepted from the other. He said..."* Now we have to ask some more questions. Who is this "he"? One of the sons of Adam. Which one? Only Allah knows. What is his name? We have no clue. What did he offer? Let's continue with what Allah said in verse 27: *"Surely I will kill you." He said, "Surely Allah only accepts from the fearer.* All of this is in just this one verse. So they both offered an offering. One son's offering was accepted, and the other son's was not. Obviously, the logic here is that the one whose offering was not accepted said to the other one (whose name we do not know from the Qur'an) that he would kill him. Only Allah accepts from the fearer, and because he feared Allah, his offering was accepted. However, because the other son did not fear Allah, his offering was not accepted.

We read in verse 28: *"If you stretch your hand against me to kill me, I will not stretch my hand to you to kill you..."* So here we read that one said to the other that if he wanted to kill him to go ahead, but the other one said that he would not kill him. Is this what the true account of Genesis in the Bible teaches us? It is amazing that Muslims will say that they believe in Moses and they believe in the Torah. Yet they do not know that the stories in the Qur'an are not in agreement with the accounts in the Bible (the book of Genesis is the first book of the Torah, which was written by Moses). The stories of Mohammed cannot be true if the accounts of the Bible are true.

Then, this son of Adam, from whom Allah accepted his offering, ended his speech by saying: *"Surely I fear Allah, the lord of the worlds."* When Muslims read in the Qur'an about the lord of the worlds, they think this is the God of the Bible. However, according to the Bible, the lord of the worlds is Satan (2 Corinthians 4:4).

In verse 29 of this same chapter in the Qur'an, he said: *"Surely I desire that you will bear my sin and your sin so that you will become among the companions of the fire, and that is the reward of the unjust."*

Wait a minute. How can one of the sons of Adam bear the sin of the other son? How can the bad one bear the sin of the good one? How can this be? Does the Qur'an teach that a man can take care of the sin of another person? Can I spend eternity in Hell for the sin of my brother?

That is exactly what Allah's word states in the Qur'an as we read once again the words of the good son telling the bad son in verse 29: *"Surely I desire that you will bear my sin and your sin so that you will become among the companions of the fire, and that is the reward of the unjust."* Muslims commonly believe, from the Qur'an, that the punishment of sin is hell fire. We see a new teaching from the Qur'an: the bad one will kill the good one and then spend eternity in hell fire to pay for his own sin and also his brother's sin. Then according to verse 30: *"So his soul persuaded him to kill his brother. So he killed him, so he became of the losers."*

Is this a true account according to the Bible? Is this what happened in the lives of Cain and Abel? Of course not, but Muslims believe that this is the true information. They believe the words of Allah, as we see once again in Qur'an 5:27 where Allah is speaking to Mohammed to recite to the Muslim believers: *"And recite to them the news with the truth of the sons of Adam..."*.

"The news with the truth" - what news? What truth? This is not the truth. This is lies. How do I know that this is not true? I know the true account, with proper and meaningful details, is written in Genesis in chapter 4.

Beginning with verses 3 and 4 we read: ³**And in the process of time it came to pass that Cain brought an offering of the fruit of the ground to the Lord. ⁴Abel also brought of the first born of his flock and of their fat.**

We see here that Cain did not bring a blood sacrifice but brought some fruit of the land. That is what he offered to the Lord. However, Abel brought an offering of the firstborn of his flock. So, how do we know the names of the sons of Adam, Cain and Abel? It is very simple. The Bible gives us this information, but in the Qur'an Mohammed did not.

Both of these brothers did not offer a *proper* sacrifice: Cain offered fruit of the land, and Abel offered an animal which was a true sacrifice. Another important question is where did Cain and Abel learn to offer sacrifices? Obviously, they learned it from their parents who revealed to them what the Lord required.

Verse 4 continued with: …**And the Lord respected Abel and his offering, ⁵but He did not respect Cain and his offering. And Cain was very angry, and his countenance fell.** The Lord accepted the offering of Abel (which was the blood sacrifice), but God **rejected Cain's offering of fruit from the soil.** God did not cover the nakedness of Adam and Eve with green leaves that came from the soil. That was their own decision, not God's. God used the death of an innocent substitute because the wages of sin is death.

As we look at the account in Genesis, after Adam and Eve sinned, they discovered they were naked (exposed in their shame). It is normal for humans to do things by their own hands. They looked around and used things to try to cover their sin. That is why people today do the same thing, especially in the cult of Islam. If they do good deeds, this will take away their evil deeds, as Allah taught Muslims in the Qur'an. Almost all false religions teach this same principle: use your own efforts (good deeds) to try and cover up your bad deeds. However, the principle of sacrifice, as taught by God in the Bible, says that the only path to forgiveness is shed blood. The justice of God must be satisfied.

The normal thing for Adam and Eve to do was to attempt to cover their nakedness with leaves of the fig tree, but that was not how God fixed their immediate problem. God covered their nakedness with *animal* skins. Once again, the most important object lesson here is not about covering their nakedness but the innocent substitute sacrificed on their behalf.

So here we see the same thing with Adam and Eve's sons. Cain and Abel were doing the same thing their parents had done. They sinned, but one of their sons, Cain, followed the old tradition of trying to cover his sin with the efforts of his hands, with good works. How do we know this? It is because the Scripture clearly teaches that he offered fruit of the soil. Maybe he was thinking this would satisfy the Lord God, the Creator.

However, Abel did what was right. He did not offer the fruit of the soil. He offered the acceptable sacrifice to God which is the shedding of the blood of a pure animal, but not just any animal. He chose the best, the firstborn of his flock, and he offered it as a true, pure sacrifice. That is why God accepted Abel's sacrifice. Not because Abel was better or smarter or more loved by God. He was accepted because he approached God in the only way that we can draw near…through an offering, a sacrificial substitute, for sin.

This is the theme we read throughout the pages of the Bible. When people sinned against God, they offered a sacrifice, and the sacrifice was always a pure animal. God ordained specific animals, clean animals and clean birds, to be used for the sacrifices. Through the shedding of their blood, man could draw near to God. For only through the shedding of blood could man receive covering for his sin because the wages of sin is death.

Noah and Sacrifices after the Flood

One of the great prophets of the Bible, which Muslims claim to believe in, is the Prophet Noah. His story is mentioned throughout the Qur'an many times. How much do Muslims actually know about Noah from just reading the Qur'an? Not very much because, as it is with every story in the Qur'an which Mohammed copied from the Bible, there is so much missing information. Small bits and pieces of information were taken out of the Bible and repeated over and over throughout the pages of the Qur'an without the necessary details to completely understand God's purposes.

Even the few details in the story of Noah, as Allah gave them to Mohammed and had it written throughout the pages of the Qur'an, are not

Chapter 9: Prelude to the Final Conflict

correct. We know from the Bible that Noah had three sons, Shem, Ham, and Japheth; but in the Qur'an, Mohammed said that Noah had one son, and sadly, this son drowned. We know from the story in the Qur'an that neither Noah's son nor his wife made it through the flood.

However, we know from the Bible that Noah's wife, his three sons, and the wives of his three sons are the only people to live through the Flood. These eight people were the ones who began life again on earth and repopulated the planet.

Another error from the story of Noah in the Qur'an is about the people who survived the flood. Mohammed stated that these people were the scum of society and believed in Noah, and they were the ones who made it through the flood!

One simple fact (which Mohammed either forgot or purposefully refused to mention in his story) was the clean animals and birds and the unclean animals and birds. Not only did Mohammed make an error in the number of animals and birds, because he said that Noah took two pairs of every kind of animal, but he forgot to tell the true numbers that God in the Bible told Noah to take on the ark: seven pairs of every clean animal and seven pairs of every clean bird.

Why is that? It is because these were the animals and birds which Noah and his sons and the generations to follow would use to offer as sacrifices. These were also the birds and animals used by Noah and his descendants to eat. That is why God told Noah to take seven pairs, not one pair as with the rest of the animals.

The one important thing which Mohammed conveniently forgot to tell us is what Noah did immediately after he exited the ark. We read in Genesis 8:18-21: [18]**So Noah went out, and his sons and his wife and his sons' wives with him.** [19]**Every animal, every creeping thing, every bird, and whatever creeps on the earth, according to their families, went out of the ark.** Once again, the Bible is very clear. As we read the Bible, we can know for sure who was on the ark. It was Noah, his wife, his three sons, and their wives. These eight people were the only ones saved in the Flood. From this verse, we know that all the animals and all the birds and all the creatures left the ark.

Now we come to the truth which Mohammed purposefully removed from the story as he rewrote it in the Qur'an. We read in verse 20 of Genesis 8: **[20]Then Noah built an altar to the Lord, and took of every clean animal and of every clean bird, and offered burnt offerings on the altar.** The Bible describes to us how Noah built an altar, but Mohammed did not tell us anything about Noah's altar. Then Noah offered clean animal and clean bird sacrifices to the Lord. This is what Mohammed did not want people to know. He did not want them to know about sacrifices or the clean animals.

Muslims in America want to force us to eat their lawful food simply because they do not eat pork. However, at the same time, they can eat dogs. They can eat camels. They can eat anything else that creeps. Did you know that Allah in the Qur'an allows Muslims to eat all kinds of creatures that come out of the water? If we read the Torah, concerning clean and unclean animals and birds, and read what God told Moses, you would be surprised. There is a huge list of animals and birds and even many creatures that live under water that Jewish people do not eat. They do not eat anything unclean (Leviticus 11).

That is not what Mohammed taught the Muslims. He taught that they could not eat pork, even though the Qur'an also states that they can eat pork if they are compelled to, as long as they did not desire it or go back for a second helping. (Qur'an 2:172)

The most important point missing from the writing of Allah in this story is that Noah offered sacrifices from the clean animals to the Lord. We read the reaction of the Lord to Noah in the Bible: **[21]And the Lord smelled a soothing aroma. Then the Lord said in His heart, "I will never again curse the ground for man's sake, although the imagination of man's heart is evil from his youth; nor will I again destroy every living thing as I have done.** The Lord was pleased with what Noah had done. The Lord accepted Noah's sacrifices.

The sacrifices of Noah and how/why the Lord accepted these sacrifices is a very important fact which we cannot find anywhere in the pages of the

Chapter 9: Prelude to the Final Conflict

Qur'an. Even though God knew that man's heart is evil and will sin again, God smelled a soothing aroma. Why? It is because this sacrifice is a picture of the coming true sacrifice of our Lord and Savior Jesus Christ, the true Lamb of God. As Noah offered up sacrifices according to God's ordinance, God was pleased with these temporary pictures of His Son.

The Sacrifices of the Covenant Between God and Abraham: Genesis 15

As I mentioned earlier, concerning the vision of Abraham in Genesis 15:5, I made the promise that we would tackle this passage again when we studied the sacrifices of Abraham. Now, let us look once again at the command of God to Abraham to bring these specific sacrifices, as we read in verse 9 of Genesis 15: **So He said to him, "Bring Me a three-year-old heifer, a three-year-old female goat, a three-year-old ram, a turtledove, and a young pigeon."** What a strange request. Why did God ask Abraham to bring these animals and birds? Was it just to look at them? No, it was for Abraham to offer them as a sacrifice, as we read in verse 10: **Then he brought all these to Him and cut them in two, down the middle, and placed each piece opposite the other; but he did not cut the birds in two."** Why did Abraham sacrifice these animals and birds? Was it to enjoy a good meal? No. Was it to feed some poor people, as Muslims do in eating the sacrifices or serving them to the poor? The answer is still no. We encourage the reader to read the entire passage in Genesis 15.

In verse 18, we read: **On the same day the Lord made a covenant with Abram, saying: "To your descendants I have given this land, from the river of Egypt to the great river, the River Euphrates -"** So now we know that these sacrifices were offered by Abraham according to the command of God. They were sacrifices used to make a covenant between God and Abraham concerning the inheritance of the Promised Land. This was fulfilled in the life of Isaac, Jacob, and the twelve sons of Jacob who became the twelve tribes of Israel, as God promised Abraham in this special covenant.

Of course, our Muslim friends, who rarely read the Bible, do not have a clue about this sacrifice of the covenant between Abram and God or the fulfillment of this promise by God. Why? It is simply because Mohammed omitted this account in the stories of the Qur'an. Muslims believe that the

Jewish people are unjustly occupying this land which belongs to the Palestinians, not realizing that (once again) Mohammed made an error in the Qur'an when he mentioned that the children of Israel inherited the Promised Land. Mohammed even called it the Holy Land. The name Holy Land was never used in the days of Moses, but used after the coming of our Lord and Savior Jesus Christ. You can read the entire story concerning the Jews' inheritance in Qur'an 5:20-26: *²⁰"And when Moses said to his people, "O my people, remember the grace of Allah on you when he made prophets among you. And he made you kings, and he gave you what he did not give anyone of the world. ²¹O my people, enter the holy land which Allah has prescribed for you, and do not turn away on your backs so you will be turned back losers." ²²They said, "O Moses, surely in it are powerful people, and surely we will not enter it until they come out of it. So if they come out of it, so surely we will enter." ²³Two men among the fearers, Allah graced on them, said, "Enter on them the door. So when you enter it, so surely you will be victorious. And on Allah, so depend, if you were believers." ²⁴They said, "O Moses, surely we will never enter it as long as they are in it. So go, you and your lord. So engage in war. Surely we are sitting down right here." ²⁵He said, "My lord, surely I do not own anything except myself and my brother, so separate between us and the transgressing people." ²⁶He said, "So surely it (the Holy land) is forbidden to them forty years; they will be lost on the earth. So do not grieve on the transgressing people."*

Abraham Offers Isaac as a Sacrifice - Genesis 22:1-9 vs Qur'an 37:99-113

Next, we will move on to another story in the Qur'an, which was copied from the Bible. Sadly, once again, Mohammed did not tell the entire story. Even though he mentioned sacrifices in this story, he did not give us the necessary details as the Bible does.

Muslims worldwide believe in Abraham and call him Prophet Abraham because Allah in the Qur'an talks about Abraham and Isaac and Jacob and Ishmael. Therefore, Muslims believe that we worship the same God. I am sorry to say, *no*. We do not.

Chapter 9: Prelude to the Final Conflict

The Abraham of the Qur'an has almost nothing to do with the actual Abraham recorded in the Bible. How do we know this? I have read the Qur'an. I have read the Bible. I have read the account of Abraham in both books. I know for sure that not only does the story in the Qur'an not match with the account in the Bible, but the Qur'an even *contradicts itself* when retelling the story of Abraham! Muslim scholars who have tried to interpret the story in the Qur'an have created all kinds of fanciful fabrications. It's not their fault. Mohammed gave them almost no solid information concerning Abraham. Their confusion is warranted.

I would like to share with you a small portion of the story in the Qur'an as we compare it to what is written in the book of Genesis in the Bible. First, we will look at the story of Abraham and the sacrificial son in Qur'an 37:99-113.

In Qur'an 37: 99, Allah said: *And he said, "Surely I am going to my lord. He will guide me."* (Abraham is speaking in this verse.) [100]*"My lord, grant me from the good."* In this verse, Abraham is praying to Allah. [101]*So we gave him the good news of a forbearing young man.* Allah here is answering Abraham's prayer and gave Abraham a son, but we do not know who this son is.

Then we continue in verse 102. [102]*So when he came to the age of walking with him, he said, "My son, surely I see in my sleep that I am slaughtering you, so see what you see." He said, "O my father, do what you are commanded. You will find me among the patient if Allah wills."* Now this little boy is walking with his father. He (Abraham) said to his son that he slaughtered him in his dream. The son replied that his father should do whatever he was commanded to do. [103]*So when they surrendered and he had laid him down on his jabīn (forehead.)* [104]*and we called him, "O Abraham,* [105]*indeed, you have believed the vision." Likewise, we surely reward the doers of good.* [106]*Surely this is a clear trial.* [107]*And we redeemed him with a great sacrifice.* In these verses, the "we" is Allah, and the "redeemed him" is Abraham's son.

[108]*And we left for him among the others.* Of course, the story in the Qur'an is not clear because we do not always know who "he" or "him" is. It is really difficult, and this is not just my opinion. This is the opinion of anyone

who reads the Qur'an, even in the original Arabic text. We do not understand who is speaking and who is being spoken to. For in this entire story, we do not know who this son is to whom Abraham is talking. Is it Isaac or Ishmael? The Qur'an never clearly says. (Are you noticing the pattern in the Qur'an in which many of the children are not named, which leads to all sorts of confusion?)

Mohammed continues: *[109]Peace be on Abraham. [110]Likewise, we reward the doers of good. [111]Surely he is of our believing servants. [112]And we gave him the good news of Isaac, a prophet among the good. [113]And we blessed on him and on Isaac, and from their offspring an obvious doer of good, and unjust to himself.*

Now we will ask a question. How can Allah tell Abraham in verse 112 that Isaac will be a prophet among the good if the entire story, beginning with verse 100 to verse 111, is not talking about Isaac? I know that Muslims believe that the son, of which the Qur'an is speaking, is Ishmael. That is not true. It is a lie. There is no evidence whatsoever in the teaching of the Qur'an that this son is Ishmael, but the opposite appears to be true. How do I know that?

As you study the interpretation of Muslim scholars about the story of Abraham, you will see that Mohammed said that Abraham sent his son Ishmael and his mother Hagar to Mecca when Ishmael was still a very young baby. Now in this story here, the son was *walking* with his father. This son was not a baby or a little boy. This son was a young man.

The story began by stating that "he" was a forbearing young man. This is not the description of Ishmael. Ishmael was a wild man as he got older. His hand was against everyone, and everyone's hand was against him. The description of this gentle young man who was walking and talking with his father was not the description of Ishmael. Also, Ishmael had already left with his mother when he was a baby for the land of Mecca, as Muslim scholars claim. Besides that, we read in verse 112 that Allah actually referred to this son by the name of Isaac, not Ishmael.

This entire, confusing story in the Qur'an is not a true story. This is not what happened in the actual history recorded in the Bible. Abraham did not

Chapter 9: Prelude to the Final Conflict

have a dream. Abraham did not say to his son that he was going to slaughter him, and neither did the son tell his father to go ahead and do it. This is a counterfeit of the true account of the sacrificial son.

Once again, Allah said in verse 107 that we (Allah) redeemed him (the son of Abraham) with a great sacrifice. In this one simple verse, Muslims skim over it quickly as if there are no facts in this verse. I think Mohammed made a mistake because in this verse he is introducing the Muslim reader to an important fact. First of all, the word *great* (azeem) is one of the names of Allah in the Qur'an. We (Allah) redeemed him (Isaac) with a great sacrifice.

This is not the teaching of the Qur'an. This is not how Muslims understand redemption. For the salvation which took place in the life of Abraham's son (Isaac), took place through a sacrifice. This sacrifice is offered by Allah himself in the Qur'an because Allah redeemed the son of Abraham with a great sacrifice.

For our Muslim friends to understand this passage and know the truth about it, we must go to the true account in the book of Genesis in the Bible for clarification. I hope and pray that, as they read the truth in Genesis, they will realize how empty and strange the writing of the Qur'an is.

The story in the Qur'an is not clear. It is missing so much information (as is true of most of the stories Mohammed copied from the Bible).

Now, let us read the entire account with details from the Bible in Genesis 22: **¹Now it came to pass after these things that God tested Abraham, and said to him, "Abraham!" And he said, "Here I am."** "After these things" refers to when Abraham sent Hagar and Ishmael away. God then spoke to Abraham.

²Then He said, "Take now your son, your only son Isaac, whom you love, and go to the land of Moriah, and offer him there as a burnt offering on one of the mountains of which I shall tell you." This was not a dream as stated in the Qur'an. This was God actually talking directly to Abraham. God told Abraham to take his son, his only son. How do we know that this was not Ishmael? It is because Abraham had sent Hagar and her son Ishmael away earlier. There is no guessing or suggesting here as to which son God was speaking about. God mentioned him by name. This son was Isaac. This was the son Abraham loved. The Bible is very clear. This verse does not need any suggestions or fabrications or interpretations. The verses of the Bible speak for themselves. Then God told Abraham where to take his son to offer him as a sacrifice: take Isaac to the land of Moriah to one of the mountains which God would tell him. The Qur'an does not give any location as to where Abraham was to sacrifice his son.

Notice, the Bible gives the important details, such as who (Abraham and Isaac), what (offer Isaac as a sacrifice), where (the land of Moriah), and later, exactly how Isaac was spared and what the sacrifice must be. All this is missing from the Qur'an.

[3]So Abraham rose early in the morning and saddled his donkey, and took two of his young men with him, and Isaac his son; and he split the wood for the burnt offering, and arose and went to the place of which God had told him. [4]Then on the third day Abraham lifted his eyes and saw the place afar off. [5]And Abraham said to his young men, "Stay here with the donkey; the lad and I will go yonder and worship, and we will come back to you." [6]So Abraham took the wood of the burnt offering and laid it on Isaac his son; and he took the fire in his hand, and a knife, and the two of them went together. Here we see that God led Abraham to a specific mountain to offer Isaac as a sacrifice. Abraham left his two servants, and only he and Isaac went to the mountain. Isaac carried the wood, and Abraham took the fire and the knife.

[7]But Isaac spoke to Abraham his father and said, "My father!" And he said, "Here I am, my son." Then he said, "Look, the fire and the wood, but where is the lamb for a burnt offering?" [8]And Abraham said, "My son, God will provide for Himself the lamb for a burnt offering." So the two of them went together. [9]Then they came to the place of which God had told him. And Abraham built an altar there and placed the wood in order; and he bound Isaac his son and laid him on the altar, upon the wood. See, it did not make any sense to Isaac. He was carrying the wood for the burnt offering, and his father was carrying the knife and the fire to light the wood. So what are we missing here? We are missing the *sacrifice*. It was very logical for Isaac to ask where the lamb was. This proves that Isaac understood that a sacrifice involved the death of a pure animal. The answer of Abraham was that God would provide for Himself the lamb.

Chapter 9: Prelude to the Final Conflict

What a great revelation! However, Mohammed missed it, and Muslims miss it also because they never read the true account in the Bible. All they know is the counterfeit story in the verses of chapter 37 of the Qur'an. All that they know is a confusing story that leaves them with more questions than answers.

As I have shared with you before, we cannot understand the true jihad of the New Testament until we understand the topic of sacrifice throughout the teaching of the Old Testament. Why? Because the fulfillment of all these sacrifices is the "true jihad" in the New Testament.

However, in the biblical account in chapter 22 of Genesis, we see our Lord and Savior Jesus Christ pictured in the obedient son, Isaac. Isaac carried the wood of the fire up the hill, and Christ carried the wood of the cross. Isaac was supposed to die and be offered as a sacrifice because he represented you and me as sinful people. Because of the justice of God, the wages of sin is death; but, instead, God provided His own Lamb to take Isaac's place. This Lamb would be offered as a substitute sacrifice for Isaac so that Isaac could live. That is the true jihad performed by God in the New Testament through our Lord and Savior Jesus Christ.

Now, let us continue with the account of Abraham and Isaac in Genesis 22:9-11. Abraham built an altar on the mountain. He placed the wood on the altar, tied up Isaac, and then laid him on the altar. Abraham took his knife and was ready to kill his son when the Angel of the Lord called from heaven and stopped him. He said, "Abraham, Abraham!" Abraham responded and said, "Here I am." In verse 12, the Angel of the Lord said: **[12]"Do not lay your hand on the lad, or do anything to him; for now I know that you fear God, since you have not withheld your son, your only son, from Me."** [13]**Then Abraham lifted his eyes and looked, and there behind him was a ram caught in a thicket by its horns. So Abraham went and took the ram, and offered it up for a burnt offering instead of his son.** [14]**And Abraham called the name of the place, The-Lord-Will-Provide; as it is said to this day, "In the Mount of the Lord it shall be provided."**

Do you see the difference between the account of Abraham as written in Genesis compared to what is written in the Qur'an? There is a huge difference between these two teachings. The truth of the account is that God provided His Lamb for an offering. We can see the fulfillment of this in John 1:29 as the Bible states: **The next day John saw Jesus coming toward him, and said, "Behold! The Lamb of God who takes away the sin of the world!**

Yes, Abraham said to his son in Genesis that God would provide for Himself a lamb for the burnt offering, and here we see John the Baptist point to the Lamb of God, Jesus Christ, who carries away the sin of the world for those who believe in Him. Even though Mohammed made a mistake and told us in the Qur'an that Allah redeemed Abraham's son with a great sacrifice, Mohammed forgot to tell us the entire story as we read the details in Genesis 22. Sadly, Mohammed denied the true fulfillment of this account as written in the Gospel of John. John the Baptist pointed to Jesus as the Lamb of God, the perfect fulfillment of Genesis 22.

Now, do you think Isaac learned anything from this? Will Isaac offer sacrifices to the Lord as well? Yes, indeed. However, that is not what **Mohammed said in the Qur'an.** He did not mention anything about Isaac, probably because he did not know anything that was written in the Bible concerning Isaac.

I would like to share with you what the Bible states concerning Isaac. To understand that Isaac offer sacrifices as his father Abraham did, we simply go to Genesis 26:23-25: [23]**Then he went up from there to Beersheba.** [24]**And the Lord appeared to him the same night and said, "I am the God of your father Abraham; do not fear, for I am with you. I will bless you and multiply your descendants for My servant Abraham's sake."** [25]**So he built an altar there and called on the name of the Lord, and he pitched his tent there; and there Isaac's servants dug a well.**

In Genesis 22:9, Abraham built an altar and offered sacrifices to the Lord. Here in Genesis 26:25, we read that Isaac also built an altar and offered sacrifices to the Lord as he learned from his father Abraham. Now we need to ask the following question. What **about Isaac's son, Jacob? Did he offer** sacrifices?

Chapter 9: Prelude to the Final Conflict

Jacob Offered Sacrifices - Genesis 31

Yes, I know that Muslims believe in the Prophet Jacob, as they always say, "Peace be upon him." However, they know almost nothing about Jacob or the details of his life. Even when their great Muslim scholar, Ibn Kathir, in his book, *The Story of the Prophets, the Beginning and the End*, told the story of Jacob, he did not tell anything about Jacob. Instead, he told us the story of Joseph as if it was the life of Jacob! This is very strange. How can we know the story of a man through the life of his son? Why didn't Mohammed write anything in the Qur'an about Jacob's life?

The truth that Jacob offered sacrifices can be found in Genesis 31:54: **Then Jacob offered a sacrifice on the mountain, and called his brethren to eat bread. And they ate bread and stayed all night on the mountain.** What did we just learn? The message of offering a sacrifice to the God of Israel was always in the Bible. It began with Adam and Eve and continued through their sons, Cain and Able, through Noah to Abraham to Isaac and to Jacob.

This information does not exist in the teaching of the **Qur'an because** Mohammed did not want his followers, the Muslim believers, to believe in the true worship of Yahweh, the God of the Bible, as we have seen throughout the Old Testament. The sacrifices were offered, and without the shedding of blood, there is no forgiveness of sin. Islam has no sacrifice; therefore, there is no forgiveness in Islam, and Mohammed rejected the sacrificial death of God's only Son Jesus.

Therefore, he did not pass on the truth of God's ultimate and true jihad. Without the sacrifice of Jesus for our sins, mankind is lost and doomed to an eternity in Hell.

The Biblical Account of Job Offering Sacrifices and Job's Story in the Qur'an

Now, let us look at the account of Job. Although the account of Job consists of forty-two chapters in the Bible, only a little information is provided in the Qur'an. For example, in Qur'an 6:84, only his name is mentioned. In Qur'an 4:163, Allah revealed to Mohammed a bunch of names of prophets, and Job's name again is only listed as a prophet. The story of Job itself is found in two chapters, Qur'an 21:83-84 and Qur'an 38:41-44. Here we see that the forty-two chapters about the account of Job in the Bible were condensed to just six verses in the Qur'an.

First, let's look at what Allah said in Qur'an 21:83-84: *[83]And Job, when he called his lord: "Surely harm has touched me, and you are the most merciful of the merciful!" [84]So we answered him. So we removed what is in him from harm, and we gave him his family and like them with them, a mercy from us and a reminder to the servants.*

That is it. That is all we learn about Job in this chapter. Job prayed to Allah and told Allah that something bad happened to him, and Allah removed whatever harm had touched him. Allah then gave him his family and another family like his family, which was a mercy to remind the servants. So now Job has two families. Is this the true account of Job? Is this how we can understand the entire forty-two chapters of Job in the Bible?

Maybe we can get more information from the only other portion about Job in Qur'an 38:41-44: *[41]And remember our servant Job when he called his lord: "Surely Satan has touched me with distress and torment!" [42] "Strike with your foot; this is a cold wash-place and a drink." [43]And we granted to him his family, and like them, with them, a mercy from us and a reminder to those who have understanding. [44] "And take a bundle in your hand, so strike with it. Do not break your oath." Surely we found him patient, blessed is the servant, surely he is repentant.*

Again, that is it, confusing as it is. That is all we learn about Job from the words of Allah in the Qur'an. Why? It is probably because that was all Mohammed had heard. He did not have any other information to add in his poetry in the pages of the Qur'an concerning Job. If Mohammed (or those who helped Mohammed rewrite the story about Job in the Qur'an) had read the account in the Bible, they could have come up with more information. Instead, forty-two chapters of the Bible were reduced to these six sparse verses in the Qur'an.

Allah reminded Mohammed in verse 41 about Job and his prayer when he stated to Mohammed that Satan had touched Job with distress and torment. Allah told Job in verse 42 to strike with his feet and there would be some

Chapter 9: Prelude to the Final Conflict

cold water with which to wash and drink. Then Allah gave him his family back and an extra family like his family. So now we know that Job had two families instead of one. Then Allah asked Job to strike with a rod so he could keep his oath. What rod? What oath?

Muslim scholars resolved this verse of Allah in the Qur'an with their fabrications. They added an entirely new story that Job's wife sold her hair to provide food for her husband. When he discovered what she had done, Job was so angry that he swore by Allah that he would strike her one hundred times. Then Muslim scholars added another fabrication. Instead of him beating her one hundred times, Job made a whip out of one hundred strands and hit her just one time. What a wonderful way for a prophet to give thanks to his wife after she sold her hair to provide him with a good meal! We learn that Job was a patient man. He was repentant. (Which is contradicted by him beating his wife.) **That is all we learn about Job's life from the Qur'an.**

We know from Scripture that the book of Job is the oldest book in the Bible. I encourage and challenge Muslims to read the forty-two chapters in **the Bible and compare them to these six verses in the Qur'an. Muslims will** be shocked to know that Mohammed knew next to nothing about Job and that Muslim scholars tried to interpret these six verses by fabricating a story about Job, his wife, and her hair.

This is evidence that these Muslim scholars are not actually scholars at all. When you invent a story, that is called *fiction*. How can the account about a man, written in forty-two chapters in the Bible, be condensed to these six verses except through fabrication as they made up this information? Where did these Muslim scholars come up with this information? It is not in the **Qur'an (Allah's word).** It is not from the hadith **(Mohammed's sayings).** What is amazing is that Mohammed, once again, removed the crucial information about Job offering sacrifices.

When you read the account of Job in the Bible, you will understand what we are trying to teach here in this book. Did Job offer sacrifices in the Old Testament? If he did offer sacrifices, why? Yes, Job offered sacrifices. He offered clean animals to cover the sins of his family. In chapter 1 of Job, we read that Job was an upright man who feared God and avoided evil. He lived in the land of Uz and had seven sons and three daughters. He was also very rich with a large household, thousands of sheep and camels, and hundreds of oxen and donkeys. He was considered among the greatest of all the people in the East.

Now Job's seven sons took turns having feasts at their homes. They each had an appointed day and would invite their three sisters to come and eat with them. The significant verse in this chapter about sacrifice is verse 5: **So it was, when the days of feasting had run their course, that Job would send and sanctify them, and he would rise early in the morning and offer burnt offerings according to the number of them all. For Job said, "It may be that my sons have sinned and cursed God in their hearts." Thus Job did regularly**.

Job was a blameless and upright man. Why? Was it because of his self-righteousness? No, it was because he obeyed the command of God. We see Job offering *sacrifices* (just like Adam, Abel, Noah, Abraham, Isaac, and Jacob). These sacrifices were offered for one reason: he said that perhaps his sons had sinned against God in their hearts. Because Job understood that the wages of sin is death, he offered these sacrifices continually because he knew that it was the only way for him, his wife, his seven sons, and his three daughters to receive forgiveness for their sin.

Did Mohammed, the false prophet of Islam, understand the facts about sacrifices in the life of Job? Do Muslim people know the real truth behind the sacrifices in the Old Testament? Obviously, and sadly, the answer is no.

Battle Plans Unfolding

Sacrifices of Moses and the Plagues in Exodus and in the Qur'an

Let us look at another important prophet and his story in the Qur'an and compare it with the account in the Bible. This is the story of Moses. I know once again that Muslims all over the world believe in and respect the Prophet Moses and believe in the Torah, but if you ask many of them what the books of Torah are, they do not have a clue. The Torah is the first five books of the Bible (the Pentateuch), and there are plenty of facts written by Moses in the Torah.

When Muslims read the story of Moses in the Qur'an, they may think they have the whole story of this great man of God. They are not aware that the **story in the Qur'an is a foolish counterfeit, missing so many of the rich** details that we find in the satisfying account of the Bible.

If only Muslims would come to know the actual information in the Bible, they would believe in the Christian faith. They would believe in the truth of the *entire* Bible. However, by and large, they have not read the Bible. They have also been taught that the Bible has been corrupted and changed. They have been indoctrinated that the only truth is in the Qur'an. Therefore, Muslims do not know the truth about the Christian faith. Sadly, they do not understand who Jesus Christ is and why He died on the cross for our sins, simply because they do not understand the importance of sacrifices.

For the purpose of this section on the sacrifices in the Old Testament, we will look at two areas. We will examine the plagues which God performed through Moses in Egypt and the sacrificial system which God established in the writings of the Torah through Moses.

I know that Muslims read the Qur'an and believe that Allah performed great miracles through Moses. We read about Moses in several places in the Qur'an (28:31-32, 27:9-12, and 7:130-133).

Obviously, Mohammed heard some of these stories from the Jewish population (probably in Mecca) and combined them. Two of these miracles were when Moses' hand turned to white (implying leprosy) and when he changed his rod into a snake. So, let me ask: were these two miracles part of the plagues God sent on Pharaoh and the Egyptian people? According to the Bible, the answer is no. The ten plagues that God brought upon Egypt had nothing to do with the leprous hand or with the rod which became a snake, but as usual, Mohammed confused everything together in the Qur'an. We read in Qur'an 27:9-12 the confusion of Mohammed and his god Allah as Allah stated: *⁹"O Moses, surely I am Allah, the dear, the wise. ¹⁰And throw down your rod!" So when he saw it shaking as though it were a jinn, he retreated backward and did not return. "O Moses, do not fear, surely the messengers will not fear in my presence, ¹¹except for those who did injustice, then changed, doing good after evil. So surely I am forgiving, merciful. ¹²And enter your hand into your pocket. It will come forth white, without evil, as one in nine signs to Pharaoh and his people, surely they were a transgressing people.*

We see here in these verses that Moses would perform nine miracles before Pharaoh. Two of these miracles were the rod that was changed to a snake and the hand of Moses that turned white (obviously Mohammed meant leprosy).

What about the rest of the nine miracles? We can find them in Qur'an 7:133: *So we sent on them the tūfān (deluge) and the locusts and the lice and the frogs and the blood, expounded signs, so they became proud. And they were a criminal people.*

So, how many miracles are in this verse? There are five. Even if we add the first two miracles, the rod which turned into a snake and the white hand, that still makes only seven miracles. So where are the rest of the nine miracles which Allah claimed to be in Qur'an 27:12? Also, the Flood (deluge) did not take place in the days of Moses. The Flood took place in the days of Noah. There is so much confusion here.

To know the true account, we must open the Bible to the book of Exodus. There were *ten* separate plagues, and they had nothing to do with the

Chapter 10: Battle Plans Unfolding

misunderstanding of Allah and Mohammed in the Qur'an. Here is the list of the ten plagues from the Bible.

The first plague was the water changed into blood in Exodus 7:14 -23.

The second plague was the frogs in Exodus 8:2-6.

The third plague was gnats or lice in Exodus 8:16-17.

The fourth plague was the flies or swarms in Exodus 8:21.

The fifth plague was the livestock disease or pestilence in Exodus 9:3.

The sixth plague was the boils in Exodus 9:8-10.

The seventh plague was the thunder and hail in Exodus 9:18 and 22-24.

The eighth plague was the locusts in Exodus 10:4-5.

The ninth plague was the darkness in Exodus 10:21-22.

The tenth plague (the most important plague) was the death of the firstborn in Exodus 11:4-5.

The final plague was quite devastating. This plague of death was not only upon the Egyptians but also upon the firstborn of their livestock. This plague was important because we see the power of the blood, the power of the sacrifice. In this plague we see God make a covenant with every household of the children of Israel.

God clearly showed Pharaoh and his people the difference between the Egyptians and the Hebrews. Some would be blessed and the others would be cursed. All the Egyptians and all those who did not believe Moses and his God, those who did not offer the sacrifice which God commanded of the Hebrews through Moses, would be punished by the death of their firstborn of their people and of their animals.

Our study continues in Exodus 11:1: **And the Lord said to Moses, "I will bring one more plague on Pharaoh and on Egypt. Afterward he will let** you go from here. When he lets you go, he will surely drive you out of here altogether.

In the first nine plagues, every time God performed one of these miracles, Pharaoh hardened his heart. Then God hardened Pharaoh's heart, too. Thus Pharaoh refused to allow the Hebrews to leave Egypt. This hardening of Pharaoh's heart was not an example of God overriding the wicked man's free will, but rather God's judgment against Pharaoh's prior rejection and rebellion.

In this last plague, God promised Moses that not only would Pharaoh allow the Hebrews to leave, but Pharaoh and his people would *beg them* to leave Egypt. Moses then spoke to Pharaoh concerning the command of the Lord. He told Pharaoh that every Egyptian firstborn, from the house of Pharaoh to the Egyptian slaves and even all the firstborn of their animals would die that night. As for the children of Israel, no harm would come to them.

The Passover Meal

So what is the night of Passover? It is very simple. God spoke to Moses, and Moses spoke to the children of Israel in Exodus 12. He told them that every household was to take an unblemished lamb or a goat for that meal, and if a family was small and could not eat the entire lamb or goat, they could share the meat with their neighbor.

The unblemished lamb or goat was sacrificed that night, and the Hebrews were to take the blood from the sacrifice and sprinkle it on the doorposts and the threshold of their doors. They were to roast the meat, and they were to eat all the meat of the sacrifice. Whatever was left over was to be burned in the fire.

In Exodus 12:12, the Lord said that on that night, He would pass over the land of Egypt and kill the firstborn of the Egyptian people and the firstborn of their livestock. Because He is Lord, God would bring judgment upon the Egyptian gods, as it were.

We read in verses 13 and 14 the establishment of the ordinance of Passover: **[13]"Now the blood shall be a sign for you on the houses where you are. And when I see the blood, I will pass over you; and the plague shall not**

Chapter 10: Battle Plans Unfolding

be on you to destroy you when I strike the land of Egypt. **[14]So this day shall be to you a memorial; and you shall keep it as a feast to the lord throughout your generations. You shall keep it as a feast by an everlasting ordinance."** This is what the Jewish people still celebrate today. It is known as the Passover Meal.

This is what we see in verses 29 through 36. We read in verses 29 and 30: **[29]And it came to pass at midnight that the Lord struck all the firstborn in the land of Egypt, from the firstborn of Pharaoh who sat on his throne to the firstborn of the captive who was in the dungeon, and all the firstborn of livestock. [30]So Pharaoh rose in the night, he, all his servants, and all the Egyptians; and there was a great cry in Egypt, for there was not a house where there was not one dead.** Then Pharaoh called Moses and Aaron and told them and the Hebrews to go away from his people and serve their Lord. He told them to take their flocks and herds with them. The Egyptians wanted the Hebrews to leave quickly because they were afraid that they would all be dead if the Hebrews remained in Egypt. Therefore, the Hebrews took their unleavened dough, and they asked the Egyptians for silver and gold articles and even clothing. Then verse 36 ended with: **Thus they plundered the Egyptians.** Did you notice that none of this part of the account was mentioned in the Qur'an or in the hadith?

The important part of this account is that God said that He would pass through the land of Egypt, and He would walk through the homes of the Egyptians. On every house that He did not see the blood on the doorposts and threshold, God would kill the firstborn of the people and the firstborn of their animals. However, the homes that had the blood on the doorposts and threshold, the homes of the Hebrews, He would pass by and not kill their firstborn.

What saved the Hebrews? It was the blood, it was their obedience to God, and it was their obedience to the command of Moses that they believed in God and offered the sacrifices. When God saw the blood, He did not harm their children. Anyone who did not obey God and did not offer the sacrifice lost their firstborn…every single house. God provided a way to be saved, and that way involved the blood of a lamb. Those who had applied the blood were saved, of those who did not, their first born perished.

Once again, we see a very great picture, for through the blood there is covering and forgiveness for sin. Without the blood, there is death. That is why the Egyptians lost every firstborn of their people and their animals. The wages of sin is death, and either a pure substitute died or the guilty would die.

Why did God allow all these plagues to take place in Egypt? It was because God wanted Moses to take His people out of the land of Egypt. The Egyptians had enslaved the Hebrews for four hundred years. When the Hebrews called out to God, He heard their plea and remembered the covenant He had made with Abraham, Isaac, and Jacob. That is why God sent Moses to take the Hebrews out of the land of Egypt. Not as Mohammed thought and taught in the Qur'an that Moses and the children of Israel inherited the land of Egypt. We see errors compiling on top of more errors across the pages of the Qur'an. Not only did Mohammed not get the story right, but he removed from it (as has been repeatedly stated before) the important truth of *sacrifice*.

The tenth plague was very clear. The Hebrews were to offer a sacrifice, a lamb or goat, as God commanded Moses, and because they did so, no harm came to them. What a great lesson we learn from this teaching found in Exodus. There was a sacrifice, and this sacrifice was a memorial because the Hebrews have continued to celebrate the Passover meal even until today.

Sacrifices Required to Be Clean Animals or Birds

As has been stated before in this book, we must study the sacrifices of the Old Testament to see the true fulfillment of the final sacrifice of the New Testament. The wages of sin is death, as we have seen in all the passages concerning jihad in the Old Testament. When people sinned, the punishment was death. However, God also provided a way for the sin of people to be covered through the sacrifice of a pure animal or a pure bird. Instead of people dying for their own sin, an innocent sacrifice was offered as a substitute and died in the place of the person.

So why did the innocent bird or innocent animal have to die for something that it had not done? This is precisely the message and meaning of sacrifices in the Old Testament. Someone who had not committed a crime, someone who had not sinned against God, would pay for the sin of someone else who had sinned against God. An innocent substitute would die in the place of the guilty, so that the guilty could be forgiven.

In this simple and beautiful picture, we understand that Christ would be the innocent, substitutionary sacrifice for you and me. Without understanding this fact, we cannot comprehend the true Christian teaching concerning God's salvation. **Without a proper understanding of sacrifice, we cannot understand the true holy war in the teachings of the New Testament because all the blood sacrifices of the Old Testament were pictures of the coming true sacrifice, the Lamb of God, Jesus Christ.**

Throughout the Qur'an, Mohammed retold the accounts of the Bible with many changes. One of the major portions he specifically removed from the biblical accounts was the offering of sacrifices. Mohammed did not tell Muslims the true, full story concerning the sacrifices of the Old Testament. He made many purposeful errors. As we have previously stated, Mohammed told the story of Abraham and his son. He stated that Allah redeemed Abraham's son with a great sacrifice as we see in Qur'an 37:107. However, according to the Qur'an, what is a sacrifice? Why does it need to be offered? What kind of things should be sacrificed? Mohammed is silent.

Mohammed's Bright Yellow Cow Is Not the Bible's Heifer

Now, we are going to focus **on another portion of the Qur'an in which** Mohammed made a similar error. Allah asked Moses to ask the children of Israel to offer a cow as a sacrifice. This is another confusing counterfeit to the true account in the Bible.

We will first look at what Allah **said in the Qur'an and then respond with the true account from the Bible.** Every chapter in the Qur'an has a name which comes from a specific word or a message in the chapter. In chapter 2, the book of "The Cow," we read what Allah said beginning with verse 67: ***And when Moses said to his people, "Surely Allah commands you to slaughter a cow." They said, "Do you take us as a scoff?"*** I wonder why the Jewish people asked Moses if he was scoffing at them because the sacrificing of pure animals was already established throughout the Bible. It would only seem to be a "scoff" if a person didn't know about offering sacrifices. Since the Qur'an does not teach about sacrifices, then it makes sense that Mohammed would change the true account to be a 'scoff' to fit within a Muslim view of the event.

From the days of Adam and Eve, Cain and Abel, Noah, and Abraham, the Hebrew people knew about sacrifice. These people had already offered thousands upon thousands of sacrifices. The story we are reading about here took place after the Hebrews had left Egypt, so these people had just recently offered the Passover lamb as a sacrifice.

We continue with the answer of Moses in the rest of verse 67: ***He said, "I seek refuge from Allah that I be of the foolish."*** Moses told them that he was not a foolish man. Allah was his help and his guidance. Moses was just telling them the truth that Allah commanded them to sacrifice a cow.

The response of the children of Israel is in verse 68: ***They said, "Call on your lord for us that he would inform us what it is."*** I can only imagine here that Moses was just a messenger between Allah and the children of Israel. So Allah would send Moses to them, and then the children of Israel would send Moses back to Allah. Then Allah would send him back to the children of Israel. Now we know from the Bible and from the Qur'an that Allah met with Moses on the top of Mt. Sinai. So Moses would go up the mountain, then back down the mountain, then back up the mountain, and then back down, etc.

Then Moses, the first *he* in the verse, told the people what the second *he*, Allah, said at the end of verse 68: ***He said, "Surely he said, 'Surely it is a cow, neither old nor young, between the two,' so do what you are commanded."***

So Moses went to the top of the mountain and told Allah that his people are willing to kill a cow, but they want to know what kind of cow. Was it a one-year-old or five-year-old or ten-year-old cow? So Allah gave Moses the answer that the cow was not old and neither was it young; it was to be somewhere in between. Really? Is this an answer?

When we read the account in the Bible in Exodus concerning the sacrifices of the Passover, God was very specific and told Moses that the lamb or goat

Chapter 10: Battle Plans Unfolding

was to be a one-year-old male, without blemish, how long they were to keep it in observation, what the Hebrews were to do with the blood, exactly how they were to cook the meat, and that the people were to eat all of the meat of the sacrifice and then burn anything that was left over. There was no confusion. There was no need to ask God, over and over, for clarification.

God did not play games with the people or with Moses and have Moses go back and forth, up and down the mountain with new questions from the people for God, and then God would give the answer to Moses to take back to the people. No, that was the fanciful imagination of Mohammed in the telling of his fictional story of "the killing of the cow."

We read in verse 69 in the Qur'an that the children of Israel said: *"Call on your lord for us that he would inform us what is its color."* You see, the Jewish people did not want to kill their own cow. They wanted to make sure they would kill the right cow of the right color and of the right age, which we do not know how old the cow is supposed to be. So here is the answer. Moses went up the mountain to ask Allah what color, and then he came back down the mountain and told the people what Allah said in the second portion of verse 69: *"Surely he said, 'Surely she is a yellow cow. Her color is bright; she pleases the beholders.'"*

A yellow cow? Where did Mohammed come up with this color? We will address the correct color when we read the account in the Bible, but let us continue with the verses of Allah in Qur'an 2:70. The children of Israel said: *"Call on your lord for us that he would inform us what she is. Surely the cows are alike to us, and surely, if Allah wills, we will be guided."*

This imaginary group of Jews weren't satisfied with the answers so far. Now they need to know exactly which cow Allah wants the Jewish people to sacrifice. Yes, we know that it has to be bright yellow but not old or young, somewhere in the middle. We can get confused because cows look alike. What a mockery of the Scripture **and a mockery of God's commands!**

Then Moses went up the mountain to ask Allah exactly which cow. We read in verse 71 that Moses told the people Allah's answer: *He said, "Surely he said, 'Surely she is a cow not worn by plowing the earth or watering the field, submissive, no blemish in her.'"*

That is exactly the description of which cow Allah is asking the Jewish people to sacrifice. Then we read the rest of verse 71: *They said, "Now you come with the truth." So they slaughtered her, and they almost did not do [it].*

What truth? What is the truth in this story? What if Moses had told them that the cow was a brown cow or an old cow or a young cow or a cow used in the field or a pregnant cow? How do they know if Moses was really telling them the truth about this cow they must kill? Were the Jewish people playing a game with Moses because they already knew the answers to these questions? Were the Jewish people examining Moses to see if he was telling the truth or if he was lying? Maybe they wanted Moses to lose weight by running up and down the mountain! How would these Jews know that *"Now, you come with the truth"*? Did they have some document to examine to verify his claims?

What a ludicrous story with multiple errors. When you know the reason why the Jewish people were commanded to kill this cow, the story becomes even more laughable. We read in verse 72 as Allah is speaking: *And when you kill a soul and disagree among yourselves about it, and Allah brings forth what you were hiding.* So if a Jewish person killed someone and they did not know who the murderer was, Allah would bring forth the truth that was hidden about the murderer. Continuing in verse 73, the *we* is Allah: *So we said, "Strike him with part of it."* The *him* in this verse is the dead person. They were to strike the murdered person with a part of the dead cow. I am not joking. This is the "word of Allah" given by Mohammed.

Verse 73 continues with: *Likewise, Allah gives life to the dead and shows you his signs, perhaps you may understand.* No one has a clue as to what this verse is talking about. There was no purpose for Moses or the people to kill a cow if it was not for a sacrifice for sin or for worship. I thank God for Ibn Kathir, Al Tabari, Qatadah, and Al Qurtobi, these great Muslim scholars who seek to help us understand what is written in the Qur'an. It takes dozens and dozens of scholars, who have lived throughout the past fourteen hundred years, to help explain just these few words. Why is that?

According to verses 72 and 73, if a Jewish man was killed and the Jewish people disagreed with each other about who the murderer was, Moses told

Chapter 10: Battle Plans Unfolding

the people to find this cow and use it to find the killer. They were to kill this cow and use her body to figure out who the killer was. The story is told by all Muslim scholars that, when they found this cow, it was forty years later. According to scholars, there really was someone who had been killed.

So, someone was killed, and his body was there for forty years! Then Moses commanded the people to search for this cow, but it took forty years to find this specific cow which the Jewish people used to figure out who killed the man! I am not making this up.

After they found the cow, they offered the owner of the cow some money, but the owner refused. He said that this was his beloved cow and turned down the money. Well, they offered him more and more money until they offered enough denarii equal to the size of the cow.

Then we read in the interpretations of the great Muslim scholars that the people sacrificed this cow and took a part from this cow. Muslim scholars have dreamed up all kinds of different interpretations. Some said it was her leg, some said it was her tail, some said it was her tongue, some have even said that it was her backbone, while others have offered that perhaps it was some other part of the cow's body. **When they struck the dead man with whatever the part was of the cow's body, the dead man came back to life** and spoke. After he told them who had killed him, he died again. These are not *my words*, these are the words of the finest Muslim scholarship over the past fourteen centuries.

We know from Scripture that the Jewish people offered sacrifices, and the history of sacrifices is throughout the Old Testament. The Jewish people offered many sacrifices to the Lord. There was the burnt offering, the peace offering, the sin offering, the guilt offering, the food and drink offering, and the red heifer offering. Mohammed stole parts of this story from the Bible and then added his humorous back-and-forth scenario. However, once we turn to the pages of the Bible, we will find out the actual reason why God asked Moses to offer the red heifer as a sacrifice.

Sadly, Muslims, who have never read the Bible and do not know the truth about what the Scripture teaches about sacrifices, believe the lies in the **Qur'an or the lies of Muslim scholars' interpretations. The extra** information Mohammed added to the story did not help him, and the fabrication created by Muslim scholars about the made-up story of the man who died, came back to life forty years later when some part of the cow struck him so that he could tell who killed him, and then died again, is nothing but a fairytale from these so-called Muslim scholars.

The Red Heifer Offering: Numbers 19:1-9 and Deuteronomy 21:1-9

Now, concerning the red heifer offering, notice that it is a red heifer, not a bright, yellow cow. (Mohammed didn't even get the color right!) There are two locations in the Bible where we will read about the red heifer offering.

The first one is found in Numbers 19:1-9. This was an ordinance given by the Lord to Moses. The offering was to be a red heifer without blemish. It was not to have any defects, and it was never to have been yoked. The heifer was to be given to Eleazar, the priest, and be taken outside of the camp and killed in his presence. At the tabernacle before the congregation, Eleazar was to sprinkle some of the blood of the heifer with his fingers seven times. Then the entire heifer was to be burned in front of Eleazar's sight. The priest was also to take cedar wood, hyssop, and scarlet and throw them in the fire with the burning heifer. Then Eleazar was to wash his clothes and bathe in water. He would be unclean until evening. After the heifer was burned, a man who was clean was to gather up the ashes and store them outside of the camp in a holy place for the people to use for purification of their sin.

The second location about offering a heifer is found in Deuteronomy 21:1-9. Here we find out what the Bible teaches concerning an unsolved murder and the use of a heifer. According to verses 1 and 2, if a murder victim was found **in the field in the land which the Lord your God is giving you to possess** and no one knew who killed that person, then the elders and judges were to measure the distance from the dead man to the surrounding cities. We read in verses 3 and 4: ³**And it shall be that the elders of the city nearest to the slain man will take a heifer which has not been worked and which has not pulled with a yoke.** ⁴**The elders of that city shall bring the heifer down to a valley with flowing water, which is neither plowed nor sown, and they shall break the heifer's neck there in the valley.**

Chapter 10: Battle Plans Unfolding

Then the priests were to come. The Lord had chosen the priests, the sons of Levi, to minister to Him and to also settle every assault and controversy among the Israelites. The elders of the city closest to the murdered man were to wash their hands over the dead heifer. In verses 7 through 9, the elders were to say: [7]**"Our hands have not shed this blood, nor have our eyes seen it.** [8]**Provide atonement, O Lord, for Your people Israel, whom You have redeemed, and do not lay innocent blood to the charge of Your people Israel." And atonement shall be provided on their behalf for the blood.** [9]**So you shall put away the guilt of innocent blood from among you when you do what is right in the sight of the Lord.**

These are the true accounts which Mohammed confused as *one sacrifice* and then added so much information from different portions of the Bible before mixing in his own humorous back-and-forth between the people and Allah. Mohammed was wrong about so many things. First of all, this was an account about *future* events. If someone was killed in the future **in the field in the land which the Lord your God is giving you to possess**, the elders and judges were to measure the distance from the dead body to the nearest cities. That is a logical thing to do. No one is going to carry a dead body from one city or field to another city or field that is farther away to hide the body. Someone could see him doing this, and he would be caught. So, most likely the murderer would live in the closest city to where the murdered man was found in the field. This is logical.

Notice that in verse 3 the elders of the closest city were to bring a heifer. The description of the heifer was given one time without the people of Moses asking Moses to ask Allah and then Allah telling Moses the answer and then Moses giving the answer to the Jewish people. No, the circle of questions and answers back-and-**forth in Qur'an 2, starting in verse 67, does** not exist in the true account of the Bible. The God of the Bible knew everything that would occur in the future and what would need to be done. He instructed Moses just *one time* before these things happened, many years before the Israelites entered the Promised Land, the land of Israel, and before any person had been killed. This was for *future* events, once they were settled in the Promised Land with cities and farms, not because someone had already been killed as in the story in the Qur'an.

The question concerning the color of the heifer was completely invented by Mohammed. As we have read in Deuteronomy, there was no specific color of heifer mentioned that the Jewish elders and judges were to kill. In my research about the bright, yellow cow in the Qur'an, I discovered that there is no such thing. No bright, yellow cow has ever been found according to livestock experts. I challenge the reader to investigate this yourself.

One must imagine that Mohammed had heard the Jews in Mecca speak of the red cow, and then he must have walked away and wondered, "How did they know to offer a *red* cow?" In his mind he confused the color and created this whole back-and-forth folly as a way for these Jews to discover all these little details. We do not know why he invented this fabrication, but it stands in direct opposition to the true account in the Bible.

When we read the Bible, we find that the only color of heifer mentioned to be killed was red, not bright yellow. This heifer was not to have been yoked or worked. This was the only description of the heifer that the elders and judges were to sacrifice. The Bible stated that the elders of the city would kill the heifer, and the priests, the sons of Levi, were to come near the sacrificed heifer. Obviously, Mohammed did not mention who was responsible to kill the heifer, and he did not mention the priests.

Another important fact that Mohammed did not mention in the story in the Qur'an is that the elders of the nearest city where the body was found were to wash their hands over the sacrificed heifer. They were to say that they had not shed the blood and their eyes had not seen who had killed the person. They themselves were not guilty of murder, and neither did they know who was. They were to ask the Lord to redeem them and not to charge the people for the person's murder. That atonement was provided on the peoples' behalf for the blood of the murdered man. As verse 8 states: [8]**Provide atonement, O Lord, for Your people Israel, whom You have redeemed, and do not lay innocent blood to the charge of Your people Israel." And atonement shall be provided on their behalf for the blood.**

So, why did the Jewish people sacrifice this heifer? It was to seek forgiveness for the innocent blood that had been shed in their land. As verse 9 states: [9]**So you shall put away the guilt of innocent blood from among you when you do what is right in the sight of the Lord.** That is the true account of why the Israelites were to kill a heifer and what to do in the case of an unknown murder.

In simple words, when we talk about sacrifice in the teaching in the Qur'an, we discover that Mohammed missed the whole idea of sacrifice completely. We cannot find any true teaching about sacrifices in the Qur'an. In the case of Abraham and his son or in the case of Moses when God commanded him to kill a cow, Mohammed copied just portions of the Bible and added fabrications and humorous scenarios to his stories. That is why we cannot find the answers for most questions, such as why the people were offering sacrifices, what the sacrifices represented, how they were to be offered, or by whom. Mohammed is silent.

As I have shared with you in the past, the sacrificial life of worship in the Jewish faith is true. It involved a substitute. Instead of the people paying for their sin, they confessed their sin to the God of Israel. As they prayed and laid their hands on the head of the animal, in a ceremonial way, their sin was removed from them and placed upon the innocent animal. Then the animal, as an innocent substitute, would be sacrificed instead of the people. The animal would take the guilt of their sin away from them. God would look at that sacrifice and then look forward in time for the one true sacrifice that He would offer on the cross, our Lord Jesus Christ. The Old Testament sacrifices were a prophetic anticipation of God's final solution to man's sin problem.

The Herd, Flock, and Bird Sacrifices: Leviticus 1

In Leviticus chapter 1, there are three different kinds of sacrifices the Jewish people could offer to the Lord. God made provisions for the various economic problems people might face. He knew that not everyone could afford a large item of livestock, such as a bullock. Therefore, He allowed a less fortunate worshiper to offer a sheep or goat or even a bird in some cases.

From the tabernacle, the Lord spoke to Moses about the kinds of offerings the people were to bring. According to verses 3 through 9, if the sacrifice was a burnt offering from a herd animal, a male without any blemish (picturing the perfect Son of God that would one day come), the person offering the sacrifice was to do this of his own free will (this teaches us that God does not force anyone to repent or worship Him). He was to lay his hand on the head of the bull, and the bull would be accepted as the atonement for him (it would die instead of the sinner). We read in verse 5: **He shall kill the bull before the Lord; and the priests, Aaron's sons, shall bring the blood and sprinkle the blood all around on the altar that is by the door of the tabernacle of meeting.** The bull was to be skinned and then cut into pieces. The priest was to lay the head, the parts, and the fat of the bull on the wood prepared for the fire on the altar as a burnt offering. Then the priest was to wash the legs and entrails of the bull with water before burning everything.

In verses 10 through 13, the same instructions were given if the burnt offering was to be a flock animal, a sheep or a goat, a male without blemish. It was to be killed on the altar's north side, and the priests were to sprinkle the blood on the altar. As with the bull, the sheep or goat was to be cut into pieces and, with its head and fat, placed on the altar's wood. After the legs and entrails had been washed with water, the priest burned all of it on the altar.

What if the person was poor and could not afford a bull or a sheep? We see in verses 14 through 17 that this person could bring a bird for the burnt sacrifice. The offering was to be turtledoves or young pigeons. In verses 15 and 16: **^{15}The priest shall bring it to the altar, wring off its head, and burn it on the altar; its blood shall be drained out at the side of the altar. ^{16}And he shall remove its crop with its feathers and cast it beside the altar on the east side, into the place for ashes.** He was to split the bird at its wings but not divide the bird entirely. Then the priest was to burn the bird on the fire of the altar.

So it did not really matter how big the sacrifice was. The offering could have been as large as a bull or as small as a dove. It all came down to the blood, the blood of an innocent substitute. The blood was taken from the sacrifice and sprinkled on the altar. Sacrifices were offered on behalf of the people for their sin.

When we read the entire Qur'an, there is no mention whatsoever about such sacrifices, even though Muslims believe that Mohammed told them the truth

Chapter 10: Battle Plans Unfolding

about Moses and about the writing of the Torah. Sadly, they do not have any idea about the meaning of the sacrifices as we have read in the Bible.

When I was growing up in Egypt, I saw Muslims celebrating Eid al-Adha, the Festival of Sacrifice. This is when Muslims all over the world celebrate how Allah provided Abraham with the great sacrifice to be offered instead of his son (whom they believe to be Ishmael). Every year millions of goats, sheep, cows, or camels are slaughtered as sacrifices by the hand of Muslims. Yet Muslims do not have any clue why they are doing this. It is an empty ritual without understanding the true meaning. If you ask believing Jews about the Passover sacrifice, they can explain it in great detail. However, if you ask a Muslim about the Festival of Sacrifice, you will only discover that it is a celebration of Abraham's son not dying. About how, why, and who, Mohammed is silent.

Muslims do not know the truth about why God commanded people to offer sacrifices in the Old Testament. Because Muslims do not know the truth, after they kill all these animals as sacrifices, they eat the flesh. They do not know that when Abraham offered the great sacrifice, he *burned* the sacrifice to the Lord. Muslims do not know that when the Jewish people offered the different sacrifices (such as the sacrifice for sin), they burned them to the Lord because these animal sacrifices took their place as a substitute to die for their sins. If only Muslims could know the truth, they would see that their festivals and sacrifices will not deliver anyone from the guilt of sin.

As we have shared many times, the sacrifice in the Old Testament is actually a picture of the true Sacrifice, the Lamb of God, our Lord and our Savior, Jesus Christ. As we study throughout the pages of the Bible, we see many accounts about sacrifices by many different prophets. Perhaps when we have gained a good grasp of what the Bible teaches us concerning sacrifice in the Old Testament, then we may come to understand the final "holy war" of the New Testament.

Rejected Sacrifices: Isaiah 1 and 43

During the lifetimes of many of the prophets, such as Isaiah, Jeremiah, Ezekiel, Elijah, and Elisha, God was opening another door for the sinful Jewish people to reconcile with Him through sacrifices. As mentioned several times before, Mohammed purposely removed the record of sacrifices in the Qur'an from what he stole from the Bible; or if he mentioned a sacrifice, he destroyed it and gave a laughable reason concerning why the Jewish people offered the sacrifice in the first place. According to the Qur'an, these sacrifices were *not* a substitutionary atonement for sinful men. However, the clear teaching of the Bible repeatedly shows that, instead of the Jewish person being put to death, a bull, sheep or goat, or even a bird was offered as a sacrifice in place of the sinful man. The wages of sin is death, and the innocent substitute paid that death with its own blood. Without this basic understanding of "the what" and "the why" of a sacrifice, we will end up with the confusion that plagued first Mohammed and now his followers over the last fourteen centuries.

As we go through the teaching of the Bible, we see that the Jewish people offered many animal sacrifices. The following is a quick list of the sacrifices that were offered on a yearly basis by the Jewish people:

The daily sacrifices offered amounted to a total of 708 lambs for the year.

The Sabbath sacrifices amounted to 96 lambs which were offered each year.

The New Moon sacrifice was an offering of 24 bulls, 12 rams, 84 lambs, and 12 goats.

The sacrifice of Passover week consisted of 14 bulls, 7 rams, 49 lambs, and 7 goats.

The Feast of Pentecost sacrifice consisted of 2 bulls, 1 ram, 7 lambs, and 1 goat.

The sacrifice for the Feast of the Trumpets was 1 bull, 1 ram, 7 lambs, and 1 goat.

The Day of Atonement sacrifice was 2 bulls, 1 ram, 7 lambs, and 3 goats.

The sacrifices of the Feast of Tabernacles were 71 bulls, 15 rams, 105 lambs, and 8 goats.

The total number of these animals offered yearly was 114 bulls, 37 rams, 1,063 lambs, and 32 goats. Therefore, the total number of all these animals offered as sacrifices were 1,246 in a regular year.

In a leap year, which contained an extra thirty days, the Jewish people offered the following:

New Moon sacrifice - 2 bulls, 1 ram, 7 lambs, and 1 goat.

Daily sacrifice - 60 more lambs

Sabbath - 8 more lambs

Thus in a leap year, an additional 79 animals were sacrificed.

These sacrifices were offered to the God of Israel every year.

(Source: http://forthewordoftruth.weebly.com/the-only-substitute.html, 06/20/2018)

Now, let me ask two very important questions. First, for Muslims who claim that their Qur'an contains everything they need out of the Bible and is the full, complete word of Allah from Adam and Eve (the Qur'an never mentioned Eve by name, just as Adam's wife) until Mohammed, why did Mohammed not mention these sacrifices in the pages of the Qur'an? Second, did God accept all these sacrifices of the Jewish people, as we read throughout the pages of the Bible, or did He reject some of their sacrifices? How can God ask the Jewish people to offer sacrifices and at the same time reject their sacrifices? The answer is in the Bible.

Yes, the Jewish people were asked to offer sacrifices, but there were *conditions* for the sacrifice to be acceptable. For example, the sacrifice was to be whole and without any blemish. That meant if the Jewish people offered a sacrifice that was blind or had a broken leg or if there were any deformities, God would not accept the sacrifice. Also, what was the condition of the heart of the people who were offering the sacrifices? Were they doing what was right before God, or were they just performing a ritual? In other words, were they offering the sacrifice in *true repentance*, or were they just doing an empty ritual while still engaging in the sinful behavior? (We see much of this kind of behavior even in some groups who call themselves Christians. They think that merely saying a few words or doing some good deed will erase the guilt of a sin which they have done and still plan to do, over and over. There is no repentance, only a sham that makes them feel forgiven while still in rebellion against God. The Jews in the Bible were no different, at times.)

For our study, let us look in two different locations in the book of Isaiah to understand why God rejected the sacrifices of the Jewish people. First, we will go to Isaiah chapter 1. I encourage you to read the entire chapter, but we will begin with verse 11: **"To what purpose is the multitude of your sacrifices to Me?" Says the Lord. "I have had enough of burnt offerings of rams and the fat of fed cattle. I do not delight in the blood of bulls, or of lambs or goats.** Notice here that the Lord gave the types of animals used for the sacrifices that we looked at earlier and told the Jewish people that He no longer delights or finds any pleasure in these sacrifices they offered. God is looking for true repentance in the offering of a sacrifice, but when a sinner (who is not repentant) offers to the Lord, the sinner is making a mockery of the seriousness of the sacrifice, and it is not accepted.

We read in verses 12 and 13: [12]**When you come to appear before Me, who has required this from your hand, to trample My courts?** [13]**Bring no more futile sacrifices; incense is an abomination to Me. The New Moons, the Sabbaths, and the calling of assemblies – I cannot endure iniquity and the sacred meeting.** Here God rejected the different sacrifices which the Jewish people had offered to God, whether it was at the time of a New Moon or a Sabbath or at any other time of meeting.

Then in verse 14 we read: **Your New Moons and your appointed feasts My soul hates; they are a trouble to Me, I am weary of bearing them.** We see that God not only rejected the Jewish people's sacrifices, but He actually hated them. Why is that? It is because *outwardly* they were doing what He asked (sacrifice) but *inwardly* there was no change of heart (repentance).

We see this clearly in verse 15: **When you spread out your hands, I will hide My eyes from you; even though you make many prayers, I will not hear. Your hands are full of blood.** This is a picture of sin. Here is the

Chapter 10: Battle Plans Unfolding

true reason why God rejected the sacrifices of the Jewish people. That is why God told the Jewish people in verses 16 and 17: **[16]"Wash yourselves, make yourselves clean; put away the evil of your doings from before My eyes. Cease to do evil. [17]Learn to do good; seek justice, rebuke the oppressor; defend the fatherless, plead for the widow."** If all of these things which God sought from the Jewish people had been practiced by them, God would have accepted their sacrifices. Otherwise, He would reject them all.

The problem was not that the Jewish people had sinned against God and offered sacrifices to cover their sin with the blood of their sacrifices. That would have been pleasing to God. The problem was that they were *still living in sin without any repentance* and doing evil while at the same time offering these sacrifices. This did not please God. There had to be true repentance, a true change of heart. The people had to do what was right, then they could offer the sacrifices, their sin would have been forgiven, and these sacrifices would have been accepted.

God desires for men to have a right relationship with Himself. That is why God extended His invitation to His people in the Old Testament, and He continues to extend the same invitation today to you and me, as we read in Isaiah 1:18-19: **[18]"Come now, and let us reason together," says the Lord. "Though your sins are like scarlet, they shall be as white as snow; though they are red like crimson, they shall be as wool. [19]If you are willing and obedient, you shall eat the good of the land; but if you refuse and rebel, you shall be devoured by the sword"; for the mouth of the Lord has spoken.**

What a great message God is sharing with us through His word! No matter what the condition of our sin or how bad our life is, if we are willing to truly repent, then He is truly willing to forgive us for our sins. He was willing to accept the sacrifices of the Old Testament in the days of Prophet Isaiah. God cannot be fooled by external obedience (sacrifices) coupled with internal disobedience (sin and rebellion). It does not matter what you do or say in some sort of religious ritual or ceremony if your heart is unrepentant. You are just fooling yourself, but not God. Believe me, God wants you to know that He is not fooled. He can see your heart. That is both comforting and terrifying.

If people do what is right, they must have true repentance by putting away evil. They must cease to do all evil things. They must learn to do what is good. So what is good? It is to rebuke the oppressor, to defend the fatherless, and to plead for the widow. That is when God can change our sin. Just as He gave the invitation to the Jewish people in the days of Isaiah, He still extends His invitation to us today. He will make our sins as white as snow after being red like scarlet. He will change our sins to be as white as wool after being as red as crimson.

So what do we learn from this passage? We see that in Isaiah chapter 1, God rejected the sacrifices of the Jewish people simply because they were living in sin without repentance. They were doing everything that was wrong and assumed that if they offered up sacrifices, their sins would be covered. They continued to live in sin and just expected that their empty, ritualistic sacrifices would help them. No, God cannot be mocked. God knows the hearts of men. If the Jewish people had been willing to do what was right and turn from their evil, God would have accepted their sacrifices. The same is true today. Ritual cannot replace reality.

Now we will look at the second passage found in Isaiah chapter 43. We will begin with verses 22 and 23: **²²"But you have not called upon Me, O Jacob; and you have been weary of Me, O Israel. ²³You have not brought Me the sheep for your burnt offerings, nor have you honored Me with your sacrifices...** Wait a minute! How can God accuse the Jewish people of not honoring Him with sacrifices? They had offered thousands of sacrifices throughout each year. They had offered these sacrifices year after year.

Verse 23 continues with: **²³I have not caused you to serve with grain offerings, nor wearied you with incense. ²⁴You have bought Me no sweet cane with money, nor have you satisfied Me with the fat of your sacrifices; but you have burdened Me with your sins, you have wearied Me with your iniquities."** Here is the reason why God rejected the sacrifices of His people. Once again, it was because of their sin and their iniquity.

Well, didn't God want them to offer sacrifices to cover their sin? Isn't that what God had required of them in order for them to receive forgiveness? So why did God reject their sacrifices here in these verses? Let me repeat, it was because their hearts were not in the right place. They did not offer their sacrifices because of true repentance. No. Instead, they offered sacrifices as if to say, "We did our part for God, and now we can do whatever we wish for ourselves." This sounds like so many who claim to be Christians in the world today, but God cannot be fooled with outward ceremonies and ritualistic religion.

The Lord continued to speak to His people in verse 25: **"I, even I, am He who blots out your transgressions for My own sake; and I will not remember your sins.** God reminded them that He would remove their sin because of His own sake; and, because of His grace, He would not remember their sin any more. [26]**Put Me in remembrance; let us contend together; state your case, that you may be acquitted.** Here we see God pleading to have the relationship back with His people. He reminded them of their sin and of their father's sin in verse 27: **Your first father sinned, and your mediators have transgressed against Me.** [28]**Therefore I will profane the princes of the sanctuary; I will give Jacob to the curse, and Israel to reproaches."** Once again, we see the punishment on God's own people. It was a justified punishment as a result of their sin.

God rejected their sacrifices because they did not honor Him. These were only two passages in the book of Isaiah in which God rejected the sacrifices of the Jewish nation because they were not offering them to please God. They only performed the sacrifices as a ritual. They wanted to keep sinning and yet look like they were worshiping God, but God cannot be fooled with empty religion.

Rejected Sacrifices: Jeremiah 7 and 17:26-27

From our study, we now understand clearly that God gave man an alternate way to be free of the punishment for his sin. That way was through sacrifice. The sacrifices of the Old Testament were a picture of the True Sacrifice, the True Jihad, which God Himself would perform through His Son, Jesus Christ. Jesus was the final, innocent substitute who would die for the sin of all mankind. This only applies to those who believe in Jesus' sacrifice. Repent and believe.

Now we will examine Jeremiah, another prophet. Jeremiah might be a new name for Muslims simply because his name is not mentioned in the Qur'an. Even though Muslims believe in thousands of prophets who came before their false prophet of the cult of Islam, Mohammed, they cannot come up with ten true prophets' names.

Jeremiah is also known by Jews and Christians as the Weeping Prophet. He wrote two books, Jeremiah and Lamentations. He prophesied about the destruction of Jerusalem in Jeremiah 6. In verse 1, he spoke to the Benjamites, his own people, and warned them about the coming evil which would bring great destruction upon Jerusalem. Even though Jeremiah described Jerusalem as a daughter of Zion and a comely, delicate woman, he continued in chapter 6 in verse 6 to explain that the city would be punished because there was oppression, violence, and wickedness in the city.

Then Jeremiah asked in verse 10: **To whom shall I speak and give warning, that they may hear? Indeed their ear is uncircumcised, and they cannot give heed. Behold, the word of the Lord is a reproach to them; they have no delight in it.**

What a sad condition! The prophet who had the message for the people could not find anyone to listen to the warning from God concerning the city. That is why God was angry with them. That is why God gave the command that they would be punished for their sin. Their homes, fields, and families would be taken away from them and be given to another people. The people of the north were about to come and take over Jerusalem. Both the young and the old would be punished. God would use the wicked to destroy the wicked.

As I have shared with you so many times before, it is amazing that Muslims will look to passages in the Bible where God used the Jewish people to punish the wicked people of the land. They point to these passages and say that this killing is like the jihad in the Qur'an. However, these same Muslims will not dare look at a passage such as this where we see God giving Jerusalem as captives with its old, its young, its women, its children, their homes, and their fields to their northern enemies as a punishment for their sins.

Why did God allow this to happen? Simply because the people were living in sin. God tells us in verse 13 that it was: **"Because from the least of them even to the greatest of them, everyone is given to covetousness; and from the prophet even to the priest, everyone deals falsely."** That was why God brought judgment upon the people of Jerusalem.

According to verse 19 in chapter 6, God repeats why He brought evil upon the people of Jerusalem. It was because they had not heeded the words of the Lord nor the Law but instead rejected them. Therefore, due to their lack of repentance, God did not accept their sacrifices as He stated in verse 20: **"For what purpose to Me comes frankincense from Sheba, and sweet cane from a far country? Your burnt offerings are not acceptable, nor your sacrifices sweet to Me."**

God rejected the sacrifices of the Jewish people because their hearts were not in the right place. They disobeyed God's command because they did not have any delight in His Law. Instead, they rejected it. They chose to live in sin rather than to live in obedience to God's command. Therefore, since God rejected the people because of their sin, He also rejected their sacrifices.

Then the Prophet Jeremiah gave the children of Judah a prophecy in chapter 7. God told the people in verses 3 and 4 to do what is right: [3]**"Amend your ways and your doings, and I will cause you to dwell in this place.** [4]**Do not trust in these lying words, saying, 'The temple of the Lord, the temple of the Lord, the temple of the Lord are these.'"** The people were depending upon the temple of the Lord to save them, but God told them that the temple of the Lord would not save them.

In verses 5-7, Jeremiah spoke to all the children of Judah: [5]**"For if you thoroughly amend your ways and your doings, if you thoroughly execute judgment between a man and his neighbor,** [6]**if you do not oppress the stranger, the fatherless, and the widow, and do not shed innocent blood in this place, or walk after other gods to your hurt,** [7]**then I will cause you to dwell in this place, in the land that I gave to your fathers forever and ever."** This was the promise that God gave, not just to the people of Judah, but to the Jewish nation. If they did what was right, God would bless them. If they did what was wrong, they would be cursed.

In verses 9-11, God asked the people of Judah: ⁹**"Will you steal, murder, commit adultery, swear falsely, burn incense to Baal, and walk after other gods whom you do not know,** ¹⁰**and then come and stand before Me in this house which is called by My name, and say, 'We are delivered to do all these abominations'?** ¹¹**Has this house, which is called by My name, become a den of thieves in your eyes?"** You see, because the Jewish people in these verses had the temple of the Lord, they depended on the temple to save them. Since they had the temple of the Lord, they thought that they could do whatever they wanted and then come to the temple and cry out to God and He would save them from their enemy. They had made their faith all about external things, offerings and buildings. Yet their hearts were far from God, and God cannot be fooled by elaborate ceremonies and impressive buildings. He sees the true condition of our hearts.

Jeremiah reminded them of what happened at Shiloh. Their fathers had the Ark of the Covenant and depended on it to save them as they went into battle against the Philistines, but the Ark did not save them. As we read previously in 1 Samuel 4:1-10, the Israelites had been defeated by the Philistines, so they decided to bring the Ark of the Covenant into their camp to save them. When the Ark arrived from Shiloh, all Israel shouted so loudly that the earth shook. The Philistines heard the noise. They became afraid, remembering what the God of Israel had done to the Egyptians with the plagues. They were afraid that the Israelites would defeat them and make them slaves. Therefore, the Philistines encouraged one another to be strong. In verse 10, the Philistines defeated Israel, killed thirty thousand of them, and captured the Ark of the Covenant.

So what do we learn from this? When Jeremiah was speaking to the Jewish people in chapter 7, he was telling them that they were depending upon the house of the Lord. They were shouting that the house of the Lord would deliver them, but the temple of the Lord will not deliver them. Ceremony and ritual mean nothing without a repentant heart.

Chapter 10: Battle Plans Unfolding

Now, we know that the Jewish people depended on the temple of the Lord because inside the temple was the Ark of the Covenant (which was the representation of God in their midst). The Ark of the Covenant did not deliver their ancestors from the Philistines, and now the temple will not save them from the kingdom of the north as the Lord stated in Jeremiah 7:14: **"Therefore I will do to the house which is called by My name, in which you trust, and to this place which I gave to you and your fathers, as I have done to Shiloh."**

In verse 15, the Lord declared what He would do to them: **"And I will cast you out of My sight, as I have cast out all your brethren – the whole posterity of Ephraim."** The Lord reminded them that when all the other tribes of Israel went to war against to tribe of Benjamin, only six hundred of the men of the tribe of Benjamin were left alive.

Then God told Jeremiah, in verse 16, not to even pray for the people: **"Therefore do not pray for this people, nor lift up a cry or prayer for them, nor make intercession to Me; for I will not hear you.** In verse 17, God asked Jeremiah if he could not see what the people were doing in the streets of Jerusalem and in the cities of Judah.

So what were the people doing in the cities and streets? God answered the question in verse 18. The children were gathering wood for fires which their fathers made and the women made cakes. For whom? For the worship of the God of Israel? No. These were not for the Lord God. It was for the false "queen of heaven," and the people poured out drink offerings to other gods. The Israelites were worshiping false gods. Because of this, the Lord told them in verses 20-22: [20]**"…Behold, My anger and My fury will be poured out on this place – on man and on beast, on the trees of the field and on the fruit of the ground. And it will burn and not be quenched."** [21]**Thus says the Lord of hosts, the God of Israel: "Add your burnt offerings to your sacrifices and eat meat.** [22]**For I did not speak to your fathers, or command them in the day that I brought them out of the land of Egypt, concerning burnt offerings or sacrifices."** God reminded them, when He brought the Israelites out of the land of Egypt, that He did not at first speak to their fathers concerning the burnt offerings or sacrifices. Now because the children of Judah were offering sacrifices to false gods, God rejected their sacrifices. So what did God command their fathers to do after leaving Egypt? In verses 23-26, God commanded them to obey His voice. He would be their God, and they would be His people. They were to walk in the ways God had commanded them to walk so it would be well with them. However, they did not obey but followed the wickedness in their hearts.

We read in verses 30-31: **³⁰"For the children of Judah have done evil in My sight," says the Lord. "They have set their abominations in the house which is called by My name, to pollute it. ³¹And they have built the high places of Tophet, which is in the Valley of the Son of Hinnom, to burn their sons and their daughters in the fire, which I did not command, nor did it come into My heart."** That was why the prophecy was given to the children of Judah through Jeremiah that the day would come when this valley would be called the Valley of Slaughter. The carcasses of the people would be eaten by the animals and the birds in this valley. That was the judgment of God on Jerusalem because they sinned against God and did evil in the eyes of the Lord. They did not obey God's word. They were evil to the point that they were offering their children as living sacrifices in the fire to false gods. They had become as bad as the previous inhabitants of the Promised Land. God would do to them what He had done to the wicked Canaanites.

It is surprising that Muslims will use verse 22 of chapter 7: **"For I did not speak to your fathers, or command them in the day that I brought them out of the land of Egypt, concerning burnt offerings or sacrifices,"** to tell us that the Bible contradicts itself, that the sacrifices were rejected by God, and that God never asked the children of Israel to offer sacrifices. What a deceptive way to interpret the verses of the Bible. They took Jeremiah 7:22 out of context and made up a doctrine out of it.

No, God accepted sacrifices, but not the sacrifices of the wicked ones among His people, those who offered many sacrifices to other gods. However, if they offered the true sacrifice after true repentance by living in obedience to God, their sacrifices would be accepted.

As we have seen in the days of Jeremiah, the Jewish people did not keep the Sabbath. They were rushing to make profit, even on the Sabbath. That is why God burned Jerusalem. We see this written clearly in Jeremiah 17:26-

27: **²⁶"And they shall come from the cities of Judah and from the places around Jerusalem, from the land of Benjamin and from the lowland, from the mountains and from the South, bringing burnt offerings and sacrifices, grain offerings and incense, bringing sacrifices of praise to the house of the Lord. ²⁷But if you will not heed Me to hallow the Sabbath day, such as not carrying a burden when entering the gates of Jerusalem on the Sabbath day, then I will kindle a fire in its gates, and it shall devour the palaces of Jerusalem, and it shall not be quenched."**

Every prophecy given by Jeremiah was fulfilled. The gates of Jerusalem were burned, and the fire was not quenched until the city was completely destroyed.

Elijah the Prophet of God vs the Prophets of Baal: 1 Kings 16:29-18

I would like to share with you another account about sacrifices in the Old Testament, which is also not mentioned in the Qur'an. In this account we read that God's people were offering sacrifices and worship to false gods. While hundreds of false prophets were offering sacrifices to these gods, there was one prophet who offered the right sacrifice to the God of Israel. We will see which sacrifice was accepted. That is how we can discern the true God from the false gods. This is a famous account for both the Jewish people and Christians alike.

Sadly, for Muslims who have never read the Bible and have never read the truth about the sacrifices, this may be the first time they will read the truth about this account. It is the account of the Prophet Elijah as written in 1 Kings.

First, I would like to give you a short summary about the kings of Israel. As we read the Scripture, we see that the line of the kings of Israel were typically ungodly kings. They had sinned against God and also caused the children of Israel to sin against God. There was no end to wars and killing during the lives of these kings. All this death and killing was the result of sin. They provoked God to anger because of their sin, and God's punishment was severe on them. When the kings sinned against God, they made the people sin against God. That is why we see so much death among the kings and the children of Israel.

There was division among the children of Israel. They divided into the northern kingdom of Israel and the southern kingdom of Judah because of their sin. We read in 1 Kings 16 beginning with verse 29 about King Ahab, the king of Israel. He ruled during the time King Asa was the king over Judah. Ahab ruled for twenty-two years in Samaria. Now, Ahab was not just a wicked king, but he did more evil in the sight of the Lord and provoked the Lord more than all the previous kings of Israel before him. He even took Jezebel, the daughter of the king of the Sidonians, as his wife. He served and worshiped Baal at the altar in the temple that he had built for Baal in Samaria. This was the condition in which Israel was living under the rule of the sinful King Ahab.

Now, we read in 1 Kings 17 about the Prophet Elijah, the Tishbite. He proclaimed to Ahab that there would not be any dew or rain in the land for years except by Elijah's word. This was the beginning of the punishment of the Lord God upon Israel. Then the Lord told Elijah to go and stay by the Brook Cherith, his water supply. Also, the Lord miraculously commanded ravens to bring bread and meat to him in the mornings and in the evenings. When the brook dried up (since there had been no rain), the Lord told Elijah to go to Zarephath.

In 1 Kings 18, we read that there was no rain for three years. Then the Lord told Elijah to go and present himself to Ahab in Samaria, and the Lord would send rain. So Elijah went to see Ahab. There was a man in charge of Ahab's house. This man was Obadiah, who feared the Lord greatly and had hidden one hundred of the prophets of God and took care of their needs. As he went to search for grass for Ahab's horses and mules, he met Elijah. Elijah told Obadiah to tell Ahab that he was here. Obadiah was afraid that if he brought the news to Ahab that Elijah was back and the Spirit of the Lord took Elijah to another place, then Ahab would kill Obadiah for lying. Elijah reassured Obadiah in verse 15 that he would present himself before Ahab that very day.

In verse 17 when Ahab saw Elijah, he called out: **"Is that you, O troubler of Israel?"** Elijah replied that it was not he who troubled Israel, but it was Ahab because he had forsaken the Lord and followed the Baals.

Chapter 10: Battle Plans Unfolding

Then Elijah told Ahab, in verse 19, to gather four hundred and fifty prophets of the false god Baal and four hundred prophets of the false goddess Asherah and to meet him on top of Mount Carmel. Many of the children of Israel assembled on the mount. There Elijah asked them how long they would be between two opinions. He told them in verse 21: **"If the Lord is God, follow Him; but if Baal, follow him."** The people did not answer. Elijah told them that he alone was the prophet of God while there were eight hundred fifty of the false prophets. It was a showdown to see who was serving the living and true God.

Elijah instructed that two bulls be brought, one for the prophets of Baal and one for Elijah. Elijah told the prophets of Baal to choose one of the bulls, cut it up, and place it on the wood. However, they were not to put fire to the wood. Instead, they were to call upon their gods. Then Elijah would call on the Lord God. The people would see who would answer with fire for their sacrifice.

According to verses 26-27, the prophets of Baal prepared the sacrifice and proceeded to call upon their god from morning to noon. They danced about the altar, but there was no answer from Baal. Then Elijah mocked them. He told them in verse 27: **"Cry aloud, for he is a god; either he is meditating, or he is busy, or he is on a journey, or perhaps he is sleeping and must be awakened."** The prophets of Baal began to cry out louder and cut themselves. They continued until the time of the evening offering, but there was still no answer from Baal. They had spent all day trying to get the attention of a god that didn't exist.

Finally, in verse 30, Elijah told the children of Israel to gather to him. He repaired the altar of the Lord using twelve stones, which represented the number of the twelve tribes of Israel. Here we see that the altar of the Lord had been broken down because of the sin of the people. That is why Elijah had to rebuild the altar of the Lord God. Then he dug a trench around the altar, put wood on it, placed the cut up bull upon the wood, and instructed that water be poured over the sacrifice and the wood. He instructed water to be poured upon the sacrifice and the wood a second time and then a third time. He also had the trenches filled with water. (This was done to prove that he wasn't secretly hiding some little spark that could flare up and then claim that it was from God.)

At the time of the evening sacrifice, Elijah simply took a few seconds to call upon the Lord in verses 36-37: **36"Lord God of Abraham, Isaac, and Israel, let it be known this day that You are God in Israel and I am Your servant, and that I have done all these things at Your word. 37Hear me, O Lord, hear me, that this people may know that You are the Lord God, and that You have turned their hearts back to You again."** Immediately, the fire of the Lord came down and consumed not only the sacrifice but also the wood, stones, dust, and the water in the trenches. When the children of Israel saw this, they fell down and worshiped the Lord God and cried out in verse 39: **"The Lord, He is God!"** At that point Elijah told the people to take hold of all the prophets of Baal, and the Prophet Elijah executed these wicked prophets at Brook Kishon.

Elijah told Ahab in verse 41: **"Go up, eat and drink; for there is the sound of abundance of rain."** That is exactly what Ahab did. He went up, ate, and drank. Then Elijah went to the top of Mount Carmel, bowed down, put his face between his knees, and told his servant to go and look toward the sea. The servant looked and reported to Elijah that there was nothing. Then Elijah told him seven times to go look again, and on the seventh time, the servant reported to Elijah that there was a small cloud coming up out of the sea. Elijah told the servant to go to Ahab and tell him to get his chariot ready and go down before the rain stopped him. Then the sky darkened and a heavy rain began. Just as the Lord had promised through Elijah.

So what do we learn from this account in the Bible? Ahab, the wicked king of Israel, caused the people to live in sin. He was worshiping the false god Baal and built altars to him. The children of Israel did not live as God commanded them to do.

However, Elijah, the true prophet of the Lord, was able to control the rain of heaven for three years. He ended the worship of Baal in Israel by killing all of Baal's false prophets after he performed these two great miracles (drought and the fire from heaven). He showed the children of Israel that the Lord God answered his prayer and that the Lord is the true God. By bringing down fire from heaven to consume the sacrifice, Elijah proved to the children of Israel that the Lord is the true God and that He accepted the true sacrifice of His prophet, Elijah.

So where are the stories of Elijah and the sacrifices of the Old Testament found in the pages of the Qur'an? You will not find this information. If Mohammed had told the truth about the sacrifices of the Old Testament, then maybe his people would come to believe in the true fulfilment of all these sacrifices in the New Testament which is the true understanding of jihad, "holy war" in the New Testament through Jesus Christ.

All these sacrifices in the Old Covenant were just a picture of the True sacrifice found in the New Covenant. That is the true understanding of holy war in the New Testament. The God of the Bible, in both the Old Testament and the New Testament, never changes. He is the same yesterday, today, and forever; and yesterday He allowed the Jewish people to offer sacrifices.

All of these sacrifices in the Old Testament were just a *covering* of their sins. However, in the New Covenant, we see the *fulfillment* of all these prophecies concerning the coming of the Lamb of God, the sacrificial One, who will die once for all mankind. Through His precious blood, He will not only bring covering for the sin of the people but *redemption*, a complete removal of sin. As we will see in the verses in both the Old and New Testaments, by His own sacrifice, God will no longer remember the sin of His people, who are now those who believe and trust in Jesus Christ as Lord and Savior.

I know that many of our Muslim friends do not believe in the death and resurrection of our Lord and Savior Jesus Christ. As a matter of fact, many of the scholarly Muslims of today have dreamed up the ludicrous idea that the deity, death, and resurrection of Christ were invented by Apostle Paul! I am not joking.

However, nothing written by Paul or Peter or John contradicts the teachings of the Old Testament. The deity, death, and resurrection of our Lord and Savior Jesus Christ is a complete fulfillment of all that was written hundreds and thousands of years before the coming in the flesh of our Lord and Savior. We know from Scripture that with Christ's death and resurrection God accomplished His true holy war in the New Testament. How could the Apostle Paul, living in the first century, invent something that was clearly laid out and revealed through hundreds of prophecies over a thousand years before Paul was born? This is how desperate modern

Muslim scholars have become. Just as their false prophet Mohammed had done before them by removing the sacrifices from the Old Testament, they are now repeating their errors and ignorance by seeking to remove the deity and death of the one True Sacrifice from the New Testament. This is wickedness! Straight from the bottom of Hell.

We all have sinned, and the wages of our sin is death. The three deaths in the Bible are spiritual death, physical death, and eternal death. Jihad in the Bible was always to remove sin, to get rid of the wicked men who lived in sin, and that is why we saw killing throughout the Old Testament. Period. It is that simple. There is no confusion. There needs to be no interpretation or explaining away.

In the New Testament, God, the Father, put Christ on the cross for your sin and mine. Instead of us sinners dying physically and spending eternity in Hell, **God's love allowed Jesus Christ to take our place on that cross** where He died for our sin. Because He rose from the dead, all those who believe and trust in Him as Lord and Savior will receive forgiveness of their sin, redemption, and eternal life. We will live forever and not be punished for our sin because He took our place as an innocent, substitutionary sacrifice. Through Him and Him alone we can be set free from the wages of our sin so that we will no longer be dead spiritually but alive by having the second birth through believing in Jesus Christ. Then when we die physically, we will have eternal life and not spend eternity in the lake of fire but will spend eternity in Heaven with Christ Jesus, our Lord and Savior and Redeemer.

My dear friend, this is the simple and loving message of the entire Bible. The entire Bible can be summed up in one verse, Romans 6:23. The Old Testament can be summed up in the first part: **"For the wages of sin is death,"** and the New Testament is summed up in the last part: **"but the gift of God is eternal life in Christ Jesus our Lord."**

Christianity is not some invention of Paul or any of the early apostles. It is the fulfillment of God's plan for the salvation for mankind. In Christ alone all the hundreds of prophecies in the Old Testament were fulfilled, some of them written over a thousand years before Jesus came in the flesh.

Chapter 10: Battle Plans Unfolding

The greatest prophecy was that the Savior must suffer and die and will not decay in the grave because He must rise from the dead on the third day. That is the teaching of the prophets in Scripture: the writings of Moses and the prophets in the Old Testament. Christ is the Prophet about whom Moses prophesied almost 3,500 years ago as written in Deuteronomy 18:15-19: [15]**"The Lord your God will raise up for you a Prophet like me from your midst, from your brethren. Him you shall hear,** [16]**according to all you desired of the Lord your God in Horeb in the day of the assembly, saying, 'Let me not hear again the voice of the Lord my God, nor let me see this great fire anymore, lest I die.'** [17]**And the Lord said to me: 'What they have spoken is good.** [18]**I will raise up for them a Prophet like you from among their brethren, and will put My words in His mouth, and He shall speak to them all that I command Him.** [19]**And it shall be that whoever will not hear My words, which He speaks in My name, I will require it of him.'"**

This is a prophecy given by God through Moses to the children of Israel concerning Christ, our Lord and Savior. Christ Jesus is the Messiah. He is the Prophet. He is the Deliverer. He is the Priest. He is the Anointed One. He is the Mediator. He is Human, and He is God. He is the Messiah who will offer Himself to die for the sins of the world.

There is so much similarity between our Lord and Savior Jesus Christ and the Prophet Moses. I know that some of our Muslim friends would love to take these verses and make them a prophecy about their false Prophet Mohammed instead of about our Lord and Savior Jesus Christ. However, this would be far from the truth.

Here are some of the similarities between Jesus and Moses. None of these descriptions fit Mohammed. Both Jesus and Moses performed miracles, but Mohammed never performed any miracles. Mohammed even admitted that he performed no miracles. The lives of Jesus and Moses were threatened when they were babies by evil kings, but Mohammed's life was never threatened as a child. Just as Moses lifted up the bronze serpent when God was punishing the children of Israel for their grumbling against Him, those who looked upon the bronze serpent were healed; so are those who look upon Jesus, who was lifted up on the cross, and believe on Him by faith will be saved from eternal death. Mohammed did not lift up any serpent, and he himself was not lifted up. Mohammed denied both the Old Testament account of Moses lifting up the serpent and the New Testament account of Jesus Christ being lifted up on the cross.

We read in Numbers 11:16-17: **[16]So the Lord said to Moses: "Gather to Me seventy men of the elders of Israel, whom you know to be the elders of the people and officers over them; bring them to the tabernacle of meeting, that they may stand there with you. [17]Then I will come down and talk with you there. I will take of the Spirit that is upon you and will put the same upon them; and they shall bear the burden of the people with you, that you may not bear it yourself alone."**

This prophecy was fulfilled, according to Luke 10:1-17, when Jesus appointed seventy disciples to teach the nations. In verse 1, we read: **After these things the Lord appointed seventy others also, and sent them two by two before His face into every city and place where He Himself was about to go.**

When we compare this to the life of Mohammed, the false prophet of Islam, we see that Mohammed did not have seventy disciples or elders. Mohammed had thousands of helpers. How were these helpers supposed to help Mohammed? They were to go fight the battles for him, to kill the Christians and the Jews, and to kill those who truly believed in Moses and those who believed and followed Jesus. As we study the life of Moses and the life of our Lord and Savior Jesus Christ, we see so many similarities. On the other hand, the opposite is true as we study the life of Mohammed because there is no connection between Mohammed and Moses; there is actually a contradiction between them.

In Deuteronomy 18:15, Moses did not say that the Lord their God would raise up for them a prophet from their cousins but that He would raise up a prophet from their midst, from their brethren. Moses was speaking to the children of Israel and not to any other people.

Mohammed did not come according to the desire of the Lord. Mohammed did not speak according to the command of the Lord. Mohammed did not hear the word of God. Mohammed did not speak in the name of God.

Chapter 10: Battle Plans Unfolding

Mohammed did not come through the promised line of Abraham, Isaac, and Jacob. Jesus Christ fulfilled all of these prophecies.

This is not the only prophecy we have concerning the Lord Jesus. There are hundreds of prophecies, and as we study them, we will see that Mohammed did not fit any of these divine glimpses into the coming Messiah. All of these prophecies work together and fit together perfectly in one Person and one Person only, and that is our Lord and Savior Jesus Christ.

For example, I would like to share with you another prophecy given by God Himself to Abraham. We read in Genesis 22:17: **"blessing I will bless you, and multiplying I will multiply your descendants as the stars of the heaven and as the sand which is on the seashore; and your descendants shall possess the gate of their enemies.** Notice here that the word used is not the singular word *descendant* but the plural word *descendants*.

However, as we continue in verse 18, we see the singular word *seed* is now used: **In your seed all the nations of the earth shall be blessed, because you have obeyed My voice."** Even though God spoke to Abraham in verse 17 concerning his seeds or descendants (plural) who would be as many as the stars in heaven and the sand on the seashore (innumerable), in verse 18 God is speaking to Abraham about the seed (singular in Hebrew) in which all the nations of the earth will be blessed because Abraham had obeyed God's voice.

The obedience of Abraham in this passage was that he was willing to offer his son, his only son Isaac, the son he loved, as a sacrifice. Notice that Ishmael had no part of this prophecy for he had been sent away earlier. God spoke to Abraham concerning Isaac, the one he was going to sacrifice. However, God had delivered his son Isaac and redeemed him with the ram which was caught in the thicket.

God blessed Abraham because of what he had done, because of what he had been willing to give up. Abraham obeyed God. Abraham believed God. Abraham did not withhold his only son and was willing to offer Isaac as a sacrifice.

That is why God blessed Abraham in verses 17 and 18 by telling Abraham that he would have many descendants and that the nations would be blessed through this one seed. God was speaking of Abraham's coming seed, the one who would bless the entire world with salvation, Abraham's greatest descendant, our Lord and Savior Jesus Christ. The nations would be blessed through this one Man by receiving forgiveness, by being redeemed from the punishment of their sin, and by offering them eternal life instead of eternal punishment in the fires of Hell. Truly all the nations of the world are blessed through our Lord Jesus Christ, the seed of Abraham.

When we read the Scripture, we see that the Bible prophecies are specifically written about our Lord and Savior. He must come from the lineage of Noah's son Shem and not from Ham or Japheth, the other two sons of Noah. Abraham was a descendant of Shem. The Messiah must come from Abraham's son Isaac and not from Ishmael or any other son of Abraham. The prophecies continue to get even more specific. He must come from Isaac's son Jacob and not from Jacob's brother Esau. He must come from the tribe of Judah, one of the twelve sons of Jacob, and not any of the other eleven sons.

The prophecies continue to narrow down on the Messiah. He must come from the family of Jesse and not from any of the other families in the tribe of Judah. He must also specifically come from the house of David and not from any of David's brothers. God was very specific, giving us hundreds of prophecies that narrow down and absolutely identify the one and only Messiah.

Was this true of Mohammed? No. He was disqualified quickly since he did not come through the line of Isaac and Jacob, he certainly wasn't from the tribe of Judah, and he had absolutely nothing to do with the family of Jesse and even less to do with the line of kings through David. It is not even *possible* that these Messianic prophecies could be fulfilled in Mohammed just due to his lineage alone, not to mention that he does not even begin to match the hundreds of other prophecies concerning the actions of the Messiah.

The fulfillment of these lineage prophecies (line of Shem, line of Abraham, line of Isaac, and Jacob and Jesse and David) all can easily be found by reading the genealogy of our Lord and Savior Jesus Christ, as written in the book of Matthew chapter 1. That is why it is very important to study the prophecies of the Old Testament and their fulfillment in the New Testament. Then we will know for sure that Christianity is not the invention of the disciples or some other people in the New Testament but the fulfillment of the prophecies written in the Old Testament. The Apostle Paul could not have written the prophecies that were recorded over a thousand years before he was even born!

Battle Plans Revealed

Old Testament Prophecies and New Testament Fulfillment of Christ's Coming

The detailed prophecies of the Old Testament will point us to the True Sacrifice, the True Lamb of God, Jesus Christ. Salvation is available only through Christ. Man can be set free once and for all. No more punishment for sin. No more killing. No more jihad. Jesus is the One who was the innocent substitute for all of mankind. He died on the cross, and God's judgment on sin and its punishment, death, has been fulfilled. He is the Savior, and in Him and Him alone, God performed the True Jihad in the New Testament. Christ entered the Holy of Holies with His own precious blood to purchase salvation for all mankind. That is the Christian faith. The wages of sin is death, and the God-man, Jesus Christ, paid our debt. He suffered the judgment that we deserved, so that we could go free. Abraham's beloved son Isaac was spared because of a sacrifice, but God's beloved Son became the sacrifice. What a picture. What a Savior!

Sadly, our Muslim friends do not believe in this because they do not believe who Jesus is or what He has done for mankind. Mohammed hid the truth about the reason for sacrifice. Mohammed even denied that Jesus actually died on the cross. Without this proper understanding, this leads Muslims to claim that this is not the true Christianity but a fabrication by Apostle Paul or some other people who introduced this false teaching in the early days of the church.

However, we know from the many, many teachings of the Old Testament that all these prophecies (written hundreds and even thousands of years before Christ came in the flesh) must be fulfilled. Many of the prophets wrote about the coming of Christ, His birth, His life, His betrayal, His arrest and trial, His death on the cross, and His resurrection. Christianity is the completion and the fulfillment of all these prophecies of the Old Testament. It is not a later "invention" but rather the perfect fulfillment of God's eternal

Chapter 11: Battle Plans Revealed

plan revealed from the beginning in the Garden of Eden to humanity's original parents.

Let us examine just the birth of the Messiah, our Lord and Savior Jesus Christ. His birth was not a coincidence. It was the fulfillment of specific writings in the books of Genesis, Numbers, Isaiah, 2 Samuel, Jeremiah, Isaiah, and Psalms. Many of these prophecies and writings of the Old Testament are fulfilled in the New Testament in Matthew's genealogy of Jesus.

It is unfortunate that often we do not read these names of the genealogy of the birth of our Lord and Savior. Many people just skip over them. Perhaps it is because we have difficulty in pronouncing these names. However, once we understand just how much prophecy is fulfilled in this list, we would be in awe of just the genealogy of our Lord alone! These are not merely a bunch of random, unimportant names. Every one of these names was tied to a prophecy, and each of these names provides a link in the line of descendants who would ultimately bring us the Savior of the world.

We read in the Bible in Matthew 1:1-2: [1]**The book of the genealogy of Jesus Christ, the Son of David, the Son of Abraham:** [2]**Abraham begot Isaac, Isaac begot Jacob, and Jacob begot Judah and his brothers.** As we continue with the list of names, we see the name of Obed, the father of Jesse, and Jesse was the father of King David. In verse 16, we read the name of Joseph, the fiancé of Mary: **And Jacob begot Joseph the husband of Mary, of whom was born Jesus who is called Christ.**

Our dear Muslim friends believe in the story in the Qur'an concerning the virgin birth because Mary was a virgin when she gave birth to her son, 'Isā. However, they do not know the entire truth about the virgin birth as it is revealed in the pages of the Bible. In Matthew 1:18-25, we read that when Joseph, the fiancé of Mary, found out that she was pregnant and he had not sexually known her yet (because he had not married her at this point), he decided to let her go away and not expose her pregnancy. If he had exposed her, there is little doubt she would have been stoned just as commanded for any woman found in adultery. While he was thinking about this in his heart, an angel spoke to him in a dream and told him not to be afraid to take Mary for his wife. The angel continued by telling Joseph that the Child was conceived by the Holy Spirit and that Mary would have a Son. The angel instructed Joseph to name the baby Jesus because the Child would save His people from their sins. Once again, even before Jesus is born we have the truth of His final sacrifice for the sins of the world!

You see, my dear Muslim friends, you believe that the name of Jesus in the Arabic language is *'Isā* **which is not even an Arabic name.** 'Isā actually has no meaning in the Arabic language. The real name of Jesus in the Hebrew language is *Yeshua*, translated in the Arabic language as Yasua, which means *Savior*. That is exactly what Joseph did. He named the baby Yeshua, for Yeshua would save His people from their sins. Mohammed removed the idea of sacrifice, and now he even changed the name of Jesus. Why would he do that? Could it be that Satan (the real Allah of Islam) didn't want the world to know that Jesus (Yeshua) was the promised Savior who would be the final sacrifice bringing eternal salvation to all who trust in Him? Why did Mohammed remove and change so many things as he conveniently borrowed various events and people from the Bible? It is quite obvious that it is a planned deception, conceived by Satan, and carried out by Mohammed, and the Bible says that Satan is the Great Deceiver. This is also a title of Allah found in Islam! In the Qur'an, it says that Allah is the Greatest Deceiver. (Qur'an 3:54 and 8:30)

This virgin birth was not a coincidence because this prophecy was given about seven hundred years before Christ's birth to the Prophet Isaiah. As we read in Isaiah 7:14: **"Therefore the Lord Himself will give you a sign: Behold, the virgin shall conceive and bear a Son, and shall call His name Immanuel."** That is exactly how it was fulfilled in Matthew 1 and in Luke 1. Mary, who was a virgin, gave birth to a Son, and they named him Immanuel, which is interpreted as *God with us*. Even to this day, many Christian songs and hymns honor this wonderfully descriptive name for Jesus: *Immanuel, God with us*. The Savior has dozens of such names and titles in the Scripture, such as: Immanuel, the Lamb of God, the Redeemer, the King of Kings and Lord of Lords, the Messiah, the Son of David, and so on.

This prophecy that a virgin would give birth to a Son, Yeshua, the Savior, and this Son who is the Lamb of God who would take away the sin of the world was given *hundreds of years* before Mary (and Paul) was even born.

Chapter 11: Battle Plans Revealed

Not only the *manner* of His birth, but also the *place* of Jesus' birth was clearly prophesied by the Prophet Micah, written more than four hundred years before the birth of our Lord. We read in Micah 5:2: **"But you, Bethlehem Ephrathah, though you are little among the thousands of Judah, yet out of you shall come forth to Me, the One to be Ruler in Israel, Whose goings forth are from of old, from everlasting."**

I wonder, when our Muslim friends read this verse, do they understand the depth of this prophecy? This prophecy is very specific as to the exact place of Jesus' birth. It was to be in Bethlehem Ephrathah, not just Bethlehem, because at the time of Jesus' birth there was another Bethlehem. The Old Testament tells us the exact place of the Savior's birth, Bethlehem Ephrathah, which was a small town out of the hundreds of towns in Judah. Notice that from this small town a Ruler of Israel would come forth "Whose going forth are from of old." The Hebrew words and phrase indicate an eternal being, One who has no beginning--God Himself.

When is the beginning of this Ruler? Every baby that has been born or will be born on earth has a beginning and an end, but this Ruler does not have a beginning or an end. Jesus Christ is not just some Jewish baby who was born two thousand years ago. No, He has no beginning or end. He is eternal. This is not just my opinion or some Christian belief in the New Testament, but it is the teaching of the Old Testament in the prophecy of Micah. The eternal deity of our Lord Jesus Christ is also repeated in the Psalms and in Prophet Isaiah's writing. In Isaiah 9:6, the prophet announced: **"For unto us a Child is born, unto us a Son is given; and the government will be upon His shoulder. And His name will be called Wonderful, Counselor, Mighty God, Everlasting Father, Prince of Peace."**

Now, why was Jesus born in Bethlehem Ephrathah? Neither Mary nor Joseph lived there. The Scripture tells us that Joseph was not living in Bethlehem before the birth of Jesus, but rather he was living in Nazareth. In Luke 2, Caesar Augustus gave a decree that all must return to their city of birth to be taxed. So Joseph took Mary and traveled to Bethlehem, the city of David, since Joseph was of the house of David. Thus he had to be registered in Bethlehem Ephrathah, and while they were there to be registered, Mary gave birth to Jesus. Christ's birth in Bethlehem was not by Mary or Joseph's choice. It was the providence of God Almighty. Mary gave birth to Jesus in Bethlehem and fulfilled the prophecy of Micah written more than four hundred years before the earthly coming of our Lord and Savior Jesus Christ. How good and powerful is our God!

Can you imagine with me just how difficult it was for a mother (who was nine months pregnant) to travel on the back of a donkey during the long ride just a few hours or days before the birth of her Son? What if the baby had been born just a few miles before they arrived in Bethlehem Ephrathah? That would have disqualified Jesus from being the promised Messiah, since God had revealed the exact place of the birth of our Savior. Jesus Christ was born in Bethlehem Ephrathah, just as God had promised.

Where was Mohammed born? In Bethlehem of Judea? No, but in Mecca, Saudi Arabia, which is about 730 miles from Bethlehem Ephrathah. Mohammed is therefore disqualified from any chance of being the Messiah or as the fulfillment of hundreds of other prophecies of the coming Prophet of whom Moses spoke.

Another great prophecy given in the Bible is that the Messiah, the Savior, will be the seed of a woman. Biblically and biologically, *the seed of a woman* seems to make no sense because women do not have *seed*. In the Scripture we always read of the seed of the man/male. Then in a fascinating event, God spoke in the Garden of Eden after Adam and Eve had sinned and told the serpent, Satan, in Genesis 3:15: **"And I will put enmity between you and the woman, and between your seed and her Seed; He shall bruise your head, and you shall bruise His heel."**

This is the first prophecy in the book of Genesis, just after Creation, as God told Satan that He would put enmity between the seed (singular in the Hebrew) of the woman and Satan. Since women properly have no seed, this prophecy must be fulfilled in some miraculous way, and the only way this can be fulfilled is that a virgin would somehow have a Son. When we study the life of Christ, we see the victory of Christ over Satan. For when we see Christ's death on the cross and resurrection from the dead, we see Satan completely demolished, and one day Satan will be thrown into the lake of fire by Christ. The seed of the woman (Jesus Christ, born of a virgin) did destroy Satan's power (sin and death) when the Promised Seed died in our place and suffered our judgment. Even at the dawn of human history, just moments after mankind's first sin, God began announcing His redemptive plan through the Son of a virgin who would redeem man! What an amazing and gracious God we serve!

Another great prophecy in the Bible is that this Messiah, the Christ, will be a Priest after the order of Melchizedek. This prophecy was given by King David one thousand years before Christ came in the flesh. In Psalm 110:4: **The Lord has sworn and will not relent, "You are a priest forever according to the order of Melchizedek."** This prophecy was fulfilled in the life of our Lord and Savior Jesus Christ as we read in Hebrew 5:6: **As He also says in another place: "You are a priest forever according to the order of Melchizedek."** This must have puzzled all of the Jewish scholars as they studied these prophecies! Why? Because many prophecies speak of the Messiah coming from the Tribe of Judah (the royal line), and yet others spoke of the Messiah as being a Priest (and all Jewish priests were of the tribe of Levi). How could one Jewish man be both a king and a priest? Surely that would require two different lineages. The answer was found in the example of Melchizedek, as stated above. **Melchizedek's priesthood was established long before Levi or Judah were even born, far back in the days of Abraham. According to the *flesh*, Jesus was of the line of David (the royal line of Judah), but He had a *spiritual* Priesthood given directly by God the Father that did not come from the Jewish line of priests through Levi. The Scripture calls Jesus our "Great High Priest," and He has a priesthood that far excels that of the tribe of Levi, and pre-dates it as well.**

What about the timing of the coming of our Lord? Could it be just anytime, maybe 2,000 years ago or 1,500 years ago or 3,000 years ago? How about in the time of Mohammed (about 1,500 years ago)? No, there was a very specific time given in the Old Testament in two different prophecies. According to both of the prophecies, Christ must be born at the time when the scepter had not passed from the tribe of Judah until the Messiah comes. In simple words, our Lord and Savior must be born before the nation of Israel lost the right to judge its own people.

This old prophecy was given by Jacob to his children as he prophesied about the future of his son Judah. Jacob said in Genesis 49:10: **The scepter shall not depart from Judah, nor a lawgiver from between his feet, until Shiloh comes; and to Him shall be the obedience of the people**.

What a great prophecy given by Jacob nearly four hundred years before the birth of Moses and almost two thousand years before the coming of Christ in the flesh. We know according to historian Josephus that the Sanhedrin of Israel lost the right to judge its own people when it lost the right to pass the death penalty in 11 A.D. Our Lord and Savior Jesus Christ was born before 11 A.D. What great prophecies, one after another, about a miraculous baby, a divine child being born, and exactly when and where He would come.

Another prophecy was that our Lord must be born before the temple of Jerusalem was destroyed (which occurred in 70 A.D. when the Roman armies under Titus demolished the city of Jerusalem and leveled the temple). If any of these prophecies had failed and not been accomplished, we would lose everything regarding the truth concerning the coming of our Lord. We read throughout the Bible, in the Old Testament, that Christ must come while the temple was still standing in Jerusalem. According to the prophecy in the book of Malachi 3:1: **"Behold, I send My messenger, and he will prepare the way before Me. And the Lord, whom you seek, will suddenly come to His temple, even the Messenger of the covenant, in whom you delight. Behold, He is coming,"** says the Lord of hosts.

Notice that the Bible declares that Christ would come to His temple, which means that Jesus Christ must be living on earth while the temple still exists. We can go to Psalm 118:26: **Blessed is he who comes in the name of the Lord! We have blessed you from the house of the Lord.** This prophecy of David was written one thousand years before the coming of our Lord in the flesh.

We can also read the prophecy of Daniel in Daniel 9:26: **"And after the sixty-two weeks Messiah shall be cut off, but not for Himself; and the people of the prince who is to come shall destroy the city and the sanctuary. The end of it shall be with a flood, and till the end of the war desolations are determined."**

Praise God that the Messiah came and was cut off. He died not for Himself but for me and you. Jerusalem was still there, and the temple was still there, just as the prophets had declared.

Chapter 11: Battle Plans Revealed

Then the prophecy in Daniel said that the people of the prince who is to come (the Romans) will destroy the city and the sanctuary. We see the fulfillment to this prophecy of Daniel, written hundreds of years earlier, as we read in Matthew 21:12-13: **[12]Then Jesus went into the temple of God and drove out all those who bought and sold in the temple, and overturned the tables of the money changers and the seats of those who sold doves. [13]And He said to them, "It is written, 'My house shall be called a house of prayer,' but you have made it a 'den of thieves.'"**

The temple was there in the days of Jesus. As I said earlier, it was destroyed later in 70 A.D. by the Romans, just as Daniel had prophesied. The prophecies concerning the timing of the coming of our Lord were fulfilled perfectly and completely during the life of Jesus Christ.

Could Mohammed have fulfilled *ANY* of these? No. Mohammed was not even born until almost exactly five hundred years *AFTER* the temple was destroyed by the Romans. Let's examine a checklist:

1. Was Mohammed born of the line of Abraham through Isaac? **No.**

2. Was Mohammed from the tribe of Judah? **No.**

3. Was Mohammed a Priest according to the order of Melchizedek? **No.**

4. Was Mohammed born of a virgin? **No.**

5. Was Mohammed born in Bethlehem? **No.**

6. Was Mohammed born before Israel lost its rights? **No.**

7. Did Mohammed visit the temple before it was destroyed? **No.**

So, our dear Muslim friends, all of these incredible prophecies and fulfillments prove that Christianity was not "invented" by some people in the early years of Christ or after our Lord's ascension. Christ's coming, life, death, burial, and resurrection were the fulfillment of over three hundred prophecies written by many prophets over hundreds and even thousands of years before Christ came in the flesh. The evidence is there in both Scripture and in history. Anyone can examine it and believe the truth. Don't take my word for it; research it for yourself. It doesn't take dozens of scholars and bizarre interpretations. It is written plainly for us so that we can have an assurance of the truth of these events and promises. God does not want you to be in doubt. He wants you to know and believe.

In 1 John 5:12-13 we read: **^{12}He who has the Son has life; he who does not have the Son of God does not have life. ^{13}These things I have written to you who believe in the name of the Son of God, that you may know that you have eternal life...** God has given us ample evidence, and He wants you to KNOW that you can HAVE eternal life. It is not a matter of "hope so" or "maybe" with God. The matter of your eternal soul is far too important. Jesus Christ, the long-promised Messiah, gave His life as a sacrifice so that you could be saved and KNOW that you HAVE eternal life. If you haven't trusted Him as your Lord and Savior, why not right now? He is waiting. He loves you. He died for you.

Sadly, many Jews claim that they are still waiting for their Messiah. However, in order to say that, they must deny what their own prophets have already written! As we have shown, in verse after verse, prophet after prophet, the Messiah had to come BEFORE the temple was destroyed. He had to come before Israel was removed as a nation. Both of those things have already happened, nearly two thousand **years ago.** Israel's Messiah has come, and the Jews did what the Scriptures said that they would do...they rejected and killed their Messiah. If only the Jews would read and believe their own book!

We read of more prophecies in the books of Matthew and Luke and the many astounding things which occurred involving the birth of the Christ Child. These amazing events had never happened before and will never happen again. They were fulfilled in only one unique person.

Another one of these prophecies about the birth of Jesus is fulfilled in Matthew 2:2 where we read about the sign from heaven when wise men from the East were asking: **"Where is He who has been born King of the Jews? For we have seen His star in the East and have come to worship Him."**

Notice that the star of the Christ Child was seen by the wise men in the East, and they came all the way to Jerusalem and then traveled to Bethlehem so that they could worship Him. This star was a miracle which God put in the heavens to point the way to the Christ Child. Just like the Old Testament prophecies provided "light" to point the way to Jesus, God even put a literal "light" in the darkness of the night to lead these Gentile seekers to His Son. What a marvelous God we serve!

We know from Matthew 2:11-15 that the wise men arrived in Bethlehem and found the Child with His mother and *worshiped* Him. Notice, they worshiped Him. Jesus was both God and man, even as a baby, just as the prophets Micah and Isaiah had prophesied. These foreign visitors presented to Him their gifts of gold, frankincense, and myrrh. After they left to return to their homes another way, an angel appeared to Joseph in a dream and told him to take the Child and Mary and go to Egypt. They were to stay there until the Lord told them to return home because Herod (the leader in Judea) was looking for the Child to kill Him (Herod would see this Child as a threat to his throne). So Joseph took his family to Egypt, and as we read in Matthew 2:15: **...and was there until the death of Herod, that it might be fulfilled which was spoken by the Lord through the prophet, saying, "Out of Egypt I called My Son."**

With many countries surrounding Israel, it would have been very easy for Mary and Joseph to take Jesus to Lebanon, Syria, Jordan, or any other nearby country, but the angel of the Lord told Joseph to go to Egypt. Going to Egypt fulfilled this prophecy from Prophet Hosea as we read in Hosea 11:1: **"...out of Egypt I called My son."** This prophecy was written hundreds of years before the birth of Jesus.

In Matthew 2:16-18, Herod became angry when he realized that the wise men had left without notifying him of the whereabouts of the Child. Therefore, he killed all the male children who were two years old and younger living in the Bethlehem area. This was another prophecy fulfilled as we read in verse 18: **"A voice was heard in Ramah, lamentation, weeping, and great mourning, Rachel weeping for her children, refusing to be comforted, because they are no more."**

This prophecy was written by Jeremiah hundreds of years earlier in Jeremiah 31:15. The children of Bethlehem would be killed, and Rachel would weep over the loss of her children for King Herod would kill her children two years old and younger. How wicked and desperate Herod must have been to slaughter little children in order to secure his power.

All of these prophecies were given to the world in order to give us the assurance that this Christ Child is the true Christ. God wants mankind to know the truth, and He has done so with great and irrefutable evidences. These prophecies must be fulfilled, even in the smallest details of what would take place at the time of His birth.

Then we read in Luke 2:8 about another fulfilled prophecy as shepherds were tending their flocks when the angel of the Lord appeared. The appearance of the angel and the glory of the Lord frightened the shepherds. The angel told the shepherds not to be afraid for he had brought them the good news that the Savior, Christ the Lord, had just been born in Bethlehem. They would find the Savior in a manger wrapped in swaddling clothes. Notice that the angel did not tell the shepherds that a good teacher or a prophet or a good man had been born that day. No, he told them that the Savior, Christ the Lord, had been born. There is only one Lord, and both the angels and shepherds knew who "the Lord" was. The Child Jesus is both God and man.

In Luke 2:25-38, we read that this Child was recognized as the Messiah. Joseph and Mary took Jesus to the temple in Jerusalem. There they met an old, devout man named Simeon, who was waiting "for the Consolation of Israel." The Holy Spirit was upon Simeon and had revealed to him that he would not die before he had seen the Lord's Christ. At the temple, he took the Christ Child in his arms and blessed God and said in verses 29-31: [29]**"Lord, now You are letting Your servant depart in peace, according to Your word;** [30] **for my eyes have seen Your salvation** [31]**which You have prepared before the face of all people…"**

What a great testimony from this old man, Simeon! He saw with his own eyes the Salvation which the Lord had prepared before all people. Salvation was through this Child, who was only eight days-old! Simeon held in his arms the fulfillment of hundreds of prophecies that God had given over the last few thousand years.

Then Simeon himself gave another prophecy, which is actually two great prophecies. The first prophecy concerned Israel, and the second prophecy concerned Mary, the mother of our Savior. In verses 34-35: [34]…**"Behold, this Child is destined for the fall and rising of many in Israel, and for a sign which will be spoken against** [35]**(yes, a sword will pierce through your own soul also), that the thoughts of many hearts may be revealed."** This is the truth we read in the passages of the Bible to learn about this Christ Child and what will take place even in His mother's broken heart. Obviously, this was a prophecy given by Simeon about the cross and what Mary would go through as she sees her Son dying on the cross. Jesus would be *physically* pierced on the cross, and Mary, His earthly mother, would be pierced *emotionally* as she watched her Son agonize for you and for me.

What we immediately learn here is that Jesus was recognized as the Messiah. We saw the sign in heaven, the star. We know that He was proclaimed by the angels. We know that He was worshiped by the Gentile wise men, and He was hunted by the wicked King Herod. All this was to fulfill many of the prophecies which were recorded in the Old Testament, most of them hundreds or thousands of years before His birth.

Prophecies and Fulfillment Concerning the Childhood of Jesus: Luke 2

Many Muslims ask questions about why we know so little about the actual childhood of Jesus. They say that we know about His birth and we know about His ministry, but they say that we know nothing in between. However, this is not entirely true. Luke 2:40 states: **And the Child grew and became strong in spirit, filled with wisdom; and the grace of God was upon Him.** When He came in the flesh on earth, even as a Child, He was not left alone. He was filled with wisdom, and He grew strong with the Spirit of God.

In Luke 2:41-49, we read that Jesus was not like any other boys of His age. When Jesus was just twelve years old, Joseph, Mary, and the rest of the family went to Jerusalem, as they did every year, for a feast. This means that Jesus was Jewish, and we know that His family followed the Mosaic Law. After the feasting days were over, the large group of worshipers headed back home, not realizing that Jesus had stayed behind in Jerusalem. They thought that Jesus was with other relatives or friends. (Remember, after Mary and Joseph were married, they had many children. This would have been a large company of people.) At the end of the day's journey, they could not find Him and returned to Jerusalem. They spent another few days searching in Jerusalem for Jesus, and when they found Him, the Child Jesus was in the temple teaching.

This twelve-year-old Child taught with such authority and understanding that the teachers were amazed at His answers. We read in verse 47: **And all who heard Him were astonished at His understanding and answers**. Notice that the teachers of the law (Jewish biblical scholars) at the temple were amazed at the answers Jesus gave and of His understanding. Jesus was not a thirty-year-old Messiah. He was just a boy of twelve, speaking and listening to the scholars of the law, and they were astonished at His understanding.

Now, we have a question. Did Jesus know He was the Son of God, even at this young age of twelve? Yes, indeed, He did. As we read in verses 48-49, we know that He did when Mary saw Him and asked Him why He had done this to them by staying behind in Jerusalem. They had been frantically searching for Him. She said in verse 48… **"Son, why have You done this to us? Look, Your father and I have sought You anxiously."**

The response of Jesus was not like any other child of twelve. Jesus was not afraid that His parents would spank Him or that He needed to apologize for staying behind. He had done nothing wrong. He was doing exactly what He was sent to do. The answer of this twelve-year-old boy is given in Luke 2:49: **And He said to them, "Why did you seek Me? Did you not know that I must be about My Father's business?**

Jesus reminded Joseph here that Joseph is not actually His father. He reminded Mary that she is only His earthly mother in the flesh, but He is her Creator God. Jesus is God the Son, and He must be about His Father's business. Jesus being in the temple at the age of twelve is Jesus being involved in His True Father's business. Then in verse 50 we read that Mary and Joseph did not understand what Jesus told them.

Sadly, here we see that Mary, the earthly mother of Jesus, the one who knew much about Jesus, the one who had been visited by the angel, the one who had experienced the miraculous pregnancy and birth, still did not understand that Jesus was in the temple to do His Father's business.

So, in these passages we learn all we need to know about the early life of the Lord Jesus. He was the miraculous, promised Son of the virgin, born in Bethlehem, Who traveled to Egypt, then back to Israel, and Who lived a perfect life of obedience doing the will of His Father in Heaven. We do not have to know every detail of every part of His life. God has revealed what is necessary in order to understand that He is the fulfillment of the prophecies and the promised Messiah Who would give His life on the cross for our salvation.

Prophecies and Fulfillment Concerning Jesus' Ministry: Isaiah 40

Now we will look at some of the prophecies concerning the ministry of Jesus Christ. The ministry of our Lord began at His baptism when He was about thirty years of age. What had He done between age twelve and age thirty? He had lived a perfect life of obedience to the Heavenly Father and was about His true Father's business. We know that there was a prophecy concerning John the Baptist written in the Old Testament in that he would come before our Lord and Savior.

John the Baptist (John "the Baptizer") was born six months before the birth of Jesus. This was not a coincidence, but this prophecy was written by Isaiah seven hundred years before Jesus' birth in Isaiah 40:3: **The voice of one crying in the wilderness: "Prepare the way of the Lord; make straight in the desert a highway for our God."**

This prophecy was fulfilled in Matthew 3:3: **For this is he who was spoken of by the prophet Isaiah, saying: "The voice of one crying in the wilderness; 'prepare the way of the Lord: make His paths straight.'"**

Isaiah wrote about John the Baptist, the man who would prepare the way for the Lord. Jesus is the Lord. That was John the Baptist's cry as he ministered to the Jewish people in the Jordan River before he met Jesus.

In verses 13-17, of Matthew chapter 3, we read that Jesus came to the Jordan River to be baptized by John. John said that it was he who should instead be baptized by Jesus. However, Jesus said in verse 15: **"Permit it to be so now, for thus it is fitting for us to fulfill all righteousness."** So John baptized Jesus. When Jesus immediately came up from the water, the heavens opened, and he, John the Baptist, saw the Spirit of God descend upon Jesus like a dove. Then a voice from heaven, in verse 17, said: **"This is My beloved Son, in whom I am well pleased."** Here is a great evidence of the true nature of the God of the Bible.

It is amazing how many times our dear Muslim friends will ask the question, "Show me a verse in the Bible that says Jesus is the Son of God." There are dozens of such verses, but this one is a great verse to not only show the Sonship of our Lord and Savior Jesus Christ but to also show the existence of the Triune God, the Father, the Son, and the Holy Spirit (known as the Trinity). For the Holy Spirit descended upon Jesus like a dove, and the voice of the Father came from heaven and said that this was His Son in whom He was pleased. In this event, we see God the Father, God the Son, and God the Holy Spirit, all present. I pray that Muslims, as they read the Old Testament prophecies and their fulfillment in the New Testament, can connect the dots and recognize that Christianity is the great plan of God for salvation.

So here we see that John the Baptist was the fulfillment of a prophecy in preparing the way for the Lord Jesus. The baptism of Jesus was the clear testimony of God the Father that Jesus is His Son. We see the whole picture of the true understanding of who God is as the Triune God throughout Scripture, both Old and New Testaments. As we look at the ministry of Jesus and examine how Jesus spoke to the people, the types of miracles He performed, and all those who believed in Him or rejected Him, we see the fulfillment of what had been prophesied hundreds of years before Jesus came to the earth in the flesh.

Chapter 11: Battle Plans Revealed

The Qur'an also talks about the miracles of Jesus and how great Jesus was as a man, as a prophet, and as a teacher, but Mohammed stopped there. Just as he had copied and changed the stories, the people and the events from the Old Testament, he also copied information about Jesus, and then changed it. Just as he removed important facts, like sacrifices because of sin, Mohammed purposefully removed any mention of Jesus as the Divine Son. Therefore, Muslims do not know the true picture of Jesus. The real reason Jesus came to earth was not to perform miracles. The real reason Jesus came to the earth was to give us eternal life which could not be accomplished unless Jesus fulfilled everything written about Him in the Old Testament prophecies concerning His sacrificial suffering, death, and resurrection. Muslims are not aware of any of this because Mohammed did not mention it. Not only that, he also contradicted and denied much of it. He denied the true nature of God, he denied that God has a Son, he denied that Jesus was anything more than a man, a prophet, and he denied that Jesus died on the cross for our sins. What a wicked and evil cult!

However, the Bible (which existed for almost five hundred years BEFORE Mohammed was even born) sets the record straight. Jesus did not come to serve God here on earth for three and a half years to just heal some of the sick or to bring some who had died back to life. The Gospel is very clear. As we read in John 3:16: **For God so loved the world...** (KJV) God did not just love the people of Israel in three and a half years of ministry, but God loved the whole world **that He gave His only Begotten Son**. (KJV) He did not send Jesus to just perform some miracles, but God sent Jesus to be a sacrificial offering to die on the cross for the sin of mankind. For **whosoever believeth in Him**, not just those living during the days of Jesus' ministry on the earth, but for all the people of the world. So they **should not perish, but have everlasting life**. (KJV) *Not perish* means not to spend eternity in Hell but to have everlasting life which is to live for eternity in Heaven. So Jesus' ministry was not just limited to the three and half years on earth but was extended to all the people of the world from Adam and Eve to the last person who accepts Jesus as Lord and Savior.

Let us examine the method that Jesus would use to speak while ministering to the people. The Scripture stated that it would be through parables. This is not my opinion or the opinion of Matthew, the writer of the gospel of Matthew. This was the plan of God, the plan of the Holy Spirit, as He inspired King David to write about the specific ministry of Jesus Christ in Psalm 78:2. Don't forget, my dear brothers and sisters, that David wrote this one thousand years before the coming of our Lord in the flesh! According to Psalm 78:2: **I will open my mouth in a parable, I will utter dark sayings of old.**

That was exactly the method of ministry used by our Lord and Savior. Jesus frequently spoke to the crowds in parables to fulfill this prophecy written by King David. We read the fulfillment of this prophecy in Matthew 13:34-35: **³⁴All these things Jesus spoke to the multitude in parables; and without a parable He did not speak to them, ³⁵that it might be fulfilled which was spoken by the prophet, saying: "I will open My mouth in parables; I will utter things kept secret from the foundation of the world.**

Even the disciples asked Jesus why He always spoke to the crowds in parables. Then the disciples would ask Him what the parable meant, and Jesus would tell them the interpretation of the parable.

Another important prophecy in the Old Testament stated that Jesus would perform many miracles. What if Jesus came like Mohammed (the false prophet of the cult of Islam) and never performed any miracles? Then we would know that Jesus was not the Son of God, not the Christ, not the Anointed One, not the Messiah, and we would have to wait for another one to come. Praise God for the prophecy of Isaiah written seven hundred years before the coming of our Lord. We read in Isaiah 35:5-6: **⁵Then the eyes of the blind shall be opened, and the ears of the deaf shall be unstopped. ⁶then the lame shall leap like a deer, and the tongue of the dumb sing.**

We will not list all the miracles Jesus performed in the fulfillment of this prophecy written by Isaiah. However, here are some examples.

In Matthew 9:27-31, two blind men came to Jesus and asked Jesus to have mercy on them. Jesus asked them if they believed He could heal them. They replied yes. When Jesus touched their eyes, they could see. Just as Isaiah had prophesied, the eyes of the blind were opened.

In Matthew 9:32-33, a mute man possessed by a demon was brought to Jesus. When Jesus cast out the demon, the mute man was then able to speak. The multitude that saw this was amazed for there had never been anything seen like this before in Israel. Just as Isaiah had prophesied, the mute (dumb) would speak.

In Matthew 17:24-27, Peter was asked if he and Jesus had paid their taxes or tribute for the temple. When Peter found Jesus, Jesus already knew why Peter was coming to Him. Jesus told Peter to go to the sea and catch a fish and look inside its mouth. So when Peter caught the fish, he found money inside the mouth of the fish to pay their taxes. How did Jesus know that Peter would catch a fish with money inside it to pay their tribute? I believe that Jesus is telling Peter here that He is not just a man. He is not just a prophet. He is God, the Knower of all things. This was another miracle that showed that Jesus is the Son of God.

In Mark 7:31-37, Jesus was in the region of Decapolis at the Sea of Galilee when the people brought a deaf-mute to Him. They begged Jesus to put His hand on the man. Then Jesus touched the man's tongue as He looked to heaven and said, "Be opened." Immediately the man's ears were opened, and he could speak plainly. They were amazed at what He had done in making the deaf-mute man hear and speak. Just as Isaiah had prophesied, the deaf would hear. These miracles were performed by Jesus to fulfill the prophecy which was written by Isaiah.

I know that our dear Muslim friends believe in the miracles of Jesus, because in the Qur'an, Allah told them about miracles. Sadly though, Muslims believe in all the lies which Mohammed added to the accounts of the Bible in his writing of the Qur'an.

For we read in Qur'an 3:49 that 'Isā (the false name for Jesus in the Qur'an) said: ..."*Indeed, I came to you with a sign from your lord. I create for you the figure of a bird from the mud. So I breathe into it, so it will become a bird by Allah's permission. And I heal the blind and the leper, and I raise the dead by Allah's permission. And I inform you about what you eat and what you store in your houses. Surely in this is a sign for you, if you were believers.*

Muslims believe in these miracles which the Qur'an claims Jesus performed. Obviously, we Christians do not believe in the lies about the creation of a bird that Muslim scholars claim Jesus did in this miracle when he was still a child. Mohammed borrowed this story from a false Gnostic text that was completely rejected by the early Christians as a forgery. It is not found in the Bible.

We know from the Scripture that the first recorded miracle that Jesus performed was not speaking from the cradle as a baby or making a bird from mud, but instead, it was changing water into wine at a wedding at Galilee when Jesus was thirty years old. You can read the entire account about Jesus performing this miracle in John 2:1-11.

Miracles of Jesus' Healing, Creating, and Raising People from the Dead: Isaiah, Psalms, and 1 Peter

Muslims believe that Jesus performed miracles. According to Qur'an 3:49, as stated above, Jesus did four great miracles. However, sadly, when Muslims read this verse, they do not comprehend what Allah said, assuming that Allah is God, as Muslims claim. If they understood what Allah stated in this one verse, they would know for sure that Jesus is not some ordinary messenger or ordinary prophet or ordinary teacher but that He is God Almighty Himself.

We see in this one verse that Mohammed described Jesus with four attributes of Allah. Let us examine this verse again together to point to four names of Allah in the Qur'an. However, before we do this, we must emphasize that I do not believe that Allah is God or Jesus is 'Isā, but since Muslims believe that Allah is God and Jesus is 'Isā, the conclusion of this examination will prove to our dear Muslim friends that the Jesus of Mohammed, 'Isā, is Allah, meaning that Jesus is God within their line of reasoning.

In Qur'an 3:49, we see four attributes of Allah as Muslims claim. In Islam, Allah has ninety-nine names. One of these names is the Creator, and here we read that Jesus in the Qur'an said, "I create for you."

The word *create,* with its various tenses and number (singular or plural), is mentioned in the Qur'an 212 times. All of them speaking of Allah, except for two places, Qur'an 3:49 and 5:110. When we examine all these 212 verses, we see that no one can share this attribute with Allah.

Chapter 11: Battle Plans Revealed

In Qur'an 7:54, we read: [54]*Surely your lord is Allah who created the heavens and the earth in six days; then he sat on the throne. He covers the night [with] the day, he pursues it swiftly, and the sun and the moon and the stars are subservient by his command.* **Is it not to him the creation and the commands?** *Tabārka* (blessed) *Allah, the lord of the worlds.* Notice here that creation only belongs to Allah.

What about Qur'an 7:191? [191]*Do they partner who cannot create anything, and they are created?* Notice that Allah here rejected the infidels' action of partnering with him those who do not create; but Jesus, according to the Qur'an, creates.

How about one more verse? In Qur'an 16:17: [17]*Is he who creates like he who does not create, do you not remember?* What a great question from Allah in the Qur'an because there is none like him or equal to him. No one else is able to create. Surprise, surprise…Jesus, son of Mary, is the only one who did create like Allah. Therefore, we must come to the conclusion that 'Isā (Jesus), son of Mary, is like Allah, and both of them are equal in creating. Notice, they both created from mud and both of them breathed life into their created creatures. Therefore, we must conclude that Jesus is God. However, Jesus, in the Bible, never created any bird out of mud. This is what was written in a Gnostic text which Christians have always rejected as a forgery, which Mohammed copied in error.

Another name for Allah in the Qur'an is the Healer. In this same passage we read that 'Isā (Jesus) said, "And I heal the blind and leper." Another name found in the Qur'an for Allah is the One Who Gives Life. The Qur'an also tells us that 'Isā said, "I raise the dead." One more name for Allah in this verse is the One Who Knows the Future, the One Who Knows the Unknown. Once again, we read that 'Isā said, "I inform you about what you eat and what you store in your houses." These are four characteristics of Allah that are given to 'Isā (Jesus), son of Mary, in this verse. I can go on and on and on about these four names attributed to Allah from the Qur'an which prove that Jesus is God according to the Qur'an itself! I am not making this up.

The sad thing about this entire story is that Muslims who have never read the Bible will use the statement *"by Allah's permission"* in Qur'an 3:49 to say that this does not make Jesus God but God just allowed Him to perform these miracles. Well, I am sorry, because even if you accept this excuse, claiming that the statement *"by Allah's permission"* is the answer for this problem, it does not solve the problem.

First of all, Allah will not share his attributes with any mortal, not with a human and not with an angel. So when we see 'Isā in the Qur'an create or heal or raise the dead, these are attributes which belong to Allah and to Allah alone and would never be shared with any human, angel, or prophet.

The second important thing is, while we see *"by Allah's permission"* in the first three attributes of Allah, when we read the last part of this verse when 'Isā said, "And I inform you about what you eat and what you store in your houses," we do not read anywhere in the Qur'an that 'Isā said, *"by Allah's permission."* This made 'Isā equal to Allah for he and Allah both know the future and hidden information. This means that 'Isā had the power in His own strength, not by Allah's permission, to know the future. The only one who knows the future, Aalam al Guob (Arabic), The Knower of the Unknown, the Knower of the Unseen, is Allah himself.

From this passage alone, we see that the Qur'an affirms that Jesus is God. It doesn't matter if it was by Allah's permission or not, for if God is God, He will not allow anyone to take part in His attributes or to share His glory in creating or raising the dead. This was Jesus, as we read in the Gospel, performing these miracles in His own strength.

We do not read in the Bible that every time Jesus performed miracles that He performed them by Allah's permission. Yes, He did not do anything against the Father's will, but at the same time, He did not "get God's permission" to do everything.

Sadly, our dear Muslim friends do not know that the disciples of Jesus were able to perform even greater miracles than the ones performed by Jesus Himself. Notice that they **did not do it by Allah's will but by the power of Jesus' name.**

Now, let us go back to the Bible to read more about the fulfillment of prophecies about the Suffering Messiah, the Savior of the world, as He performed many more miracles during His three years of ministry.

We read of the miracle Jesus performed in Mark 8:22-26 when He healed the blind man's eyes. Only the Creator of the eye can heal the eye. Jesus touched this blind man, and then he could see. Just like Isaiah had said, the coming Messiah would give sight to the blind, and He did on more than one occasion.

Remember, Jesus is the One who created man in the beginning. John wrote in John 1:3: **All things were made through Him, and without Him nothing was made that was made.** He is the One who created man's eyes. He is the One who created man's ears and tongues. He is the One who is able to fix all things that needed to be fixed in the bodies of people. Jesus healed the lepers as recorded in Luke 17:11-19. Jesus raised many from the dead. As the Creator of nature, He has power over all nature, including disease and death.

An example of Jesus raising the dead is found in Luke 7:11-18. Jesus was traveling, along with some of His disciples, to the city of Nain. As He neared the city, the only son of a widow had died and was being carried out of the city to be buried. The Lord saw the mother of this son and had compassion on her. Then Jesus touched the coffin and told the man to arise. That is exactly what happened. The man who was dead then sat up and spoke.

What was the reaction of the people who had accompanied the woman? In verse 16, we read that fear came upon the crowd and that they glorified God and said: **"A great prophet has risen up among us"; and, "God has visited His people."** Yes, indeed, it was not just a great prophet but God Himself visiting His people.

Another account of Jesus raising the dead is found in John 11:1-16. This is the account of Jesus bringing Lazarus back to life. Lazarus and his two sisters, Mary and Martha, lived in Bethany and were dear friends whom Jesus loved. When Jesus heard that Lazarus was ill, He chose to delay two more days before traveling to Bethany. Jesus told His disciples in verse 11: **"Our friend Lazarus sleeps, but I go that I may wake him up."** The disciples replied in verse 12: **"Lord, if he sleeps he will get well."** Jesus knew what the disciples did not know. He was speaking of the death of

Lazarus and not that Lazarus was just sleeping as the disciples thought. So Jesus plainly told them that Lazarus was dead.

When Jesus and the disciples arrived in Bethany to comfort Mary and Martha, Lazarus had already been dead in the tomb for four days. As soon as Martha heard that Jesus was there, she met Him and said to Jesus that Lazarus would not have died if He had been there. However, Jesus told her that her brother would rise again. In verses 24-26, we read: [24]**Martha said to Him, "I know that he will rise again in the resurrection at the last day."** [25]**Jesus said to her, "I am the resurrection and the life. He who believes in Me, though he may die, he shall live.** [26]**And whoever lives and believes in Me shall never die."**

What a bold statement our Lord and Savior Jesus Christ made. This has never been claimed by any man or prophet before. Because Jesus is God, He can proclaim this statement. Then we read that Jesus went to the tomb, and in the shortest verse in the Bible, verse 35, we read: **"Jesus wept."**

It is amazing that Muslims will look at a verse like this and ask, "How can Jesus be God? If Jesus is God would He weep like a woman?" Yes, indeed. Jesus wept because He loved Lazarus, and all the people who saw Jesus weeping knew how much Jesus loved him. Some have offered that perhaps Jesus wept because Lazarus was a picture of the tragedy that sin had brought upon His creation. Sin leads to death, and Lazarus in the tomb was yet another example of the horrible legacy of sin and death in the world. Or perhaps Jesus wept because of the unbelief of many in the crowd. Or perhaps because He knew that soon some of these same people who will witness Him raising the dead will be calling out for Him to be crucified. In any case, the Lord loved Lazarus, and we know that His heart was broken for the pain and suffering that the family was going through.

Then some of the people in the crowd questioned that if Jesus could heal the blind, could He not have kept Lazarus from dying? In verse 38, Jesus told them to remove the stone from the tomb. Martha reminded Jesus that Lazarus had been dead for four days and by now there would be such a stench from the decomposing body. Then Jesus said to her in verse 40: **"Did I not say to you that if you would believe you would see the glory of God?"** When they took the stone away, Jesus looked up and thanked

God for hearing Him and for God always hearing Him. He said this so that the people would believe that God had sent Him. After Jesus said this, in verse 43, He cried out loudly and said: **"Lazarus, come forth!"** Then Lazarus came out of the tomb still bound in grave clothes, and Jesus told the people to unwrap him. Lazarus returned to life!

Now, what was the reaction of the people when they saw all this? The Bible states in verse 45 that many of the Jewish people, who had come to be with Mary and Martha and saw Lazarus raised from the dead, then believed in Jesus.

Prophecies on the Nation of Israel Rejecting Jesus and Gentiles Believing in Jesus: Isaiah and 1 Peter

Jesus performed many great miracles, but the greatest miracle was yet to come. Now, did all the Jews believe in Jesus as they saw this great miracle of raising Lazarus? The normal assumption would be yes. They had seen Him make the blind to see and the lame to walk, open the ears of the deaf, and raise people from the dead. However, if the entire nation of Israel believed in Jesus, that would mean we would have a bigger problem: the Old Testament prophecies would then not be fulfilled. When we read the Old Testament prophecies given by Isaiah throughout his book, we see that the Gentiles will believe in the coming Messiah, Jesus Christ, while many of His own people, the Jews, would reject Him.

We read in Isaiah 8:14: **He will be as a sanctuary, but a stone of stumbling and a rock of offense to both the houses of Israel, as a trap and a snare to the inhabitants of Jerusalem.**

Also, we read in Isaiah 28:16: **Therefore thus says the Lord God: "Behold, I lay in Zion a stone for a foundation, a tried stone, a precious cornerstone, a sure foundation; whoever believes will not act hastily."**

Another prophecy is given in Isaiah 49:6: **Indeed He says, "It is too small a thing that You should be My Servant to raise up the tribes of Jacob, and to restore the preserved ones of Israel; I will also give You as a light to the Gentiles, that You should be My salvation to the ends of the earth."**

Here we see that Christ will be the Light, not only for Israel, but also for the Gentile people, those who have no God. Now they will have Christ to be the Light and lead them to believe in the God of Israel. This changed the body of believers from just the land of Israel to the entire world as we see today, two thousand years later. Now there are Christians all over the world. The prophecies of Isaiah are fulfilled. The Gentiles have believed in Him.

Isaiah also prophesied in Isaiah 50:6: **I gave My back to those who struck Me, and My cheeks to those who plucked out the beard; I did not hide My face from shame and spitting.**

This is a clear and literal prophecy which we will address in more detail as we study what the Scripture declared concerning the cross and the suffering of our Lord and Savior Jesus Christ. However, here we see a clear verse in which Isaiah prophesied that the Messiah would be rejected by His own people. That is exactly what happened.

Finally, we read in Isaiah 60:3: **The Gentiles shall come to your light, and kings to the brightness of your rising**.

I would like to share a couple of prophecies written by King David one thousand years before the coming of our Lord and Savior in the flesh. These passages declare that Jesus will be rejected by His own people.

In Isaiah 53, we have an entire chapter dedicated to the coming Messiah who would also die for the sins of the world. In verses 2 and 3 we read of His rejection by the Jews: [2]**He has no form or comeliness; and when we see Him, there is no beauty that we should desire Him.** [3]**He is despised and rejected by men, a Man of sorrows and acquainted with grief. And we hid, as it were, our faces from Him; He was despised, and we did not esteem Him.**

We read in Psalm 22:7-8: [7]**All those who see Me ridicule Me; they shoot out the lip, they shake the head, saying,** [8]**"He trusted in the Lord, let Him rescue Him; let Him deliver Him, since He delights in Him!"**

In this passage we see a prophecy by David saying that not only would our Lord be rejected, but He would also be mocked.

Also, David wrote in Psalm 118:22: **This stone which the builders rejected has become the chief cornerstone.**

Yes, indeed, there are many prophecies in the Bible that tell us that God's Chosen People, the Jews, rejected Christ who is the Cornerstone, who is our God who came in the flesh. Thank God, for the news we find in prophecy, that we, the Gentiles, will believe in Him.

Let us look at the fulfillment of these prophecies. We read in 1 Peter 2:7-8: **⁷Therefore, to you who believe, He is precious; but to those who are disobedient, "the stone which the builders rejected has become the chief cornerstone," ⁸and "A stone of stumbling and a rock of offense."**

Prophecies of the Last Week of Jesus on Earth: Zechariah 9, Psalm 41, Matthew 21, Luke 19

Let us now look at the last week of the life of our Lord and Savior Jesus Christ here on earth. This proves to our Muslim friends that the Christian faith is not something newly fabricated in the New Testament, but rather, it is the fulfillment of prophecies found in the older writings of the Old Testament.

Jesus entered Jerusalem just five days before He was nailed to the cross. The Bible describes this event written by Prophet Zechariah hundreds of years earlier in Zechariah 9:9: **"Rejoice greatly, O daughter of Zion! shout, O daughter of Jerusalem! behold, your King is coming to you; He is just and having salvation, lowly and riding on a donkey, a colt, the foal of a donkey."**

This is perfectly fulfilled in the Scripture. Jesus did not enter Jerusalem riding on a camel or a horse or even walking on foot, as was His usual method of travel. Our Lord, Jesus Christ, came into Jerusalem riding a donkey as we read in Matthew 21 beginning in verse 1. As they neared Jerusalem, Jesus sent two of His disciples to go to the village, and there they would find a donkey with her colt.

Why did Jesus need these donkeys? These were the donkeys needed to fulfill the prophecy written by Prophet Zechariah in the Old Testament. As we read in Matthew 21:4-5: **⁴All this was done that it might be fulfilled** which was spoken by the prophet, saying: ⁵"Tell the daughter of Zion, 'behold, your King is coming to you, lowly, and sitting on a donkey, a colt, the foal of a donkey.'"

We know that this is exactly what happened. When the disciples brought Jesus the donkey and colt, they laid their clothes on the donkey and colt for Jesus to sit upon. The multitude of people also laid their clothes or cut branches on the road in front of Jesus. Then the multitude of people around Jesus cried out in verse 9 shouting: **"Hosanna to the Son of David! 'Blessed is He who comes in the name of the Lord!' Hosanna in the highest!"**

We read about this same account in Luke 19:32-37. When we read this account of Jesus entering the city of Jerusalem and of the whole city shouting and rejoicing about receiving their king, how can this end in the cross? Surely this will end in Jesus becoming their King!

Reading up to this point in the life of our Lord and Savior, it must seem that He will rule over Israel. He will be the King who will free the Jewish people and reunite the nation. He is the Son of David who will bring liberty and freedom for the Jewish nation. However, that is not the end of the story. We have another prophecy in the Bible which teaches that Jesus will be betrayed.

This is what was written by King David a thousand years before Jesus entered Jerusalem in Psalm 41:9: **Even my own familiar friend in whom I trusted, who ate my bread, has lifted up his heel against me.**

We see the fulfillment of this prophecy in Matthew 26:47-50. Judas Iscariot, one of the twelve disciples, who ate the Passover bread with Jesus in the Upper Room, led a large armed group of men sent by the chief priests and elders, to turn Jesus over to the Jewish authorities. The sign with which he betrayed Jesus was with a kiss. When Judas greeted and kissed Jesus, Jesus said in verse 50: **"Friend, why have you come?"** Then the men with Judas arrested Jesus.

I believe when Jesus called Judas *friend* here, He was letting us know that this is the fulfillment of the prophecy of King David. Judas had lived with Jesus and the other disciples for three and a half years. He was very familiar with Jesus, and he became the friend who betrayed Jesus so the prophecy would be fulfilled.

Judas had spoken earlier to the chief priests and asked them how much money they would give him to betray Jesus. The price of thirty pieces of silver was offered, which he accepted. Do you think this was a coincidence or was it the incredible fulfillment of yet another prophecy given hundreds of years earlier that the Messiah would be sold for thirty pieces of silver?

According to the Old Testament prophecy found in Zechariah 11:12: **Then I said to them, "If it is agreeable to you, give me my wages; and if not, refrain." So they weighed out for my wages thirty pieces of silver.** Did you pay attention to what the Bible stated? Zechariah wrote the exact amount that would be given, not twenty-five pieces or forty pieces of silver but exactly thirty pieces. If they would have given Judas twenty-nine or thirty-one, then Jesus would not have been the prophesied Messiah. It is interesting to note that thirty pieces of silver was also the price for purchasing or redeeming a slave, at the time of Jesus.

We read the fulfillment of this prophecy in the New Testament in Matthew 26:14-16: [14]**Then one of the twelve, called Judas Iscariot, went to the chief priests** [15]**and said, "What are you willing to give me if I deliver Him to you?" And they counted out to him thirty pieces of silver.** [16]**So from that time he sought opportunity to betray Him.**

Now, we ask one more detailed question. What will Judas do with this thirty pieces of silver? Will he buy some goods or a house? What will happen to this money? It will be thrown onto the floor. We read this in the prophecy given in Zechariah 11:13: **And the Lord said to me, "Throw it to the potter" – that princely price they set on me. So I took the thirty pieces of silver and threw them into the house of the Lord for the potter.** This was the prophecy that the money would be thrown into the house of the Lord.

Let us see if this prophecy was fulfilled in the New Testament. According to Matthew chapter 27, the chief priests and elders bound Jesus and then took Him to Pontius Pilate who was the Roman governor. When Judas saw that Jesus had been condemned, he was sorry for what he had done. He took the thirty pieces of silver back to the chief priests and elders, telling them in verse 4 that he had **"sinned by betraying innocent blood."**

In verse 5 we read: **Then he threw down the pieces of silver in the temple and departed, and went and hanged himself.** Judas did not return the money to their hands, and he did not put the money in the box of the temple treasury. He threw the money down on the temple floor. This was the exact fulfillment of the Old Testament prophecy given by Zechariah.

So, will the priests and Jewish people just leave the silver on the floor, or will they collect the silver off the floor to pay some temple expense? No. We have the exact prophecy concerning what they did with this thirty pieces of silver in the last part of Zechariah 11:13 which stated that this money would go to the potter.

The fulfillment of this is found in Matthew 27:6-10. We read in verses 6-8: **⁶But the chief priests took the silver pieces and said, "It is not lawful to put them into the treasury, because they are the price of blood." ⁷And they consulted together and bought with them the potter's field, to bury strangers in. ⁸Therefore that field has been called the Field of Blood to this day.** This fulfilled Zechariah's prophecy.

What a great line of prophecies we see here given by Prophet Zechariah in the Old Testament and fulfilled in the New Testament. The Bible revealed to us that Jesus would be betrayed by one of His close friends. That is exactly what happened. Jesus was betrayed by Judas, one of His disciples. The prophecy of the Old Testament told that Jesus would be sold for thirty pieces of silver. Again, that is exactly what happened. Judas betrayed Jesus for thirty pieces of silver. The prophecy stated that the thirty pieces of silver would be thrown onto the floor of the temple. That is what Judas did. The prophecy of Zechariah foretold that the thirty pieces of silver would be given to the potter. That is how the thirty pieces of silver were used. The silver was used to buy a potter's field called the Field of Blood. All of these prophecies were fulfilled in the last few hours of Jesus' life on earth.

Prophecies of the Death of Jesus Fulfilled

Let me remind you again that jihad in the Bible is a holy war in which people must die for their sin. It is a justifiable war to bring holiness and righteousness to people's lives here on earth. In the Old Testament, clean animals and clean birds were offered as substitute sacrifices for the sins of mankind. These Old Testament sacrifices were pictures of the coming True Sacrifice in the New Testament. God chose to perform jihad by taking the life of His own Son instead of demanding the lives of you and me. We are sinners and deserve to die and spend eternity in Hell, but God chose the Savior, Jesus (His Hebrew name is Yeshua which means Savior), to die on the cross so that jihad in the New Testament would be fulfilled. Once and for all, Christ went to the cross, and by His own blood, He entered the inner sanctuary of the Temple, Holy of Holies. Because of His precious blood, we no longer have to offer any sacrifices or die for our own sins. This is the message of the Christian faith: that those who believe in Him will not perish but will have everlasting life.

Muslims do not believe in any of these biblical facts, the deity of Christ, His death, and His resurrection. If you ask Muslims why, they will respond that these are lies that were added to the Bible by Paul and other early Christians. Sadly, Muslims have no idea that Christ and His salvation was the plan of God from the beginning. Since we have biblical manuscripts (such as the Dead Sea Scrolls) which date back to almost two centuries before the birth of Jesus, it is now impossible to claim that the Bible was "changed later by Paul." **We have biblical texts hundreds of years older than** Paul, and those documents speak of the God-man Messiah, who would be born in Bethlehem from a virgin, live a perfect life, then be betrayed and crucified as a sacrifice for our sins, and finally rise from the dead. Paul and other early Christians cannot change documents that were already written long before they were born!

However, when it comes to the idea of changing Scripture, I wonder how **many Muslims realize that the Qur'an was written over five hundred years AFTER the Bible was completed? We have manuscripts from the Bible that are almost a thousand years older than the Qur'an, and those ancient** documents teach about sacrifice, the deity of Christ, His sinless life, betrayal, crucifixion, and resurrection. Since Mohammed removed those fundamental truths from the segments he copied from the Bible, it is **Mohammed (not the Apostle Paul) who changed "truth." It is impossible for** Paul to have changed documents that existed before he was born, but it can be proven conclusively that Mohammed tried to edit and change what

Muslims know about the Bible in order to fit his own personal religious and political agenda. Muslims often say "the Bible has been corrupted." Yes, it has been…by Mohammed, in the Qur'an!

The truths of the Bible are not an "invention." God Himself spoke to mankind through hundreds of prophecies to conclusively show that the day would come when Christ would appear in the flesh and be born and die and rise again on the third day. All of these prophecies in the Old Testament show that the Christian faith is not the invention of some later people but the application and fulfillment to all the prophecies written throughout the years from the days of Adam and Eve until Christ came in the flesh.

With that settled, now we will look at the details of the last hours of Jesus' life of earth. He had been arrested and was dragged before various leaders and courts. So did Jesus defend Himself? It is only common sense for an innocent man to defend himself. If a person is accused of a crime, especially if that person was a righteous (innocent) person, he will defend himself. However, Jesus did not do that. Why? The answer is very simple. This was also to fulfill a prophecy found in Isaiah 53:7. Let me remind you that Isaiah wrote this prophecy nearly seven hundred years before Christ came in the flesh. We read: **"He was oppressed and He was afflicted, Yet He opened not His mouth; He was led as a lamb to the slaughter, And as a sheep before its shearers is silent, So He opened not His mouth."**

This is what will happen to the Messiah, He will be crucified and will be slaughtered as a lamb, a sacrificial lamb. That is exactly what happened to Jesus, the Lamb of God. He did not defend Himself or do anything to prevent His slaughter because He came to die for mankind. If Jesus, the God-man, would have defended Himself, then no army on earth could have crucified Him. He was born to die, and so He remained silent.

We find the fulfillment of this prophecy in Mathew 27:12: **And while He was being accused by the chief priests and elders, He answered nothing.** We see here that Pilate (who was overseeing the "trial") is quite frustrated. He does not know what to do to be able to set Jesus free. He knows that Jesus is innocent, but at the same time, Jesus is not defending Himself. In verse 13 Pilate asked Jesus if He heard all the things of which the people were accusing Him. We read in verse 14: **But He answered him not one** word, so that the governor marveled greatly. Jesus did not open His mouth, and by doing this, He fulfilled the prophecy in Isaiah written hundreds of years earlier.

Another prophecy written by the Prophet Isaiah is found in Isaiah 50:6 which predicts that Jesus would be beaten and spit upon: **"I gave My back to those who struck Me, And My cheeks to those who plucked out the beard; I did not hide My face from shame and spitting."**

In this passage, Isaiah is prophesying about the physical abuse that the Messiah would endure. We see the fulfillment of this in Matthew 26:67: **"Then they spat in His face and beat Him; and others struck Him with the palms of their hands."** He also wrote about what happened at the time of the crucifixion in 27:26-30. Here we see that Pilate released another prisoner. [26]…**and when he had scourged Jesus, he delivered Him to be crucified**. The soldiers then took Jesus, stripped him, put a scarlet robe on him, set a crown of thorns on his head, placed a staff in his hand, and knelt before Jesus to mock him by saying, "Hail, king of the Jews." [30]**Then they spat on Him, and took the reed and struck Him on the head.**

All of these horrific sufferings took place in the final hours of Jesus' life in order to fulfill the prophecies written in the Old Testament. All that was written by the Old Testament prophets concerning Jesus Christ have been fulfilled. Perfectly. When you consider the hundreds of different prophecies, there is only one human being in all of human history who could and did fulfill them ALL, and that was our Lord and Savior Jesus Christ.

Let's continue with another prophecy found in Isaiah 53:12. In this prophecy we see that Jesus will be crucified among transgressors (criminals/sinners): **"Therefore I will divide Him a portion with the great, And He shall divide the spoil with the strong, Because He poured out His soul unto death, And He was numbered with the transgressors, And He bore the sin of many, And made intercession for the transgressors."**

Jesus must be crucified among the transgressors, and the fulfillment of this prophecy is found in Matthew 27:38. **Then two robbers were crucified**

with Him, one on the right and another on the left. He was crucified between two thieves (criminals or transgressors).

It is very sad that our dear Muslim friends do not know what prophecy is or what the fulfillment of prophecy is. A prophecy is when God reveals what will happen in the future. Only God knows the future, so only God can speak prophetically through a prophet. Muslims do not realize that without prophecy, a man cannot properly be called a prophet. If they knew that, they would never believe in Mohammed as a "prophet," but they do believe that Mohammed is a prophet. However, if you ask Muslims to produce any evidence or proof that he was a prophet and ask them to share one of Mohammed's prophecies, they cannot produce any evidence for their belief. They will look at you as if they do not understand your question. As I just stated, for without prophecy, a man cannot be a prophet. If Mohammed is a prophet, then please tell us even one of his prophecies.

I remember when I was speaking in a university in Tennessee that a bunch of Muslim students came to attend my seminar. One of the students asked me that if Jesus is God, why did Jesus on the cross cry, "My God, My God, why hast thou forsaken me?"

I asked this student if he believed in the book of Psalms. He replied, "Yes, I believe in the Zabor, the book of David." (The Zabor is what Muslims call the Psalms in the Bible.) So I asked him if he had ever read Psalm 22. He did not even know that there are chapters in the book of Psalms because Muslims are only taught that David wrote the Zabor, the book of Psalms. Few have ever read the Psalms. They do not know what is in it because Mohammed only mentioned one verse out of the entire 150 chapters in the book of Psalms. The verse is found in Qur'an 21:105: [105]*And indeed, we wrote in the Psalms after the reminder: "Surely my good servant will inherit the earth."* That is all that Muslims know about Psalms.

I asked another student nearby to open to Psalm 22. In a few minutes, the student read the entire chapter. There we saw the cross, and there we saw the crucifixion. I explained to the Muslim student that when Jesus was on the cross crying, **"My God, my God, why hast thou forsaken me,"** it was not because Jesus was seeking God to take Him off the cross. He was actually leading all the Jews standing under the cross to Psalm 22 to let

Chapter 11: Battle Plans Revealed

them know that what was written in this Psalm has been fulfilled. One of the great verses in Psalm 22 is verse 16. It is also written in Zechariah 12:10. These verses state that Jesus would be crucified, and it details that His hands and His feet would be pierced!

This prophecy is one of the most amazing prophecies in the Bible. Why? Well, at the time of David's writing in Psalms, which was one thousand years before Christ, there were no crucifixions. Crucifixion wasn't even invented until hundreds of years AFTER Psalm 22 was written by David. The Jews did not know about crucifixion. David did not know what it meant for a man to have his hands and feet pierced. Then, under the inspiration of the Holy Spirit, David wrote of future events in great detail.

Imagine with me, if we are reading a book written by an author about four or five hundred years ago, and he wrote about a crime that had been committed by a person who killed someone during a robbery. Then he wrote that the court decreed that the criminal would be put to death in the electric chair. Notice that this story was written four or five hundred years before the discovery of electricity. Now, how did this author know about electricity? Do you think the people reading his book back then when it was written had any idea what electricity was or that without electricity there could not be an electric chair? His readers would have had no clue as to what this meant in the book. It meant nothing to them, and that is exactly how it was with David. He did not know what crucifixion entailed. Crucifixion was invented by the Greeks and modified by the Romans. That was three to four hundred years before Christ died on the cross for you and for me.

David wrote to us about crucifixion six hundred years earlier than the invention of the use of crucifixion in Psalm 22:16: **"For dogs have surrounded Me; The congregation of the wicked has enclosed Me, They pierced My hands and My feet;**

David was not writing this about himself in this verse. He died an honorable death in his own bed at the age of seventy-three. He was never pierced in his hands or his feet. His prophetic writing described the death of the Messiah in the far-off future. In this graphic poetry, the Messiah would be surrounded by dogs (a common term for vile, wicked people), and they will piece His hands and His feet. Jesus was indeed surrounded in his trials and tortured by wicked people, and then they pierced His hands and His feet.

We read in Zechariah12:10: **"And I will pour on the house of David and on the inhabitants of Jerusalem the Spirit of grace and supplication; then they will look on Me whom they pierced. Yes, they will mourn for Him as one mourns for his only son, and grieve for Him as one grieves for a firstborn."** The fulfillment of such prophecies is seen in the New Testament as we see Jesus nailed on the cross by His hands and His feet. He was also pierced in His side to fulfill this prophecy in Zechariah. We read the fulfillment of this prophecy in John 19:34: **But one of the soldiers pierced His side with a spear, and immediately blood and water came out.**

Recently I saw a video online about a doctor, an atheist who then became a Christian. He had been trying everything in a vain attempt to disprove Christianity, but he became a Christian because of this one verse. Blood and water came from the side of our Lord and Savior Jesus Christ on the cross which took place after Jesus gave up His spirit. This had been prophesied in Zechariah in chapter 12, verse 10. This doctor did research to disprove this. As a medical fact, he learned that if a person is dead and then his side is pierced, blood and water will come out separately. Because of this medical phenomenon and other evidences, this doctor became a Christian. He was an honest skeptic. He looked at the evidence, and the evidence (from fulfilled prophecy to the medical facts to the empty tomb) convinced him of the truth about Jesus Christ.

Many, many atheists have become Christians (such as C.S. Lewis, Lee Strobel, Josh McDowell) after trying to disprove Christianity. By seeking to deny it, they all discovered that it was true and then accepted Christ as their Lord and Savior. God is not afraid of our skepticism or questions. He has provided enough evidence in nature, in Scripture, and in history. If a person sincerely wants to know the truth, God has provided mountains of irrefutable evidence. The question is: are we willing to accept the truth?

A few years ago, a controversy arose over the movie, *The Passion*, made by Mel Gibson. The question was: Who killed Jesus? Was it the Jews, or was it the Romans? The fact is Jesus was not killed by either. He was killed by

Chapter 11: Battle Plans Revealed

God the Father. The reason God the Father had to kill his own Son, Jesus, was for you and me. It was God performing a holy war for mankind instead of all of us who have sinned being put to death. God chose His Son to die on the cross as a substitute for all of mankind's sin. His salvation is open freely to anyone to receive. It is for those Jews and Gentiles who accept Him and believe in Him, and they will have eternal life. Dear reader, have you looked at the evidence and accepted Him? He will save you. He died to save you.

What if Jesus had come to our world a few years earlier than the time He did come, would He have been crucified? If Jesus was killed by the Jews, would He have been crucified? No, the Jews typically killed by stoning. In that case, He would have broken bones. This fact would not fit with the prophecies, which clearly state that the Christ would not have any broken bones. (Psalms 34:20) If Jesus had been a full Roman citizen, He would have been killed by decapitation. However, **Jesus was a Jew under Rome's** domination at a precise point in history. The punishment for Him was crucifixion, exactly what all the prophets had said a thousand years before. The timing and manner of the fulfillment of the prophecies about the way Jesus would die had to fit with Old Testament prophecies.

In the cross we clearly see the love of God, for He chose to substitute His Son for the sins of all mankind. Remember, Muslims claim that the crucifixion did not happen. They claim that the death of Jesus and His resurrection were inventions by Paul or other Christians in the early days of Christianity. Through the Old Testament prophecies and their fulfillment in the New Testament, we clearly see that this account of Jesus was not some made-up story as Muslims claim. They are the ones making a false claim. Muslims cannot prove it. Non-Christian historians living near the time of Jesus tell us about the crucifixion of Jesus as well. The Old Testament Scriptures prophesied it, and secular historians have reported about it. Jesus came, Jesus died, Jesus was buried, and Jesus arose from the grave.

Christianity is not some invention or some new thought or belief about God. It is actually the fulfillment of the plan of God which was given to the world through the prophets throughout the Old Testament. Muslims believe in the Prophet David and in the Prophet Moses, but sadly, Muslims do not know what David and Moses wrote about the crucifixion and the death and resurrection of our Lord Jesus, which was prophesied over a thousand years before it actually happened.

The Old Testament Scriptures are clear: the Messiah must be crucified, and the only way Jesus would be crucified was to be judged by the Romans. If the Jews had the power to kill their own people at that time, He would have been put to death as a blasphemer because He claimed to be God. As I have already stated, the Jewish punishment of death was by stoning. We read that Jesus was found guilty of blasphemy in Matthew 26:65: **Then the high priest tore his clothes, saying, "He has spoken blasphemy! What further need do we have of witnesses? Look, now you have heard His blasphemy!"**

When Jesus came to this world, He came at the right time. When He died, He died in the right way. When we study Jewish history, we see that Judah lost its power to judge its own people around 11 A.D. After that time, the Romans assumed that power. So when Jesus was born, Judah still had the power to kill their own criminals; but at the time of the trial of Jesus, around 30 A.D., Israel did not have that power. Therefore, Jesus must be judged and executed by the Roman standard. At this time, the Romans conducted capital punishment for certain crimes by crucifixion. The timing of Jesus' coming was perfect, and the time of His death was perfect. This was another fulfillment of prophecy.

Another important prophecy given by David was written in Psalm 22:18 and could not be fulfilled if the Jews had the power to put Jesus to death. This prophecy concerned the casting of lots on the ground for the clothes of Jesus. When the Jews stoned someone, they did not remove the criminal's clothing. However, when the Romans crucified a criminal, they stripped the criminal naked. David wrote in this verse: **They divide My garments among them, and for My clothing they cast lots.**

Here is the fulfillment of this prophecy in John 19:23-24: [23]**Then the soldiers, when they had crucified Jesus, took His garments and made four parts, to each soldier a part, and also the tunic. Now the tunic was without seam, woven from the top in one piece.** [24]**They said therefore among themselves, "Let us not tear it, but cast lots for it, whose it shall**

Chapter 11: Battle Plans Revealed

be," that the Scripture might be fulfilled which says: "They divided My garments among them, And for My clothing they cast lots."

Therefore, the prophecy of David was fulfilled perfectly as Jesus was crucified and nailed naked upon the cross as the soldiers cast lots for his garment.

What about the date of the crucifixion? Could Jesus be crucified at just any time of the year? No, it must be at a specific time. A very specific time. A very specific day. Jesus must be crucified on the Passover night because Jesus is the true Lamb of God, He is the fulfillment of the Old Testament Passover. Earlier, when we studied sacrifices in the Old Testament, the last of the ten plagues brought upon the Egyptians was the destroyer passing over the land of Egypt to kill the firstborn.

God told the Hebrews to sacrifice a lamb and put the blood of the lamb on the door posts so that the destroyer would pass over their homes saving their firstborn children and their animals from the destroyer/death. Many of my Egyptian people died along with many of their animals that night. While the firstborn Egyptians and animals died, the Hebrews and their animals were delivered from death. On that night, Pharaoh let the Hebrews go. Moses and his people left Egypt. This was the Passover. The firstborn died, and the people were set free. What a beautiful picture of the salvation provided by our Lord and Savior Jesus Christ, the only begotten Son of God.

Since the Jews left Egypt, they have celebrated the Passover meal even until the time that Jesus went to the cross, which once again was the fulfillment of prophecy. It was exactly on that day of Passover that Jesus was crucified on the cross, because Christ is our Passover as we read in 1 Corinthians 5:7: **Therefore purge out the old leaven, that you may be a new lump, since you truly are unleavened. For indeed Christ, our Passover, was sacrificed for us.** What perfect timing!

Jesus fulfilled the prophecies written in Psalm 22 a thousand years before Jesus went to the cross. We encourage you to read all of Psalm 22. This chapter describes what will happen to the Suffering Messiah on the cross beginning in verse 1: **My God, My God, why have You forsaken Me?** We see verse 1 fulfilled in Matthew 27:46 as Jesus cried out: "**Eli, Eli,** lama sabachthani?" that is, "My God, My God, why have You forsaken Me?"

On the cross, Jesus became thirsty. We read in Matthew 27:34: **They gave Him sour wine mingled with gall to drink.** and in Matthew 27:48: **Immediately one of them ran and took a sponge, filled it with sour wine and put it on a reed, and offered it to Him to drink.** Why was He given sour wine? This was another Old Testament prophecy which Jesus fulfilled. This prophecy was written by David in Psalm 69:21: **They also gave me gall for my food, and for my thirst they gave me vinegar to drink.**

When we read the Old Testament, we can see Christ, the sacrificial Lamb of God that God Himself provided, even earlier than in the days of the Hebrews and the Passover night. We see this in the days of Abraham in Genesis 22. If you remember, Isaac asked his father Abraham about the lamb because he had only seen the wood, the knife, and the fire. In Genesis 22:8, Abraham answered his son saying that God will provide His lamb for the sacrifice.

God did provide Jesus Christ, His Lamb, as the sacrifice, not only as a substitute for Isaac but also for all mankind! John the Baptist said in John 1:29, as he pointed to Jesus: **"Behold! The Lamb of God who takes away the sin of the world!"** This is the sacrificial Lamb of God. He is the true Passover Lamb. He was crucified for all mankind. He was crucified for you and for me.

Through Jesus, both the justice of God and the love of God meet. For God's justice requires that all men be put to death because all men have sinned. Yet God's love requires Him to forgive. How can God forgive guilty men for their sin unless the sacrifice is offered? As it is written in the Scripture, without bloodshed there is no forgiveness of sin, and Jesus did shed His precious blood. Therefore, we can have forgiveness.

The Point of the Sword

Jesus' Death on the Cross: Psalms, Zechariah, Matthew, John

Let us look at what took place on the cross. According to the Scripture, they were not to break the bones of the Passover lamb to be sacrificed, and we know from Scripture that they did not break any of Jesus' bones. In Psalms 34:20, David said that not one of His bones will be broken. Someone may say that this verse was just a simple prophecy. As we read the description of the gospel message, as Jesus was on the cross, the soldiers were commanded to break the legs of the thieves to speed up the process of their death. Without the ability to push on the nail through their feet, crucifixion victims would quickly suffocate because they could not raise up to take a breath.

However, when they came to break Jesus' legs, they saw that He was already dead. Instead, they pierced His side with a spear. This is another prophecy fulfilled, as we read the prophecies written by David in Psalm 34:19-20: [19]**Many are the afflictions of the righteous, But the Lord delivers him out of them all.** [20]**He guards all his bones; Not one of them is broken**.

Not one bone can be broken. The lamb to be offered by the Jewish people as the Passover meal could not have any blemish or any broken bones. The Bible clearly states that it had to be a whole, healthy, spotless lamb. We read the fulfillment of this prophecy by the Lamb of God, Jesus, in John 19:33: **But when they came to Jesus and saw that He was already dead, they did not break His legs.**

As Jesus and the two thieves were upon the crosses, the Sabbath was drawing near. It was getting late. The soldiers needed to remove these bodies off of the crosses before the day ended. The only way to speed their deaths was to break their legs. The soldiers broke the legs of the two thieves, but when the soldiers came to Jesus, they saw that He was already dead and did not break His legs. This fulfilled the prophecy given by David one thousand years earlier: that they would not break any of His bones.

As I earlier stated, the soldiers instead pierced Jesus with a spear in His side. This action fulfilled another prophecy which predicted that He must be speared in His side, which is found in Zechariah 12:10: ...**then they will look on Me whom they pierced**... We read the fulfillment of this prophecy in John 19:34: **But one of the soldiers pierced His side with a spear, and immediately blood and water came out.** Why did the soldiers pierce Jesus in His side? It was simply to make sure He was dead before they removed His body from the cross.

When Jesus died, according to Matthew 27:50, He gave up His spirit. Now what happened to the body of Jesus? We know from Scripture that He was not a rich man. Jesus did not have a home or even a regular place to lay His head. He told Peter to catch a fish that had money in its mouth just to be able to pay their taxes. He did not even own a donkey to ride when He entered Jerusalem. So where would He be buried? Did you know that even the place where Jesus was to be buried was prophesied? God is a God of details.

The Holy War of the New Testament: Isaiah, Psalms, Matthew, Hebrews

The only "Holy War" which God practiced in the New Testament was the killing of His own Son for the sins of mankind. In the justice of God, all men must die because all men have sinned. In the love of God, Jesus was willing to die in our place and take our sins upon Himself. So where would He be buried? The prophecy of His burial is found in Isaiah 53:9: **And they made His grave with the wicked – But with the rich at His death, Because He had done no violence, Nor was any deceit in His mouth**.

Here we see that, according to Isaiah, the Messiah must be buried in a rich man's tomb. This prophecy was fulfilled in Matthew 27:57-60: [57]**Now when evening had come, there came a rich man from Arimathea, named Joseph, who himself had also become a disciple of Jesus.** [58]**This man went to Pilate and asked for the body of Jesus. Then Pilate commanded the body to be given to him.** [59]**When Joseph had taken the**

Chapter 12: The Point of the Sword

body, he wrapped it in a clean linen cloth, [60]and laid it in his new tomb which he had hewn out of the rock; and he rolled a large stone against the door of the tomb, and departed.

Will this be the end of Jesus and His ministry? Will His holy body stay in the tomb and decay and rot like every other dead person, or will He rise again? We read the prophecy in Psalm 16:7-10: [7]**I will bless the Lord who has given me counsel; My heart also instructs me in the night seasons. **[8]**I have set the Lord always before me; Because He is at my right hand I shall not be moved.** [9]**Therefore my heart is glad, and my glory rejoices; My flesh also will rest in hope.** [10]**For You will not leave my soul in Sheol, Not will You allow Your Holy One to see corruption.**

David was clearly telling us that his body will not experience the corruption of decay that always follows death. However, whose body is he talking about? David died and was buried, and the Jews know where he is buried. His body saw corruption and decayed. The tomb of David is well-known; however, the tomb of Jesus is empty. His body is not there for He rose on the third day.

This prophesy, written a thousand years before the coming of Christ in the flesh, was used by the Apostle Peter. In the first sermon given by him after Jesus' resurrection, Peter explained to the huge gathering of Jews that David was prophesying concerning Christ in that His body would not decay. We read Peter's sermon in Acts 2:31-36 in which Christ's soul did not remain in Hades and neither did His body decay, but that He was raised up. The disciples and others were witnesses of this, and Jesus now sits at the right hand of the Father. It was not David who ascended into the heavens but Jesus. David's body decayed, but not the body of Jesus. This was the fulfillment of David's prophecy; it is Jesus who sits at the right hand of God and that God made Jesus both Lord and Christ.

Another prophecy which foretold that Jesus would ascend into Heaven was prophesied in Psalm 68:18: **You have ascended on high, You have led captivity captive; You have received gifts among men, Even from the rebellious, That the Lord God might dwell there.**

This prophecy was fulfilled as we read in Acts 1:9: **Now when He had spoken these things, while they watched, He was taken up, and a cloud received Him out of their sight.**

Where is Jesus right now? He ascended on high. He is sitting on the right hand of the Father. We can read this prophecy in Psalm 110:1: **The Lord said to my Lord, "Sit at My right hand, Till I make Your enemies Your footstool."**

The Lord is telling the Lord. Who is the first Lord? Who is the second Lord? David is writing here about the Lord (God the Father) speaking to the Lord (God the Son) and telling the Son that He will have His enemies as His footstool.

We read the fulfillment of this prophecy in Hebrews 1:3: **Who being the brightness of His glory and the express image of His person, and upholding all things by the word of His power, when He had by Himself purged our sins, sat down at the right hand of the Majesty on high.**

Jesus is the Son of God who came and lived a perfect life on earth, died, was buried, resurrected, and then ascended to Heaven. We read the prophecy in the Old Testament, the prophecy of David, that Jesus is the Son of God in Psalm 2:7 where God said: **"I will declare the decree: The Lord has said to Me, 'You are My Son, Today I have begotten You.'"**

We also read about this prophecy in Isaiah 9:6: **For unto us a Child is born, Unto us a Son is given; And the government will be upon His shoulder. And His name will be called Wonderful, Counselor, Mighty God, Everlasting Father, Prince of Peace**.

God wants you to know that Jesus is the Son of God. He spoke of it many times in the Scriptures. Muslims often ask, "Where is it found in the Bible that Jesus says that He is the Son of God?" They ask this question because they think that we do not have the answer for this. Sadly, they ask this question because they do not know that the Bible, in both the Old and New Testaments, declares that Jesus is the Son of God dozens and dozens of times. As we have seen earlier at the baptism of Jesus by John the Baptist in Matthew 3, God the Father declared from heaven that Jesus is His beloved

Son and that the Father is well pleased with Him. One verse is enough to prove it, but there are many such verses in the Holy Bible.

Jesus Himself, as He left earth to go into heaven, spoke to His disciples and gave them the Great Commission in Matthew 28:18-19. Jesus commanded them to baptize the new believers in the name of the Father, the Son, and the Holy Spirit. Once again, we see the triune Godhead of Father, Son, and Holy Spirit. In the Old Testament as well, we read of the Father, the Son, and the Holy Spirit, for example, in Genesis 1:1-3. In verse 1 we learn of God the Father, Elohim. In verse 2 we learn of God, the Holy Spirit, who was hovering over the water. In verse 3 we learn about the Word of God, the Creator of all things, Jesus, the Son of God.

The Resurrection of Jesus Christ: Luke

After the resurrection, our Lord and our Savior gave His disciples understanding concerning His coming, His life, His death, and His resurrection. All of this had been prophesied in the Old Testament by Moses in the Torah, in the prophets, and by David in the Psalms. From beginning to end, the Old Testament reveals the truth about the coming Messiah, Savior, Redeemer, Substitute, and Lamb of God.

After His resurrection, we read of a fascinating discussion. Jesus appeared to two men while they were walking and talking on the road to Emmaus. He asked them what they were talking about. They began sharing all of the events surrounding the crucifixion of Jesus. Then Jesus told these two men in Luke 24:25: **"O foolish ones, and slow of heart to believe in all that the prophets have spoken!"** Notice that Jesus told them that His death, burial, and resurrection was what had been prophesied. Then Jesus continued in verses 26 and 27: **[26]Ought not the Christ to have suffered these things and to enter into His glory?" [27]And beginning at Moses and all the Prophets, He expounded to them in all the Scriptures the things concerning Himself.** As the Holy Spirit led Luke to write these truths, Jesus is referring here to what had been prophesied about Himself throughout the Old Testament written by Moses (the Law) and the prophets and David hundreds of years before the coming of Jesus Christ in the flesh. These prophecies have been thoroughly explained in this book.

I know that Muslims believe in the prophets. In the Qur'an, Allah instructed them to believe in the prophets and the books written before the Qur'an. Allah meant the "book of Moses," the "book of David," and the "book of Jesus." These are the books that Muslims are told to believe about the Old and New Testaments.

I know that some Muslims believe that there were one thousand prophets while others will say that there were ten thousand prophets. Others will disagree and say that there were hundreds of thousands of prophets. In Islam, there are plenty of different opinions on how many prophets there were in the Old Testament. However, if you ask them to name ten prophets from the Old Testament, sadly, even Muslim leaders and imams cannot come up with ten correct names of the prophets.

If you ask Muslims if they believe in the Prophet Moses, they will say yes. Then you need to ask a specific question, such as: "What do you know about Moses' writings and prophecies concerning the Messiah?" Then you will see that they cannot give an answer. They do not know what Moses said about the Messiah Jesus. They do not know what David said about the Messiah Jesus. This goes on and on with every other Old Testament prophet. Muslims do not know any of the prophecies of the prophets of the Old Testament regarding Jesus' birth, life, suffering, betrayal, piercing, death, resurrection, and ascension. In many ways, it is not their fault. Mohammed did not tell them the truth. Mohammed carefully selected what he wanted from the Old and New Testaments and then mixed it with his own ideas and agenda. He changed it; he corrupted it.

So you see, my Muslim friends, it is not just about words. You say you believe in these prophets. Then you need to know who the "prophet" was that you claim to believe and his sayings. You need to know what his prophecy was and the message of his prophecy. Then (and only then) can you say that you believe in Moses and the message of Moses or that you believe in David and the message of David. Anyone can claim to be a prophet. Words are cheap; words mean nothing by themselves. The claims of a prophet must be backed up and confirmed with evidence.

If you have never read what is written in the Bible about Moses and you only count on what is written in the Qur'an about him, then you are in deep

Chapter 12: The Point of the Sword

trouble because Mohammed did not give you any solid information about Moses. What is written about Moses in **the Qur'an is nothing but a foolish counterfeit of the true account of Moses in the Bible. Mohammed corrupted the story of Moses in the Qur'an, as well as the story of Noah, the story of Adam, the story of Jesus, and the rest of the stories in the Qur'an. Mohammed is the one who tried to change the Bible. The Qur'an came over five hundred years after the Bible, and through comparison it is easy to see which one was corrupted.** The early Christians (such as Paul) could not have changed manuscripts that were written hundreds of years before they were born. This is impossible. However, it is possible (and we can prove) that Mohammed changed the documents five hundred years AFTER they were written by selectively choosing what he wanted and then adding his own fabrications in the Qur'an.

Please read the Scripture. If you would come to know the prophecies of the prophets, who lived before the coming of Jesus in the flesh, from Moses to Malachi, you would know that the message of Christianity is true. Jesus is God's Son who died on the cross for our sins, was buried, and arose. However, you have chosen to believe in your (false) prophet Mohammed, who did not have a second witness or any miracles to prove that he is a prophet. His sinful life was a great evidence that he could not be a prophet. **You believe in the lies he told you in the Qur'an concerning the prophets** and the books of the prophets. Read what the prophets actually said, not just what someone else said about them over a thousand years later!

When you actually read the Bible and compare the accounts of the Bible to **the stories of the Qur'an, you will see that you have been deceived with many lies.** I can prove this with just one verse from the Qur'an. A famous verse. In a moment, we will examine **Qur'an 4:157. In this one verse, a Muslim is forced to denounce all the truth declared by the prophets** throughout the entire Old Testament (over three hundred prophecies) and is forced to ignore them by believing in this one ambiguous verse in the Qur'an written by a man who lived five hundred years after Jesus' death, burial, and resurrection. Is that reasonable? One verse is worth more than three hundred other verses?

My dear friend, please answer this one question: Have you ever personally investigated Mohammed to determine if he was a true prophet or if the writings of the Qur'an are true? How do you know that a man without any prophecy is a "prophet"? What evidence is there that he spoke for God? Many people down through time have claimed to be prophets for God, such as Joseph Smith (Mormonism). Why don't you believe in him or any of the others?

We have overwhelming evidence from history and fulfilled prophecy that validate that the writings of the Old and New Testaments are completely true. So where is Mohammed's evidence? Where is the validation? The world has been waiting for over 1,400 years. Verifying evidence has yet to emerge. How much longer should we wait for God to validate someone who claims to speak for Him?

Let's be honest. We know that people can be deceitful, and the world is filled with those who would seek to take advantage of others. It doesn't matter if they are from the deserts of the Middle East or the mountains of Tibet or the plains of America. Therefore, the Lord gave us wisdom and discernment to carefully consider and test people and their motives as well as their truthfulness. God would have us to be wise and extremely careful when it comes to trusting people who claim to speak for Him. Just because someone claims to be a prophet (and there have been many false prophets over the last few thousand years), this does not mean that we should take their word for it. The Old and New Testaments command us to test and prove anyone who claims to speak for God. When it comes to Mohammed, we only have his word. That's all. No evidence, no prophecies, and no miracles. Unfortunately, his word also contradicts what all of the other prophets who came before him (who have been proven to be true with fulfilled prophecies) have said. Jesus said that if the blind follows the blind, they will both fall into the ditch. Be careful who you follow.

Now, as I promised, let us examine the one verse that forces Muslims to deny both the entire Old Testament and the New Testament of the Bible. Allah said in Qur'an 4:157: *And their saying, "Surely we killed the Christ 'Isā, son of Mary, the messenger of Allah." And they did not kill him, and they did not crucify him; but it was made to appear to them, and surely those who disagree about him are in doubt of him. They do not have any knowledge of him except following the conjecture, and they did not kill him*

Chapter 12: The Point of the Sword

for certain. Then Mohammed covered this verse with verse 158: *Yet Allah raised him up to himself. And Allah was dear, wise.*

It is amazing that **Muslims blindly believe Mohammed's lies in which he told them that 'Isā (he meant Jesus) did not die on the cross and that he was never crucified.** Mohammed used this one ambiguous verse, a single verse in which Allah did not bother to tell us how it was made to appear to the Jews that 'Isā was the one who was nailed on the cross but that it was not him. Instead, it was someone who looked like him. This is a very strange passage. It makes God out to be a deceiver (which Allah admits to doing in several verses).

When you read the interpretation of Muslim scholars concerning this confusing and bizarre verse, they will give you contradicting stories to help Muslims understand that it was *not* Jesus who died on the cross but merely someone who *looked like* Him. It is amazing that Muslims must believe that Allah deceived all Christians (in the six hundred years between Christ and Mohammed) to believe in a lie that it was merely someone who looked like Jesus, who died on the cross, and who was not Jesus Himself!

Once again, here is the message of Christianity. God performed **"holy war"** in the New Testament by causing Jesus to sacrificially die on the cross for our sins. We are all sinners, but you and I do not have to die for our sins. All we need to do is to repent and believe on the substitute Sacrifice, the Lamb of God, Jesus Christ. Then we can be forgiven and set free from the punishment of our sins. No more killing. No more holy war because the Holy One died for the sins of the world, once forever and once for all.

Holy war is over. Death and killing is over. God's justice has been accomplished when He put His Son, Jesus Christ, on the cross for the sin of mankind because the wages of sin is death. The gift of God is eternal life. Notice...it is a gift. It is *free*. Why? Because Jesus paid for it. Justice has been served when Jesus took the place of all humanity on the cross. He died so that all may be saved. All those who will trust in Him and accept His **substitutionary death will have eternal life. That is God's absolute** promise, and God cannot lie. That is why God no longer requires any man to kill another man to provide justice for sin.

So, someone may ask: "What about the people who commit murder? Shouldn't they be put to death?" That is a great question, and God has already answered it. The death of Christ on the cross does not abrogate (replace) His own laws of the Bible concerning the punishment for murder. The law was written in the Ten Commandments in Exodus 20:13: **You shall not murder.** So what if a man commits murder? Will he be punished? The answer can be found in Genesis 9:6: **Whoever sheds man's blood, by man his blood shall be shed; for in the image of God He made man.** Also, in Leviticus 24:17 we read: **Whoever kills any man shall surely be put to death.** A similar message can be found in Exodus 21:12: **He who strikes a man so that he dies shall surely be put to death.**

Also, in Numbers 35:30-31, in which we see the importance of the role of witnesses, the Scripture states: **³⁰Whoever kills a person, the murderer shall be put to death on the testimony of witnesses; but one witness is not sufficient testimony against a person for the death penalty. ³¹Moreover you shall take no ransom for the life of a murderer who is guilty of death, but he shall surely be put to death.** We as Christians do not believe in personal revenge as written in Romans 12:19: **Beloved, do not avenge yourselves, but rather give place to wrath; for it is written, "Vengeance is Mine, I will repay," says the Lord.**

How about what is written in Matthew 5:21, when Jesus said: **"You have heard that it was said to those of old, 'You shall not murder, and whoever murders will be in danger of the judgment.'"** The judgment of murder is death, but it is not to be carried out by the person who lost a loved one or by any member of his family. It will be carried out by the government. It is called Capital Punishment, not Personal Revenge. For in that case, it will be justice done according to the laws of the land, and we can read this clearly as it is written in Romans 13:1-2.

For we learn from this important passage that every soul must live in submission to those who have been put in authority, for every power is given to those who are in authority, which is given ultimately by God. This does not mean that God condones the actions of every leader or government. Rather that God has established human government to keep law and order. Even bad government in a world of sinners is better than no government. The wicked hearts of people need to be kept in check by human government and human justice.

So here is the conclusion, I personally will not take revenge on a person who commits a murder on my loved one. I will forgive him. However, if the law of the land hands down the sentence of capital punishment, then I must submit to the laws of the land.

As it used to be in the days of the Old Testament, God killed men by all kinds of circumstances such as floods, plagues, poison, fire, sword, or whatever means that He chose to punish people for their sin. When both Jews and Gentiles sinned, God punished them both by death.

As for the New Testament, the death of Jesus Christ was the only "holy war" performed which was accomplished by God Himself. As we have seen above, the death of Christ was the fulfillment of hundreds of prophecies prophesied by many of the prophets in the Old Testament. The suffering Messiah must come in flesh through the line of David. He must be born of a virgin in Bethlehem. He must live a sinless life. He must minister to the Jewish people during the time of the temple. He must be rejected. He must be betrayed. He must be tried and found guilty even though there was no sin in Him. He must be put to death on the cross. He must be crucified among **criminals. He must be pierced. He must be buried in a rich man's tomb. He** must rise on the third day. He must be ascended on high, and He will come back to judge the living and the dead. His coming back to judge the living and the dead is one of the few prophecies concerning Jesus that is still awaiting fulfillment. However, this prophecy could be fulfilled at any time. Come, Lord Jesus, come.

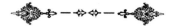

Clearing The Fog of War

Muslims Claim Christianity Was Spread by the Sword in Matthew 10:34

However, Muslims will immediately claim that this is not true. They will say that holy war is not over in the Bible and Christianity is not a loving religion. They claim there are many verses in the Bible which teach that Christianity was spread by the sword, and then they always point to the Crusades (which were a thousand years AFTER the life, death, and resurrection of Jesus). They will ask, "Do you know how many Muslims were killed by the hands of the Christians in their barbaric attacks on innocent Muslim men, women, and children?"

First, let us look at the verses in the New Testament where Muslims claim that Christians are allowed to fight and that Jesus commanded His disciples to take up the sword and fight. Jesus said that He did not come to the world to give peace but to bring a sword (Matthew 10:34). Muslims have twisted these words of Jesus to mean that Jesus Himself will slaughter those who will not believe in Him. This is not a joke. Sadly, there are a few verses in the Bible that Muslims will take and twist to teach such lies. Mohammed only used fragments of the Scripture and mixed it with his own ideas, and modern Muslim scholars do the same.

Throughout my writings, I have used many quotes from the Qur'an. I never attempt to interpret any of the verses of the Qur'an. I believe that the only ones who can interpret the Qur'an correctly are the Muslim scholars such as Ibn Kathir, Al Qurtobi, Al Tabari, Al Jalalain, and so on. I will not attempt to interpret the Qur'an. I only read the verses of the Qur'an and only use the interpretations of Muslim scholars. This is fair, don't you think?

This is the same advice which I give to Muslims. Do not interpret the Bible by yourself. If you do not know how to interpret your own Qur'an, then how can you interpret the Bible? If you desire to understand the true interpretation, the true meaning of the words of God, and the words of Jesus

Chapter 13: Clearing the Fog of War

in the New Testament, you need to go to Christian scholars as I went to Muslim scholars when I read the verses of the Qur'an to be able to understand the Qur'an. You need to go to Christian scholars and read their interpretations of the Bible. Then you can come to the true understanding of what is written in the Bible and what Jesus meant by what He said. Let me assure you, the majority of the Bible requires very little interpretation. God speaks clearly as He shares history, poetry, wisdom, and prophecy. However, there are passages that do require more thoughtful investigation and interpretation. Jesus often spoke in parables, and then He would explain the interpretation of those parables to His disciples privately.

In the many hundreds of times that I have spoken, at length, with Muslims from all over the world, they typically read the interpretations of the Bible given by some ignorant, foolish Muslim who seeks to twist the Scripture by adding or removing words in the verses and adding or removing periods to end a sentence of the Bible however they wish. That is how they come up with the false understanding of what Jesus said about the sword and what the New Testament teaches about war and death. However, is this right and fair? No.

Once again, before reading these verses, which Muslims often misunderstand, I want to restate that holy war, jihad, in the New Testament ended when Jesus Christ gave up His spirit on the cross after dying to pay the penalty for our sins. From this point on, there is no more killing, no more holy war in the New Testament.

Hermeneutics. This is a fancy word which means the science of interpreting the Bible. When we read a passage in the Bible, we need to consider the setting, the culture, the people receiving the message, what the author meant by what he said in the text, how the people understood the message, and how the people practiced the message. Then we bring the same teaching of the same message to our daily lives, and we practice these same verses in the same manner in which the earlier recipients understood and practiced the message.

Now, it is important to point out that not every passage or verse contains something for us to obey or practice. Much of the Bible is a faithful historical record. We can read about the Flood or Creation or the birth of

Jesus, and there is nothing to do or obey in those passages. However, we still can learn from them. We can learn about the nature of God or the wickedness of man or how to handle various situations or temptations. Not every verse can be "obeyed" or "practiced."

It is also important to point out that not every verse applies to every person. There are some passages (primarily in the Old Testament) that were only given to Jews for a specific reason or time period, for example, the rules and regulations of the gathering of the daily manna. Those rules no longer apply today because the manna ceased the moment the Jews entered the Promised Land. Some passages only apply to those who have already been saved by Jesus, and some passages are warnings only to those who are still undecided and unsaved. You cannot just pop the Bible open and point randomly at a verse and say, "This is what God wants me to do." That is nonsense.

Some of the Bible wasn't written to you, but that doesn't mean that we can't learn something from all of it. If I read a letter from President George Washington to Benjamin Franklin, I might be able to learn about how the Founding Fathers felt about the events happening at America's birth, but that letter was not written TO me. Nevertheless, I can still learn from it. Sadly, there is so much error and false teaching in churches today because they do not **"rightly divide the word of truth"** as Paul encouraged us to do in 2 Timothy 2:15. They take every verse as if it contains something for us to obey today. As Christians, we do not bring sacrifices to a temple for our sins because those passages about animal sacrifices ended when Christ offered Himself, once for all, to pay for our sins. Just imagine someone who has rejected Jesus Christ, and they read the verse in Revelation in which God promises to **"wipe away every tear from their eyes"** in Heaven. This verse is a blessed promise to the child of God, but it was not written to a sinner who has rejected Christ. They will be judged for their sins with weeping and gnashing of teeth.

Remember, all of the Bible was written **FOR** you, but not all of the Bible was written **TO** you.

So, when we read the Bible, we must understand WHO God is speaking to and WHAT is the circumstance. Ask yourself if this passage is written to

Chapter 13: Clearing the Fog of War

the Jews, to Gentiles, to Christians, or to the lost? We need to understand the context of the passage in order to get the proper understanding. In other words, when Jesus taught, what did Jesus mean by what He said and who was He talking to or about? How did the disciples understand His teachings? What was the cultural setting at the time when Jesus taught His message? How did the disciples practice the teachings of Jesus? Today, if it is a passage giving us an example to follow or a command to obey, then we must practice the verses in **the same manner. This isn't new.** This is how we live our lives and interact with each other every day. We speak to each other, and we have to know the context, the person speaking, and the situation. Then we can understand one another. The same is true in studying the Scriptures.

Let us investigate verses in which Muslims claim that Jesus taught His disciples to perform the holy war of killing the infidels. First, we read in Matthew 10:34: **"Do not think that I came to bring peace on earth. I did not come to bring peace but a sword."**

Jesus said that He came to earth to bring a sword, and Muslims believe from this one verse that most likely Jesus bought swords for each of His disciples. Perhaps all Christians should follow the command of Jesus and carry a sword to perform jihad for the sake of Allah. Perhaps from this verse we can imagine that Jesus commanded and provoked His disciples to go out and perform jihad for the sake of Allah as Mohammed told his followers to fight for the sake of Allah, engage in war, and kill the infidels. This is the kind of nonsense that I hear as I travel the world and interact with many Muslims.

Is this the real understanding of Jesus' words in verse 34? He did not come to bring peace but to bring a sword? Is this how we understand the teachings of Jesus by just picking out one verse like Matthew 10:34 and making complete doctrines and entire lifestyles out of it? Or should we read the entire passage and ask ourselves some questions such as: what was the cultural setting for this passage, how does this verse fit in the context of the teachings of Jesus in this passage, or how did the disciples understand and practice what Jesus said? Then we can understand what Jesus meant by what He said in verse 34. Even more than that, we should look at all the teachings of Jesus throughout the Bible to really understand what He really meant in Matthew 10:34. We cannot understand Jesus' teaching in any verse in the Bible without reading the verse within the context of the passage and within the rest of the teachings of the Bible concerning this verse or topic.

The Bible is not like the Qur'an. In the Qur'an, almost every verse is a new thought. When you read the verses of the Qur'an, Mohammed jumps from one topic to another topic, usually in the very next verse. There is very little continuity in the verses of the Qur'an. It is rare to read more than two or three verses before an entirely new topic or subject is brought up by Mohammed. Yet, in the Bible, there are entire BOOKS of the Old and New Testaments that are one continuous account of the life of a prophet or of Jesus Christ. Every verse connects with the verse before and the verse after as it tells the wonderful story of God's redemptive love for mankind, but the Qur'an is a confusing mess of ideas, as if shook up in a bag and then dumped on the page.

Muslims always give the same excuse to me when I open the Qur'an and read a verse in which it clearly teaches to hate, to kill the Jew or the Christian, or to terrorize someone. Muslims will tell me that I am taking the verse "out of context." It is difficult not to laugh when they tell me that. For the jumbled style of the writing of Mohammed throughout the entire Qur'an is verses without any context whatsoever. Many verses in the Qur'an are not connected to the previous verses or the following verses. Ten verses in a row might give ten or fifteen different topics. There is little to no context and little or no continuity.

Then Muslims will give many other excuses for why the verse teaches what it teaches. Sadly, all their excuses are unsuccessful. The truth about the command of Allah in the Qur'an, when he told the Muslims in Qur'an 5:51 not to take the Jews and Christians as friends, is exactly what he meant. When Allah commands a Muslim to kill Christians or Jews "who do not believe in Allah" or who do not "forbid what Allah and his messenger (Mohammed) forbid" in Qur'an 9:29, that is exactly what he meant. There is no connection whatsoever with the teaching of this verse with previous verses or verses which follow in that chapter of the Qur'an. So, what does it mean when a Muslim says to read the verse "in context" when there is no context. The verse simply stands alone. It is a direct command without anything to add or take away from it in the verses around it.

However, that is not what we find in the Bible. With the exception of some of the Proverbs and Psalms, most of the Bible is an historical, theological, or prophetic narrative that has wonderful and understandable continuity. When we look at Matthew 10:34, we know that this verse has been put in a body of the teachings of our Lord and Savior. That is why we must read the text and read the interpretation of the text by Christian scholars. That is how we know the true meaning of the teachings of our Lord and Savior Jesus Christ. That is what we will do right now.

The True Teaching of Jesus in Matthew 10:34

So, let us go back to the beginning of Matthew 10 starting with verse 1. Here Jesus called His disciples to follow Him. Jesus gave them the authority, the power, to cast out demons in His name and also to heal sickness and get rid of every disease. Then in verses 2-4, the names of Jesus' disciples are given. **We know that there were twelve disciples, not** twelve armies that Mohammed prepared for invading the world. His armies had hundreds of thousands of Muslim believers who loved death more than life. Here Jesus is doing the opposite. These twelve disciples were sent to give life to the dead and to bring healing to the sick and the weak. That is the opposite message of Mohammed, the false prophet of the cult of Islam. The message of Jesus would spread with love and forgiveness, not compulsion at the end of a bloody sword.

Then in verse 5 Jesus told His disciples not to go to the Gentiles and not to the city of the Samaritans. Jesus instead commanded His disciples to only **go to the Jews.** Muslims read the verse and say, "Look! **Jesus did not come to the world. He did not send His disciples to the world. He only came to the Jews, but Mohammed came to the whole world.**" No, my dear Muslim friends, you need to read the entire Bible to see the true answer to your claim.

It was only in the early days of His ministry that Jesus sent His disciples to the Jews. However, after He died on the cross and rose from the dead (but before He left earth), He commissioned His disciples in the Great

Commission and told them to now go to the ends of the world. The ends of the world means **anyone** in the world: to everyone in everyplace, to the Jew and the Gentile, to the Hebrew and the Greek, to the black and the white, to the free and the slave, and to the Muslims because we are all one in Christ Jesus. In John 3:16 we read: **"For God so loved the world…"** It does not say, "For God so loved the Jews." No, it was because **"God so loved the world that He gave His only begotten Son…"**

In verses 7 and 8 of Matthew chapter 10, Jesus told His disciples to preach that the **"kingdom of heaven is at hand."** Then He told them what to do. They must **"heal the sick, cleanse the lepers, raise the dead, and cast out demons."** So how much will they make in this business? Nothing. It was free because they had freely received, and now they were to freely give. This was not a business. This service was freely given. It was a ministry of grace.

Then Jesus gave them more advice in verses 9 and 10. He told them not to take money (gold, silver, etc.) with them. He would supernaturally provide for them on their journey. Jesus would take care of their needs as they served Him. He even told them not to take extra clothing or shoes. They would not have to worry about anything, not what they would eat or what they would wear or where they would sleep. God would provide for all their needs.

In verse 11, Jesus instructed them that when they came to a city or village to search for someone who was a worthy believer in whose home they could stay. They were to stay with this person the entire time they were in the city, and the disciples were to give their peace to the house and household. However, if the person was not worthy, their peace would return back to the disciples and they were to leave.

So what happened if someone refused to listen to the message of Christ? What would be the reaction of the disciples? Will the disciples get angry and perform jihad on the people of a city who reject Jesus? Will they call down fire from heaven to burn up the wicked? Will they start killing those who reject the love of God, or will they move on with their ministry to another city?

Chapter 13: Clearing the Fog of War

We read the answer to these questions in Matthew 10:14-15: **And whoever will not receive you nor hear your words, when you depart from that house or city**, shake the sword in the air and shout "Allah Akbar" and start killing all the people in the house and fight everyone in the city as Prophet Mohammed, the prophet of Islam, did. No, no, no, my dear brothers and sisters, that is not what Jesus said. He said if people did not accept them or believe in their message or were not interested in it, they were to **"shake off the dust from your feet."** They were to simply leave. God has given to people a free will. If they will not accept Christ, then move on and preach to others.

The disciples were not to shake a sword in the air with their *hands* as Muslims do. They were to shake the dust off of their *feet* and go on. What a great difference between the teachings of our Lord and Savior Jesus Christ and the teachings of the false prophet of Islam, Mohammed.

Jesus is saying to His disciples and all Christians that He did not want them to defend themselves while in His service. Jesus Himself will be the One to do that. The proof is in verse 15: **Assuredly, I say to you, it will be more tolerable for the land of Sodom and Gomorrah in the day of judgment than for that city!**

In verse 16, we see the mission of Jesus: **Behold, I send you out as sheep in the midst of wolves. Therefore be wise as serpents and harmless as doves.** He is not sending His disciples on a peaceful mission. There will be great dangers. He is sending them out to perform great miracles, heal the sick, raise the dead, cast out demons, and strengthen the people. Jesus is sending them out as sheep among wolves. We know what wolves do to sheep. They devour the sheep. That is why Jesus advised His disciples to be wise as serpents and at the same time to be harmless like doves. They were bringing the true message of the true Messiah, and many of the wicked religious leaders of the land would gladly kill them to shut them up.

Then Jesus told His disciples in verses 17 and 18: [17]**But beware of men, for they will deliver you up to councils and scourge you in their synagogues.** [18]**You will be brought before governors and kings for My sake, as a testimony to them and to the Gentiles.** This was a prophecy in which Jesus described to His disciples what would happen to them. They would be brought before councils, governors, kings, and the synagogues. This is exactly what happened to Peter, James, John, Paul, and the other disciples so that they could give their testimony about Jesus Christ to the Jews and to the Gentiles. Then Jesus instructed them not to worry when this happened as to what they should say or do because the Father (through the Holy Spirit) would give them divine words to speak.

Jesus told the disciples in verses 21 and 22 about the identity of those who would be the ones to deliver up and betray His followers to be put to death. It would be brother delivering up his brother, father delivering up his own child, and children delivering up their parents. This is what would happen in the Church among the Christians. The disciples and the Church would be hated because of Jesus. In the same family there would be one brother who would be a follower of the Messiah Jesus and another brother who would reject Him. There would be a believing child and yet a stubborn and unrepentant parent. The truth about Jesus will divide even brother from brother and father from child. Even the strongest earthly relationships will be divided because of Jesus Christ. I have personally witnessed this in my own life, in my own family, and among my friends.

In verses 23-27, Jesus continued by telling His disciples that when they are persecuted in a city to escape to another city. There is no student better than his teacher or servant better than his master. It would be perfect for a student to be like his teacher and a servant to be like his master. Then Jesus reminded His disciples that the unbelieving people called Him Beelzebub (a false god or demon). However, Jesus instructed the disciples not to be afraid of them because everything will be known one day. What Jesus told them in the darkness, they will say in the light. What they heard Jesus whisper in their ears, they will shout from the housetops.

There is a great verse I always quote when someone asks me, "Aren't you afraid, Usama, that someday a Muslim will harm you for what you are doing in this ministry?" It is verse 28: **"And do not fear those who kill the body but cannot kill the soul. But rather fear Him who is able to destroy both soul and body in hell."**

I also know that the Scripture assures me in verses 29-31 that I am better than a bird. My Lord watches over the birds of the air and feeds them and takes care of them, and I am more valuable than the birds to my loving God. I also do not know how many hairs I have on my head, but my Lord has them numbered. He will keep me safe according to His will. He knows, and He cares.

Then Jesus told His disciples in verses 32 and 33: [32]**"Therefore whoever confesses Me before men, him I will also confess before My Father who is in heaven.** [33]**But whoever denies Me before men, him I will also deny before My Father who is in heaven."** It is amazing that Mohammed taught his Muslim believers that it is okay to deny their faith at the time of persecution as long as their faith was secure in their hearts. According to Qur'an 16:106: *[106]Whoever becomes an infidel in Allah after he believed, except one who was compelled and his heart is secure in faith; but whoever opens his chest to the infidelity, so on them wrath from Allah, and they will have great torment.*

However, born-again Christians are killed all over the world every day by the hand of Muslims because they simply obey Jesus' command in verses 32 and 33. True, born-again Christians will never deny their Lord and Savior even if the Muslims or other radicals behead every one of us.

However in Islam, Mohammed taught his followers to lie just to keep themselves safe until they have the upper hand. It is okay for Muslims to pretend to be friends with Americans. They can pretend to be loving and peaceful to the Christians and Jews as it is written in Qur'an 3:28: *[28]Believers do not take the infidels for friends, rather than the believers, and whoever does this so he has nothing to do with Allah, except that you should guard yourself from them, cautiously. And Allah himself warns you, and to Allah is the final return.*

Muslims continue to do this until they get the upper hand, and then they must kill the last one of the non-believers as written in Qur'an 47:35: *[35]So do not be weak and do not call for peace when you have the upper hand. And Allah is with you, and he will not leave from you [for] your works.*

Infidels are non-believers, those who do not believe in Mohammed, those who do not believe in Allah, and those who do not believe in the wicked, barbaric cult of Islam. As written in Qur'an 9:29: *Engage in war with those who do not believe in Allah nor in the last day. Nor forbid what Allah and his messenger forbid, nor believe in the religion of the truth (Islam) among those who have been given the book until they pay the jizya (tribute) out of hand and they are subdued.*

Now, let's go back to Matthew 10 to look at the verse that Muslims read when they fabricate an interpretation of it in order to make the verse teach that Jesus commanded His followers to engage in holy war and kill others in His name just like Mohammed commanded his followers. In verse 34, Jesus said: **"Do not think that I came to bring peace on earth. I did not come to bring peace but a sword."**

First, let's see how Muslims understand this verse. They understand this verse to mean that Jesus did not come to the world to bring peace but to bring war because the Christians will carry the sword and go out and fight and perform jihad for the sake of Allah. Really?

Is that true? Did Jesus come to the world to bring peace or to bring war? Was Jesus successful in bringing war to this world? How many battles did Jesus engage in? Did Jesus' disciples engage in any war? Did any of the early Christians for the first one hundred, two hundred, three hundred, four hundred, or five hundred years engage in any war? How about the first one thousand years?

I know that Muslims will point to the Crusades. The Crusades began after the first one thousand years of Christianity. Why did the Crusades take place? Who was responsible for the Crusades?

Throughout the first one thousand years of the Church, Christians did not engage in war. Our Lord Jesus and all His disciples never engaged in any war. Jesus came to bring peace. As a matter of fact, we read in Luke 2:13-14 that when Jesus was born, the angels praised God and said: **"Glory to God in the highest, and on earth peace, goodwill toward men!"** That was the shout of the angels when Jesus was born.

When Paul was writing to the Gentiles, he said in Ephesians 2:12-17 that before Christ, we the Gentiles were foreigners concerning Israel and the promises given to Israel, and there was no hope for us in this world. However, if we are saved, then we are in Christ Jesus and are no longer far away but near through His blood because Jesus is our peace. He made the two of us as one. The Jews and the Gentiles are no longer separated but are one. The enmity between the Jews and the Gentiles will be demolished.

For when Christ died on the cross, the curtain wall inside the Holy of Holies (that separated us from God) was torn from the top to the bottom. Now God can communicate with us without any separation with those who believe in Jesus Christ. Because Jesus died on the cross, we are His temple, and His spirit dwells in us. Christ Himself is our peace. So how can Jesus say that He did not come to earth to bring peace but a sword if He Himself is our peace? Thank God for the blood of Jesus Christ who makes us clean and makes us one and gave His life to bring such a great salvation to Gentiles like me.

So what is the true meaning when Jesus said that He did not come to bring peace but a sword? To understand this verse, we need to read the following verses. Jesus said in verses 35 and 36: [35]**"For I have come to 'set a man against his father, a daughter against her mother, and a daughter-in-law against her mother-in-law;'** [36]**and 'a man's enemies will be those of his own household.'"** Do you understand what Jesus is saying here? Jesus did not say, "I did not come to bring peace but a sword so each one of you disciples must take up a sword and fight." No, He is talking about the family. He is not talking about the enemies of the land or other cities or other countries. He is talking about the enemies of the believer within his own household. If people would just read two or three more verses, they would see that Jesus gave the simple interpretation: Jesus brings division even in close relationships. Brother against brother, and father against child. There is no middle ground when it comes to the truth of the God-man Jesus.

Here Jesus is telling the disciples that they will be hated by their own fathers, mothers, sisters, brothers, sons, and daughters. That is the enemy. The enemy of the Christian believer is even those who live in his own household. Jesus did not tell His disciples (and is not telling us Christians today) to carry a sword to kill our own family members! This is the same Jesus who taught us to *love* our enemies, to *pray* for those who persecute us, and to *bless* those who curse us. If your enemy is hungry, give him something to eat; and if your enemy is thirsty, give him something to drink.

He is not teaching us to kill our own family members. Never. Not even once.

Jesus continued in verses 37-39: **³⁷"He who loves father or mother more than Me is not worthy of Me. And he who loves son or daughter more than Me is not worthy of Me. ³⁸And he who does not take his cross and follow after Me is not worthy of Me. ³⁹He who finds his life will lose it, and he who loses his life for My sake will find it."**

We can easily understand what Jesus meant in verse 34 when He said that He did not come to this world to bring peace but a sword. Jesus is telling us that we have to make a decision. The sword is to separate, the sword is to split apart, and the sword is to make a choice. Do we love our fathers, mothers, brothers, sisters, sons, and daughters more than Jesus Christ? Are we willing to set all of this aside to follow Jesus alone? Jesus brings division. Are we willing to leave all and follow Him?

If we care more about our families than the call of God to believe in Jesus and take Him as Lord and Savior in our lives, then we are not ready to truly receive and follow Christ. We must make a decision when it comes to Jesus Christ, and sometimes that decision will divide us from those we are close to. That is what Jesus meant by the sword. Jesus is telling us, in order to be a true Christian, that not only do we have to put God first in our lives but we have to put ourselves last. You have to be willing to die for Jesus. You must carry the cross.

I know so many of our Muslim friends do not understand what it means for a person to carry a cross. The Romans forced a criminal who was condemned to death to carry his own cross on his back to the place where he was to be crucified. We as Christians have died to this world. We follow Jesus, not to go out and kill others but for us to die daily for Him. If we choose to love a family member or a friend more than Jesus, then we are not truly following Him. If we are willing to die for Jesus, then that is when we save our lives.

I have met so many times with Muslim friends who have decided not to accept Jesus as Lord and Savior because they are so concerned about their parents and their brothers and sisters or they fear for their lives. It is very sad to see Muslims who know there is no truth in Islam and are convinced, 100 percent, that Mohammed is a false prophet and know that the only way of salvation is through Jesus Christ, but because of the fear of some family member or fear for their own lives, they refuse to accept Jesus Christ as their Savior. That is the great test. Jesus divides.

Are you willing to accept Jesus Christ as Lord and Savior, even if it will cause you to be separated from your family and friends or maybe even cost you your life if you are a Muslim who becomes a Christian? Honor killing is the teaching of Allah in Qur'an 6:151 where Allah gives Muslims the right to kill anyone who becomes a Christian: *...And do not kill the soul which Allah forbids except with a just cause...* Muslim scholars will tell you that one of the "just causes" for killing someone is when a person abandons Islam for another faith. They can be killed.

But Jesus never spoke of a Christian killing someone for not believing. The "sword" Jesus spoke of here in this passage He Himself explained a few words later. This is the true meaning of Jesus' words, "Do not think that I come to bring peace but a sword." He was talking about splitting the family apart: the father from the sons, the mother-in-law from the daughter-in-law, and the sisters from the brothers. Jesus was not taking about jihad or holy war but the resolve of people accepting Him as Lord and Savior for they will be separated from their families. They may even be killed for His sake. Just as a sword cuts and divides, so will the decision to follow Jesus Christ. It may be a painful separation from your own family.

Let's be clear, the sword was not for the disciples or Christians to go and fight. Not Jesus, not His disciples, nor any Christians for about the first thousand years ever went to war for the "sake of God." There are no verses calling for them to go to war for God in the New Testament. Instead, Christians were the ones attacked and persecuted. It was the Christians who were kicked out of their homes and cities and countries. It is the price that Christians pay to be a follower of Jesus. This is the true fulfillment of the prophecy of our Lord and Savior in that He did not come to bring peace but the sword. If you decide to follow Jesus, be ready to be divided from even your own family.

My dear Muslim friends, how many of Jesus' disciples or early Christians, for the first thousand years, understood or practiced Matthew 10:34 as you claim? The answer is…none. Think about that. None. Now, compare that to the history of Mohammed. How many wars and battles and killings did Mohammed himself engage in, and how many more did his early followers engage in? Dozens? Hundreds? Thousands? And how many people have died due to Islamic warfare in the centuries since the false prophet of Islam came preaching intolerance and vengeance and the spoils of war? Tens of thousands? Hundreds of thousands? Millions? Some historians have estimated that at least 500 million people have died due to Islamic aggression since Mohammed began preaching his intolerant new faith.

Muslims always like to talk about the Crusades as examples of "Christian Holy War" (when they were actually politically-motivated wars used to restrict the expansion of Muslim aggression in the Middle East). Let's look at the numbers. Most historians agree that the total number of Jews, Christians, and Muslims killed during the 177 years of the Crusades is about 1.5 million people. Now this includes those who died in travel (about 5 percent), those who died from diseases (a high number), or those who died when captured and sent off into slavery. **That's about 8,500 people per YEAR or about 23 people per day.** Now, compare that to the estimated 500 million that Islam has killed during its 1,500 years of conquest. By the numbers, Islam is over 300 times more bloody and violent than all of the Crusades combined.

The other important point to remember is that NOWHERE in the entire New Testament is the Christian ever called upon to kill another person. They are not called to kill for the faith (or lack of it) or for possessions or for wives or for land. Not even once. The Crusades were political wars, typically fought because of: (1) the greed of the European leadership who used **"God" and "religion" as a way to stir up people to join the battles** or (2) to stop or slow the advancement of the Islamic aggressors who were working their way through the Middle East and on to Europe. These weren't actually religious wars per se, but rather territorial wars to stop the advancing Islamic armies as they bathed nation after nation in blood in their conquest of fulfilling Mohammed's commands.

Once again, nowhere in the New Testament is the Christian believer called upon to kill anyone for anything. Never even once. However, compare this to Islam and the Qur'an. There are dozens and dozens of passages which encourage Muslim believers and followers of Mohammed to fight and kill and terrorize. The Crusades, on the other hand, were actually a denial of the teachings of Jesus. The Crusades were fought in disobedience to the clear teachings of love and forgiveness given by Jesus. The Crusades, at best, were territorial wars fought to stop the advancement of Islamic expansion or perhaps wars of political greed. Period. Just because people invoked the "name of God" does not mean that the Crusades were "Christian" or "godly." But Mohammed and the Qur'an command the Muslim believers to fight until there is no religion left but Islam.

More Verses that Muslims Say Teach Jihad or War in the New Testament: Luke 12:49-51 and Luke 22:36 and 38

Let us look into the book of Luke to read another passage that Muslims use to claim that Jesus somehow commanded His disciples to engage in war. Luke provides for us the same teaching in which Christ did not come to bring peace but division. Luke used the word *division* instead of *sword*. Luke knew what the sword would do. It would divide the family, one from another. Jesus said in Luke 12:49-51: **⁴⁹"I came to send fire on the earth, and how I wish it were already kindled! ⁵⁰But I have a baptism to be baptized with, and how distressed I am till it is accomplished! ⁵¹Do you suppose that I came to give peace on earth? I tell you, not at all, but rather division."** Here are the words of Jesus telling us He did not bring peace (harmony) to earth but division.

What division is Jesus bringing? We see the answer in verses 52 and 53: **⁵²"For from now on five in one house will be divided: three against two, and two against three. ⁵³Father will be divided against son and son against father, mother against daughter and daughter against mother, mother-in-law against her daughter-in-law and daughter-in-law against her mother-in-law."**

The division, the "sword," is interpreted by Jesus Himself! We do not even need to read Christian scholars or seek out the opinion of Bible teachers. Jesus explains that the sword is division between family members. This happened back two thousand years ago, and it is happening today. For who can understand this better than anyone else but Muslims who received Jesus Christ as their Lord and Savior? There are innumerable accounts about Muslims who became Christians and then were hated by their own families, and many of them were even killed by their own family members. As I mentioned before, this is called honor killing in Islam. Allah commanded **Muslim believers in the Qur'an to kill Muslims who commit the sin of apostasy** (by leaving Islam and becoming a Christian). It is a fact of recent history that Muslims will even kill their own family members who have become a follower of Jesus Christ. Jesus indeed brings a sword, the sword of division.

Another passage that Muslims often misunderstand and attempt to use to teach that Jesus Christ is not a loving, peaceful prophet as Christians claim is in Luke 22. Muslims argue that Christianity is not the loving, peaceful religion that Christians say it is but actually claim that in this passage Jesus gave His disciples a direct command to carry swords. He even told them to sell their clothes so they could buy swords to perform jihad for the sake of Allah. So is this true? Once again, the obvious answer is no.

First, we will look at two verses, Luke 22:36 and 38: [36]**Then He said to them, "But now, he who has a money bag, let him take it, and likewise a knapsack; and he who has no sword, let him sell his garment and buy one...** [38]**So they said, "Lord, look, here are two swords." And He said to them, "It is enough."**

Here is how Muslims understand these two short verses: Jesus instructed His disciples to sell their own clothes to buy swords. The disciples told Jesus that there were two swords in the upper room, and Jesus said that these two swords were enough to start the war. Is that what Jesus meant? Once again...no.

I would like to share with you the true interpretation of this passage. We first need to go back and look at verse 35 (this is called reading in context): **And He said to them, "When I sent you without money bag, knapsack, and sandals, did you lack anything?" So they said, "Nothing."**

Chapter 13: Clearing the Fog of War

When we studied Matthew 10 earlier, we saw that Jesus' twelve disciples were sent by Him to the house of Israel to do miracles: to give life to the dead, cast out demons in His name, and bring healing to the sick and the weak. Jesus commanded His disciples to do these miracles for free. In verses 9 and 10, Jesus told His disciples not to take any money or any extra food or clothing with them on their journey. Jesus would provide whatever they needed. That is what Jesus is reminding them of here in verse 35.

Jesus then gave them new instructions in Luke 22:36 and 38. When Jesus sent them out in Matthew 10, Jesus was with them, and He took care of them. Now, in Luke, He is telling them that He will no longer be with them, and they will have to make their own preparations for their journey. Now they will need to take care of themselves. As we read above, Jesus told them in verse 36: **"But now, he who has a money bag, let him take it, and likewise a knapsack; and he who has no sword, let him sell his garment and buy one.**

What is the sword which Jesus is talking about? The Greek word used for sword in this verse is *makhaira*. It is used 29 times in the New Testament and 156 times in the Old Testament (the Septuagint/Greek translation). So what is a makhaira? Is it a big sword about three or four feet long like the one Mohammed and his followers carried all the time with which to perform jihad in which they used to kill people three or four feet away from them or to chop off their heads?

No, a makhaira is just a large knife, such as a small sword. It is also known as a dagger.

So what would the disciples do with this small sword or knife? They certainly could not use it to perform jihad or do battle, but there were plenty of uses in the cultural setting in which the disciples lived. This knife was used for protection from thieves or wild animals or to cut meat such as fish. It was not to launch jihad against the enemy of Christianity, for now Jesus is about to leave His disciples.

William MacDonald said in his discussion of this passage that the disciples will be poor and they will be hungry. They will meet so many dangers in their ministry. For the time being, they will need to take care of themselves.

(*Believer's Bible Commentary*, 2008, page 1403) That is why they needed a bag of money. That is why they needed dishes in which to carry their food. If they did not have a sword, then they were to sell some of their clothes to buy a sword (a large knife, not a real "sword" that would be used in combat). Remember, this was a two-edged knife or small sword, not the sword of Islam. This is not a weapon of conquest or of battle, but rather a tool to be used for everyday needs of cutting, slicing, and defense.

Can we prove (through the rest of the teachings of Jesus throughout the Bible) what He meant by the "sword"? Was it a sword to perform jihad or a sword to protect themselves from thieves or wild animals? Did Jesus teach anywhere else in the Bible that His disciples were to carry swords to fight the enemy and perform jihad like Mohammed and his followers? Never even once! Think about that. Not even one time. In fact, just the opposite. Jesus said that if someone attacked you for your faith, you were not to resist. If they strike your face, turn the other cheek; if they take your shirt, give them your coat as well. Jesus never advocated fighting or killing.

The True Teachings of Jesus Instructing His Disciples to Buy a Sword: John 18:36 and Matthew 26:52

Let's see what Jesus said in John 18:36: **"My kingdom is not of this world. If My kingdom were of this world, My servants would fight, so that I should not be delivered to the Jews; but now My kingdom is not from here."**

Would the disciples of Jesus need to carry a three or four-foot long sword to have the kingdom on earth? No, Jesus very clearly teaches in this passage that His kingdom is not of this physical world. He will not ask His disciples or His followers to form an army and carry swords to bring a kingdom on earth. (This proves that the Crusades had nothing to do with Jesus or Christianity. The Crusades were a politically motivated, disobedient denial of the clear teachings of Jesus Christ.)

Another passage of Jesus' teaching about the relationship between Christians and any of our enemies is found in Matthew 26:52 when Jesus told Peter: **"Put your sword in its place: for all who take the sword will perish by the sword."** What is going on here? This is referring to when

Chapter 13: Clearing the Fog of War

Judas came with the multitude armed with swords, the chief priest, and the elders to arrest Jesus. Peter, the great fisherman, used his makhaira, his knife, and all he was able to do was cut the ear of the high priest's servant. Think about that…it wasn't a weapon of war. The only damage he inflicted was wounding an ear. So much for conquering the world!

Now, this is important: what did Jesus do? Did He command all the other disciples to immediately yank out their weapons and attack the infidels? No. What did He do? He *healed* the servant's ear, and then He looked at Peter and told him to put his knife away for those who take the knife will perish by the knife. Jesus did not encourage Peter to use his knife to kill some of these people who came to arrest Him and put Him to death. Jesus did not defend Himself, and He rebuked Peter for cutting the ear of the servant. If Jesus was about violence and killing, then why did He heal His enemy when they came to arrest Him?

Jesus taught His disciples and all Christians in Matthew 5:43-45: **⁴³"You have heard that it was said, 'You shall love your neighbor and hate your enemy.' ⁴⁴But I say to you, love your enemies, bless those who curse you, do good to those who hate you, and pray for those who spitefully use you and persecute you, ⁴⁵that you may be sons of your Father in heaven; for He makes His sun rise on the evil and on the good, and sends rain on the just and on the unjust.'"**

What a great teaching from a great Master, our Lord and Savior Jesus Christ. Christians must be like their Father in Heaven. Christians must love their enemies. So how could Jesus (who taught His disciples to love their enemies), now in this verse, teach His disciples to carry swords and go out to kill their enemies? That is not what Jesus taught or practiced as we read throughout the pages of the New Testament. (But violence and killing is what Mohammed taught and practiced as we read the pages of the Qur'an and the hadith.)

Remember, what did Jesus mean by the *sword*? Again, this was a small sword or knife with two edges which could be used to defend one's self from wild animals or thieves or cut and slice meat. It was not an attack weapon, not a sword to perform jihad.

So what about Luke 22:38 in which the disciple said to Jesus: **"Lord, look, here are two swords." And He said to them, "It is enough."**

William MacDonald also wrote in his *Believer's Bible Commentary* that the disciples of Jesus misunderstood what Jesus had said because they thought that they could stop the Jews from taking Jesus to be put to death. However, this was not at all what the Lord meant by what He said.

Would two small knives be enough to keep the mob from taking Jesus to be put on the cross? The entire reason that Jesus was born and lived among us was so that he could die on the cross. He is the Lamb of God who came to take away the sin of the world. He did not want His disciples (or anyone else) to stop Him from going to the cross.

When Jesus said to them that it was enough, I believe Jesus meant enough of this conversation because they did not understand what He was telling them at the time. Many times in the gospel accounts we have the Lord rebuking His disciples for not understanding many of His clear and simple teachings. They did not even fully understand His coming and His death and resurrection until after His resurrection when Jesus showed His disciples what was written in the prophecies in the Old Testament concerning all the events that were fulfilled in His life.

That is when they finally understood every word that He taught them. Then they understood about His role in the world as the Savior and their new role in the world as the carriers of His great message of salvation. Then did they purchase weapons and begin raising an army to kill the Romans and the infidels? No. They went out joyfully and preached the gospel of the grace of God to Jew and Gentile alike.

If you want to know what Jesus meant, then look at the lives of His early followers. We see peace, love, and forgiveness. Not swords, violence, blood, and war. In fact, most of the early disciples of Jesus died by the sword, but not one of them killed a person with the sword even in self-defense. So, no, Jesus never taught or commanded or practiced war in the New Testament.

Chapter 13: Clearing the Fog of War

The Slaughter of Those Who Refused to Believe in Jesus: Luke 19:27

Muslims read in the Qur'an that Allah commanded Mohammed and his Muslim followers to behead (decapitate by the sword) those who do not submit to Islam. We see this clearly in Qur'an 47:4 when Allah said: *So when you meet those who became infidels, so strike the necks (decapitating) until you have made a great slaughter among them.* This is also found in Qur'an 8:12: *When your lord revealed to the angels: "I am with you, so make firm those who believed. I will cast the terror into the hearts of those who became infidels. So strike above their necks (decapitation), and strike off (chop off) every finger from them."*

When we read verses like these in the Qur'an, we see that Islam is not the loving, peaceful religion that the media seems to adore and promote. Muslims go to the Bible and read a random verse or two and come up with an unwarranted conclusion that Mohammed, the prophet of Islam, is no different than Jesus, the "prophet" of Christianity. Where do we see Jesus beheading people? Where do they read this? Nowhere!

Let us read Luke 19:27 where Jesus said: **"But bring here those enemies of mine, who did not want me to reign over them, and slay them before me."** Jesus is asking that His enemies, the ones who did not want Jesus to rule over them, be brought before Him to be killed.

Now, hold on...do Muslims ever bother to read the verses just before verse 27? Have they ever read this passage in context? What was Jesus talking about? What was the connection between this verse and the previous verses in the same chapter? No, they do not bother to read these verses. This is a smart move by every scheming Muslim, those who try to make Jesus look like Mohammed. Mohammed slayed so many Christians and Jews who refused to submit to him, and here (they claim), "We see Jesus doing the same thing! Jesus is asking for His enemies to be slain before Him because they did not want Jesus to rule over them."

Well, my dear Muslims friends, that is not what is going on in Luke. We have to go back and read the previous verses, and then read verse 27 within the context. In the first ten verses of this chapter, we see that Jesus was passing through Jericho on His way to Jerusalem to be put to death on the cross. Below is a short summary of the passage in context.

There was a very rich man in Jericho by the name of Zacchaeus, the chief tax collector. He wanted to see Jesus, and since he was such a short man and could not see over the crowd, he climbed high up into a sycamore tree to gain a better view. When Jesus saw him, He told Zacchaeus to come down because He, Jesus, was going to his, Zacchaeus', home. However, when the crowd heard that Jesus was going home with Zacchaeus, they grumbled about Jesus entering a "sinner's house." (The Jews especially hated tax collectors, much like people today despise the I.R.S.) While at his home, Zacchaeus told Jesus that he would give to the poor and make restitution for what he had wrongly taken from the people. There was now a new heart in Zacchaeus. He was saved, a follower of Jesus. We read what Jesus said to him in verses 9 and 10: [9]**"...Today salvation has come to this house, because he also is a son of Abraham;** [10]**for the Son of Man has come to seek and to save that which was lost."**

After this encounter with Zacchaeus in Jericho, Jesus left to go to Jerusalem. He was going there in order to be crucified on the cross and die for the sin of the world and then rise from the dead on the third day to bring salvation. His kingdom would be accomplished after His resurrection. However, that was not what was in the hearts and minds of some of his followers, including His own disciples. They still did not understand that Jesus had been born to DIE. They were still looking for a political Messiah, not a spiritual Savior. They were thinking Jesus would be appointed king over Israel in Jerusalem and take the throne of King David, His father according to the flesh. They were thinking of a physical, earthly seat of power, but Jesus was headed to a cross, not a throne. He was King, but He was also our substitute, our Savior.

Verse 11 states: **Now as we heard these things, He spoke another parable...** Did you read this, my Muslim friends? Jesus spoke in another *parable*. As we covered earlier, parables are not "true" accounts of actual events. Rather, they are made-up stories that are used to help teach another truth (usually a non-physical, spiritual truth). This was the method Jesus used to speak to the people of Israel. That is how He taught the children of Israel. This also fulfilled a prophecy given by David. When the Messiah would come, He would speak to the crowds in parables. We read this in Psalm 78:2: **I will open my mouth in a parable; I will utter dark sayings of old.** That was how Jesus spoke to the crowds.

Why did Jesus speak in parables? As we finish verse 11, it was "**…because He was near Jerusalem and because they thought the kingdom of God would appear immediately.**" The followers of Jesus got it wrong, and Jesus used a parable in verses 11-27 to correct their misunderstanding concerning His entry into Jerusalem. It is like Jesus is telling them that He was not going to Jerusalem right now to become the king of Israel because there are events that must happen *before* Israel will have Him as king (namely His death, burial, and resurrection). These must occur first before Jesus can be appointed King, not only over Jerusalem, but over the entire earth in His thousand-year kingdom that we often call "The Millennium."

The parable begins in verse 12 (notice…Jesus Himself said it was a *parable*): **Therefore He said: "A certain nobleman went into a far country to receive for himself a kingdom and to return. ¹³So he called ten of his servants, delivered to them ten minas…** A mina is worth about three month's salary in Jesus' day. **…and said to them, 'Do business till I come.' ¹⁴But his citizens hated him…**

The citizens of the country did not just dislike the nobleman, they hated him. **…and sent a delegation after him, saying, 'We will not have this man to reign over us.' ¹⁵"And so it was that when he** (that is the nobleman) **returned, having received the kingdom, he then commanded these servants, to whom he had given the money, to be called to him, that he might know how much every man had gained by trading.** The master wanted to know how much each servant had gained by investing the money he had given to them.

¹⁶Then came the first, saying, 'Master, your mina has earned ten minas.' Notice the servant said that it was the master's mina, not his own money, which he had invested. This mina earned ten minas. **¹⁷And he said to him, 'Well done, good servant; because you were faithful in a very little, have authority over ten cities.' ¹⁸And the second came, saying, 'Master, your mina has earned five minas.' ¹⁹Likewise he said to him, 'You also be over five cities.'** This servant also invested the master's mina and made five minas more. The master then gave this servant authority over five cities.

[20]**Then another came, saying, 'Master, here is your mina, which I have kept put away in a handkerchief.** [21]**For I feared you, because you are an austere man. You collect what you did not deposit, and reap what you did not sow.'**

Notice that the first two men were faithful with the master's money. They acknowledged that the money belonged to him. It was the master's money with which they used to make a profit. However, this third servant was a wicked servant. He told the master that the master collected what he did not deposit. Really? It was the master's money to start with, and instead of investing the master's money, this servant just hid it away.

[22]**And he said to him, 'Out of your own mouth I will judge you, you wicked servant. You knew that I was an austere man, collecting what I did not deposit and reaping what I did not sow.** [23]**Why then did you not put my money in the bank, that at my coming I might have collected it with interest?'** If this servant did not want to work with the master's money, he should have at least put the money in the bank to earn basic interest, but instead, he chose to ignore the gift he had received from the master.

[24]**And he said to those who stood by, 'Take the mina from him, and give it to him who has ten minas.'** [25]**(But they said to him, 'Master, he has ten minas.')** [26]**'For I say to you, that to everyone who has will be given; and from him who does not have, even what he has will be taken away from him.** Everyone who is faithful with the talents given to him will be given more, but everyone who is lazy will have his talents taken away from him.

Then we come to verse 27 which our dear Muslim friends do not understand. The king said: [27]**But bring here those enemies of mine, who did not want me to reign over them, and slay them before me.'"** So how does verse 27 fit within the context of this parable, this story? Remember that this is a *parable* for the future to come.

The interpretation of this parable is that Jesus was entering Jerusalem. People thought that this was the time for Jesus to set up His kingdom on earth. However, Jesus is telling them no. That is not what is going to happen for this is His *first* coming (to die). In His second coming, He will be the King to rule from Jerusalem over the entire world. Right now, though, He is going to Jerusalem for another reason. He was going to bring salvation not judgment.

In this parable Jesus is telling His disciples that the Jewish nation not only will reject Him to reign over them but they will also reject His followers. That is exactly what the Jews did to the early Christians, just like when they **stoned Stephen. The Jews martyred many of Jesus' followers.**

Jesus gives gifts or talents, and we all have gifts. What we do with our gifts is what we are talking about here concerning these three servants. Every one of us will stand before Jesus with all the talents He has given to us, and we will have to give an account of what we have done with them. There are three different examples in this parable: the one who made ten more minas, the one who made five more minas, and the one who made nothing and considered Jesus to be an unjust master because He will harvest what He did not plant when He comes back to the earth.

I pray that we will all stand before Christ with the talents which He has given us and also stand with the gifts in our hands which we gained by using these talents. Please, my fellow believer in the Lord Jesus Christ, please do not be like the lazy servant who just gave many excuses why he did nothing with the talents the master had graciously given him. What will you say to Jesus on the day of judgment? Will you do what is right? Will you do your duty before Jesus and live a life of ministry that brings profit from the talents He has given us for His glory and our benefit?

God has blessed all of us with many gifts. Use them for His kingdom. Use them for His service. At least, give someone else some of your talent so that he can use it for the glory of the Lord. Remember that the master told the wicked servant that he should have at least put the mina in the bank to earn basic interest (which would have required almost no effort at all. The wicked man had no excuse!)

So if you have a gift and do not know how to use it or are tempted to be lazy in using it, then give the gift to someone who will use it to make a profit for the Lord. Help others to do the work of the kingdom of God. Be faithful in the things which the Lord has given you. Use your gifts as wisely as you can so that you will not be standing before Christ on the day of judgment and be called a wicked or unprofitable servant.

All those who love the Lord and serve Him with their talents will have a larger reward for a bigger ministry. Everyone who is lazy, whatever he had will be taken away from him as a punishment and be given to those who work hard for the ministry of Christ.

The punishment for the people of the city who refused to have Jesus as their King was on them. The punishment was death. This was not just a story in a parable. In real life, anyone who refuses to have Jesus as his Lord and Savior will be punished eternally in the second death.

Remember, in the beginning of this book, we discussed sin and the punishment of sin. Sin (rebellion) leads to spiritual death which leads to physical death which then leads to eternal death if you have not repented of your sin and accepted the free gift of salvation provided by Jesus Christ. That is why we have jihad in the Bible. In the Old Testament, God allowed physical death for those who refused Him as King to rule over them. God is no respecter of people. The wages of sin is death. Jesus is God who became a true man, He became sin for us, He died on the cross for us, He was buried, and He arose from the grave.

All of those who believe and trust in Jesus Christ are the children of God, also called "born-again" Christians. For all those who reject Jesus, the day is coming when He comes back to judge the dead and the living, and every single person who has not trusted in Him will be put to death in the Second Death, the eternal death of Hell. That is what Luke 19:27 is talking about. It is a day of judgment, not as Mohammed did by killing Christians and Jews for not believing in his "prophethood."

There is not one single verse in the teaching of the New Testament in which Jesus commanded someone to kill someone else, and Jesus did not behead

Chapter 13: Clearing the Fog of War

anyone. Now, compare that to the life and teachings of Mohammed, as recorded in the Qur'an and in the hadith and in history.

Think about Jesus, and then think about Mohammed.

One is a Savior; the other is a savage.
One died, was buried, and arose from the grave; the other died, and his body remains and rots in the grave.
One told His followers to love; the other commanded his followers to fight.
One conquers by love and forgiveness; the other conquers by fear and the sword.
And finally, one *gave* His life so that we could have the riches of Heaven; the other *took* life so that he himself could have the riches of earth.

Summary

In closing, let me summarize. Death in the Bible is justifiable because the wages of sin is death. God warned that sin and rebellion would lead to death, and there are three deaths: *spiritual* death (separation from God), *physical* death, and *eternal* death. As we look through history, God does not punish people randomly and for no reason, but rather due to the requirements of a just punishment. They sinned against Him so they must die.

God, as Creator of all life, can choose to end physical life in any manner He deems fit. God used the flood in Noah's day. He used fire in Sodom and Gomorrah. He used the sword in the time of Moses and Joshua. He used serpents to kill His own people when they sinned against Him. Many times He used the enemy, the wicked people in the land, to punish His own people, the Jews, when they sinned against Him. He even used the Jews to kill the Jews many times. He used plagues to punish His people and the Egyptians and the Philistines for their sins. Remember, God is no respecter of persons. Throughout the Bible, we see that the wages of sin is death.

Throughout the Old Testament, sacrifices were offered as a substitute for us. Instead of you and me dying for our sin (justly), we could offer an innocent, unblemished animal as a substitute to die in our place. However, all these sacrifices were just a simple picture of the coming True Sacrifice, Jesus Christ, the Lamb of God. Those animal sacrifices had no power or magic to remove sin. They merely looked ahead in faith to the coming True Sacrifice who would remove sins once and for all. God accepted those pictures of His Son and was satisfied.

Jesus Christ is God the Son who became a true man through a humble virgin. Jesus is God who became flesh. He lived a perfect life on earth, but He was rejected by His own people and betrayed by one of His closest friends. He was found guilty, even though He had never sinned. He became sin for us, He died on the cross, He was buried, and He arose from the grave.

All those who repent of their sins and trust in Him are called the children of God or born-again Christians or the saved. For all those who reject Jesus Christ as Lord and Savior, the day is coming when He will come back to judge the dead and the living. Then He will cast everyone who did not repent and trust in Him to the second death (eternal fire of Hell).

That is what Luke 19:27 is talking about. It is a day of judgment, but not as Mohammed did by killing Christians and Jews who refused to believe in his false "prophethood." As stated earlier, there is not one single verse in the teaching of the New Testament where Jesus commanded someone to kill someone else, and Jesus Himself never killed anyone. This parable in Luke 19:11-27 is just that…a *parable*. I hope and I pray that you will realize the truth of the words of Jesus. He Himself gave us the interpretation. It is there for all who are willing to read and accept it.

The first coming of Jesus was to accomplish His *spiritual* kingdom. As we see this clearly in Jesus' own words in John 18:36: **Jesus answered, "My kingdom is not of this world. If My kingdom were of this world, My servants would fight, so that I should not be delivered to the Jews; but now My kingdom is not from here."** Once again, on the day of judgment, Jesus will rule over the earth, and what we read in the parable of Luke 19:27 will be reality. This parable will be fulfilled.

Finally, as we close this examination of "jihad" in the Bible, I would like to share a few thoughts about a topic that is often misused or misunderstood by Muslims: the Crusades. Most people know very little about this period of history. When did the Crusades take place and where? It is amazing that many people speak of the Crusades as if this was the practice of Christianity throughout the history of the Church! However, that is not even remotely true. For over a thousand years after Jesus died, was buried, and arose from the grave, Christians did not fight any of their enemies. The first crusaders marched to Turkey in August of 1096. The fight itself did not begin until May of 1097, and it was successful by June 3, 1098.

We are probably all familiar with the common expression, "a day late and a dollar short." That is exactly what happened with the crusaders. No matter how much success they were able to accomplish, it was a lost cause. Even though historians can distinguish at least ten Crusades, the Europeans did not really accomplish their goal. What was their goal? It was to free the lands which had been taken by the Muslim invaders. Mohammed and his army invaded the first Jewish city roughly around 625 A.D. The name of the city was Yathrib, but Mohammed changed its name to Medina. The crusaders did not start their war until 1097 (over four hundred years later). The Crusades were not a knee-jerk reaction. These were political and territorial wars fought after hundreds of years of Islamic aggression and land acquisition.

However, it was a lost cause. Why? Because by the time the Crusades started, Muslims had already invaded the Middle East. They continued to conquer all of the northern countries of Africa (from Egypt to Morocco) and also in Asia from Saudi Arabia to Turkey and even all the way to India! In 1098, the crusaders were able to take Turkey's capital back, but sadly, the crusaders were not able to keep it under their control.

Muslim armies continue to dominate and control all of these countries. These fifty-seven Muslim countries were never set free or returned to their own original peoples. So where was the success of the Crusades? Even after September 11, all of these so-called "won" wars were simply a loss of blood and money. Islam has continued to dominate and enslave the peoples who were conquered centuries ago.

So in simple words, the crusaders waited four hundred seventy-two years to attempt to restore the lands from the hands of the Muslim invaders. These types of territorial wars have gone on since nearly the beginning of mankind. The Crusades were nothing new, and they are certainly not a "religious" war in the strictest sense. Jesus never commanded any of His followers to "kill the infidels" or to fight for land or spoils. The fact that many of the European soldiers claimed to be Christians does not magically put God's "Stamp of Approval" on a political war that He never commanded.

The Crusades were merely the *reaction* to the Muslim's *action*. Period. Now, on a purely political and earthly level, I cannot see anything inherently wrong for Christians to fight in these Crusades, even though they were not able to free the lands, but at least they were able to end the Muslim invasion of Europe (at that time). If any of these Europeans were fighting

Chapter 14: Summary

for "religious" reasons, they did so in denial and disobedience to the clear teachings of Jesus.

If the schools and media in Europe had taught the true history of the Crusades, just up to fifty years ago, I doubt that there would be any Muslims in Europe today. However sadly, all over the West, when Muslims and liberals talk about the Crusades, I feel that Christians are ashamed of themselves simply because they are ignorant of the true knowledge of what took place in these battles.

My primary disagreement about the Crusades is in the false teachings which were promoted by the spiritual leaders in Europe. For example, these greedy leaders falsely promised the crusaders that if they were to die while fighting, they would go to Heaven. Obviously, that is a false teaching according to Jesus Himself. Salvation is a free gift and has nothing to do with dying in a battle. Anyone who fought and died (on either side) and did not know Jesus Christ as Lord and Savior, is now in Hell.

I recently was in the city of New Orleans, Louisiana, where I met a taxi driver by the name of Mohammed. We had a discussion for a few hours as I shared with him many of the facts about Islam. Then, he suddenly mentioned the Crusades as if it was the last option for him to make some type of equality between the violence of Islam and the violence of the crusaders. My answer to him was this: "What would you expect from the Christian men of Europe when they saw the Muslim invaders, after taking over the Middle East, beginning to march into Europe from Spain in the west and in the east from Turkey? What should these European Christian men do? Should they just have given up their lands and families and let the Muslim invaders take over as they did in the fifty-seven countries that they had already invaded, or should they fight to keep their lands free from these savage Muslim invaders?"

You see, my friend, the European crusaders were not *invading* Muslim countries. The crusaders were trying to free countries like Turkey, Egypt, and Syria, and at the same time, they were doing everything they could to stop the Muslims from invading their own lands in Europe. Mr. Mohammed, the taxi driver, did not and *could not* argue the point.

Other skeptics will throw out other simple challenges like: "What about the cases where we see people claiming to be Christians doing evil acts like blowing up abortion clinics or bombing buildings or committing suicide? What is the answer for this problem?"

The answer is very simple. Just like we do not judge all police officers because of a few "bad cops" who have abused their power, we also do not judge Christianity by what a few individual people say or do. We judge Christianity by the teachings of the New Testament and the commands of Jesus as He gave them. Similarly, we should evaluate Islam, not by the sayings or actions of the Muslim believers in the 21st Century, but by the words of Allah in the Qur'an and the commands of Mohammed in the hadith. That is exactly what we will be investigating in jihad (the "unholy" war) as revealed in the Qur'an in volume 2 of this book series.

May God bless you richly as you seek to know the truth of these things, but more importantly, may each of us come to know the Lord Jesus, the Promised Messiah, the Final Sacrifice, the Lamb of God, and the One who endured the Final Jihad so that we could be saved from our sins and from an eternal Hell. Dear reader, if you do not yet know Him, please repent of your sin and rebellion and trust the One who loves you, who died for you, and now who waits to save you. If you are willing, He is willing to save you. He promised.

"For the wages of sin is death, but the gift of God is eternal life in Christ Jesus our Lord." (Romans 6:23)

Coming Soon!

OTHER RESOURCES BY USAMA DAKDOK

BOOKS

The Generous Qur'an

The only accurate English translation of the Qur'an available anywhere! It is a one-of-a-kind resource that exposes the true nature of Islam's most holy book. This book is not just for Jews, Christians, or Muslims, but for anyone who speaks English and is seeking an understanding of what is actually contained in the Qur'an—the basis of the Islamic faith.

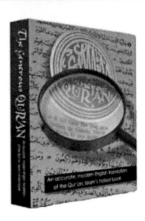

Exposing the Truth About the Qur'an

This 2-volume set discusses the hundreds of geographical, historical, moral, theological, legal, scientific, and linguistic errors contained in Islam's holiest book. It also explores the striking differences between the Qur'anic and the much older Biblical accounts of familiar events and people, such as the Creation, the Flood, Adam and Eve, Noah, Abraham, Moses, and Jesus. After fourteen centuries of blind adherence, now is the time for critical and thoughtful examination.

LIVE PRESENTATIONS

Did you know you can schedule Usama to speak at your church or special event? Get ready for a hard-hitting, take-no-prisoners approach to relevant topics.

The "Revealing the Truth About..." Series
- Islam
- Qur'an
- Sharia
- ISIS
- Jihad and Terrorism of Islam

Other Presentations
- The Infiltration of Islam in America
- Lies in the Textbooks
- Women in Islam
- Slavery in Islam
- Islam and Science
- and many more...

For more information or to book Usama, visit:
http://www.thestraightway.org/presentations

WEBSITE

Please visit our website, where you'll find additional **FREE** resource materials to equip you with the knowledge needed to confront the growing threat of Islam.
Articles, videos, books, live radio shows, program archives, and more.

http://www.thestraightway.org/

▶ YouTube

https://www.youtube.com/user/usamaway/videos

NOTES

NOTES

NOTES

NOTES